CORE & SHELL DEVELOPMENT

Version 2.0

REFERENCE GUIDE

First Edition June 2006

Copyright

The U.S. Green Building Council authorizes you to view the LEED-CS Version 2.0 Reference Guide for your individual use. In exchange for this authorization, you agree to retain all copyright and other proprietary notices contained in the original LEED-CS v2.0 Reference Guide. You also agree not to sell or modify the LEED-CS v2.0 Reference Guide or to reproduce, display or distribute the LEED-CS v2.0 Reference Guide in any way for any public or commercial purpose, including display on a website or in a networked environment. Unauthorized use of the LEED-CS v2.0 Reference Guide violates copyright, trademark, and other laws and is prohibited.

Note that the text of the federal and state codes, regulations, voluntary standards, etc., reproduced in the LEED-CS v2.0 Reference Guide is either used under license to the U.S. Green Building Council or, in some instances, is in the public domain. All other text, graphics, layout, and other elements of content contained in the LEED-CS v2.0 Reference Guide are owned by the U.S. Green Building Council and are protected by copyright under both United States and foreign laws.

Trademark

LEED® is a registered trademark of the U.S. Green Building Council.

Disclaimer

None of the parties involved in the funding or creation of the LEED-CS Version 2.0 Reference Guide, including the U.S. Green Building Council, its members, its contractors or the United States government make any warranty (express or implied) or assume any liability or responsibility, to you or any third parties for the accuracy, completeness or use of, or reliance on, any information contained in the LEED-CS v2.0 Reference Guide, or for any injuries, losses or damages (including, without limitation, equitable relief) arising out of such use or reliance.

As a condition of use, you covenant not to sue, and agree to waive and release the U.S. Green Building Council, its members, its contractors and the United States government from any and all claims, demands and causes of action for any injuries, losses or damages (including, without limitation, equitable relief) that you may now or hereafter have a right to assert against such parties as a result of your use of, or reliance on, the LEED-CS v2.0 Reference Guide.

U.S. Green Building Council

1015 18th Street NW, Suite 508

Washington, DC 20036

ISBN # 1-932444-05-X

Acknowledgements

The LEED-CS Reference Guide has only been made possible through the efforts of many dedicated volunteers, staff members and others in the USGBC community. The Reference Guide drafting was managed and implemented by USGBC staff and consultants and included review and suggestions by many TAG members and the CS Core Committee. We especially extend our deepest gratitude to all of our LEED committee members who participated in the development of this guide, for their tireless volunteer efforts and constant support of USGBC's mission. They are—

LEED-CS Core Committee

Jerry Lea (Chair), Hines Corporation
Christine Magar (Vice-Chair), Greenform
Peter Bartels, Power Construction Company, LLC
Clark Bisel, Flack + Kurtz
Gary Gardner, Davis Gardner Gannon Pope Architecture
Art Gensler, Gensler
Russell Perry, SmithGroup
Joe Van Belleghem, BuildGreen Developments, Inc.
Ken Wilson, Envision Design
Sally Wilson, CB Richard Ellis
Jerry Yudelson, Interface Engineering, Inc.
Special thanks to Rand Ekman and Heather Beaudoin from OWP/P for their contributions to the LEED-CS Reference Guide and Pilot Program.

Energy & Atmosphere TAG

Greg Kats (Chair), Capital-E
Marcus Sheffer (Vice-Chair), 7group
Saad Dimachkieh, HOK Architects
Chad Dorgan, Farnsworth Group, Inc.
Jay Enck, Commissioning & Green Building Services
Donald Fournier, Building Research Council
Ellen Franconi, IPMVP and AEC
Jonathan Heller, Ecotope, Inc.
Tia Heneghan, Sebesta Blomberg
John Hogan, City of Seattle Department of Planning and Development
Bion Howard, Building Environmental Science
Michael Lorenz, Kling
Cheryl Massie, Flack + Kurtz
Brenda Morawa, BVM Engineering, Inc.
Erik Ring, CTG Energetics, Inc.
John Schinter, Jones Lang LaSalle
Mick Schwedler, Trane Company
Gordon Shymko, IPMVP and G.F. Shymko & Associates
Michael Zimmer, Thompson Hine LLP

Indoor Environmental Quality TAG

Bob Thompson (Chair), EPA Indoor Environments Management Branch
Steve Taylor (Vice-Chair), Taylor Engineering
Jude Anders, Johnson Controls, Inc.
Terry Brennan, Camroden Associates
Brian Cloward, Mithun
Larry Dykhuis, Herman Miller, Inc.
Greg Franta, Ensar Group, Inc.
Francis Offerman, Indoor Environmental Engineering
Christopher Schaffner, The Green Engineer
Dennis Stanke, Trane Company

Materials & Resources TAG

Nadav Malin (Chair), BuildingGreen, Inc.
Kirsten Ritchie (Vice-Chair), Scientific Certification Systems
Paul Bertram, PRB Design
Chris Dixon, Mithun
Ann Edminster, Design AVEnues
Lee Gros, Lee Gros, Architect and Artisan
Debra Lombard, RETEC
Nancy Malone, Siegel & Strain Architects
Dana Papke, California Integrated Waste Mgmt. Board
Wayne Trusty, Athena Institute
Denise Van Valkenburg, Steelcase
Melissa Vernon, Interface Flooring Systems
Mark Webster, Simpson Gumpertz & Heger
Gabe Wing, Herman Miller, Inc.

Sustainable Sites TAG

Bryna Dunn (Chair), Moseley Architects
Susan Kaplan (Vice-Chair), Battery Park City Authority
Gina Baker, Burt Hill
Ted Bardacke, Global Green USA
Stephen Benz, Judith Nitsch Engineering, Inc.
Mark Brumbaugh, Brumbaugh & Associates
Meg Calkins, Department of Landscape Architecture, Ball State University
Stewart Comstock, Maryland Department of the Environment
Jay Enck, Commissioning & Green Building Services
Ron Hand, E/FECT. Sustainable Design Solutions
Richard Heinisch, Acuity Lighting Group
Michael Lane, Lighting Design Lab
Marita Roos, Andropogon Associates
Zolna Russell, Hord Coplan Macht, Inc.
Eva Wong, U.S. EPA Heat Island Reduction Initiative (HIRI)

Water Efficiency TAG

David Sheridan (Chair), Aqua Cura
John Koeller (Vice-Chair), Koeller and Company
Gunnar Baldwin, TOTO USA, INC.
Neal Billetdeaux, JJR
David Carlson, Columbia University
Bill Hoffman, City of Austin, Water Conservation
Heather Kinkade-Levario, ARCADIS
Geoff Nara, Civil & Environmental Consultants
Shabbir Rawalpindiwala, Kohler Company
Stephanie Tanner, U.S. Environmental Protection Agency
Bill Wall, Clivus New England, Inc.
Bill Wilson, Environmental Planning & Design, LLC

This reference guide was printed on 100% post-consumer waste paper, processed chlorine free, and printed with non-toxic, soy-based inks using 100% wind power. By using these materials and production processes, the U.S. Green Building Council saved the following resources:

Trees*	Solid Waste	Liquid Waste	Electricity	Greenhouse Gases	Sulfur & Nitrogen Oxides
78	6,990 lbs.	65,564 gallons	10,032 kWh	16,668 lbs.	36 lbs.

*One harvested tree = approx. 575 lbs.

Table of Contents

LEED-CS ratings:

❏ Certified   23-27 points

❏ Silver   28-33 points

❏ Gold   34-44 points

❏ Platinum   45-61 points

Foreword from the USGBC

The built environment has a profound impact on our natural environment, economy, health and productivity. Breakthroughs in building science, technology and operations are now available to designers, builders, operators and owners who want to build green and maximize both economic and environmental performance.

The U.S. Green Building Council (USGBC) is coordinating the establishment and evolution of a national consensus effort to provide the industry with tools necessary to design, build and operate buildings that deliver high performance inside and out. Council members work together to develop industry standards, design and construction practices and guidelines, operating practices and guidelines, policy positions and educational tools that support the adoption of sustainable design and building practices. Members also forge strategic alliances with key industry and research organizations, federal government agencies and state and local governments to transform the built environment. As the leading organization that represents the entire building industry on environmental building matters, the Council's unique perspective and collective power provides our members with enormous opportunity to effect change in the way buildings are designed, built, operated and maintained.

USGBC Membership

The Council's greatest strength is the diversity of our membership. The USGBC is a balanced, consensus nonprofit representing the entire building industry, consisting of over 6,500 companies and organizations. Since its inception in 1993, the USGBC has played a vital role in providing a leadership forum and a unique, integrating force for the building industry. Council programs are—

❑ Committee-Based

The heart of this effective coalition is our committee structure in which volunteer members design strategies that are implemented by staff and expert consultants. Our committees provide a forum for members to resolve differences, build alliances and forge cooperative solutions for influencing change in all sectors of the building industry.

❑ Member-Driven

The Council's membership is open and balanced and provides a comprehensive platform for carrying out important programs and activities. We target the issues identified by our members as the highest priority. We conduct an annual review of achievements that allows us to set policy, revise strategies and devise work plans based on member needs.

❑ Consensus-Focused

We work together to promote green buildings and in doing so, we help foster greater economic vitality and environmental health at lower costs. The various industry segments bridge ideological gaps to develop balanced policies that benefit the entire industry.

Contact the U.S. Green Building Council

1015 18th Street NW, Suite 508
Washington, DC 20036
(202) 828-7422 Office
(202) 828-5110 Fax
www.usgbc.org

Introduction

I. Why Make Your Building Green?

The environmental impact of the building design, construction and operation industry is significant. Buildings annually consume more than 30% of the total energy and more than 60% of the electricity used in the U.S. Each day five billion gallons of potable water is used solely to flush toilets. A typical North American commercial construction project generates up to 2.5 pounds of solid waste per square foot of completed floor space. Development shifts land usage away from natural, biologically-diverse habitats to hardscape that is impervious and devoid of biodiversity. The far reaching influence of the built environment necessitates action to reduce its impact.

Green building practices can substantially reduce or eliminate negative environmental impacts and improve existing unsustainable design, construction and operational practices. As an added benefit, green design measures reduce operating costs, enhance building marketability, increase worker productivity, and reduce potential liability resulting from indoor air quality problems. For example, energy efficiency measures have reduced operating expenses of the Denver Dry Goods building by approximately $75,000 per year. Students in day-lit schools in North Carolina consistently score higher on tests than students in schools using conventional lighting fixtures. Studies of workers in green buildings reported productivity gains of up to 16%, including reductions in absenteeism and improved work quality, based on "people-friendly" green design. At a grocery store in Spokane, Washington, waste management costs were reduced by 56% and 48 tons of waste was recycled during construc-

tion. In other words, green design has environmental, economic and social elements that benefit all building stakeholders, including owners, occupants and the general public.

Commercial buildings and speculative developments can also benefit from a reduction in operating costs, tenant retention and improved market position. For example, a 734,073 sq.ft. commercial office building in Atlanta, Georgia, was designed with a computer modeled reduction of its annual energy cost by 22.2% from the ASHRAE/IESNA 90.1-2004 baseline, for a modeled annual energy cost savings of $238,000.00. A 109,000 sq.ft. commercial office building in Port Huron, Michigan reduced its building water use by 32.2% below the Energy Policy Act of 1992. And, a 172,000 sq.ft. multiple building retail project in Savannah, Georgia computer modeled an annual energy cost reduction across five buildings by 31.0% from the ASHRAE/IESNA 90.1-2004 baseline, for a modeled annual cost savings of $27,980.00. This same project was able to reduce 173,000 sq.ft. of site water use requirements for irrigation to zero by utilizing only on site captured rainwater.

II. LEED® Green Building Rating System

A. History of LEED®

Following the formation of the U.S. Green Building Council (USGBC) in 1993, the membership quickly realized that a priority for the sustainable building industry was to have a system to define and measure "green buildings." The USGBC began to research existing green building metrics and rating systems. Less than a year after formation, the membership followed up on the initial findings with the establishment of a committee to focus solely on this topic. The diverse initial composition of the committee included architects, realtors, a building owner, a lawyer, an environmentalist and industry representatives. This cross section of people and professions added a richness and depth both to the process and to the ultimate product.

The first LEED Pilot Project Program, also referred to as LEED Version 1.0, was launched at the USGBC Membership Summit in August 1998. After extensive modifications, the LEED Green Building Rating System Version 2.0 was released in March 2000. This rating system is now called the LEED Green Building Rating System for New Commercial Construction and Major Renovations, or LEED-NC. The current version of LEED-NC is version 2.2.

As LEED has evolved and matured, the program has undertaken new initiatives. In addition to a rating system specifically devoted to building operational and maintenance issues, LEED addresses the different project development/delivery processes that exist in the U.S. building design and construction market. Currently, the LEED product portfolio is being expanded to the following areas:

**Rating System
Product Portfolio**

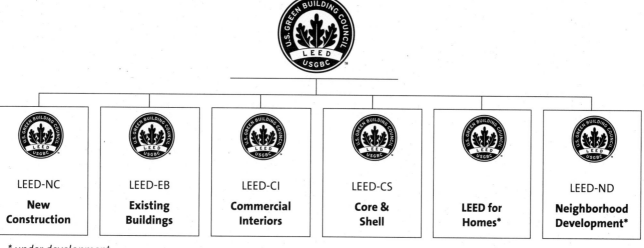

LEED-NC — **New Construction**

LEED-EB — **Existing Buildings**

LEED-CI — **Commercial Interiors**

LEED-CS — **Core & Shell**

LEED for Homes*

LEED-ND — **Neighborhood Development***

* under development as of May 2006

LEED for Core & Shell (LEED-CS) is part of the growing portfolio of rating system products serving specific market sectors.

B. Features of LEED®

The LEED Green Building Rating System is a voluntary, consensus-based, market-driven building rating system based on existing proven technology. It evaluates environmental performance from a whole building perspective over a building's life cycle, providing a definitive standard for what constitutes a "green building." The development of the LEED Green Building Rating System was initiated by the USGBC Membership, representing all segments of the building industry, and has been open to public scrutiny.

The rating system is organized into five environmental categories: Sustainable Sites, Water Efficiency, Energy & Atmosphere, Materials & Resources, and Indoor Environmental Quality. An additional category, Innovation & Design Process, addresses sustainable building expertise as well as design measures not covered under the five environmental categories.

LEED is a measurement system designed for rating new and existing commercial, institutional and residential buildings. It is based on accepted energy and environmental principles and strikes a balance between known established practices and emerging concepts.

It is a performance-oriented system where credits are earned for satisfying criterion designed to address specific environmental impacts inherent in the design, construction and O&M of buildings. Different levels of green building certification are awarded based on the total credits earned. The system is designed to be comprehensive in scope, yet simple in operation.

C. The Future of LEED®

The green design field is growing and changing daily. New technologies and products are coming into the marketplace and innovative designs are proving their effectiveness. Therefore, the Rating System and the Reference Guide will evolve as well. Teams wishing to certify with LEED should note that they will need to comply with the version of the rating system that is current at the time of their registration.

The USGBC will highlight new developments on its website on a continuous basis at www.usgbc.org.

III. LEED for Core & Shell Overview and Process

The Leadership in Energy and Environmental Design® (LEED) Green Building Rating System for Core & Shell Development (LEED-CS) is a set of performance standards for certifying the sustainable design and construction of speculative and core and shell buildings. It has been developed as part of the U.S. Green Building Council's ongoing effort to provide a national standard for what constitutes a "green building." The intent of which is to assist in the creation of high performance, healthful, durable, affordable and environmentally sound buildings.

The LEED for Core & Shell Rating System is a market specific application, which recognizes the unique nature of core and shell development. The LEED-CS Rating System acknowledges the limited level of influence a developer can exert in a speculatively developed building. For example, some key building areas, interior space layout, interior finishes, lighting, mechanical distribution, and other tenant related systems are often outside the direct control of the developer. LEED-CS encourages the implementation of green design and construction practices in areas the developer can control and fosters a synergistic relationship, which allows future tenants to capitalize on green strategies implemented by the developer. It is the responsibility of the owner/developer to properly identify which LEED rating system to use for the LEED building certification as further described herein.

LEED-CS is designed to be complementary to the LEED for Commercial Interiors Green Building Rating System (LEED-CI). The LEED-CI and LEED-CS rating systems establish green building criteria for both owner/developers and tenants.

LEED-CS addresses:

❑ Site selection

❑ Water efficiency in core and shell building systems

❑ Energy optimization of the core and shell systems and provisions for fit out of tenant spaces to optimize operational building energy use

❑ Materials and resource guidelines for construction of building core and shell

❑ Indoor Environmental Quality planning of the building core and shell to ensure tenant fit out is able to make optimal use of Indoor Environmental Quality attributes including thermal comfort, daylight and views as well as prevention of contamination from indoor pollutants

A. When to Use LEED-CS

The LEED-CS Rating System was developed to serve the speculatively driven development market where project teams routinely do not control all aspects of a building's design and construction. The scope of LEED-CS is limited to those elements of the project under the direct control of the owner/developer. Depending on how the project is structured, this scope can range significantly from project to project. The LEED-CS Rating System has been developed to address a variety of project types and a broad project range.

Scope of Construction

❑ LEED-CS can be used for projects where the developer controls the design and construction of the entire core and shell base building including

MEP/FP systems, but has no control over the design and construction of the tenant fit-out. Examples of this type of project are a commercial office building, medical office building, retail center, warehouse, or lab facility.

❑ LEED-CS can also be used for projects that have limited control of the building systems. This is often found in retail development. Projects with limited scope should review the specific credit requirements for guidance.

❑ In projects that are designed and constructed to be partially occupied by the owner/developer, it is assumed the owner/developer has direct influence over the portion of the work that would typically be tenant interior construction. For projects of this type to utilize the LEED-CS Rating System, the owner/tenant must occupy 50% or less of the building's leasable space. Projects with greater than 50% of the building's tenant space occupied by a owner/tenant should utilize LEED-NC.

Core & Shell and Tenant Space Guidance

Due to the particular nature of core and shell project development the project team may not know the tenant make up and the resulting occupant count during the building's design. To guide core and shell projects, a default occupancy count table has been developed. For some credits, projects will need to refer to this default occupancy count table to determine credit compliance. The method of determining occupancy must be consistent across all credits in a submittal. The default occupancy count table is included as Appendix 1.

Included as Appendix 2 are the Core & Shell Energy Modeling Guidelines. These guidelines are intended to ensure that projects in different markets with different project teams are approaching the energy modeling requirements in a similar manner, and that a minimum benchmark for energy optimization is established. Guidance is included for how to model both designed core and shell spaces and tenant spaces that are not part of the project design and construction scope.

To assist project teams in defining the owner/tenant division in the project design as well as certification review process, the Core & Shell/Tenant Interiors Checklist has been developed. This checklist is attached as Appendix 3.

B. LEED-CS Registration

Project teams interested in obtaining LEED-CS Certification for their project must first register this intent with the USGBC. Projects can be registered on the USGBC website (www.usgbc.org) in the LEED section, under Register Your Project. The website includes information on registration costs for USGBC member companies as well as non-members. Registration is an important step that establishes contact with the USGBC and provides access to software tools, errata, critical communications and other essential information.

C. Credit Interpretation Rulings

In some cases, the design team may encounter challenges in applying a LEED-CS prerequisite or credit to their particular project. These difficulties arise from instances where the Reference Guide does not sufficiently address a specific issue or there is a special conflict that requires resolution. To address such issues, the USGBC has established the LEED-CS Credit Interpretation Ruling (CIR) process (separate from the CIR page found in other LEED rating systems). See the LEED-CS section of the USGBC website for more information at www.usgbc.org.

The Credit Interpretation process is summarized as follows:

1. Project teams should review the CIR webpage to read previously posted credit interpretation requests and USGBC responses. Many questions can be resolved by reviewing existing CIRs and the LEED-CS v2.0 Reference Guide. Note that CIRs for other rating systems (LEED-EB, LEED-CI and LEED-NC) are not necessarily applicable.

2. If no existing Credit Interpretation Rulings are relevant to the project, the LEED project team should submit an on-line credit interpretation request. The description of the challenge encountered by the project team should be brief but explicit; should be based on prerequisite or credit information found in the Rating System and Reference Guide; and should place a special emphasis on the Intent of the prerequisite or credit. If possible, the project team should offer potential solutions to the problem and solicit approval or rejection of their proposed interpretation. Follow the detailed instructions in the "CIR Guidelines" document available on the CIR webpage in the LEED section of the USGBC website.

3. USGBC will rule on your request electronically according to the posted schedule, either through a posting on the CIR Page or via e-mail correspondence.

D. LEED-CS Precertification Application

Overview

LEED-CS Precertification is a unique aspect of the LEED-CS program. Precertification is formal recognition by USGBC given to a candidate project for which the owner/developer has established a goal to develop a LEED-CS building. LEED-CS Precertification is granted to projects after USGBC has reviewed early design stage documentation. This documentation, which reflects a studied and realistic set of project goals and intentions, forms the basis for an award of Precertification at the project's anticipated LEED-CS certification level. Precertification is not required for a documented and completed building nor is it confirmation of, or a commitment to, achieve LEED-CS certification. Precertification is not LEED Certification.

Value

Precertification provides the core & shell owner/developer with the ability to market to potential tenants and financiers the unique and valuable green features of a proposed building.

Submittal and Review

Once a project is registered as a LEED-CS project with the USGBC, the project team may complete the LEED-CS precertification letter templates and submit the project for precertification. This is a voluntary submittal at the discretion of the project team.

Because much of the value of precertification occurs early in a project's development, the project team's documentation and the USGBC's review is less comprehensive than the final LEED-CS certification application. Project teams are required to provide confirmation that the project intends to meet the requirements of a credit. This is provided using the LEED-CS precertification letter templates on the appropriate design team member's letterhead for each credit pursued, with a brief description of the strategy and/or technology that will be employed. The owner/developer is also required to provide a signed letter template declaring that they are in agreement with the intention and strategies as indicated on each credit-specific letter template submitted.

The LEED-CS Project Scope checklist will also need to be submitted. This checklist includes information about building use, LEED-CS occupancy numbers and core and shell scope. It serves as a design team tool and also provides the USGBC with useful building information for the review.

The project is reviewed and a LEED-CS precertification level (certified, silver, gold or platinum) is granted. A certificate and letter are provided to the project. The review will allow the developer to market the project's intention to achieve a particular LEED-CS certification level. This precertification process is not intended to be a supplementary comprehensive review of a project's submittal for the anticipated LEED-CS certification level. LEED-CS certification review must still occur with the USGBC's established two-phase application (Design and Construction). Because of the many factors inherent in project design, construction and project documentation and review, it is possible that the final certification review will not correspond exactly to the Precertification review. Project team members should be aware that it is incumbent upon the team to demonstrate that the credit requirements have been met at the design and construction certification reviews.

E. LEED-CS Certification Application

Once a project is registered, the project design team begins to collect information and perform calculations to satisfy the prerequisite and credit submittal requirements. Since submittal documentation should be gathered throughout design and construction, it is helpful to designate a LEED team leader who is responsible for managing the compilation of this information by the LEED-CS project team. The Letter Templates that are provided through the LEED project resources webpage, located in the LEED section of the USGBC website, should be used. These templates contain embedded calculators, and are instrumental in documenting fulfillment of credit requirements and prompting for correct and complete supporting information.

Two-Phase Application

A feature of LEED-CS v2.0 is the option of splitting a LEED-CS certification application into two phases. Rather than submitting all documentation for a project at the end of the construction phase, project teams will be able to submit designated "design phase credits" at the end of the design phase for review by USGBC. Design phase credits are those credits that USGBC can reasonably adjudicate based on design phase documentation. For example, if a project site meets the LEED-CS Sustainable Sites Credit 3: Brownfield Redevelopment Requirements, USGBC can assess the likelihood of the project achieving this credit prior to the completion of construction. It is important to remember that LEED credit is not awarded at the design review stage. Project teams are notified of the likelihood of their project to achieve a LEED credit if construction is executed in accordance with design phase plans. Projects must submit verification that design elements were implemented as planned after completion of construction. A list of the potential design phase credits can be found in the LEED section of the USGBC website. Project Teams are allotted one design phase review. At the completion of construction, the balance of attempted credits, verification of design phase credits, and additional documentation for any design phase credits that has changed since the design phase review are documented and submitted for USGBC review. See **Table 1** for a complete listing of design and construction phase credits.

F. Review and Certification

To earn LEED-CS certification, the applicant project must satisfy all of the prerequisites and a minimum number of points to attain the established LEED-CS project ratings as listed below. Having satisfied the basic prerequisites of the program, applicant projects are then rated according to their degree of compliance within the rating system. All LEED-CS projects will need to comply with the version of LEED-CS that is current at the time of project registration.

Credit Compliance

Overview

The LEED-CS Rating System is written for core and shell development and is intentionally neutral regarding requirements for tenant build-out. A core and shell rating can be attained without making any requirements of a tenant. A tenant can choose to pursue or not to pursue a LEED for Commercial Interiors (LEED-CI) rating with no impact on the building's LEED-CS rating. However, if a developer chooses to make specific lease requirements part of their tenant negotiation, and these requirements meet the criteria of a particular credit in the LEED-CS Rating System, the LEED-CS project may be able to receive a point for this credit even if the work is not part of the core and shell design and construction.

The following describes this approach to credit compliance and may be used, as applicable, throughout the rating system.

Requirements

Meet LEED-CS Credit requirements through either

❑ Design and construction of the building core and shell;

OR

❑ Establishment of tenant requirements that meet the LEED-CS credit requirements, but will be implemented as part of the tenant controlled build-out.

Submittals

❑ Provide the LEED letter template, signed by the building owner/developer for the credit being pursued,

Table 1: Design & Construction Phase Credits

Sustainable Sites	Design Submittal	Construction Submittal
SSp 1: Construction Activity Pollution Prevention		*
SSc 1: Site Selection	*	
SSc 2: Development Density & Community Connectivity	*	
SSc 3: Brownfield Redevelopment	*	
SSc 4.1: Alternative Transportation, Public Transportation Access	*	
SSc 4.2: Alternative Transportation, Bicycle Storage & Changing Rooms	*	
SSc 4.3: Alternative Transportation, Low-Emitting & Fuel-Efficient Vehicles	*	
SSc 4.4: Alternative Transportation, Parking Capacity	*	
SSc 5.1: Site Development, Protect or Restore Habitat		*
SSc 5.2: Site Development, Maximize Open Space	*	
SSc 6.1: Stormwater Management, Quantity Control	*	
SSc 6.2: Stormwater Management, Quality Control	*	
SSc 7.1: Heat Island Effect, Non-Roof		*
SSc 7.2: Heat Island Effect, Roof	*	
SSc 8: Light Pollution Reduction	*	
SSc 9: Tenant Design & Construction Guidelines	*	
Water Efficiency		
WEc 1.1: Water Efficient Landscaping: Reduce by 50%	*	
WEc 1.2: Water Efficient Landscaping: No Potable Water Use or No Irrigation	*	
WEc 2: Innovative Wastewater Technologies	*	
WEc 3.1: Water Use Reduction, 20%	*	
WEc 3.2: Water Use Reduction, 30%	*	
Energy & Atmosphere		
EAp 1: Fundamental Commissioning of the Building Energy Systems		*
EAp 2: Minimum Energy Performance	*	
EAp 3: Fundamental Refrigerant Management	*	
EAc 1: Optimize Energy Performance	*	
EAc 2: On-Site Renewable Energy	*	
EAc 3: Enhanced Commissioning		*
EAc 4: Enhanced Refrigerant Management	*	
EAc 5.1: M&V— Base Building	*	
EAc 5.2: M&V— Tenant Sub-metering	*	
EAc 6: Green Power		*

continued on page 20

Table 1: Design & Construction Phase Credits

Materials and Resources	Design Submittal	Construction Submittal
MRp 1: Storage and Collection of Recyclables	*	
MRc 1.1: Building Reuse: Maintain 25% of Existing Walls, Floors & Roof		*
MRc 1.2: Building Reuse: Maintain 50% of Existing Walls, Floors & Roof		*
MRc 1.3: Building Reuse: Maintain 75% of Walls, Floors & Roof		*
MRc 2.1: Construction Waste Management: Divert 50% from Disposal		*
MRc 2.2: Construction Waste Management: Divert 75% from Disposal		*
MRc 3: Materials Reuse: 1%		*
MRc 4.1: Recycled Content: 10% (post-consumer + 1/2 pre-consumer)		*
MRc 4.2: Recycled Content: 20% (post-consumer + 1/2 pre-consumer)		*
MRc 5.1: Regional Materials: 10% Extracted, Processed & Manufactured Regionally		*
MRc 5.2: Regional Materials: 20% Extracted, Processed & Manufactured Regionally		*
MRc 6: Certified Wood		*
Indoor Environmental Quality		
EQp 1: Minimum IAQ Performance	*	
EQp 2: Environmental Tobacco Smoke (ETS) Control	*	
EQc 1: Outdoor Air Delivery Monitoring	*	
EQc 2: Increased Ventilation	*	
EQc 3: Construction IAQ Management Plan, During Construction		*
EQc 4.1: Low-Emitting Materials, Adhesives & Sealants		*
EQc 4.2: Low-Emitting Materials: Paints & Coatings		*
EQc 4.3: Low-Emitting Materials: Carpet Systems		*
EQc 4.4: Low-Emitting Materials: Composite Wood & Agrifiber Products		*
EQc 5: Indoor Chemical & Pollutant Source Control	*	
EQc 6: Controllability of Systems: Thermal Comfort	*	
EQc 7: Thermal Comfort: Design	*	
EQc 8.1: Daylight and Views: Daylight 75% of Spaces	*	
EQc 8.2: Daylight and Views: Views for 90% of Spaces	*	

based on the core and shell design and construction.

OR

The LEED letter template for the credit pursued indicating that 100% of leased square footage complies with credit requirements. Lease or sales agreements may be requested.

AND

100% of the unleased square footage shall comply with the credit requirements when leased. A statement signed by the owner/developer that all leases and/or sales agreements will comply may be requested.

The USGBC recognizes the realities and complexity of tenant fit out and the difficulties associated with the enforcement of a 100% compliance path requirement. As a result, in certain instances, a minor portion (defined as a 10% variance) of the final fully occupied tenant spaces may not meet the 100% requirement. Under such situations, the committee acknowledges the 100% assurance has been met.

Design Phase Review

Once USGBC has received your complete design phase application and the design phase fee (which is a portion of the total certification fee), the USGBC will formally rule on your application by designating each attempted credit as either *Anticipated* or *Denied*. No certification award will be given at this time, nor will any credits be awarded. This process serves to allow project teams the opportunity to assess the likelihood of credit achievement, and requires follow through to ensure the design is executed in the construction phase according to design specifications.

Construction Phase Review

At the completion of construction, the project team will submit all attempted credits for review. If the project team had elected to have a design phase review and any of the design phase *Anticipated* credits have changed, additional documentation must be submitted to substantiate continued compliance with credit requirements. For design phase *Anticipated* credits that have not substantively changed, the project team must submit a verification that the design has been executed per requirements in the construction phase. Once USGBC has received the complete application and fee (the remainder of the total certification fee, if a design review has been conducted), the USGBC will formally rule on your full application. All applicant-verified design phase credits that were designated as *Anticipated* and have not changed since the design phase review will be declared as *Achieved*. All other credits will be designated as either *Achieved* or *Denied*.

Appeals

Appeals may be filed either after the design phase review or the final review. Please see the LEED-CS section of the USGBC website for more information on appeals.

Figure 1 (*following page*) illustrates the general sequence of submittals for LEED-CS precertification and certification. The activities are indicated in relation to the typical project delivery phase.

Fees

Certification fee information can be found in the LEED-CS section of the USGBC website. The USGBC will acknowledge receipt of your application and proceed with application review when all project documentation has been submitted.

The LEED-CS ratings are awarded according to the following scale—

❑ Certified   23-27 points

❑ Silver   28-33 points

❑ Gold   34-44 points

❑ Platinum   45-61 points

Figure 1: Sequence of Submittals for LEED-CS Precertification and Certification

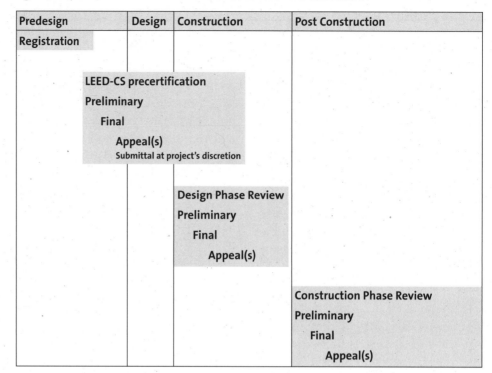

Predesign	Design	Construction	Post Construction
Registration			

LEED-CS precertification
Preliminary
Final
Appeal(s)
Submittal at project's discretion

Design Phase Review
Preliminary
Final
Appeal(s)

Construction Phase Review
Preliminary
Final
Appeal(s)

The USGBC will recognize buildings that achieve one of these rating levels with a formal letter of certification and a mountable plaque.

G. Updates & Addenda

This is the first edition of the LEED-CS Version 2.0 Reference Guide, dated May 2006. As LEED-CS continues to improve and evolve, updates and addenda will be made available to substitute and augment the current material. The USGBC cannot be held liable for any criteria set forth herein, which may not be applicable to later versions of LEED-CS. Updates and addenda will be accumulated between revisions and will be formally incorporated in major revisions. In the interim between major revisions, the USGBC may use its consensus process to clarify criteria.

When a project registers for certification, the prerequisites, credits, and credit rulings current at the time of project registration will continue to guide the project throughout its certification process.

IV. LEED-CS Version 2.0 Reference Guide

The LEED-CS v2.0 Reference Guide is a supporting document to the LEED-CS Green Building Rating System. The Guide is intended to assist project teams in understanding LEED-CS criteria and the benefits of complying with each criterion. The Guide includes examples of strategies that can be used in each category, case studies of buildings that have implemented these strategies successfully, and additional resources that will provide more information. The guide does not provide an exhaustive list of strategies for meeting the criteria as subsequent strategies will be developed and employed by designers that satisfy the Intent of each credit. Nor does it provide all of the information that design teams need to determine the applicability of a credit to their project.

Prerequisite and Credit Format

Each prerequisite and credit is organized in a standardized format for simplicity and quick reference. The first section summarizes the key points regarding the measure and includes the Intent, Requirements, and some Potential Technologies & Strategies for achieving the credit. The subsequent sections provide supportive information to help interpret the measure, examples, and links to various resources.

If your project team encounters an out-of-date web link in the Reference Guide, please go to the root website, which should take the form of www.organization.com with no additional text following. Then you may be able to navigate through the website to find the referenced document. Please contact the USGBC at (202) 828-7422 if you are unable to locate a resource.

Greening Opportunity Icons

Throughout this Reference Guide, you will see this icon:

This icon will assist projects that are proceeding with the intention of certifying with LEED-EB, following their LEED-CS certification. It identifies credits that involve measures that are significantly more cost-effective and convenient to implement during design and construction than they are during the operation of the building. These credits are—

SSc 2:   Development Density & Community Connectivity

SSc 4.1:   Alternative Transportation: Public Transportation Access

EAc 1:   Optimize Energy Performance

EAc 3:   Enhanced Commissioning

EAc 5:   Measurement & Verification

MRc 4:   Recycled Content

MRc 5:   Regional Materials

MRc 6:   Rapidly Renewable Materials

MRc 7:   Certified Wood

EQc 1:   Outdoor Air Delivery Monitoring

EQc 6.2:   Controllability of Systems: Thermal Comfort

EQc 7:   Thermal Comfort

EQc 8:   Daylight and Views

This icon will also assist you in identifying the credits and considerations that are important for a LEED-CI pursuit. This will assist the project team with identifying the core and shell building issues that can assist a tenant or buyer with pursuing a LEED-CI certification. It identifies credits that either directly assist with the LEED-CI pursuit, or that provide a core and shell systems capability that can be utilized by the tenant or buyer.

Case Study

National Business Park 318
Annapolis Junction, Maryland

Photo courtesy of: Jeffery Sauers

National Business Park 318 (NBP 318) is a four-story, 125,681-sq.ft. office building, which was fully leased during construction and earned LEED-CS Pilot Gold Certification. NBP 318 is located in a 285-acre business community and is one of three buildings on a business campus arranged around a central sculpture plaza that allows for pedestrian connectivity. NBP 318 had a $2.84 per sq.ft. green construction premium with a $0.70 per sq.ft. annual energy savings. The analysis showed a six-month return on investment, after costs were offset by energy savings, waste reduction and other green practices. Some other attributes include highly filtered air, extremely efficient mechanical systems, water usage reduction of 40% and an extensive green housekeeping program. Sustainable features include: a stormwater management system that removes 80% of the total suspended solids and more than 50% of average annual post-development phosphorous; heat island reduction through the use of a white roof; reduced light pollution with exterior lighting designed to prevent spillage beyond the site; alternative transportation opportunities with bicycle storage and changing rooms to encourage tenant employees to bike to work; and tenant design and construction guidelines to promote green practices by tenants.

Sustainable Sites

Buildings affect ecosystems in a variety of ways. Development of greenfield or previously undeveloped sites consumes land. Development projects must also be sensitive to encroaching on agricultural lands, compromising existing wildlife habitat, and exacerbating local and regional erosion. The impacts of increased impervious surfaces to stormwater runoff should be controlled to mimic natural conditions and protect water quality in receiving waters. Sedimentation caused by erosion may hinder regional waterway navigation, disrupt aquatic life and reduce the quality of local/regional recreation areas. Heat from the sun is absorbed by buildings and paved surfaces and is radiated back, increasing temperatures in surrounding urban areas. External lighting systems may cause light pollution to the night sky and interfere with nocturnal ecology.

A building's location also affects ecosystems based on the occupants' options for travel to and from the site. According to the Federal Bureau of Transportation Statistics, vehicle use in America has nearly tripled, from 1 to 2.85 trillion miles per year, between 1970 and 2002. Vehicles are responsible for approximately 20% of U.S. greenhouse gas emissions annually (NRDC). Vehicle fuel consumption and emissions contribute to climate change, smog and particulate pollution, all of which have negative impacts on human health. The infrastructure required to support vehicle travel (parking and roadway surfaces, service stations, fuel distribution networks, etc.) increase the consumption of land and nonrenewable resources, alter stormwater flow and absorb heat energy, exacerbating heat island effect.

Project teams undertaking building projects should be cognizant of the inherent impacts of development on land consumption, ecosystems, natural resources and energy use. Preference should be given to buildings with high performance attributes in locations that enhance existing neighborhoods, transportation networks, and urban infrastructures. During initial project scoping, preference should be given to sites and land use plans that preserve natural ecosystem functions and enhance the health of the surrounding community.

Establishing sustainable design objectives and integrating building location and sustainable features as a metric for decision making encourages development and preservation or restoration practices that limit the environmental impact of buildings on local ecosystems.

Sustainable Sites Credit Characteristics

For single building developments, the LEED submittal is typically the entire project scope and is generally limited to the site boundary, however, it is not uncommon for a LEED for Core and Shell building to be a portion of a larger multiple building development. In situations like this the project team may determine the limits of the project submitting for LEED Certification differently than the overall site boundaries. This **LEED Project Boundary** is the portion of the project site that is submitting for LEED certification and must be used consistently across all Sustainable Sites prerequisites and credits.

Table 1 shows which credits were substantially revised from LEED-NC Version 2.2, which credits are eligible to be submitted in the Design Phase Submittal, and which project team members are likely to carry decision-making responsibility for each credit. The decision-making responsibility matrix is not intended to exclude any party, rather to emphasize those credits that are most likely to require strong participation by a particular team member.

Table 1: SS Credit Characteristics

Credit	Significant Change from LEED-NC v2.2	Design Submittal	Construction Submittal	Owner Decision-Making	Design Team Decision-Making	Contractor Decision-Making
SSp1: Construction Activity Pollution Prevention			*		*	*
SSc1: Site Selection		*		*		
SSc2: Development Density & Community Connectivity		*		*	*	
SSc3: Brownfield Redevelopment		*		*		
SSc4.1: Alternative Transportation, Public Transportation Access		*		*		
SSc4.2: Alternative Transportation, Bicycle Storage & Changing Rooms	*	*			*	
SSc4.3: Alternative Transportation, Low-Emitting & Fuel-Efficient Vehicles	*	*		*	*	
SSc4.4: Alternative Transportation, Parking Capacity		*		*	*	
SSc5.1: Site Development, Protect or Restore Habitat			*	*	*	*
SSc5.2: Site Development, Maximize Open Space		*		*	*	
SSc6.1: Stormwater Management, Quantity Control		*			*	
SSc6.2: Stormwater Management, Quality Control		*			*	
SSc7.1: Heat Island Effect, Non-Roof			*		*	*
SSc7.2: Heat Island Effect, Roof		*			*	*
SSc8: Light Pollution Reduction	*	*			*	
SSc9: Tenant Design & Construction Guidelines	*	*		*	*	

Construction Activity Pollution Prevention

Required

Intent

Reduce pollution from construction activities by controlling soil erosion, waterway sedimentation and airborne dust generation.

Requirements

Create and implement an Erosion and Sedimentation Control (ESC) Plan for all construction activities associated with the project. The ESC Plan shall conform to the erosion and sedimentation requirements of the 2003 EPA Construction General Permit OR local erosion and sedimentation control standards and codes, whichever is more stringent. The Plan shall describe the measures implemented to accomplish the following objectives:

❑ Prevent loss of soil during construction by stormwater runoff and/or wind erosion, including protecting topsoil by stockpiling for reuse.

❑ Prevent sedimentation of storm sewer or receiving streams.

❑ Prevent polluting the air with dust and particulate matter.

The Construction General Permit (CGP) outlines the provisions necessary to comply with Phase I and Phase II of the National Pollutant Discharge Elimination System (NPDES) program. While the CGP only applies to construction sites greater than 1 acre, the requirements are applied to all projects for the purposes of this prerequisite. Information on the EPA CGP is available at: http://cfpub.epa.gov/npdes/stormwater/cgp.cfm.

Potential Technologies & Strategies

Create an Erosion and Sedimentation Control Plan during the design phase of the project. Consider employing strategies such as temporary and permanent seeding, mulching, earth dikes, silt fencing, sediment traps and sediment basins.

Summary of Referenced Standard

Storm Water Management for Construction Activities (U.S. EPA Document No. EPA

832R92005), Chapter 3

U.S. Environmental Protection Agency Office of Water, www.epa.gov/OW

Internet download link for Chapter 3 (72 pages): www.epa.gov/npdes/pubs/chap03_conguide.pdf

Download site for all sections: http://yosemite.epa.gov/water/owrccatalog.nsf, search by title index. Hardcopy or microfiche (entire document, 292 pages): National Technical Information Service (order # PB92-235951), www.ntis.gov, (800) 553-6847

This standard describes two types of measures that can be used to control sedimentation and erosion. Stabilization measures include temporary seeding, permanent seeding and mulching. All of these measures are intended to stabilize the soil to prevent erosion. Structural control measures are implemented to retain sediment after erosion has occurred. Structural control measures include earth dikes, silt fencing, sediment traps and sediment basins. The application of these measures depends on the conditions at the specific site.

Approach and Implementation

Erosion on existing sites typically results from foot traffic killing the vegetation, steep slopes where stormwater sheet flow exceeds vegetation holding power, runoff that exceeds vegetation holding power, or vehicle traffic on unpaved areas. Identifying and eliminating these and other causes will minimize soil loss and preserve receiving water quality.

This prerequisite effectively extends NPDES requirements for construction activities, which currently only apply to projects 1 acre and larger, to all projects pursuing LEED certification.

Typically, the civil engineer identifies erosion-prone areas and soil stabilization measures. The contractor then adopts a plan to implement the measures presented by the civil engineer and responds to rain events and other activities accordingly. It is recommended that the Erosion and Sedimentation Control (ESC) Plan be incorporated into the construction

Table 1: Technologies for Controlling Erosion & Sedimentation

Control Technology	Description
Stabilization	
Temporary Seeding	Plant fast-growing grasses to temporarily stabilize soils
Permanent Seeding	Plant grass, trees, and shrubs to permanently stabilize soil
Mulching	Place hay, grass, woodchips, straw, or gravel on the soil surface to cover and hold soils
Structural Control	
Earth Dike	Construct a mound of stabilized soil to divert surface runoff volumes from distributed areas or into sediment basins or sediment traps
Silt Fence	Construct posts with a filter fabric media to remove sediment from stormwater volumes flowing through the fence
Sediment Trap	Excavate a pond area or construct earthen embankments to allow for settling of sediment from stormwater volumes
Sediment Basin	Construct a pond with a controlled water release structure to allow for settling of sediment from stormwater volumes

drawings and specifications, with clear instructions regarding responsibilities, scheduling and inspections.

If a Storm Water Pollution Prevention Plan (SWPPP) is required for the project via the National Pollutant Discharge Elimination System (NPDES) or local regulations, an ESC Plan may already be required. In that case, the only action required is to confirm that the plan meets the Requirements of this prerequisite and is implemented. If an ESC Plan is not required for purposes other than LEED, use the Referenced Standard listed above as a guideline on how to compose the plan.

Core and Shell Concerns

There are no core and shell-specific issues regarding implementation.

Calculations

There are no calculations associated with this prerequisite.

Exemplary Performance

There is no Exemplary Performance point available for this prerequisite.

Precertification Submittal Documentation

Provide the LEED-CS Precertification Submittal Templates, which include the following:

❑ Narrative describing how the project intends to accomplish the prerequisite requirements on the credit-specific Submittal Template signed by the appropriate design team member

❑ Confirmation of this intent from the owner/developer on the LEED-CS Precertification Submittal Template

Certification Submittal Documentation

This prerequisite is submitted as part of the **Construction Submittal**.

Photo Credit: CTG Energetics, Inc.

Example of Structural Control. Silt fence: fabric filter media removes sediment from stormwater volumes flowing through the fence.

Design and Construction Credit Compliance

The following project data and calculation information is required to document credit compliance using the LEED-CS v2.0 Submittal Templates:

❑ Provide copies of the project drawings to document the erosion and sedimentation control measures implemented on the site.

❑ Provide confirmation regarding the compliance path taken by the project (NPDES Compliance or Local Erosion Control Standards).

❑ Provide a narrative to describe the Erosion and Sedimentation control measures implemented on the project. If a local standard has been followed, please provide specific information to demonstrate that the local standard is equal to or more stringent than the referenced NPDES program.

Tenant Sales or Lease Agreement Credit Compliance

This compliance method is not available for this prerequisite.

Considerations

Environmental Issues

The loss of topsoil is the most significant on-site consequence of erosion. Topsoil is the soil layer that contains organic matter, plant nutrients and biological activity. Loss of topsoil greatly reduces the soil's ability to support plant life, regulate water flow, and maintain the biodiversity of soil microbes and insects that controls disease and pest outbreaks. Loss of nutrients, soil compaction, and decreased biodiversity of soil inhabitants can severely limit the vitality of landscaping. This can lead to additional site management and environmental concerns, such as increased use of fertilizers, irrigation and pesticides; and increased stormwater runoff that heightens the pollution of nearby lakes and streams.

The off-site consequences of erosion from developed sites include a variety of water quality issues. Runoff from developed sites carries pollutants, sediments and excess nutrients that disrupt aquatic habitats in the receiving waters. Nitrogen and phosphorous from runoff hasten eutrophication by causing unwanted plant growth in aquatic systems, including algal blooms that alter water quality and habitat conditions. Algal blooms can also result in decreased recreation potential and diminished diversity of indigenous fish, plant and animal populations.

Sedimentation also contributes to the degradation of water bodies. The build-up of sedimentation in stream channels can lessen flow capacity, potentially leading to increased flooding. Sedimentation also affects aquatic habitat by increasing turbidity levels. Turbidity reduces sunlight penetration into the water and leads to reduced photosynthesis in aquatic vegetation, causing lower oxygen levels that cannot support diverse communities of aquatic life.

Economic Issues

Erosion and sedimentation control measures are required in most areas in order to minimize difficult and expensive mitigation measures in receiving waters. The cost of erosion and sedimentation control on construction sites will include some minimal expense associated with installing and inspecting measures, particularly before and after storm events. The cost will vary depending on the type, location, topography and soil conditions of the project.

Resources

Please see the USGBC website at www.usgbc.org/resources for more specific resources on materials sources and other technical information.

In addition to the resources below, check with state and local organizations for information on erosion and sedimentation control specific to your region.

Websites

CPESC Inc.

www.cpesc.net

(828) 655-1600

Search the directory on this website to find certified erosion and sedimentation control professionals in your state.

Environment Canada's Freshwater Web – Sediment Page

www.ec.gc.ca/water/en/nature/sedim/e_sedim.htm

(819) 953-6161

This site includes information on the environmental effects of sedimentation.

EPA Erosion and Sediment Control Model Ordinances

www.epa.gov/owow/nps/ordinance/erosion.htm

(202) 566-1155

This resource, developed by the EPA, is geared towards helping municipalities draft ordinances for erosion and sedimentation control and might serve as a helpful tool in developing company policies for meeting this LEED-CS Prerequisite.

Erosion Control Technology Council

www.ectc.org

(651) 554-1895

This nonprofit organization develops performance standards, testing procedures, and guidance on the application and installation of rolled erosion control products.

International Erosion Control Association (IECA)

www.ieca.org

(970) 879-3010

This organization's mission is to connect, educate and develop the worldwide erosion and sediment control community.

Soil Erosion and Sedimentation in the Great Lakes Region

www.great-lakes.net/envt/pollution/erosion.html

(734) 971-9135

This resource from the Great Lakes Information Network provides links to general resources, education and training opportunities, materials, manuals, maps and other resources related to soil erosion, sedimentation and watershed management.

Definitions

Erosion is a combination of processes in which materials of the earth's surface are loosened, dissolved or worn away, and transported from one place to another by natural agents (such as water, wind or gravity).

Eutrophication is the accumulation of nutrients that encourage dense algal growth. The decay of which depletes oxygen in shallow waters.

Sedimentation is the addition of soils to water bodies by natural and human-related activities. Sedimentation decreases water quality and accelerates the aging process of lakes, rivers and streams.

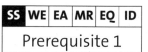

SS | WE | EA | MR | EQ | ID

Prerequisite 1

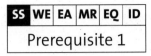

SS	WE	EA	MR	EQ	ID
Prerequisite 1					

Site Selection

1 Point

Intent

Avoid development of inappropriate sites and reduce the environmental impact from the location of a building on a site.

Requirements

Do not develop buildings, hardscape, roads or parking areas on portions of sites that meet any one of the following criteria:

❑ Prime farmland as defined by the United States Department of Agriculture in the United States Code of Federal Regulations, Title 7, Volume 6, Parts 400 to 699, Section 657.5 (citation 7CFR657.5)

❑ Previously undeveloped land whose elevation is lower than 5 feet above the elevation of the 100-year flood as defined by FEMA (Federal Emergency Management Agency)

❑ Land that is specifically identified as habitat for any species on Federal or State threatened or endangered lists

❑ Within 100 feet of any wetlands as defined by United States Code of Federal Regulations 40 CFR, Parts 230-233 and Part 22, and isolated wetlands or areas of special concern identified by state or local rule, OR within setback distances from wetlands prescribed in state or local regulations, as defined by local or state rule or law, whichever is more stringent

❑ Previously undeveloped land that is within 50 feet of a water body, defined as seas, lakes, rivers, streams and tributaries which support or could support fish, recreation or industrial use, consistent with the terminology of the Clean Water Act

❑ Land which prior to acquisition for the project was public parkland, unless land of equal or greater value as parkland is accepted in trade by the public landowner (Park Authority projects are exempt)

Potential Technologies & Strategies

During the site selection process, give preference to those sites that do not include sensitive site elements and restrictive land types. Select a suitable building location and design the building with the minimal footprint to minimize site disruption of those environmentally sensitive areas identified above.

Summary of Referenced Standards

U.S. Department of Agriculture Definition of Prime Agricultural Land as stated in

United States Code of Federal Regulations Title 7, Volume 6, Parts 400 to 699, Section 657.5 (citation 7CFR657.5)

www.gpoaccess.gov/cfr/index.html (Go to "Browse and/or search the CFR.")

See also "Identification of Important Farmlands": http://a257.g.akamaitech.net/7/257/2422/11feb20051500/edocket.access.gpo.gov/cfr_2005/janqtr/pdf/7cfr657.5.pdf

This standard states: "Prime farmland is land that has the best combination of physical and chemical characteristics for producing food, feed, forage, fiber, and oilseed crops, and is also available for these uses (the land could be cropland, pastureland, rangeland, forest land, or other land, but not urban built-up land or water). It has the soil quality, growing season, and moisture supply needed to economically produce sustained high yields of crops when treated and managed, including water management, according to acceptable farming methods. In general, prime farmlands have an adequate and dependable water supply from precipitation or irrigation, a favorable temperature and growing season, acceptable acidity or alkalinity, acceptable salt and sodium content, and few or no rocks. They are permeable to water and air. Prime farmlands are not excessively erodible or saturated with water for a long period of time, and they either do not flood frequently or are protected from flooding. Examples of soils that qualify as prime farmland are Palouse silt loam, 0 to 7 percent slopes; Brookston silty clay loam, drained; and Tama silty clay loam, 0 to 5 percent slopes."

Federal Emergency Management Agency (FEMA) 100-Year Flood Definition

Federal Emergency Management Agency

www.fema.gov

(202) 646-4600

This referenced standard addresses flood elevations. FEMA defines a 100-Year Flood as the flood elevation that has a 1% chance of being reached or exceeded each year. It is not the most significant flood in a 100-year period. Instead, 100-year floods can occur many times within a 100-year period. See the FEMA website for comprehensive information on floods and other natural disasters such as wildfires and hurricanes.

Endangered Species Lists

U.S. Fish and Wildlife Service's List of Threatened and Endangered Species

www.fws.gov/endangered/

This referenced standard addresses threatened and endangered wildlife and plants. The

Service also maintains a list of plants and animals native to the United States that are candidates for possible addition to the federal list.

National Marine Fisheries Service's List of Endangered Marine Specieswww.nmfs.noaa.gov/pr/species/esa_species.htm

Consult state agencies for state-specific lists of endangered or threatened wildlife and plant species.

Definition of Wetlands in the United States Code of Federal Regulations, 40 CFR,

Parts 230-233, and Part 22

www.gpoaccess.gov/cfr/index.html

(888) 293-6498

This referenced standard addresses wetlands and discharges of dredged or filled material into waters regulated by states. The definition of wetland areas pertaining to this credit, found in Part 230, is as follows:

"Wetlands consist of areas that are inundated or saturated by surface or ground water at a frequency and duration sufficient to support, and that under normal circumstances do support, a prevalence of vegetation typically adapted for life in saturated soil conditions."

Approach and Implementation

One of the most important factors in creating sustainable buildings is locating them on an appropriate site. Developing a building on an inappropriate site can result in the loss of prime farmland or key habitat. Before a project site is selected, evaluate the potential environmental disturbance that will occur as a result. Channel development into previously developed areas to prevent sprawl and habitat loss.

Avoid developing sites that exhibit any of the characteristics listed in the restricted criteria. Consider the proposed use of the building, and set a preference for previously developed sites that complement the use, thereby reducing associated parking needs and vehicular miles traveled. The site selection process might include landscape architects, ecologists, environmental engineers and civil engineers, as well as local professionals who can provide site-specific expertise. Have a government official, ecologist or other qualified professional perform a site survey to inventory the important environmental characteristics, including wetlands, sloped areas, unique habitat areas and forested areas. Zoning requirements of the local municipality and the community master plan should be integrated to the greatest extent possible. Community coordination and consideration of public comments can help preempt negative community reaction.

Where feasible, integrate neighboring activities to create a development with shared amenities and spaces. When designing the building, consider a smaller footprint, and set aside large contiguous areas for natural space on the project site to minimize disruption of the environmentally sensitive areas identified above. Build in dense blocks to limit the development footprint and site disturbance to the smallest area possible. Incorporate site features into the design such as natural features that already exist on the site, natural shelter from trees or terrain, natural areas for outdoor activities, and water features for thermal, acoustic and aesthetic benefit.

Calculations

There are no calculations associated with this credit.

Exemplary Performance

There is no Exemplary Performance point available for this credit.

Precertification Submittal Documentation

Provide the LEED-CS Precertification Submittal Templates, which include the following:

❑ Narrative describing how the project intends to accomplish the credit requirements on the credit-specific Submittal Template signed by the appropriate design team member

❑ Confirmation of this intent from the owner/developer on the LEED-CS Precertification Submittal Template

Certification Submittal Documentation

This credit is submitted as part of the **Design Submittal**.

Design and Construction Credit Compliance

The following project data and calculation information is required to document credit compliance using the LEED-CS v2.0 Submittal Templates:

❑ Provide confirmation that the project site does not meet any of the prohibited criteria. Special circumstances for individual projects and site compliance should be noted.

AND (For Projects with Special Circumstances)

❑ Provide a narrative to describe any special circumstances or non-standard compliance paths taken by the project.

Tenant Sales or Lease Agreement Credit Compliance

This compliance method is not available for this credit.

Considerations

Environmental Issues

As non-urban development increases, the importance of prudent site selection increases as well. Prevention of habitat encroachment is an essential element of sustainable site selection. The best strategy for selecting a building site is to choose a previously developed site. Since these sites have already been disturbed, damage to the environment is limited and sensitive land areas can be preserved. The site surrounding a building defines the character of the building and provides the first impression for occupants and visitors to the building. Creative and careful site designs can integrate the natural surroundings with the building(s), providing a strong connection between the built and natural environments and minimizing adverse impacts on the non-built portions of the site.

Habitat preservation is the most effective means to meet the requirements of the Endangered Species Act and to minimize developmental impacts on indigenous wildlife. Not building on inappropriate sites preserves these areas for wildlife, recreation and ecological balance. Building on inappropriate sites such as floodplains can be detrimental to ecosystems.

Economic Issues

Site selection can play an important role in the way that the public responds to, and is involved with, the proposed development. Channeling development away from sensitive ecological areas in favor of previously disturbed sites can encourage public support for a project and speed public review periods, thus minimizing or preventing obstacles traditionally encountered during project scoping. Economically, this can also save on mitigation costs that a developer would incur if the proposed development were approved within a sensitive area.

Appropriate site selection can reduce the risk of property damage due to natural events such as landslides, floods, sinkholes and soil erosion. Higher first costs may be encountered due to site survey and selection activities. Increased property values can offset these costs in the future. Proper site selection can also avoid potential loss of property due to potential litigation resulting from harm to endangered species.

Resources

Websites

ESRI

www.esri.com/hazards/makemap.html

This software company creates tools for GIS mapping. Its website includes an option to make a map of all of the flood areas within a user-defined location.

Natural Resources Defense Council

www.nrdc.org

(212) 727-2700

NRDC uses law, science, and a large membership base for protection of wildlife and wild places to ensure a safe and healthy environment.

Print Media

Constructed Wetlands in the Sustainable Landscape by Craig Campbell and Michael Ogden, John Wiley & Sons, 1999.

Holding Our Ground: Protecting America's Farms and Farmland by Tom Daniels and Deborah Bowers, Island Press, 1997.

Saved By Development: Preserving Environmental Areas, Farmland by Rick Pruetz, Arje Press, 1997.

Wetland Indicators: A Guide to Wetland Identification, Delineation, Classification, and Mapping by Ralph W. Tiner, Lewis Publishers, 1999.

Definitions

A **Community** is an interacting population of individuals living in a specific area.

The **Development Footprint** is the area on the project site that has been impacted by any development activity. Hardscape, access roads, parking lots, non-building facilities and building structure are all included in the development footprint.

An **Ecosystem** is a basic unit of nature that includes a community of organisms and their nonliving environment linked by biological, chemical and physical process.

An **Endangered Species** is an animal or plant species that is in danger of becoming extinct throughout all or a significant portion of its range due to harmful human activities or environmental factors.

Previously Developed Sites are those that previously contained buildings, roadways, parking lots, or were graded or altered by direct human activities.

A **Threatened Species** is an animal or plant species that is likely to become endangered within the foreseeable future.

Wetland Vegetation consists of plants that require saturated soils to survive, as well as certain tree and other plant species that can tolerate prolonged wet soil conditions.

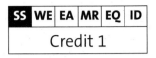

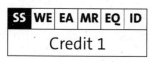

Credit 1

Development Density & Community Connectivity

Credit 2

1 Point

Intent

Channel development to urban areas with existing infrastructure, protect greenfields and preserve habitat and natural resources.

Requirements

OPTION 1 — DEVELOPMENT DENSITY

Construct or renovate building on a previously developed site AND in a community with a minimum density of 60,000 sq.ft. per acre net. (Note: density calculation must include the area of the project being built and is based on a typical two-story downtown development.)

OR

OPTION 2 — COMMUNITY CONNECTIVITY

Construct or renovate building on a previously developed site AND within 1/2 mile of a residential zone or neighborhood with an average density of 10 units per acre net AND within 1/2 mile of at least 10 Basic Services AND with pedestrian access between the building and the services.

Basic Services include, but are not limited to–

1) Bank; 2) Place of Worship; 3) Convenience Grocery; 4) Day Care; 5) Cleaners; 6) Fire Station; 7) Beauty; 8) Hardware; 9) Laundry; 10) Library; 11) Medical/Dental; 12) Senior Care Facility; 13) Park; 14) Pharmacy; 15) Post Office; 16) Restaurant; 17) School; 18) Supermarket; 19) Theater; 20) Community Center; 21) Fitness Center; and 22) Museum.

Proximity is determined by drawing a 1/2-mile radius around the main building entrance on a site map and counting the services within that radius.

Potential Technologies & Strategies

During the site selection process, give preference to urban sites with pedestrian access to a variety of services.

Can assist in certification under LEED for Existing Buildings Operations and Maintenance

Can assist tenants in certification under LEED for Commercial Interiors

Summary of Referenced Standard

There is no standard referenced for this credit.

Approach and Implementation

The general approach for achieving this credit is to give preference to sites within an existing urban fabric. Work with local jurisdictions and follow the urban development plan to meet or exceed density goals. Consider synergies with neighbors and choose sites based on infrastructure, transportation and quality-of-life considerations. Sites with redevelopment plans that will achieve the required development density by the completion of the project should not be excluded from consideration. This credit can be achieved by choosing to develop a site where community revitalization is occurring provided the required development density or basic services adjacency is in place or in construction by the project's completion.

Calculations

Option 1 — Development Density

To determine the development density of a project, both the project density and the densities of surrounding developments must be considered. The calculations detailed below refer to the building(s) that define the LEED-CS pursuing certification, the project site area, and the area and density of the surrounding buildings.

Note: The LEED-CS Submittal Template can be used to perform these calculations.

1. Determine the total area of the project site and the total square footage of the building. For projects that are part of a larger property (such as a campus), define the project area that is defined in the LEED project's scope. The project area must be defined consistently throughout LEED documentation.

2. Calculate the development density for the project by dividing the total square footage of the building by the total site area in acres. This development density must be equal to or greater than 60,000 sq.ft. per acre (see **Equation 1**).

3. Convert the total site area from acres to sq.ft. and calculate the square root of this number. Then multiply the square root by three to determine the appropriate density radius. (Note: the square root function is used to normalize the calculation by removing effects of site shape.) (See **Equation 2**.)

4. Overlay the density radius on a map (see **Figure 1**) that includes the project site and surrounding areas, originating from the center of the site. This is the density boundary.

5. For each property within the density boundary and for those properties that intersect the density boundary, create a table with the building square footage and site area of each property. Include all properties in the density calculations except for undeveloped public areas such as parks and water bodies. Do not include public roads and right-of-way areas. Information on neighboring properties can be obtained from your city or county zoning department.

Equation 1

$$\text{Development Density (sq.ft./acre)} = \frac{\text{Gross Building Square Footage (sq.ft.)}}{\text{Project Site Area (acres)}}$$

Equation 2

$$\text{Density Radius (LF)} = 3 \times \sqrt{\text{Property Area [acres]} \times 43{,}560 \text{ [sq.ft./acre]}}$$

Figure 1: An illustration of a Sample Area Plan

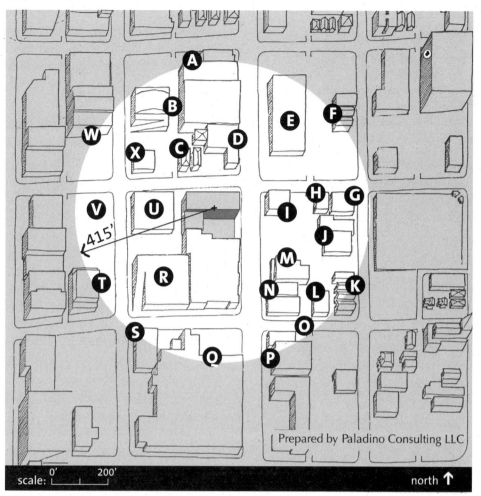

Prepared by Paladino Consulting LLC

scale: 0' 200'

north ↑

6. Add all the square footage values and site areas. Divide the total square footage by the total site area to obtain the average property density within the density boundary. The average property density of the properties within the density boundary must be equal to or greater than 60,000 sq.ft. per acre.

Example

The following example illustrates the property density calculations: A 30,000-sq.ft. building is located on a 0.44-acre urban site and the calculations are used to determine the building density. The property density is above the minimum density of 60,000 sq.ft. per acre required by the credit (see **Table 1**).

Table 1: Property Density Calculation

Project Buildings	Building Space [SF]	Site Area [acres]
Project	30,000	0.44
Density [SF/acre]		**68,182**

Table 2: Density Radius Calculation

Density Radius Calculation	
Site Area [acres]	0.44
Density Radius [LF]	415

Next, the density radius is determined. A density radius of 415 feet is calculated (see **Table 2**). The density radius is applied to an area plan of the project site and surrounding area. The plan identifies all properties that are within or are

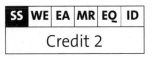
intersected by the density radius. The plan includes a scale and a north indicator.

Table 3 summarizes the information about the properties identified on the map (see **Figure 1**). The building space and site area are listed for each property. These values are summed and the average density is calculated by dividing the total building space by the total site area.

For this example, the average building density of the surrounding area is greater than 60,000 sq.ft. per acre, thus, the example qualifies for one point under this credit.

OR

Option 2 — Community Connectivity

To determine the connectivity of a project, both residential and commercial adjacencies must be considered. The calculation process is described in the following steps:

Prepare a site map (**Figure 2**) and draw a 1/2-mile radius around the main building entrance. Radiuses may be drawn around multiple entrances for projects with multiple buildings or more than one main entrance. The combination of the area in these radiuses would then be considered the project radius. Mark all residential developments within the radius. At least one area zoned for residential development of 10 units per acre or greater must be present within the radius for the project to earn this credit.

Mark all commercial buildings within the radius. At least 10 community services must be present within the radius for the project to earn this credit.

Services may include: Bank, Place of Worship, Convenience Grocery, Day Care, Cleaners, Fire Station, Beauty, Hardware, Laundry, Library, Medical/Dental, Senior Care Facility, Park, Pharmacy, Post Office, Restaurant, School, Supermarket, Commercial Office, and Community Center. Other services will be considered on a project-by-project basis.

With the exception of restaurants, no service may be counted more than once in the calculation. Up to 2 restaurants may be counted towards achievement of this credit. Only count those services for which there is pedestrian access between the service and the project. Pedestrian access is assessed by confirming that pedestrians can walk to the services without

Table 3: Sample Area Properties

Buildings within Density Radius	Building Space [SF]	Site Area [acres]	Buildings within Density Radius	Building Space [SF]	Site Area [acres]
A	33,425	0.39	N	28,740	0.30
B	87,500	1.58	O	6,690	0.15
C	6,350	0.26	P	39,000	0.39
D	27,560	0.32	Q	348,820	2.54
E	66,440	1.17	R	91,250	1.85
F	14,420	1.36	S	22,425	0.27
G	12,560	0.20	T	33,650	0.51
H	6,240	0.14	U	42,400	0.52
I	14,330	0.22	V	-	0.76
J	29,570	0.41	W	19,200	0.64
K	17,890	0.31	X	6,125	0.26
L	9,700	0.31	Y	5,000	0.30
M	24,080	0.64	Z	4,300	0.24
			Total Building Space [SF]	997,665	
			Total Site Area [acres]		16.04
			Average Density [SF/acres]		**62,199**

U.S. Green Building Council

Figure 2: Example Map for Community Connectivity (Source: Google Maps)

being blocked by walls, highways or other barriers.

Prepare a table (see **Table 4**) listing each of the identified services, the business name, and the service type to confirm compliance.

Exemplary Performance

There is no Exemplary Performance point available for this credit.

Table 4: Example Community Connectivity Tabulation

Service Identification (Corresponds to Uploaded Vicinity Plan)	Business Name	Service Type
1	Restaurant 1	Restaurant
2	Grocery 1	Convenience Grocery
3	Urgent Care 1	Medical
4	Pharmacy 1	Pharmacy
5	Gym 1	Fitness
6	Hair Care 1	Beauty
7	Bank 1	Bank
8	Restaurant 2	Restaurant
9	Cleaners 1	Cleaners
10	Post Office 1	Post Office

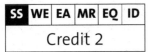

Precertification Submittal Documentation

Provide the LEED-CS Precertification Submittal Templates, which include the following:

❑ Narrative describing how the project intends to accomplish the credit requirements on the credit-specific Submittal Template signed by the appropriate design team member

❑ Confirmation of this intent from the owner/developer on the LEED-CS Precertification Submittal Template

Certification Submittal Documentation

Design and Construction Credit Compliance

This credit is submitted as part of the **Design Submittal**.

The following project data and calculation information is required to document credit compliance using the LEED-CS v2.0 Submittal Templates:

Option 1 — Development Density

❑ Provide a site vicinity plan showing the project site and the surrounding sites and buildings. Sketches, block diagrams, maps, and aerial photos are all acceptable for this purpose. Draw the density boundary on the drawing or note the drawing scale.

❑ Provide a project site and building area (sq.ft.).

❑ Submit a listing of site and building areas for all surrounding sites within the density radius.

OR

Option 2 — Community Connectivity

❑ Provide a site vicinity drawing showing the project site, the 1/2 mile community radius, and the locations of the community services surrounding the project site. Sketches, block diagrams, maps and aerial photos are all acceptable for this purpose. Indicate either the 1/2-mile radius on the drawing or note the drawing scale.

❑ Provide a project site and building area (sq.ft.).

❑ Submit a listing (including business name and type) of all community services within the 1/2-mile radius.

AND (For Projects With Special Circumstances — Either Compliance Path)

❑ Provide an optional narrative to describe any special circumstances or non-standard compliance paths taken by the project.

Tenant Sales or Lease Agreement Credit Compliance

This compliance method is not available for this credit.

Considerations

Environmental Issues

Consider the functional adjacencies of the site with respect to transportation and productivity. Community developments with at least 10 of the basic services listed in this credit within a 1/2-mile radius reduce transportation impacts. Making access to basic services walkable may improve productivity by reducing the time spent driving between services and accessing parking. In addition, occupant health can be improved by increased levels of physical activity.

Urban redevelopment affects all areas of site design including site selection, transportation planning, building density and stormwater management. Urban sites often involve the rehabilitation of an existing building, with a reduction of construction waste and new material use. The potential trade-offs of sites in dense areas are limited open space and possible negative IEQ aspects such as contaminated soils, undesirable air quality or limited daylighting applications.

Economic Issues

A significant economic benefit of infill development is the reduction or elimination of new infrastructure, including roads, utility services and other amenities already in place. If mass transit serves the urban site, significant cost reductions are possible by downsizing the project parking capacity. Urban infill development sometimes requires significant additional costs when compared with suburban development due to site constraints, contaminated soils and other issues. Municipal and county incentives for urban infill projects may also be available.

Community Issues

Urban sprawl affects quality of life because commuters must spend increasing amounts of time in their automobiles. In addition, families often need more vehicles to accommodate family needs, resulting in a higher cost of living and less free time. The redevelopment of urban areas helps restore, invigorate and sustain established urban living patterns, creating a more stable and interactive community.

Resources

Please see the USGBC website at www. usgbc.org/resources for more specific resources on materials sources and other technical information.

Websites

Congress for New Urbanism

www.cnu.org

Urban Land Institute

ULI Washington

www.washington.uli.org

(703) 390-9217

The Urban Land Institute is a nonprofit organization based in Washington D.C. that promotes the responsible use of land in order to enhance the total environment.

The International Union for the Scientific Study of Population

www.iussp.org

33 1 56 06 21 73

The IUSSP promotes scientific studies of demography and population-related issues.

Print Media

Changing Places: Rebuilding Community in the Age of Sprawl by Richard Moe and Carter Wilkie, Henry Holt & Company, 1999.

Density by Design: New Directions in Residential Development by Steven Fader, Urban Land Institute, 2000.

Green Development: Integrating Ecology and Real Estate by Alex Wilson, et al., John Wiley & Sons, 1998.

Once There Were Greenfields: How Urban Sprawl Is Undermining America's Environment, Economy, and Social Fabric by F. Kaid Benfield, et al., Natural Resources Defense Council, 1999.

Suburban Nation: The Rise of Sprawl and the Decline of the American Dream by Andres Duany, et al., North Point Press, 2000.

Definitions

Building Density is the floor area of the building divided by the total area of the site (square feet per acre).

Greenfields are sites that have not been previously developed or built on, and which could support open space, habitat or agriculture.

Pedestrian Access implies that pedestrians can walk to the services without being blocked by walls, freeways or other barriers.

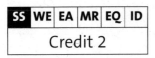

SS WE EA MR EQ ID

Credit 2

Property Area is the total area within the legal property boundaries of a site and encompasses all areas of the site including constructed areas and non-constructed areas.

Site Area is defined the same as property area.

The **Square Footage** of a building is the total area in square feet of all rooms including corridors, elevators, stairwells and shaft spaces.

Brownfield Redevelopment

Intent

Rehabilitate damaged sites where development is complicated by environmental contamination, reducing pressure on undeveloped land.

Requirements

Develop on a site documented as contaminated (by means of an ASTM E1903-97 Phase II Environmental Site Assessment or a local Voluntary Cleanup Program) OR on a site defined as a brownfield by a local, state or federal government agency.

Can assist tenants in certification under LEED for Commercial Interiors

Potential Technologies & Strategies

During the site selection process, give preference to brownfield sites. Identify tax incentives and property cost savings. Coordinate site development plans with remediation activity, as appropriate.

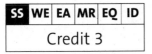

Credit 3

Summary of Referenced Standards

ASTM E1903-97 Phase II Environmental Site Assessment

ASTM International

www.astm.org

This guide covers a framework for employing good commercial and customary practices in conducting a Phase II environmental site assessment of a parcel of commercial property. It covers the potential presence of a range of contaminants that are within the scope of CERCLA, as well as petroleum products.

EPA Brownfields Definition

U.S. EPA Sustainable Redevelopment of Brownfields Program

www.epa.gov/brownfields

With certain legal exclusions and additions, the term "brownfield site" means real property, the expansion, redevelopment, or reuse of which may be complicated by the presence or potential presence of a hazardous substance, pollutant or contaminant (source: Public Law 107-118, H.R. 2869 – "Small Business Liability Relief and Brownfields Revitalization Act"). See the website for additional information and resources.

Approach and Implementation

Gain community support by highlighting the environmental, economic and community-related benefits of brownfield redevelopment. Negotiate with local municipalities and landowners for below-market purchase prices for brownfield real estate. Also, obtain tax incentives by meeting the locally applicable requirements of EPA brownfield tax credits. The advantages and disadvantages of brownfield redevelopment should be carefully considered during the site selection process.

Utilize remediation experts to develop a master plan for site remediation. Prioritize site remediation activities based on available funds and specific site considerations, and establish time frames for completing remediation activities. Test for toxicity and hazardous levels of pollution on the proposed site. To earn this credit, a site with existing hazardous substances present or potentially present must be selected, and remediation efforts must be performed to identify, contain and mitigate the hazard.

Clean the site using established technologies that have minimal disruption on the natural site features, both above ground and underground. Consider in-situ remediation schemes that treat contaminants in place instead of off-site. Once remediation is complete, continue to monitor the site for the identified contaminants to ensure that contamination problems do not return.

Remediation efforts on brownfield sites are sometimes costly and time-intensive due to the potentially extensive effort required to characterize the contamination, evaluate cleanup options and perform cleanup activities. However, substantially lower property costs can offset remediation costs and time delays. The cost of remediation strategies varies by site and region. Several remediation strategies should be considered in order to identify the strategy with the greatest benefit and lowest cost to the property owner. The appropriate technology for a specific site depends on the contaminants present, hydrogeologic conditions and other factors. Traditional remediation efforts for contaminated groundwater are termed "pump-and-treat." Pump-and-treat technologies involve pumping contaminated groundwater to the surface and treating the water using physical or chemical processes. Contaminated soils can be remediated in a variety of ways. Advanced technologies such as bioreactors and in-situ applications are sometimes more cost-effective than hauling large quantities of contaminated soil to an approved disposal facility. Innovative remediation efforts such as solar detoxification technologies are currently being developed and are expected to reduce remediation costs in the future. It is important to consider the environmental implications of all remediation strategies being investigated for your project to ensure the solution does not cause problems elsewhere.

Calculations

There are no calculations associated with this credit.

Exemplary Performance

There is no Exemplary Performance point available for this credit.

Precertification Submittal Documentation

Provide the LEED-CS Precertification Submittal Templates, which include the following:

❑ Narrative describing how the project intends to accomplish the credit requirements on the credit-specific Submittal Template signed by the appropriate design team member

❑ Confirmation of this intent from the owner/developer on the LEED-CS Precertification Submittal Template

Certification Submittal Documentation

Design and Construction Credit Compliance

This credit is submitted as part of the **Design Submittal**.

The following project data and calculation information is required to document credit compliance using the LEED-CS v2.0 Submittal Templates:

❑ Provide confirmation whether the project site was determined contaminated by means of an ASTM E1903-97 Phase II Environmental Site Assessment or the site was defined as a brownfield by a local, state or federal government agency.

❑ Provide a detailed narrative describing the site contamination and remediation efforts undertaken by the project.

Tenant Sales or Lease Agreement Credit Compliance

This compliance method is not available for this credit.

Considerations

Environmental Issues

Many potential building sites in urban locations have been abandoned due to real or potential contamination from previous industrial or municipal activities. These sites can be remediated and redeveloped for reuse. Environmental and economic concerns are key issues when evaluating brownfield redevelopment. Costs incurred to remediate site contamination and land prices can be additive or can offset each other. Perception of the building site by the building owner and future building occupants must also be weighed. Building owners may be wary of cleanup requirements and the potential for liability associated with contaminants migrating off-site and impacting downstream neighbors. Building occupants may worry about health risks from breathing contaminated air or coming into contact with contaminated soil. These concerns must be investigated and resolved before making the final decision to redevelop a brownfield site.

Remediation efforts remove hazardous materials from brownfield sites' soil and groundwater. This reduces the exposure of humans and wildlife to health risks as

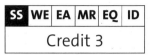

SS	WE	EA	MR	EQ	ID

Credit 3

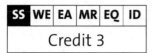
a result of environmental pollution. Redevelopment of brownfield sites provides an alternate option to developing on greenfield sites. Preservation of greenfield sites for future generations decreases the overall environmental impact of development. Brownfields often have existing infrastructure improvements in place including utilities and roads, reducing the need for further environmental impacts due to construction of new infrastructure. In some instances, rather than remediate the contamination, it may be more sensible to leave contaminants in place, choosing instead to stabilize and isolate the contaminants from human exposure.

Brownfields can offer an attractive location and are often inexpensive when compared to comparable uncontaminated properties. It is essential to weigh the value of the remediated property against cleanup costs to determine if the site is economically viable for redevelopment. Developers have been reluctant to redevelop brownfield sites in the past due to potential liability associated with taking responsibility for the cleanup of others' contamination. In recent years, the EPA and many state and local government agencies have begun to provide incentives for brownfield redevelopment by enacting laws that reduce the liability of developers who choose to remediate contaminated sites. Before embarking on a brownfield development effort, it is important to contact state and local regulators to determine the rules governing these sites and available financial assistance programs. It may also be helpful to contact the regional EPA's Office of Solid Waste and Emergency Response (OSWER), which may provide site characterization and remediation support.

Economic Issues

Remediation and reclamation of contaminated sites can contribute to social and economic revitalization of depressed or disadvantaged neighborhoods. Local liabilities can be turned into valuable community assets and catalyze increased community investment. Clean up of contaminated properties can renew and augment a sense of community pride in local residents.

Resources

Please see the USGBC website at www. usgbc.org/resources for more specific resources on materials sources and other technical information.

Websites

Brownfields Technology Support Center

www.brownfieldstsc.org

A public cooperative effort that provides technical support to federal, state and local officials on items related to site investigation and cleanup.

EPA Sustainable Redevelopment of Brownfields Program

www.epa.gov/brownfields

A comprehensive site on brownfields that includes projects, initiatives, tools, tax incentives and other resources to address brownfield remediation and redevelopment. For information by phone, contact your regional EPA office.

Print Media

ASTM Standard Practice E1739-95: Risk-Based Corrective Action Applied at Petroleum Release Sites

American Society for Testing & Materials

www.astm.org

(610) 832-9585

This document is a guide for risk-based corrective action (RBCA), a decision making process that is specific to cleaning up petroleum releases at contaminated sites. It presents a tiered approach to site assessment and remedial actions. It also includes a comprehensive appendix with risk calculations and sample applications.

EPA OSWER Directive 9610.17: Use of Risk-Based Decision-Making in UST Correction Action Programs

U.S. Environmental Protection Agency, Office of Underground Storage Tanks

www.epa.gov/swerust1/directiv/od961017.htm

(703) 603-7149

This document addresses the application of risk-based decision-making techniques to properties where leaking underground storage tanks (USTs) have created risks to human health and the environment. Guidelines are included to assist in making decisions in a manner consistent with federal law, specifically CERCLA and RCRA programs. Risk-based decision-making is a method that utilizes risk and exposure assessment methodology to determine the extent and urgency of cleanup actions. The goal is to protect human health and the environment. This standard includes several examples of state programs that use risk-based decision-making in leaking UST legislation.

Definitions

Bioremediation involves the use of microorganisms and vegetation to remove contaminants from water and soils. Bioremediation is generally a form of in-situ remediation, and can be a viable alternative to landfilling or incineration.

CERCLA refers to the Comprehensive Environmental Response, Compensation, and Liability Act (CERCLA), commonly known as Superfund. CERCLA addresses abandoned or historical waste sites and contamination. It was enacted in 1980 to create a tax on the chemical and petroleum industries and provided federal authority to respond to releases of hazardous substances.

Ex-Situ Remediation involves the removal of contaminated soil and groundwater. Treatment of the contaminated media occurs in another location, typically a treatment facility. A traditional method of ex-situ remediation is pump-and-treat technology that uses carbon filters and incineration. More advanced methods of ex-situ remediation include chemical treatment or biological reactors.

In-Situ Remediation involves treatment of contaminants in place using technologies such as injection wells or reactive trenches. These methods utilize the natural hydraulic gradient of groundwater and usually require only minimal disturbance of the site.

RCRA refers to the Resource Conservation and Recovery Act. RCRA focuses on active and future facilities. It was enacted in 1976 to give the EPA authority to control hazardous wastes from cradle to grave, including generation, transportation, treatment, storage and disposal. Some non-hazardous wastes are also covered under RCRA.

Remediation is the process of cleaning up a contaminated site by physical, chemical or biological means. Remediation processes are typically applied to contaminated soil and groundwater.

Risk Assessment is a methodology used to analyze for potential health effects caused by contaminants in the environment. Information from the risk assessment is used to determine cleanup levels.

Site Assessment is an evaluation of above-ground (including facilities) and subsurface characteristics, including the geology and hydrology of the site, to determine if a release has occurred, as well as the extent and concentration of the release. Information generated during a site assessment is used to support remedial action decisions.

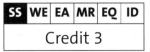

SS | WE | EA | MR | EQ | ID
Credit 3

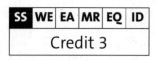

SS	WE	EA	MR	EQ	ID
Credit 3					

Alternative Transportation

Public Transportation Access

Intent

Reduce pollution and land development impacts from automobile use.

Requirements

Locate project within 1/2 mile of an existing—or planned and funded—commuter rail, light rail or subway station.

OR

Locate project within 1/4 mile of one or more stops for two or more public or campus bus lines usable by building occupants.

Potential Technologies & Strategies

Perform a transportation survey of future building occupants to identify transportation needs. Site the building near mass transit.

Can assist in certification under LEED for Existing Buildings Operations and Maintenance

Can assist tenants in certification under LEED for Commercial Interiors

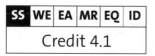
Summary of Referenced Standard

There is no standard referenced for this credit.

Approach and Implementation

Select a site that has convenient access to existing transportation networks to minimize the need for new transportation lines. Local telephone books and community websites provide maps and directories that will be helpful in determining the transportation options available. Look for functional and direct sidewalks, paths and walkways to existing mass transit stops. Provide incentives such as transit passes to encourage occupants to use mass transit.

If a light rail or subway station is sited, planned and funded at the time the project is completed, it satisfies the intent of the credit.

Calculations

Use an area drawing to indicate mass transit stops within 1/2 mile of the project. Remember that the project is required to be within a 1/2 mile pedestrian route to a commuter rail, light rail or subway station or within 1/4 mile of two or more bus lines. **Figure 1** shows two bus lines within 1/4 mile of the project location. The map includes a scale bar and a north indicator.

Figure 1: Sample Area Drawing

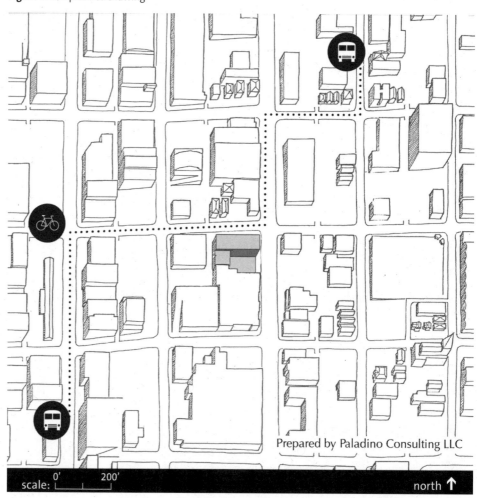

Prepared by Paladino Consulting LLC

scale: 0' 200'   north ↑

Exemplary Performance

Projects may be awarded one innovation point for Exemplary Performance in alternative transportation, SS Credit 4, by instituting a comprehensive transportation management plan that demonstrates a quantifiable reduction in personal automobile use through the implementation of multiple alternative options.

Precertification Submittal Documentation

Provide the LEED-CS Precertification Submittal Templates, which include the following:

❑ Narrative describing how the project intends to accomplish the credit requirements on the credit-specific Submittal Template signed by the appropriate design team member

❑ Confirmation of this intent from the owner/developer on the LEED-CS Precertification Submittal Template

Certification Submittal Documentation

Design and Construction Credit Compliance

This credit is submitted as part of the **Design Submittal**.

The following project data and calculation information is required to document credit compliance using the LEED-CS v2.0 Submittal Templates:

Commuter Rail Service

❑ Provide a site vicinity drawing showing the project site and the location of all (existing/proposed) fixed rail stations within 1/2 mile of the site.

❑ Provide a listing of each fixed rail station and the distance from the station to the project site (miles).

OR

Bus Service

❑ Provide a site vicinity drawing showing the project site and the location of all existing bus stops within 1/4 mile of the site.

❑ Provide a listing of each bus line that serves the site vicinity and the distance from the bus stop to the project site (miles).

Tenant Sales or Lease Agreement Credit Compliance

This compliance method is not available for this credit.

Considerations

Environmental Issues

The environmental effects of automobile use include vehicle emissions that contribute to smog and air pollution as well as environmental impacts from oil extraction and petroleum refining. Increased use of public transportation can improve air quality. A surprisingly large number of people are willing to use alternative means of transportation such as mass transit if it is convenient and facilities are provided to encourage their use. Encouraging the use of mass transit reduces the energy demand for transportation needs and affects building sites by reducing the space needed for parking lots, which encroach on green space on the building site. Minimizing parking lots reduces the building footprint and sets aside more space for natural areas or greater development densities.

Reduction in private vehicle use reduces fuel consumption and air and water pollutants in vehicle exhaust. On the basis of passenger miles traveled, public transportation is approximately twice as fuel efficient as private vehicles. Another benefit of public transportation is the associated reduction in the need for infrastructure used by vehicles. Parking facilities and roadways for automobiles have negative impacts on the environment because impervious surfaces like asphalt increase stormwater runoff while contributing to urban heat island effects.

Economic Issues

Many occupants view proximity to mass transit as a benefit and this can influence the value and marketability of the building. For building occupants, costs associated with traveling to and from the workplace can be significantly reduced if access to public transportation is available. For this reason, providing access to public transportation may yield an economic benefit associated with attracting and retaining employees. Existing building project teams have little to no control over their building's proximity to mass transit. If a building is not near mass transit, a shuttle can be provided to earn this credit, but this would be an added operating cost for the building.

Reducing the size of parking areas based on anticipated use of public transit by building occupants may alter operating costs associated with parking lot maintenance. If local utilities charge for stormwater based on impervious surface area, minimization of these areas can result in lower stormwater charges.

Resources

Please see the USGBC website at www. usgbc.org/resources for more specific resources on materials sources and other technical information.

Websites

Office of Transportation and Air Quality

U.S. Environmental Protection Agency

www.epa.gov/otaq/

This U.S. EPA website provides information on the types and effects of air pollution associated with automobile use, information for consumers, and links to resources for organizations interested in promoting commuter choice programs.

Best Workplaces for Commuters

www.bestworkplacesforcommuters.gov/index.htm

(888) 856-3131

This program, established by the U.S. EPA and DOT, publicly recognizes employers for their exemplary commuter benefits programs. It provides tools, guidance and promotions to help employers incorporate commuter benefits into their employee benefits plan, reap financial benefits and gain national recognition.

Advanced Transportation Technology Institute

www.atti-info.org

A nonprofit organization that advances clean transportation technologies through research, education and technology transfer in order to promote a healthy environment and energy independence.

Definitions

Mass Transit is a publicly or privately operated transportation service that provides transportation, for the general public, to multiple fixed stops on a scheduled basis. Mass transit vehicles are typically capable of serving 10 or more occupants, such as buses, trolleys, light rail, etc.

Public Transportation is bus, rail or other transportation service for the general public operating on a regular, continual basis that is publicly or privately owned.

Alternative Transportation

Bicycle Storage & Changing Rooms

Can assist tenants in certification under LEED for Commercial Interiors

Intent

Reduce pollution and land development impacts from automobile use.

Requirements

CASE 1

For commercial or institutional buildings with a total gross square footage of less than 300,000 sq.ft., provide secure bicycle racks and/or storage (within 200 yards of a building entrance) for 3% or more of all building users (calculated on average for the year), AND provide shower and changing facilities in the building, or within 200 yards of a building entrance, for 5% of Full-Time Equivalent (FTE) occupants.

CASE 2

For projects with a total gross square footage greater than 300,000 sq.ft., provide secure bicycle storage for 3% of the occupants for up to 300,000 sq.ft., then an additional 5% for the occupants for the space over 300,000 sq.ft. Mixed-use buildings with a total gross square footage greater than 300,000 sq.ft. must apply this calculation for each use in the building, AND provide shower and changing facilities in the building, or within 200 yards of a building entrance, for 5% of Full-Time Equivalent (FTE) occupants.

CASE 3

For residential buildings or the residential portion of a mixed-use building, provide covered storage facilities for securing bicycles for 15% or more of building occupants in lieu of changing/shower facilities.

See Appendix 1 — Default Occupancy Counts for occupancy count requirements and guidance.

Potential Technologies & Strategies

Design the building with transportation amenities such as bicycle racks and showering/changing facilities.

Summary of Referenced Standard

There is no standard referenced for this credit.

Approach and Implementation

Select a site that provides convenient access to safe bicycle pathways and secure bicycle storage areas for cyclists. Provide shower and changing areas for cyclists that are easily accessible from bicycle storage areas.

During the site selection process, consider potential building occupants and users and determine if the available bike routes and their compatibility with mass transit options meet their needs. Look for functional and direct paths that can be used by bicycle commuters. This information will help determine the size, type and location of bike racks and showering facilities for the project. Commercial office buildings should consider the regional commuting patterns and provide amenities appropriately. Retail developments should consider bicycle usage for both employees and retail customers.

There are a number of different types of secure bike storage systems, and design and costs will vary. Secure bicycle storage means that bikes can be individually locked and stored (i.e. in a bicycle rack). For residential projects, bike storage must be covered to protect bicycles from weather as well as theft.

For projects that are located on a multiple building development, showering facili-

Equation 1

$$\text{FTE Occupants} = \frac{\text{Occupant Hours}}{8}$$

Equation 2

$$\text{FTE Occupants} = \frac{\text{Building Gross Square Foot}}{\text{Gross Square Foot per FTE}}$$

ties can be shared between buildings as long as the facilities are within 200 yards of the entrance to the building pursuing LEED certification.

Calculations

Case 1

To determine the number of secure bicycle spaces and changing/showering facilities required for the building, use the calculation methodology as follows:

1. Identify the total number of full-time and part-time building occupants.

2. Calculate the Full-Time Equivalent (FTE) building occupants based on a standard 8-hour occupancy period. An 8-hour occupant has an FTE value of 1.0 while a part-time occupant has a FTE value based on their hours per day divided by 8 (see **Equation 1**). Note that FTE calculations for the project must be used consistently for all LEED-CS credits. In buildings with multiple shifts, use only the highest volume shift in the FTE calculation but consider shift overlap when calculating building users.

Core and shell buildings projects may not have identified the final occupancy count. Projects that do not know the occupancy count must utilize the default occupancy counts provided in Appendix 1 (see **Equation 2**). Projects that do know the tenant occupancy must use these numbers as long as the gross square foot per employee is not greater than that in the default occupancy count table.

3. Estimate the Transient occupants, such as visitors and customers, for the facility.

4. Calculate building users by combining FTE occupants and Transient occupants.

5. Calculate the average annual building users by performing this calculation for at least three (3) use periods dur-

ing the year—peak, low, and typical. This is particularly important for retail development projects. Other building types such as commercial office buildings or medical office buildings may vary only slightly, if at all, during the year.

6. The minimum number of **secure bicycle spaces** required is equal to 3% of the average annual building users (see **Equation 3**). Secure bicycle spaces include bicycle racks, lockers and storage rooms. These spaces should be easily accessible by building occupants during all periods of the year, and be provided free of charge.

7. The required number of **changing** and **showering facilities** is equal to 5% of the FTE occupants. Showering facilities can be unit showers or group showering facilities. (See **Equation 4**.)

Case 2

Many core and shell buildings, particularly in the commercial office market, have a gross square footage greater than 300,000 sq.ft. For buildings of this scale, the bicycle storage requirement is determined based on the FTE occupants for the square footage up to 300,000 (per use) and then again for the square footage above 300,000 sq.ft. To determine the number of secure bicycle spaces and changing/showering facilities required for the building, follow the calculation methodology below:

1. To determine the minimum number of bicycle spaces, perform the calculations outlined in Case 1, steps 1 through 6. For multiple use buildings, perform this calculation for each use.

2. Prorate the Average Annual Building Users for the building square footage less than or equal to 300,000 sq.ft. (see **Equation 5**), and the building square footage greater than 300,000 sq.ft. (see **Equation 6**) for each building use.

3. For each use greater that 300,000 gross square feet, the additional secure bicycle storage spaces required is equal to 5% of the average annual building users calculated for the remaining building square feet (see **Equation 7**).

4. The required number of changing and showering facilities is equal to 5% of the FTE occupants. Showering facilities can be unit showers or group showering facilities (see **Equation 3**).

Equation 3

Secure Bicycle Spaces = Average Annual Building Users x 0.03

Equation 4

Showering Facilities = FTE Occupants x 0.05

Equation 5

Average Annual Building Users (</= 300,000sq.ft.) =
Average Annual Building Users x 300,000sq.ft. / building square footage

Equation 6

Average Annual Building Users (> 300,000 sq.ft.) = Average Annual Building Users x
(building square footage – 300,000 sq.ft.) / building square footage

Equation 7

Secure Bicycle Spaces = Average Annual Building Users (> 300,000 sq.ft.) x 0.05

Equation 8

Showering Facilities = FTE Occupants x 0.05

Equation 9

Secure Bicycle Spaces = occupants x 0.15

Case 3

The minimum number of secure and covered bicycle spaces required is equal to 15% of the building occupants for residential projects. Changing and shower facilities in addition to those in the residential units are not required (see **Equation 9**).

Example: Case 1 — commercial office building less than 300,000 gross square feet

Many core and shell buildings are mid size, single-use commercial office buildings. These buildings are often programmed for single shift occupancy. An example of the calculations for this type of building follows.

Building square footage: **125,000 sq.ft.**

Gross square feet per employee (from Appendix 1 or tenant use as applicable): **250 sq.ft./FTE**

FTE occupants = 125,000 / 250 = **500**

Secure Bicycle Spaces = 500 x 0.03 = **15 bicycle spaces**

Shower and changing facilities = 500 x 0.05 = 2.5, therefore provide **3**

Example: Case 2 — mixed use commercial office building and retail greater than 300,000 gross square feet

Many urban core and shell buildings are large, multi-use buildings with a retail base and commercial office above. This example will illustrate a 580,000 gross square foot single shift occupancy. An example of the calculations for this type of building follows.

Building square footage:

| Commercial Office | 560,000 |
| Retail | 20,000 |

Gross square feet per employee (from Appendix 1 or tenant use as applicable):

| Commercial Office | 250 |
| Retail | 550 |

Building Total (SF)	**560,000**		
Building Usage (SF)	Commercial Office:		560,000
	Retail:		20,000
SF per Employee	Commercial Office:		250
	Retail:		650

Determining FTE Occupants / Commercial:

$$\frac{560,000}{250} = 2,240$$

Determining FTE Occupants / Retail:

$$\frac{20,000}{550} = (36.38)\ \mathbf{37}$$

Retail Transient Occupants			
Low	200		
High	570		
Typical	350	**Average +**	**373**
Total Retail FTE Occupants:			410
			+2,240
Total FTE Occupants:			2,277

To determine FTE occupants:

Commercial Office FTE occupants 560,000 / 250 = **2,240**

There are no transient office users.

Retail FTE occupants = 20,000 / 550 = 36.36, therefore **37**

Retail Transient occupants

Low	200
High	570
Typical	350
Average	373
Total Retail occupants	**410**
Total FTE occupants	**2277**

To determine secure bicycle storage:

Commercial office secure bicycle spaces is calculated separately for the first 300,000 sq.ft. and for the remaining square footage and added together.

Average Annual Building Users (</= 300,000 sq.ft.) = 2240 x (300,000 sq.ft. / 560,000 sq.ft.). = 1200 Users

Average Annual Building Users (> 300,000 sq.ft.) = 2240 x [(560,000 sq.ft. – 300,000 sq.ft.) / 560,000 sq.ft] = 1040 Users

Bicycle storage spaces for the users prorated for the first 300,000 sq.ft. of the building

Secure Bicycle Spaces = 1200 x 0.03 = **36 bicycle spaces**

Plus

Bicycle storage spaces for the users prorated for the building square footage above 300,000sq.ft.

Secure Bicycle Spaces = 1040 x 0.05 = 5.2 therefore **6 spaces**

The secure bicycle spaces for the retail spaces are calculated similarly. However, because the retail space is less than 300,000 sq.ft., there is no need to prorate the space.

410 occupants x0.03 = 12.3 therefore **13 spaces**

Total bicycle storage required is **55 spaces**

Shower and changing facilities = 2277 x 0.05 = 11.38, therefore provide **12**

Exemplary Performance

Projects may be awarded one innovation point for exemplary performance in alternative transportation, SS Credit 4, by instituting a comprehensive transportation management plan that demonstrates a quantifiable reduction in personal automobile use through the implementation of multiple alternative options.

Precertification Submittal Documentation

Provide the LEED-CS Precertification Submittal Templates, which include the following:

❑ Narrative describing how the project intends to accomplish the credit requirements on the credit-specific Submittal Template signed by the appropriate design team member

❑ Confirmation of this intent from the owner/developer on the LEED-CS Precertification Submittal Template

Certification Submittal Documentation

Design and Construction Credit Compliance

This credit is submitted as part of the **Design Submittal**.

The following project data and calculation information is required to document credit compliance using the LEED-CS v2.0 Submittal Templates:

❑ Provide building square footage per .use.

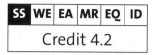

SS | WE | EA | MR | EQ | ID

Credit 4.2

❑ Provide the FTE occupancy counts and Transient occupancy counts for the project.

❑ Provide total FTE occupancy counts.

❑ Provide number of bike racks per use per building square footage.

❑ Provide number of showers provided.

❑ Provide project drawings to show the location(s) of the secure bicycle storage areas and shower/changing facilities.

Tenant Sales or Lease Agreement Credit Compliance

This compliance method is available to core and shell projects that incorporate into tenant sales or lease agreements requirements for the installation of secure bicycle storage and shower/changing facilities as part of the tenant scope of work. Provide the LEED letter template for the credit pursued indicating the following:

❑ That 100% of leased square footage complies with credit requirements. Lease or sales agreements may be requested. Agreements will need to provide the number of bike racks and shower/changing facilities required per use per tenant square footage.

❑ That 100% of the unleased square footage shall comply with the credit requirements when leased. A statement signed by the owner/developer that all leases and/or sales agreements will comply may be requested.

❑ Provide building square footage per use.

❑ Provide the FTE occupancy counts and Transient occupancy counts for the project.

❑ Provide total FTE occupancy counts.

❑ Provide the number of bike racks and shower/changing facilities per use per building square footage.

In addition, provide the following project data and calculation information based on project type:

Non-Residential Buildings

❑ Confirm the quantity of shower/changing facilities provided and their distance from the building entry.

Residential Buildings

❑ No additional documentation is required.

Mixed Non-Residential and Residential Buildings

❑ Confirm the number of residential units and residential FTE occupants for the project.

❑ Confirm the quantity of shower/changing facilities provided for the non-residential portion of the project and their distance from the building entry.

AND (For Projects With Special Circumstances — Any Compliance Path)

❑ Provide an optional narrative to describe any special circumstances or non-standard compliance paths taken by the project.

Considerations

Environmental Issues

The environmental effects of automobile use include vehicle emissions that contribute to smog and air pollution as well as environmental impacts from oil extraction and petroleum refining. Bicycling as an alternative to personal vehicle operation offers a number of environmental benefits. Bicycle commuting produces no emissions and has zero demand for petroleum-based fuels. Bicycle commuting also relieves traffic congestion, reduces noise pollution, and requires far less infrastructure for roadways and parking lots. Roadways and parking lots produce stormwater runoff, contribute to the urban heat island effect, and encroach on green space.

Bicycles are more likely to be used for relatively short commuting trips. Displacing vehicle miles with bicycling even for short trips carries a substantial environmental benefit, since a large portion of vehicle emissions occur in the first few minutes of driving following a cold start, as emissions control equipment is less effective at cool operating temperatures.

Economic Issues

The initial project cost increase for bike storage areas and changing facilities or showers is typically low relative to the overall project cost. Building occupants can realize health benefits through bicycle and walking commuting strategies. Bicycling and walking also exposes people to the community, encouraging interaction among neighbors and allowing for enjoyment of the area in ways unavailable to automobile passengers.

Resources

Please see the USGBC website at www. usgbc.org/resources for more specific resources on materials sources and other technical information.

Websites

Advanced Transportation Technology Institute

www.atti-info.org

(423) 622-3884

A nonprofit organization that advances clean transportation technologies through research, education and technology transfer in order to promote a healthy environment and energy independence.

Definitions

Full-Time Equivalent (FTE) building occupant is a measurement equal to one person occupying a building for an eight hour schedule per workday.

For some building types the occupancy use will fluctuate at different times of the year. This is particularly true for commercial retail establishments. The Average Annual Building Users is the average number of building users occupying the building for an eight hour schedule per workday taken at the peak use period for the year, the low use period for the year, and the average use period for the year.

Mass Transit includes transportation facilities designed to transport large groups of persons in a single vehicle, such as buses or trains.

Public Transportation is bus, rail or other transportation service for the general public operated on a regular, continual basis that is publicly or privately owned.

Secure Bicycle Storage is an internal or external space dedicated to the secure storage of bicycles. This should be available to all building users and may include lockers and storage rooms.

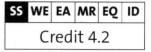

SS | WE | EA | MR | EQ | ID

Credit 4.2

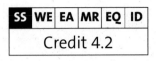

Alternative Transportation
Low-Emitting & Fuel-Efficient Vehicles

Intent

Reduce pollution and land development impacts from automobile use.

Requirements

OPTION 1

Provide preferred parking for low-emitting and fuel-efficient vehicles for 5% of the total vehicle parking capacity of the site.

OR

OPTION 2

Install alternative-fuel refueling stations for 3% of the total vehicle parking capacity of the site (liquid or gaseous fueling facilities must be separately ventilated or located outdoors).

For the purposes of this credit, low-emitting and fuel-efficient vehicles are defined as vehicles that are either classified as Zero Emission Vehicles (ZEV) by the California Air Resources Board or have achieved a minimum green score of 40 on the American Council for an Energy Efficient Economy (ACEEE) annual vehicle rating guide.

"Preferred parking" refers to the parking spots that are closest to the main entrance of the project (exclusive of spaces designated for handicapped) or parking passes provided at a discounted price.

For project types that demonstrate market barriers to the definition of "preferred parking closest to the main entrance," alternatives to may be considered on a case-by-case basis.

See Appendix 1—Default Occupancy Counts for occupancy count requirements and guidance.

Potential Technologies & Strategies

Provide transportation amenities such as alternative fuel refueling stations. Consider sharing the costs and benefits of refueling stations with neighbors.

Summary of Referenced Standard

There is no standard referenced for this credit.

Approach and Implementation

Establishing alternative fuel refueling stations requires the consideration of a number of legal, technical and safety issues, which vary by fuel type. Consider the following while developing alternative fuel station infrastructure:

❑ Consider building occupants to determine which alternative fuel type is in highest demand.

❑ Compare the environmental and economic costs/benefits of different alternative fuel types to determine which alternative fuel type would provide the highest benefit.

❑ Investigate local codes and standards for refueling stations in the area.

❑ Compare different fuel station equipment options and fuel availability. Depending on the type of alternative fuel provided, equipment requirements will differ in terms of expense and complexity of installation. Lack of availability may limit the feasibility of providing refueling stations for some types of fuels.

❑ Learn about the safety issues associated with alternative fuel types. Ensure that appropriate building personnel are trained to operate and maintain refueling stations.

The establishment of preferred parking for low emitting and fuel-efficient vehicles requires consideration of the building use. For commercial office buildings the location of these designated spaces should be closest to the main entrance of the project. Because retail developments often require that employee parking is not adjacent to the main entrance, alternatives will be considered. Mixed-use projects should consider the traffic patterns related to each use.

Calculations

Option 1

To determine the number of alternative fuel vehicle parking spaces required (5%), multiply the total number of parking spaces in the project by 0.05.

Option 2

To determine the number of alternative fuel vehicle fueling stations required (3%), multiply the total number of parking spaces in the project by 0.03.

Exemplary Performance

Projects may be awarded one innovation point for exemplary performance in alternative transportation, SS Credit 4, by instituting a comprehensive transportation management plan that demonstrates a quantifiable reduction in personal automobile use through the implementation of multiple alternative options.

Precertification Submittal Documentation

Provide the LEED-CS Precertification Submittal Templates, which include the following:

❑ Narrative describing how the project intends to accomplish the credit requirements on the credit-specific Submittal Template signed by the appropriate design team member

❑ Confirmation of this intent from the owner/developer on the LEED-CS Precertification Submittal Template

Certification Submittal Documentation

This credit is submitted as part of the **Design Submittal**.

Design and Construction Credit Compliance

The following project data and calculation information is required to document credit compliance using the LEED-CS v2.0 Submittal Templates:

❑ Provide the total parking capacity of the site.

In addition, provide the following project data and calculation information based on the appropriate compliance path:

Option 1 — Preferred Parking for Low-Emitting/Fuel Efficient Vehicles

❑ Provide project drawings to show the location(s) of the preferred parking spaces for low-emitting/fuel-efficient vehicles.

❑ Confirm the number of preferred parking spaces provided.

Option 2 — Alternative Fuel Refueling Stations

❑ Provide project drawings to show the location(s) of the alternative fuel refueling stations.

❑ Confirm the fuel type, number of stations, and fueling capacity for each station for an 8-hour period.

AND (For Projects With Special Circumstances — Any Compliance Path)

❑ Provide an optional narrative to describe any special circumstances or non-standard compliance paths taken by the project.

Tenant Sales or Lease Agreement Credit Compliance

This compliance method is not available for this credit.

Considerations

Environmental Issues

Operation of vehicles significantly contributes to global change and air quality problems through the emission of greenhouse gases (GHGs) and other pollutants generated from combustion engines and fuel evaporation. Motor gasoline is estimated to account for 60 % of all carbon dioxide (a major GHG) emitted in the United States in the last 20 years. Personal vehicles also generate large portions of the air pollutants responsible for smog and ground-level ozone, both of which have negative effects on human health.

Alternative fuel and alternative technology vehicles offer the possibility of reducing air pollutants from vehicular travel as well as the environmental effects of producing gasoline. However, the extent to which alternative vehicles produce an environmental benefit depends on the complete lifecycle of their fuels and the vehicle technology. For example, electric vehicles generate zero greenhouse gases (GHGs) during operation, but the amount of GHGs emitted during the production of the electricity that these vehicles run on varies greatly depending on the electricity source. Furthermore, alternative fuels may be superior to conventional gasoline on the basis of one pollutant, but carry a higher pollution load for another pollutant. Because the environmental benefit of alternative fuel and alternative technology vehicles depend on complete fuel-cycle energy-use and emissions, carefully consider available vehicle technologies and fuel sources before purchasing vehicles or installing fuel stations.

Economic Issues

Initial costs for alternative vehicles are higher than for conventional vehicles, and this may delay their purchase. Federal, state and local government may offer tax incentives for purchasing alternative vehicles, which can help offset their higher initial costs. Different alternative fuel vehicles need different refueling stations, and the costs vary. Hybrid vehicles are gaining traction in the marketplace, which should start to drive down their cost. For fuel-efficient vehicles, reduced operating costs on a per-mile basis can offset higher initial purchase prices or higher fuel costs.

Resources

Please see the USGBC website at www. usgbc.org/resources for more specific resources on materials sources and other technical information.

Websites

Alternative Fuels Data Center

www.afdc.doe.gov

A section of the DOE Office of Transportation Technologies website that has information on alternative fuels and alternative fueled vehicles, a locator for alternative refueling stations and other related information.

American Council for an Energy-Efficient Economy (ACEEE)

www.greenercars.com

Online searchable green car guide based on a combination of fuel efficiency and tailpipe emission levels. Also offers hard-copy Green Guide to Cars and Trucks, an annual publication of the American Council for an Energy-Efficient Economy.

CARB Cleaner Car Guide

www.driveclean.ca.gov/en/gv/home/index.asp

(916) 323-6169

The California Air Resources Board (CARB) has developed a comprehensive searchable buyer's guide to find the cleanest cars on the market, and lists advantages that clean vehicles offer.

California Certified Vehicles List

www.arb.ca.gov/msprog/ccvl/ccvl.htm

This site provides a list of all vehicles certified by the California Air Resources Board.

Clean Cities Vehicle Buyer's Guide For Consumers

www.eere.energy.gov/cleancities/vbg/

The Vehicle Buyer's Guide for Consumers explains the alternative fuel and advanced technology vehicles, including hybrid and neighborhood electric vehicles available. You can use this site to learn more about the vehicle technologies; obtain pricing and technical specifications; locate the nearest alternative fuel station; contact a dealer, industry expert or manufacturer; research financial incentives and laws in your state; and more.

Clean Cities Vehicle Buyer's Guide For Fleets

www.eere.energy.gov/cleancities/vbg/fleets

The Vehicle Buyer's Guide for Fleets is designed to educate fleet managers and policy makers about alternative fuels and vehicles to help them determine whether the Energy Policy Act of 1992 (EPAct) affects them. Use the site to determine if your fleet is covered under EPAct; obtain pricing and technical specifications for light and heavy-duty AFVs; find an alternative fueling station in your area; or research information about state AFV purchasing incentives and laws.

CREST

www.crest.org/hydrogen/index.html

The Center for Renewable Energy and Sustainable Technology's fuel cell and hydrogen page.

Electric Auto Association

www.eaaev.org

This nonprofit education organization promotes the advancement and widespread adoption of electric vehicles.

Electric Drive Transportation Association

www.electricdrive.org

This industry association promotes electric vehicles through policy, information and market development initiatives.

Fuel Economy Website

www.fueleconomy.gov/feg

This U.S. Department of Energy site allows comparisons of cars based on gas mileage (mpg), greenhouse gas emissions, air pollution ratings, and safety information for new and used cars and trucks.

Natural Gas Vehicle Coalition

www.ngvc.org/ngv/ngvc.nsf

The Natural Gas Vehicle Coalition consists of natural gas companies, vehicle and equipment manufacturers, service providers, environmental groups and government organizations.

Rocky Mountain Institute Transportation Page

www.rmi.org/sitepages/pid18.php

This website offers information on the environmental impact of transportation, and extensive information about Hypercar vehicles.

Union of Concerned Scientists Clean Vehicle Program

www.ucsusa.org/clean_vehicles

This site provides information about the latest developments in alternative vehicles, the environmental impact of conventional vehicles, and information for consumers such as the guide Buying a Greener Vehicle: Electric, Hybrids, and Fuel Cells.

Definitions

Alternative Fuel Vehicles are vehicles that use low-polluting, non-gasoline fuels such as electricity, hydrogen, propane or compressed natural gas, liquid natural gas, methanol and ethanol. Efficient gas-electric hybrid vehicles are included in this group for LEED purposes.

Hybrid Vehicles are vehicles that use a gasoline engine to drive an electric generator and use the electric generator and/or storage batteries to power electric motors that drive the vehicle's wheels.

Preferred Parking generally refers to parking spots that are closest to the main entrance of the project, exclusive of spaces designated for handicapped, or to parking passes provided at a discounted price. Some project types that demonstrate market barriers to this definition may propose an alternative definition on a case-by-case basis.

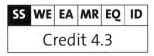

SS | WE | EA | MR | EQ | ID
Credit 4.3

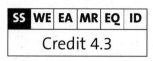

Alternative Transportation

Parking Capacity

Intent

Reduce pollution and land development impacts from single occupancy vehicle use.

Can assist tenants in certification under LEED for Commercial Interiors

Requirements

OPTION 1 — NON-RESIDENTIAL

❑ Size parking capacity to not exceed minimum local zoning requirements.

OR

OPTION 2 — NON-RESIDENTIAL

For projects that provide parking for less than 3% of FTE building occupants:

❑ Provide preferred parking for carpools or vanpools, marked as such, for 3% of total provided parking spaces.

OR

OPTION 3 — RESIDENTIAL

❑ Size parking capacity to not exceed minimum local zoning requirements, AND provide infrastructure and support programs to facilitate shared vehicle usage such as carpool drop-off areas, designated parking for vanpools, or car-share services, ride boards, and shuttle services to mass transit.

OR

OPTION 4 — ALL

Provide no new parking.

"Preferred parking" refers to the parking spots that are closest to the main entrance of the project (exclusive of spaces designated for handicapped) or parking passes provided at a discounted price.

See Appendix 1 — Default Occupancy Counts for occupancy count requirements and guidance.

Potential Technologies & Strategies

Minimize parking lot/garage size. Consider sharing parking facilities with adjacent buildings. Consider alternatives that will limit the use of single occupancy vehicles.

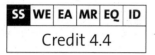
Summary of Referenced Standard

There is no standard referenced for this credit.

Approach and Implementation

The intent of this credit is to limit availability of parking as a means of encouraging the use of alternative forms of transportation to and from the site. Select a project site that is easily accessible from residential areas by bicycle or public transportation. Once the site is selected, determine the expected number of cars likely to drive to the site and compare this number to local zoning requirements. If parking demand is expected to be less than that required by local codes, consider seeking a variance with the appropriate authorities to provide less parking. However, any on-site parking reductions should be carefully balanced with community needs to avoid needlessly burdening surrounding neighborhoods with excessive street parking.

Where possible, develop transportation demand management strategies in order to reduce the number of parking spaces required to meet the needs of occupants. Transportation demand strategies may include the publishing of an employee roster with addresses to assist people in finding carpool partners, creating incentive programs for carpooling, providing a ride share board, or setting parking fees at a level sufficient to encourage carpooling.

Calculations

Option 1 — Non-Residential

Determine the minimum number of parking spaces required by local zoning requirements. Total the parking spaces provided for the project (excluding service lots) and verify that the project parking does not exceed the minimum required.

Option 2 — Non-Residential

For projects that provide parking for less than 3% of FTE building occupants—

1. Identify the total number of full-time and part-time building occupants.

2. Calculate the Full-Time Equivalent (FTE) building occupants based on a standard 8-hour occupancy period. An 8-hour occupant has an FTE value of 1.0 while a part-time occupant has a FTE value based on their hours per day divided by 8 (see **Equation 1**). Note that FTE calculations for the project must be used consistently for all LEED-CS credits. In buildings with multiple shifts, use only the highest volume shift in the FTE calculation but consider shift overlap when determining peak building users.

Core and shell buildings projects may not know the final occupancy count. Core and shell projects must utilize the default occupancy counts provided in Appendix 1 (see **Equation 2**). Projects that do know the tenant occupancy must use these numbers as long as the gross square foot per employee is not greater than that in the default occupancy count table.

3. Determine if the total number of provided parking spaces is less than 3% of FTE occupants.

4. Designate preferred parking equivalent to 3% of the total provided project parking as reserved carpool/vanpool spaces.

Option 3 — Residential

No calculations are needed for residential projects beyond what is needed to comply with local zoning requirements.

Equation 1

$$\text{FTE Occupants} = \frac{\text{Occupant Hours}}{8}$$

Equation 2

$$\text{FTE Occupants} = \frac{\text{Building Gross Square Foot}}{\text{Gross Square Foot per FTE}}$$

Option 4 — All

No calculations are required for this compliance path.

Exemplary Performance

Projects may be awarded one innovation point for Exemplary performance in alternative transportation, SS Credit 4, by instituting a comprehensive transportation management plan that demonstrates a quantifiable reduction in personal automobile use through the implementation of multiple alternative options.

Precertification Submittal Documentation

Provide the LEED-CS Precertification Submittal Templates, which include the following:

❑ Narrative describing how the project intends to accomplish the credit requirements on the credit-specific Submittal Template signed by the appropriate design team member

❑ Confirmation of this intent from the owner/developer on the LEED-CS Precertification Submittal Template

Certification Submittal Documentation

This credit is submitted as part of the **Design Submittal**.

Design and Construction Credit Compliance

The following project data and calculation information is required to document credit compliance using the LEED-CS v2.0 Submittal Templates:

❑ Provide the FTE occupancy for the project.

❑ Provide the total parking capacity of the site.

❑ Confirm the appropriate project compliance path.

In addition, provide the following project data and calculation information based on the appropriate compliance path:

Option 1 — Non-Residential

❑ Provide the number of parking spaces required for the project per local code or ordinance.

❑ Provide the number of carpool/vanpool spaces that are on-site.

Option 2 — Non-Residential

❑ Provide the number of carpool/vanpool spaces that are on-site.

Option 3 —Residential

❑ Provide a description of the infrastructure/programs that are in place to support and promote ridesharing.

Option 4 — All

❑ There are no additional items required for this compliance path.

AND (For Projects With Special Circumstances — Any Compliance Path)

❑ Provide an optional narrative to describe any special circumstances or non-standard compliance paths taken by the project.

Tenant Sales or Lease Agreement Credit Compliance

This compliance method is not available for this credit.

Considerations

Environmental Issues

Reducing the use of private automobiles saves energy and avoids environmental problems associated with automobile use, such as vehicle emissions that contribute to smog and other air pollutants, and the environmental impacts associated with oil extraction and petroleum refining. The environmental benefits of carpooling are significant. For example, 100 people who carpooled (2 people per car) 10 miles to work and 10 miles home instead of driv-

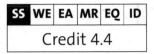
ing separately would prevent emission of 7.7 pounds of hydrocarbons, 55 pounds of carbon monoxide, 3.3 pounds of nitrogen oxides, 990 pounds of carbon dioxide and 50 gallons of gasoline per day.

Parking facilities for automobiles also have negative impacts on the environment, since asphalt surfaces increase stormwater runoff and contribute to urban heat island effects. By restricting the size of parking lots and promoting carpooling, buildings can reduce these effects while benefiting from reduced parking requirements and more and healthier green space.

Economic Issues

Carpooling reduces the size of the parking areas needed to support building occupants, allowing the building to accept more occupants without enlarging the parking area. Carpooling may reduce the cost of land added for parking as well as infrastructure needed to support vehicles. Reduction in parking areas can decrease the amount of impervious surfaces on a site. This may result in reduced stormwater charges, as some local utilities charge for stormwater based on impervious surface area. Also, many municipalities and state governments offer tax incentives for carpooling programs, since fewer cars on the road reduces pollution, traffic congestion and wear and tear to roadways.

Resources

Please see the USGBC website at www. usgbc.org/resources for more specific resources on materials sources and other technical information.

Websites

Advanced Transportation Technology Institute

www.atti-info.org

(423) 622-3884

A nonprofit organization that advances clean transportation technologies through research, education and technology transfer in order to promote a healthy environment and energy independence.

Definitions

A **Carpool** is an arrangement in which two or more people share a vehicle for transportation.

Preferred Parking generally refers to the parking spots that are closest to the main entrance of the project, exclusive of spaces designated for handicapped, or to parking passes provided at a discounted price. Some project types that demonstrate market barriers to this definition may propose an alternative definition on a case-by-case basis.

Site Development

Protect or Restore Habitat

Intent

Conserve existing natural areas and restore damaged areas to provide habitat and promote biodiversity.

Requirements

On greenfield sites, limit all site disturbance to 40 feet beyond the building perimeter; 10 feet beyond surface walkways, patios, surface parking and utilities less than 12 inches in diameter; 15 feet beyond primary roadway curbs and main utility branch trenches; and 25 feet beyond constructed areas with permeable surfaces (such as pervious paving areas, stormwater detention facilities and playing fields) that require additional staging areas in order to limit compaction in the constructed area.

OR

On previously developed or graded sites, restore or protect a minimum of 50% of the site area (excluding the building footprint) with native or adapted vegetation. Native/ adapted plants are plants indigenous to a locality or cultivars of native plants that are adapted to the local climate and are not considered invasive species or noxious weeds. Projects earning SS Credit 2 and using vegetated roof surfaces may apply the vegetated roof surface to this calculation if the plants meet the definition of native/adapted.

Greenfield sites are those that are not previously developed or graded and remain in a natural state. Previously developed sites are those that previously contained buildings, roadways, parking lots, or were graded or altered by direct human activities.

Potential Technologies & Strategies

On greenfield sites, perform a site survey to identify site elements and adopt a master plan for development of the project site. Carefully site the building to minimize disruption to existing ecosystems and design the building to minimize its footprint. Strategies include stacking the building program, tuck-under parking and sharing facilities with neighbors. Establish clearly marked construction boundaries to minimize disturbance of the existing site and restore previously degraded areas to their natural state. For previously developed sites, utilize local and regional governmental agencies, consultants, educational facilities, and native plant societies as resources for the selection of appropriate native or adapted plant materials. Prohibit plant materials listed as invasive or noxious weed species. Native/adapted plants require minimal or no irrigation following establishment, do not require active maintenance such as mowing or chemical inputs such as fertilizers, pesticides or herbicides, and provide habitat value and promote biodiversity through avoidance of monoculture plantings.

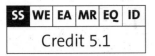

Summary of Referenced Standard

There is no standard referenced for this credit.

Approach and Implementation

Preserve and enhance natural site elements including existing water bodies, soil conditions, ecosystems, trees and other vegetation. Identify opportunities for site improvements that increase the area of native/adapted vegetation or other ecologically appropriate features. Activities may include removing unnecessary paved areas and replacing them with landscaped areas, or replacing excessive turf-grass areas with native or adapted plantings to promote biodiversity and provide habitat.

During the construction process, establish clearly marked construction and disturbance boundaries and note these site protection requirements in construction documents. Delineate lay down, recycling and disposal areas, and use paved areas for staging activities. Erect construction fencing around the drip line of existing trees to protect them from damage and soil compaction by construction vehicles. Consider the costs/benefits of contractual penalties if destruction of protected areas outside of the construction boundaries occurs. Coordinate infrastructure construction to minimize the disruption of the site and work with existing topography to limit cut-and-fill efforts for the project.

For urban projects earning SS Credit 2, consider installing a vegetated roof. Select native or adapted, non-invasive species, and ensure that the roof structure is designed to support the added weight of the planting beds. Research the species that are likely to utilize this space (primarily birds and insects) and select plants that will help support these species by providing food, forage or nesting areas.

Calculations

There are no calculations associated with this credit.

Exemplary Performance

The project may be awarded one innovation point for exemplary performance in restoring or protecting a minimum of 75% of the site area (excluding the building footprint) with native or adapted vegetation on previous developed or graded sites.

Precertification Submittal Documentation

Provide the LEED-CS Precertification Submittal Templates, which include the following:

❑ Narrative describing how the project intends to accomplish the credit requirements on the credit-specific Submittal Template signed by the appropriate design team member

❑ Confirmation of this intent from the owner/developer on the LEED-CS Precertification Submittal Template

Certification Submittal Documentation

This credit is submitted as part of the **Construction Submittal**.

Design and Construction Credit Compliance

The following project data and calculation information is required to document credit compliance using the LEED-CS v2.0 Submittal Templates:

❑ Provide the project site area. For multiple building projects where the LEED project boundary is not the project site area, provide an overall site plan with project boundaries indicated for each development parcel.

- ❏ Provide the project building footprint area.

- ❏ Provide a narrative describing the project's approach to this credit. Include information regarding any special circumstances or considerations regarding the project.

In addition, provide the following project data and calculation information based on the appropriate compliance path:

Greenfield Sites

- ❏ Provide a copy of the project's site/grading drawings highlighting the designated site disturbance boundaries.

Previously Developed/Graded Sites

- ❏ Provide the area (sq.ft.) of the site that has been restored using native and/or adaptive planting.

- ❏ Provide a copy of the project's site/landscape plan that provides information regarding the restored site area and the planting materials.

Tenant Sales or Lease Agreement Credit Compliance

This compliance method is not available for this credit.

Considerations

Environmental Issues

Development on building sites often damages site ecology, indigenous plants and regional animal populations. Ecological site damage can be reduced by restoring native and adapted vegetation and other ecologically appropriate features on the site, which in turn provides habitat for fauna. Other ecologically appropriate features are natural site elements beyond vegetation that maintain or restore the ecological integrity of the site. They may include water bodies, exposed rock, bare ground, or other features that are part of the historic natural landscape within the region and provide habitat value. When construction occurs on the site, protection of open space and sensitive areas through the use of strict boundaries reduces damage to the site ecology, resulting in preservation of wildlife corridors and habitat.

Projects that comply with SS Credit 2 are often developing on previously developed land. For these projects the installation of a vegetated roof surface may provide a number of benefits including improved habitat, reduction in the urban heat island effect, and stormwater control.

Economic Issues

Native or adapted plantings typically reduce maintenance costs over their lifetime by minimizing inputs of fertilizers, pesticides and water. In many cases, trees and vegetation raised off site are costly to purchase and may not survive transplanting. Additional trees and other landscaping, as well as soil remediation and water elements, can incur first costs. It may be advantageous to implement site restoration in phases to spread costs out over time. Strategic plantings can shade the building and site impervious areas, which can decrease cooling loads during warm months and reduce energy expenditures.

Resources

Please see the USGBC website at www.usgbc.org/resources for more specific resources on materials sources and other technical information.

Websites

American Society of Landscape Architects

www.asla.org

ASLA is the national professional association representing landscape architects. The website provides information about products, services, publications and events.

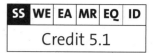

SS | WE | EA | MR | EQ | ID

Credit 5.1

Ecological Restoration

http://ecologicalrestoration.info

This quarterly print and online publication from the University of Wisconsin-Madison Arboretum provides a forum for people interested in all aspects of ecological restoration.

Lady Bird Johnson Wildlife Center

www.wildflower.org

The center, located in Austin, Texas, has the mission of educating people about the environmental necessity, economic value and natural beauty of native plants. The website offers a number of resources, including a nationwide Native Plant Information Network and a National Suppliers Directory.

North American Native Plant Society

www.nanps.org

A nonprofit association dedicated to the study, conservation, cultivation and restoration of native plants. Its website contains links to state and provincial associations.

Plant Native

www.plantnative.org

This organization is dedicated to moving native plants and nature-scaping into mainstream landscaping practices.

Society for Ecological Restoration International

www.ser.org

Nonprofit consortium of scientists, planners, administrators, ecological consultants, landscape architects, engineers, and others with the mission of promoting ecological restoration as a means of sustaining the diversity of life and reestablishing an ecologically healthy relationship between nature and culture.

Soil and Water Conservation Society

www.swcs.org

An organization focused on fostering the science and art of sustainable soil, water, and related natural resource management.

Print Media

Design for Human Ecosystems: Landscape, Land Use, and Natural Resources, by John Tillman Lyle, Island Press, 1999.

This text explores methods of landscape design that function like natural ecosystems.

Landscape Restoration Handbook by Donald Harker, Marc Evans, Gary Libby, Kay Harker, and Sherrie Evans, Lewis Publishers, 1999.

This resource is a comprehensive guide to natural landscaping and ecological restoration, and provides information on 21 different ecological restoration types.

Definitions

Adapted (or Introduced) Plants are those that reliably grow well in a given habitat with minimal attention from humans in the form of winter protection, pest protection, water irrigation or fertilization once root systems are established in the soil. Adapted plants are considered to be low maintenance but not invasive.

The **Building Footprint** is the area on a project site that is used by the building structure and is defined by the perimeter of the building plan. Parking lots, landscapes and other non-building facilities are not included in the building footprint.

The **Development Footprint** is the area on the project site that has been impacted by any development activity. Hardscape, access roads, parking lots, non-building facilities and building structure are all included in the development footprint.

Greenfield sites are those that are not previously developed or graded and remain in a natural state.

Invasive Plants are both indigenous and non-indigenous species or strains that are characteristically adaptable, aggressive, have a high reproductive capacity and tend to overrun the ecosystems they inhabit. Collectively they are one of the great threats to biodiversity and ecosystem stability.

The **LEED Project Boundary** is the portion of the project site submitted for LEED certification. For single building developments, this will be the entire project scope and is generally limited to the site boundary. For multiple building developments, the LEED Project Boundary may be a portion of the development as determined by the project team.

Local Zoning Requirements are local government regulations imposed to promote orderly development of private lands and to prevent land use conflicts.

Native (or Indigenous) Plants refers to plants adapted to a given area during a defined time period and that are not invasive. In America, the term often refers to plants growing in a region prior to the time of settlement by people of European descent.

Open Space Area is the property area minus the development footprint, or as defined by local zoning requirements. Open space must be vegetated and pervious, with exceptions only as noted in the SS Credit 5.2 compliance language. For projects located in urban areas that earn SS Credit 2, open space also includes non-vehicular, pedestrian oriented hardscape spaces.

Previously Developed sites are those that previously contained buildings, roadways, parking lots, or were graded or altered by direct human activities.

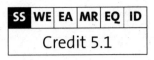

SS	WE	EA	MR	EQ	ID
Credit 5.1					

Site Development

Maximize Open Space

Intent

Provide a high ratio of open space to development footprint to promote biodiversity.

Requirements

OPTION 1

Reduce the development footprint (defined as the total area of the building footprint, hardscape, access roads and parking) and/or provide vegetated open space within the project boundary to exceed the local zoning's open space requirement for the site by 25%.

OR

OPTION 2

For areas with no local zoning requirements (e.g., some university campuses, military bases), provide vegetated open space area adjacent to the building that is equal to the building footprint.

OR

OPTION 3

Where a zoning ordinance exists, but there is no requirement for open space (zero), provide vegetated open space equal to 20% of the project's site area.

ALL OPTIONS:

❑ For projects located in urban areas that earn SS Credit 2, vegetated roof areas can contribute to credit compliance.

❑ For projects located in urban areas that earn SS Credit 2, pedestrian oriented hardscape areas can contribute to credit compliance. For such projects, a minimum of 25% of the open space counted must be vegetated.

❑ Wetlands or naturally designed ponds may count as open space if the side slope gradients average 1:4 (vertical:horizontal) or less and are vegetated.

Potential Technologies & Strategies

Perform a site survey to identify site elements and adopt a master plan for development of the project site. Select a suitable building location and design the building with a minimal footprint to minimize site disruption. Strategies include stacking the building program, tuck-under parking and sharing facilities with neighbors to maximize open space on the site.

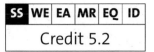

Summary of Referenced Standard

There is no standard referenced for this credit.

Approach and Implementation

Choose a development footprint and location that minimizes disturbance to the existing ecosystem. Consider issues such as building orientation, daylighting, heat island effects, stormwater generation, significant vegetation, existing green corridors, and other sustainable building issues. Once the site and building location have been determined, design and construct a compact parking, road and building footprint layout in order to preserve open land and provide connections to adjacent ecosystems. Reduce footprints by tightening program needs and stacking floor plans.

In areas with no zoning requirements, designated open space that is equal to the building footprint can be separate from the project site as long as the open space is preserved as such for the life of the building.

When designing green roofs, attention must be given to support, waterproofing and drainage. Green roofs typically include a waterproof and root repellant membrane, a drainage system, filter cloth, a lightweight growing medium and plants. Modular systems are available, with all layers pre-prepared into movable interlocking grids, or individual layers can be installed separately.

Open space in an urban context that includes hardscape surfaces should be pedestrian oriented and accessible, and provide for passive or active recreation opportunities. Examples of urban open space include pocket parks, accessible roof decks, plazas and courtyards.

Calculations

Option 1

Determine the zoning requirement for open space. Set-back requirements and lot coverage requirements only qualify as open space requirements if the areas they set aside are required to be vegetated. Calculate the open space required for this credit as shown in **Equation 1**.

Option 2

In cases where there is no local zoning requirement, the open space requirement is equal to the building footprint. This option is designed to address campus situations where it may be difficult to define the project's site area.

Option 3

In cases where local codes require zero open space, determine the total project site area and multiply by 0.20 to determine the open space required for credit achievement, as shown in **Equation 2**. This option is designed to address situations where the code is silent on open space, and zoning conditions where there is no requirement for open space. This is commonly the case in urban centers that allow zero lot line (no set-back) development.

This requirement can be met through open space provided at grade or, for projects located in urban areas that earn SS Credit 2, on the roof.

Equation 1

Total Open Space Required = Open Space Required by Zoning x 1.25

Equation 2

Total Open Space Required = Total Project Site Area x 0.20

Example: high-rise commercial office build-ing in an urban center

A 670,000 square foot commercial office building has an overall site area of 116,700 square feet. The zoning requirement for the site is that a minimum of 20% net lot area shall be public open space. The project is in an urban center and complies with SS Credit 2 and has provided the following open space.

Pedestrian oriented hardscape	27,900 sq.ft.
Vegetated open space on structure	27,500 sq.ft.
Vegetated open space on grade	500 sq.ft.
Total open space	55,900 sq.ft.

The percentage of open space provided is 48%

The percentage of vegetated open space to total open space is 51%

Exemplary Performance

Projects may be awarded an innovation point for exemplary performance by demonstrating that they have doubled the amount of open space required for credit achievement. All designated open space shall be within the LEED project boundary. For example, projects with local zoning requirements must increase the amount of open space provided by 50% instead of by 25%; projects with no local zoning requirements must provide open space equal to two times the building footprint; and urban projects where zero open space is required must provide open space equal to 40% of the site area.

Precertification Submittal Documentation

Provide the LEED-CS Precertification Submittal Templates, which include the following:

❑ Narrative describing how the project intends to accomplish the credit requirements on the credit-specific Submittal Template signed by the appropriate design team member

❑ Confirmation of this intent from the owner/developer on the LEED-CS Precertification Submittal Template

Certification Submittal Documentation

This credit is submitted as part of the **Design Submittal**.

Design and Construction Credit Compliance

The following project data and calculation information is required to document credit compliance using the LEED-CS v2.0 Submittal Templates:

❑ Provide the project site area. For multiple building projects where the LEED Project boundary is not the project site area, provide an overall site plan with project boundaries indicated for each development parcel.

❑ Provide the project building footprint area.

❑ Provide a copy of the project's site/landscape drawings highlighting the dedicated vegetated open space.

❑ Provide an optional narrative describing any special circumstances or considerations regarding the project's credit approach.

In addition, provide the following project data and calculation information based on the appropriate compliance path:

Option 1

❑ Provide the area (sq.ft.) of open space required by local zoning codes/ordinances.

❑ Provide the area (sq.ft.) of the vegetated dedicated open space provided by the project.

Option 2

❏ Provide the area (sq.ft.) of the vegetated dedicated open space provided by the project.

Option 3

❏ Provide the area (sq.ft.) of the vegetated dedicated open space provided by the project.

Tenant Sales or Lease Agreement Credit Compliance

This compliance method is not available for this credit.

Considerations

Environmental Issues

Open space provides habitat for vegetation, which in turn provides habitat for local wildlife. Even small open spaces in urban areas can provide refuges for wildlife populations, which have become increasingly marginalized. Plants that specifically support local species such as insects and other pollinators can help sustain populations up the food chain. Open space also helps reduce urban heat island effect, increases stormwater infiltration, and provides the human population on the site with a connection to the outdoors

Economic Issues

Preserving topsoil, plants and trees on the site can reduce landscaping costs for the building. Even in cases where rent values are high and the incentive for building out to the property line is strong, well designed open space can significantly increase property values. Reducing the footprint of a structure on a given site can have varying economic impacts. Building a vertical structure with the same square footage as a horizontal structure may add a small percentage to first costs depending on building size and use. A structure with a smaller footprint is generally more resource-efficient, resulting in reduced material and energy costs. A more compact building with coordinated infrastructure can reduce initial project costs, as well as operations and maintenance costs. Reduced earthwork, shorter utility lines, and reduced surface parking and paved areas all can reduce initial project costs. Compact paving areas and buildings reduce operations and maintenance costs.

Resources

Please see the USGBC website at www. usgbc.org/resources for more specific resources on materials sources and other technical information.

Websites

North American Native Plant Society

www.nanps.org

(416) 631-4438

A nonprofit association dedicated to the study, conservation, cultivation and restoration of native plants. Contains links to state/provincial associations.

Soil and Water Conservation Society

www.swcs.org

(515) 289-2331

An organization focused on fostering the science and art of sustainable soil, water and related natural resource management.

Green Roofs for Healthy Cities

www.greenroofs.org

A nonprofit industry association consisting of public and private organizations and individuals committed to developing a market for green roof infrastructure products and services in cities across North America.

Print Media

Beyond Preservation: Restoring and Inventing Landscapes by A. Dwight Baldwin et al., University of Minnesota Press, 1994.

Design for Human Ecosystems: Landscape, Land Use, and Natural Resources by John Tillman Lyle and Joan Woodward, Milldale Press, 1999.

Landscape Restoration Handbook by Donald Harker, Lewis Publishers, 1999.

Definitions

Adapted (or Introduced) Plants are those that reliably grow well in a given habitat with minimal attention from humans in the form of winter protection, pest protection, water irrigation or fertilization once root systems are established in the soil. Adapted plants are considered to be low maintenance but not invasive.

The **Building Footprint** is the area on a project site that is used by the building structure and is defined by the perimeter of the building plan. Parking lots, landscapes and other non-building facilities are not included in the building footprint.

The **Development Footprint** is the area on the project site that has been impacted by any development activity. Hardscape, access roads, parking lots, non-building facilities and building structure are all included in the development footprint.

Greenfield Sites are those that are not previously developed or graded and remain in a natural state.

Invasive Plants are both indigenous and non-indigenous species or strains that are characteristically adaptable, aggressive, have a high reproductive capacity and tend to overrun the ecosystems they inhabit. Collectively they are one of the great threats to biodiversity and ecosystem stability.

The **LEED Project Boundary** is the portion of the project site submitted for LEED certification. For single building developments, this will be the entire project scope and is generally limited to the site boundary. For multiple building developments, the LEED Project Boundary may be a portion of the development as determined by the project team.

Local Zoning Requirements are local government regulations imposed to promote orderly development of private lands and to prevent land use conflicts.

Native (Indigenous) Plants refers to plants adapted to a given area during a defined time period and that are not invasive. In America, the term often refers to plants growing in a region prior to the time of settlement by people of European descent.

Open Space Area is the property area minus the development footprint or as defined by local zoning requirements. Open space must be vegetated and pervious, with exceptions only as noted in the SS Credit 5.2 compliance language. For projects located in urban areas that earn SS Credit 2, open space also includes non-vehicular, pedestrian oriented hardscape spaces.

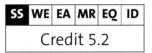

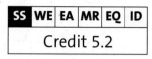

Stormwater Design

Quantity Control

Intent

Limit disruption of natural hydrology by reducing impervious cover, increasing on-site infiltration, and managing stormwater runoff.

Requirements

OPTION 1 — EXISTING IMPERVIOUSNESS IS LESS THAN OR EQUAL TO 50%

a. Discharge Rate and Quantity

Implement a stormwater management plan that prevents the post-development peak discharge rate and quantity from exceeding the pre-development peak discharge rate and quantity for the one- and two-year, 24-hour design storms.

OR

b. Stream Channel Protection

Implement a stormwater management plan that protects receiving stream channels from excessive erosion by implementing a stream channel protection strategy and quantity control strategies.

OR

OPTION 2 — EXISTING IMPERVIOUSNESS IS GREATER THAN 50%

Implement a stormwater management plan that results in a 25% decrease in the volume of stormwater runoff from the two-year, 24-hour design storm.

Potential Technologies & Strategies

Design the project site to maintain natural stormwater flows by promoting infiltration. Specify vegetated roofs, pervious paving, and other measures to minimize impervious surfaces. Reuse stormwater volumes generated for non-potable uses such as landscape irrigation, toilet and urinal flushing and custodial uses.

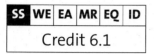

Summary of Referenced Standard

There is no standard referenced for this credit.

Approach and Implementation

The approach to this credit may vary significantly depending on the condition of the project site at the beginning of the project. If the project is being constructed on a largely undeveloped site, the goal is to preserve stormwater flows and design the project to respond to the natural soil conditions, habitat, and rainfall characteristics. If the project is a redevelopment of a previously developed site, the goal is typically to improve stormwater management in a way that restores the natural functions of the site to the maximum extent practicable.

The approach to this credit also varies dramatically between different regions and climate zones. The strategies employed in an urban environment where water is discharged to concrete channels and then the ocean are different from the strategies employed at an inland site that discharges to a small stream and lake system.

The most effective method to minimize stormwater runoff volume is to reduce the amount of impervious area. By reducing impervious area, stormwater infrastructure can be minimized or deleted from the project. Strategies to minimize or mitigate impervious surfaces may include—

❑ Smaller building footprint

❑ Pervious paving materials

❑ Stormwater harvesting for reuse in irrigation and/or buildings

❑ Green roofs

❑ Bioswales/vegetated filter strips

❑ Retention ponds

❑ Clustering development to reduce paved surfaces (roads, sidewalks, etc.)

Guidelines for Capturing and Reusing Stormwater Runoff

Stormwater captured (or harvested) in cisterns, rain barrels, or other devices, is a primary source of water in many parts of the world. Stormwater should not be used for potable needs if there are sources available that pose less risk to public health. However, harvested stormwater may be used to reduce potable water needs for uses such as landscape irrigation, fire suppression, toilet and urinal flushing and custodial uses.

Storage and reuse techniques range from small-scale systems (e.g., rain barrels) to underground cisterns that may hold large volumes of water. Whether large or small, stormwater harvesting system designs should consider the following:

1. Water need for the intended use—how will the harvested water be used and when will it be needed? For example, if the water is used to irrigate landscaping for four summer months, the amount of water needed and the how often the storage unit will refill must be considered. Usage requirements and the expected volume and frequency of rainfall must be determined.

2. Drawdown—storage system design must provide for the use or release of water between storm events for the design storage volume to be available.

3. Drainage Area—the size and nature (e.g., percent imperviousness) of the area draining to the storage system determines how much runoff will be available for harvesting.

4. Conveyance System—reused stormwater and graywater systems must not be connected to other domestic or commercial potable water systems. Pipes and storage units should be clearly marked (e.g., "Caution: Reclaimed Water, Do Not Drink").

5. Pretreatment—screens or filters may be used to remove debris and sedi-

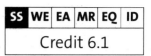
ment from runoff and to minimize pollutants.

6. Pressurization—uses for harvested rainwater may require pressurization. For example, most irrigation systems require a water pressure of at least 15 psi to function properly. Stored water has a pressure of 0.43 psi per foot of water elevation, and the water pressure at the bottom of a ten-foot vault would be 4.3 psi (10 ft. x 0.43 psi). Pressurization (e.g., a pump, pressure tank and filter) costs more and creates a more useable system.

The amount of runoff reduced by a stormwater harvesting system may be considered equal to its storage volume. However, volume calculations must also consider how often the system is emptied and the interval between storm events.

Example:

Rainwater will be harvested from a 10,000 sq.ft. roof (100% imperviousness). The system will be designed to capture the runoff from 90% of the average annual rainfall (1 inch of rainfall for humid watersheds). The volume of the proposed storage system is the amount of runoff captured (Vr) which is calculated below in **Equation 1**.

Another design consideration: if the tank must be emptied before subsequent storm events.

Use a tank that is 10 ft x 10 ft x 8 ft deep. The total storage volume (V_s) = 800 cu.ft. Using a design storm interval of three

days (72 hours), the drawdown rate (Q_r) is calculated below in **Equation 2**.

In this example, the captured rain must be drained within 3 days or at a minimum rate of 1.4 gpm for the tank to be emptied for the next storm.

Different municipalities, state and local governments have various design requirements for capturing and reuse of stormwater runoff. These requirements range from where stormwater may be captured and used, to length of time stormwater can be held in a cistern, to the type of water treatment required before reuse. Designers should check with the governing administrative authority to determine parameters which will affect collection, use and distribution of captured stormwater.

Calculations

There are two compliance paths for this credit—one for largely undeveloped sites and one for largely developed sites.

Option 1—Existing Imperviousness Is Less Than Or Equal To 50% (Largely Undeveloped Sites)

Option 1-a: Discharge Rate and Quantity

Determine the pre-development discharge rate and quantity for the project. These values are typically calculated by the civil engineer using the surface characteristics of the site and data on storm event frequency, intensity and duration. Calculate

Equation 1

$$V_r = \frac{(P)(R_v)(A)}{12"} = \frac{(1')(0.95)(10,000\ SF)}{12"} = 791.67\ c.f.\ (5,922\ gal)$$

Where, R_v = 0.05 + (0.009) (I) = 0.05 + (0.009) (100) = 0.95
R_v = Volumetric Runoff Coefficient
I = Percent Imperviousness

Equation Source: 2000 Maryland Stormwater Design Manual, Vol. I & II (MDE, 2000)

Equation 2

$$Q_r = \frac{800\ c.f.}{259,200\ sec} = 0.003\ cfs\ or\ 1.37\ gpm$$

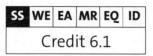
rate and quantity for the one-year and two-year, 24-hour design storms.

Determine the post-development discharge rate and quantity for the project consistent with the pre-development calculations. The post-development rate AND quantity must be equal to or less than the pre-development values to earn this credit.

Option 1-b: Stream Channel Protection

Describe the project site conditions, the measures taken, and controls implemented as part of the project scope that prevent excessive stream velocities and the associated erosion. Include in the description numerical values for pre-development and post-development conditions to demonstrate that the rate and quantity of stormwater runoff in the post-development condition are below critical values for the relevant receiving waterways.

Figure 1 (source Figure 1.4), excerpted from the Maryland Stormwater Design Manual, diagrams the potential increases in critical discharge rate from development.

Option 2—Existing Imperviousness Is Greater Than 50% (Largely Developed Sites)

Determine the pre-development discharge rate and quantity for the project. These values are typically calculated by the civil engineer using the surface characteristics of the site and data on storm event frequency, intensity, and duration. Calculate rate and quantity for the one-year and two-year, 24-hour design storms.

Determine the post-development discharge rate and quantity for the project consistent with the pre-development calculations. The post-development rate AND quantity must be at least 25% less than the pre-development values to earn this credit.

Exemplary Performance

There is no exemplary performance point available for this credit.

Figure 1: Increased Frequency of Flows Greater than the Critical Discharge Rate in a Stream Channel after Development

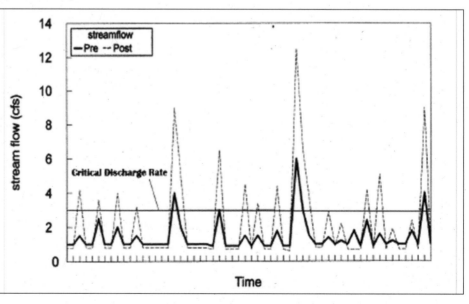

Precertification Submittal Documentation

Provide the LEED-CS Precertification Submittal Templates, which include the following:

❑ Narrative describing how the project intends to accomplish the credit requirements on the credit-specific Submittal Template signed by the appropriate design team member

❑ Confirmation of this intent from the owner/developer on the LEED-CS Precertification Submittal Template

Certification Submittal Documentation

Design and Construction Credit Compliance

This credit is submitted as part of the **Design Submittal**.

The following project data and calculation information is required to document credit compliance using the LEED-CS v2.0 Submittal Templates:

Option 1—Existing Imperviousness Is Less Than Or Equal TO 50%

❑ Provide the pre-development site run-off rate (cfs).

❑ Provide the pre-development site run-off quantity (cf).

❑ Provide the post-development site runoff rate (cfs).

❑ Provide the post-development site runoff quantity (cf).

OR

❑ Provide a narrative describing the project site conditions, measures taken, and controls implemented to prevent excessive stream velocities and associated erosion.

Option 2—Existing Imperviousness Is Greater Than 50%

❑ Provide the pre-development site run-off rate (cfs).

❑ Provide the pre-development site run-off quantity (cf).

❑ Provide the post-development site runoff rate (cfs).

❑ Provide the post-development site runoff quantity (cf).

Tenant Sales or Lease Agreement Credit Compliance

This compliance method is not available for this credit.

Considerations

Environmental Issues

The intent of this credit is to limit the disruption of the natural stormwater flows that results from development. Undeveloped land has a certain capacity to absorb rainfall in the soils, vegetation and trees. Clearing of vegetation and/or construction of impervious surfaces (i.e., roads, parking lots and buildings) reduces the capacity of the land to absorb rainfall and increases the amount of stormwater runoff.

As areas are constructed and urbanized, surface permeability is reduced, resulting in increased stormwater runoff volumes that are transported via urban infrastructure (e.g., gutters, pipes and sewers) to receiving waters. These stormwater volumes contain sediment and other contaminants that have a negative impact on water quality, navigation and recreation. Furthermore, conveyance and treatment of stormwater volumes requires significant municipal infrastructure and maintenance. Reducing the generation of stormwater volumes helps maintain the natural aquifer recharge cycle and assists in restoring depleted stream base flows. In addition, stormwater volumes do not have to be conveyed to receiving waters by the municipality, and receiving waters are not impacted.

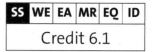

SS	WE	EA	MR	EQ	ID

Credit 6.1

Figure 2: Water Balance at a Developed and Undeveloped Site (Source: Schueler, 1987)

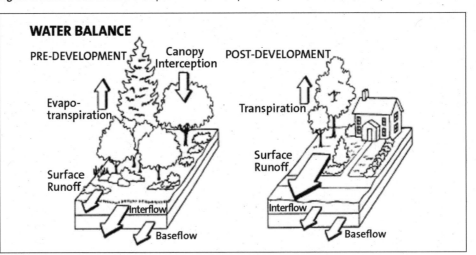

Figure 3: Relationship Between Impervious Cover and the Volumetric Runoff Coefficient (Source: Schueler, 1987)

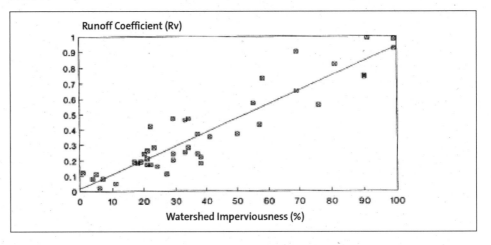

The geometry and health of streams is closely linked to stormwater runoff velocities and volumes. Increases in the frequency and magnitude of stormwater runoff due to development can cause increased bankfull events. As a result, the stream bed and banks are exposed to highly erosive flows more frequently and for longer periods. The resultant impacts may include channel-widening or down-cutting or both.

Figures 2 and 3 (Source Figures 1.1 and 1.2), excerpted from the Maryland Stormwater Design Manual show the impact of development of stormwater flows and the increase in the volumetric runoff coefficient as a function of site imperviousness.

Economic Issues

If natural drainage systems are designed and implemented at the beginning of site planning, they can be integrated economically into the overall development. Water detention and retention features require cost for design, installation and maintenance. However, these features can also add significant value as site amenities if planned early in the design. Smaller stormwater collection and treatment systems lessen the burden on municipalities for maintenance and repair, resulting in a more affordable and stable tax base.

Synergies and Trade-Offs

Stormwater runoff is affected significantly by site topography, site design, and especially quantity of impervious surface area to support transportation amenity design. It may be possible to reuse stormwater for non-potable water purposes such as flushing urinals and toilets, custodial applications, and building equipment uses. It is helpful to perform a water balance to determine the estimated volumes of water available for reuse. Stormwater runoff volumes can also be reduced by designing the building with underground parking, a strategy that also reduces heat island effects. Pervious paving systems usually have a limit on transportation loads and may pose problems for wheelchair accessibility and stroller mobility. If stormwater volumes are treated on site, additional site area may need to be disturbed to construct treatment ponds or underground facilities. Application of green roofs reduces stormwater volumes that may be intended for collection and reuse for non-potable applications.

Resources

Websites

Please see the USGBC website at www. usgbc.org/resources for more specific resources on materials sources and other technical information.

Stormwater Best Management Practice Design Guide. EPA/600/R-04/121A, September 2004.

www.epa.gov/ORD/NRMRL/pubs/ 600r04121/600r04121a.pdf

Maryland Stormwater Design Manual

www.mde.state.md.us/Programs/ WaterPrograms/SedimentandStormwater/ stormwater_design/index.asp

Definitions

Impervious Surfaces promote runoff of precipitation volumes instead of infiltration into the subsurface. The imperviousness or degree of runoff potential can be estimated for different surface materials.

Stormwater Runoff consists of water volumes that are created during precipitation events and flow over surfaces into sewer systems or receiving waters. All precipitation waters that leave project site boundaries on the surface are considered to be stormwater runoff volumes.

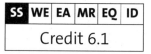

SS | WE | EA | MR | EQ | ID

Credit 6.1

Case Study

East Hills Center
Grand Rapids, Michigan

Photo courtesy of: Bazzani Associates

East Hills Center is a LEED-CS Gold Certified, 7200-sq.ft. single story office and retail condominium development. The building is located in an urban setting and is an infill new construction project. Four of the five condominium spaces had committed owners before the building broke ground. A notable sustainable feature is the zero stormwater discharge management. All stormwater is collected, retained and released back to the environment on-site. A vegetated roof garden collects the stormwater that falls on the roof and also reduces heat island effect. The building's biofiltration area has no connections to the city's storm sewers. Several passive solar design strategies are integrated in the East Hills Center project. Another design element is the south facing glass with a canopy and light shelf combination. The canopy reduces the amount of direct solar heat gain while the light shelf reflects daylight into the occupant's space. A thermally isolated concrete slab has also been incorporated into the design.

Stormwater Design

Quality Control

Intent

Reduce or eliminate water pollution by reducing impervious cover, increasing on-site infiltration, eliminating sources of contaminants, and removing pollutants from stormwater runoff.

Requirements

Implement a stormwater management plan that reduces impervious cover, promotes infiltration, and captures and treats the stormwater runoff from 90% of the average annual rainfall[1] using acceptable best management practices (BMPs).

BMPs used to treat runoff must be capable of removing 80% of the average annual post development total suspended solids (TSS) load based on existing monitoring reports. BMPs are considered to meet these criteria if (1) they are designed in accordance with standards and specifications from a state or local program that has adopted these performance standards, or (2) there exists in-field performance monitoring data demonstrating compliance with the criteria. Data must conform to accepted protocol (e.g., Technology Acceptance Reciprocity Partnership [TARP], Washington State Department of Ecology) for BMP monitoring.

Potential Technologies & Strategies

Use alternative surfaces (e.g., vegetated roofs, pervious pavement or grid pavers) and nonstructural techniques (e.g., rain gardens, vegetated swales, disconnection of imperviousness, rainwater recycling) to reduce imperviousness and promote infiltration, thereby reducing pollutant loadings.

Use sustainable design strategies (e.g., Low Impact Development, Environmentally Sensitive Design) to design integrated natural and mechanical treatment systems such as constructed wetlands, vegetated filters, and open channels to treat stormwater runoff.

In the United States, there are three distinct climates that influence the nature and amount of rainfall occurring on an annual basis. Humid watersheds are defined as those that receive at least 40 inches of rainfall each year, Semi-arid watersheds receive between 20 and 40 inches of rainfall per year, and Arid watersheds receive less than 20 inches of rainfall per year. For this credit, 90% of the average annual rainfall is equivalent to treating the runoff from:

(a) Humid Watersheds – 1 inch of rainfall;

(b) Semi-arid Watersheds – 0.75 inches of rainfall; and

(c) Arid Watersheds – 0.5 inches of rainfall.

Summary of Referenced Standard

Guidance Specifying Management Measures for Sources of Non-Point Pollution in Coastal Waters, January 1993 (Document No. EPA 840B92002)

Internet location: www.epa.gov/owow/nps/MMGI

Hardcopy or microfiche (entire document, 836 pages): National Technical Information

Service (order # PB93-234672): www.ntis.gov, (800) 553-6847

U.S. Environmental Protection Agency Office of Water: www.epa.gov/OW

This document discusses a variety of management practices that can be incorporated to remove pollutants from stormwater volumes. Chapter 4, Part II addresses urban runoff and suggests a variety of strategies for treating and infiltrating stormwater volumes after construction is completed. See the Resources section later in this credit for a summary of best management practices listed in the EPA document.

Approach and Implementation

This credit may be achieved using either non-structural or structural stormwater management measures or a combination of the two.

Non-Structural Measures

Non-structural strategies, such as vegetated swales, disconnection of impervious areas, and pervious pavement, can be used to promote infiltration and limit runoff. In these cases, you are "capturing and treating" runoff by allowing it to naturally filter into the soil and vegetation. Pollutants are broken down by microorganisms in the soil and plants.

Structural Measures

Structural measures, such as rainwater cisterns, manhole treatment devices and ponds can be used to remove pollutants from runoff from impervious areas and sometimes reuse the water for irrigation or building flush fixtures.

Non-structural measures are often preferred because they may be less costly to construct and maintain and they help recharge groundwater supplies.

Structural measures are preferred on urban or constrained sites and make it possible to effectively clean the runoff with minimal space allocation and land use. For existing sites with greater than 50% imperviousness, structural techniques may include restoration and repair of deteriorated storm sewers, or separation of combined sewers.

The most effective method to minimize stormwater runoff volume and treatment requirements is to reduce the amount of impervious area. Strategies to minimize or mitigate impervious surfaces may include—

❑ Smaller building footprint

❑ Pervious paving materials

❑ Stormwater harvesting for reuse in irrigation and/or buildings

❑ Green roofs

❑ Bioswales/vegetated filter strips

❑ Retention ponds

❑ Clustering development to reduce paved surfaces (roads, sidewalks, etc.)

Calculations

As part of the stormwater management plan process, describe the Best Management Practices (BMPs) employed to capture and/or treat stormwater runoff. Describe how each measure contributes to reducing imperviousness and/or increasing infiltration. Describe how each measure is sized to capture and/or treat 90% of the annual rainfall volume.

Determine the annual rainfall using the following guidelines:

Humid watersheds are defined as those that receive at least 40 inches of rainfall each year, Semi-arid watersheds receive between 20 and 40 inches of rainfall per year, and Arid watersheds receive less than 20 inches of rainfall per year. For this credit, 90% of the average annual rainfall is equivalent to treating the runoff from—

1. Humid Watersheds – 1 inch of rainfall;

2. Semi-arid Watersheds – 0.75 inches of rainfall; and

3. Arid Watersheds – 0.5 inches of rainfall.

Where non-structural controls involving infiltration are employed, determine the soil type(s) and associated infiltration rates. Confirm that the soils have the capacity to infiltrate water at a rate and quantity sufficient to absorb at least 90% of the annual rainfall volume.

Where structural controls are used, confirm that the equipment has the capacity to treat at least 90% of the annual rainfall volume. If individual measures are designed to handle less than 90% of the annual rainfall volume, describe how the measures work together to satisfy the requirement.

Water that is infiltrated on-site is assumed to be 100% treated for the purposes of this credit.

Stormwater control measures (or BMPs) that discharge water off-site must meet the following criteria (repeated from the credit requirement):

1. Achieve 80% total suspended solids (TSS) removal.

AND

2. Be designed in accordance with standards and specifications from a state or local program that has adopted these performance standards.

OR

Be supported by in-field performance monitoring data demonstrating compliance with the criteria. Data must conform to accepted protocol (e.g., Technology Acceptance Reciprocity Partnership [TARP], Washington State Department of Ecology) for BMP monitoring.

Exemplary Performance

There is no exemplary performance point available for this credit.

Precertification Submittal Documentation

Provide the LEED-CS Precertification Submittal Templates, which include the following:

❑ Narrative describing how the project intends to accomplish the credit requirements on the credit-specific Submittal Template signed by the appropriate design team member

❑ Confirmation of this intent from the owner/developer on the LEED-CS Precertification Submittal Template

Certification Submittal Documentation

This credit is submitted as part of the **Design Submittal**.

Design and Construction Credit Compliance

The following project data and calculation information is required to document credit compliance using the LEED-CS v2.0 Submittal Templates:

Non-Structural Controls

❑ Provide list of Best Management Practices (BMPs), including a description

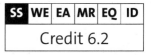

of the function of each BMP and the percent annual rainfall treated.

Structural Controls

❏ Provide list of structural controls, including a description of the pollutant removal of each control and the percent annual rainfall treated.

AND

❏ Provide an optional narrative describing any special circumstances or considerations regarding the approach to the credit.

Tenant Sales or Lease Agreement Credit Compliance

This compliance method is not available for this credit.

Considerations

Environmental Issues

As areas are constructed and urbanized, surface permeability is reduced, resulting in increased stormwater runoff volumes that are transported via urban infrastructure (e.g., gutters, pipes and sewers) to receiving waters. These stormwater volumes contain sediment and other contaminants that have a negative impact on water quality, navigation and recreation. Furthermore, conveyance and treatment of stormwater volumes requires significant municipal infrastructure and maintenance.

Stormwater pollution sources include atmospheric deposition, vehicle fluid leaks, and mechanical equipment wastes. During storm events, these pollutants are washed away and discharged to downstream waters.

Synergies and Trade-Offs

Stormwater runoff is affected significantly by site selection and site design. It may be possible to reuse stormwater for non-potable water purposes such as flushing urinals and toilets, custodial applications, and

building equipment uses. It is helpful to perform a water balance to determine the estimated volumes of water available for reuse. Stormwater runoff volumes can also be reduced by consolidating the building footprint and designing the building with underground parking, a strategy that also reduces heat island effects. Pervious paving systems usually have a limit on transportation loads and may pose problems for wheelchair accessibility and stroller mobility. If stormwater volumes are treated on site, additional site area may need to be disturbed to construct treatment ponds or underground facilities. Application of green roofs reduces stormwater volumes that may be intended for collection and reuse for non-potable applications.

Resources

Please see the USGBC website at www. usgbc.org/resources for more specific resources on materials sources and other technical information.

Websites

Stormwater Best Management Practice Design Guide. EPA/600/R-04/121A, September, 2004.

www.epa.gov/ORD/NRMRL/pubs/ 600r04121/600r04121a.pdf

Maryland Stormwater Design Manual

www.mde.state.md.us/Programs/ WaterPrograms/SedimentandStormwater/ stormwater_design/index.asp

Technology Acceptance and Reciprocity Partnership

www.dep.state.pa.us/dep/deputate/ pollprev/techservices/tarp/

Definitions

Total Suspended Solids (TSS) are particles or flocs that are too small or light to be removed from stormwater via gravity settling. Suspended solid concentrations are typically removed via filtration.

Heat Island Effect

Non-Roof

1 Point

Can assist tenants in certification under LEED for Commercial Interiors

Intent

Reduce heat islands (thermal gradient differences between developed and undeveloped areas) to minimize impact on microclimate and human and wildlife habitat.

Requirements

OPTION 1

Provide any combination of the following strategies for 50% of the site hardscape (including roads, sidewalks, courtyards and parking lots):

❑ Shade (within 5 years of occupancy)

❑ Paving materials with a Solar Reflectance Index (SRI)[2] of at least 29

❑ Open grid pavement system

OR

OPTION 2

Place a minimum of 50% of parking spaces under cover (defined as underground, under deck, under roof, or under a building). Any roof used to shade or cover parking must have an SRI of at least 29.

Potential Technologies & Strategies

Shade constructed surfaces on the site with landscape features and utilize high-reflectance materials for hardscape. Consider replacing constructed surfaces (i.e., roof, roads, sidewalks, etc.) with vegetated surfaces such as vegetated roofs and open grid paving or specify high-albedo materials to reduce the heat absorption.

The Solar Reflectance Index (SRI) is a measure of the constructed surface's ability to reflect solar heat, as shown by a small temperature rise. It is defined so that a standard black (reflectance 0.05, emittance 0.90) is 0 and a standard white (reflectance 0.80, emittance 0.90) is 100. To calculate the SRI for a given material, obtain the reflectance value and emittance value for the material. SRI is calculated according to ASTM E 1980-01. Reflectance is measured according to ASTM E 903, ASTM E 1918, or ASTM C 1549. Emittance is measured according to ASTM E 408 or ASTM C 1371. Default values for some materials will be available in this LEED-CS v2.0 Reference Guide.

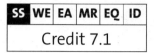
Summary of Referenced Standard

There is no standard referenced for this credit.

Approach and Implementation

Limit the amount of impervious hardscape areas on the site in order to limit heat island effect. For features such as parking lots, roads and walkways, use open grid pavement systems that are at least 50% pervious, which remain cooler due to reduction of impervious surface area and increased evaporation from the open cell vegetation. Use light colored paving surfaces, and shade paved areas with landscaping. Utilize a parking deck to reduce parking footprint by 50%.

Darker paving materials, such as asphalt, generally exhibit low reflectance and consequently low SRI values. Grey or white concrete has a higher reflectance and a higher SRI. Concrete made with white cement may cost up to twice as much as that made with gray cement. Some blended cements (e.g., slag cements) are very light in color and cost the same or slightly less than portland-only based gray cement (Source: "Albedo: A Measure of Pavement Surface Reflectance," R&T Update #3.05, June 2002, American Concrete Pavement Association, www.pavement.com/techserv/RT3.05.pdf). Micro surfaces and coatings over asphalt pavement can be used to attain the required SRI value for this credit. Coatings and integral colorants can be used in cementitious pavers or cast-in-place parking surfaces to improve solar reflectance.

Vegetation can shade buildings and pavements from solar radiation and cool the air through evapotranspiration. Provide shade using native or adaptive trees, large shrubs and non-invasive vines. Trellises and other exterior structures can support vegetation to shade parking lots, walkways and plazas. Deciduous trees allow buildings to benefit from solar heat gain during the winter months. On site locations where tree planting is not possible, use architectural shading devices to block direct sunlight radiance.

Alternatively, place parking under cover. This can include using multi-story or subterranean parking structures, or placing parking under a shade structure. Parking cover must also meet the same SRI requirements as non-roof impervious surfaces.

Calculations

Option 1

1. Identify all non-roof hardscape surfaces on the project site and sum the total area (T).

2. Identify all of the hardscape surfaces that have an open grid paving system that are at least 50% pervious and sum the total area (O).

3. Identify all of the hardscape features that have an SRI of at least 29 and sum the total area (R).

SRI is calculated using the LEED Submittal Template by inserting both emissivity and reflectance values into the worksheet and pressing "Click to Calculate SRI." Emittance is calculated according to ASTM E 408 or ASTM C 1371 and Reflectance is calculated according to ASTM E 903, ASTM E 1918, or ASTM C 1549. Alternatively, **Table 1** provides a list of SRI values for typical paving materials; where these materials are used, the SRI values from this table may be used in lieu of obtaining specific Emissivity and Reflectance measurements.

4. Identify all of the hardscape features that will be shaded by trees or other landscape features. Shade coverage shall be calculated at 10a.m., noon and 3p.m. The mean of these three values will be used as the effective shaded

Material	Emissivity	Reflectance	SRI
Typical New Gray Concrete	0.9	0.35	35
Typical Weathered* Gray Concrete	0.9	0.20	19
Typical New White Concrete	0.9	0.7	86
Typical Weathered* White Concrete	0.9	0.4	45
New Asphalt	0.9	.05	0
Weathered Asphalt	0.9	.10	6

* Reflectance of surfaces can be maintained with cleaning. Typical pressure washing of cementious materials can restore reflectance close to original value. Weathered values are based on no cleaning.

area. Calculate the effective shaded area (S).

5. Sum the open space paving, high reflectance paving and shaded areas to get the qualifying area (Q) as in **Equation 1**.

(Note that each surface should be counted only once. For example, a 10-sq.ft. area that is 55% pervious, has an SRI of 30 and is shaded by a tree contributes only 10 square feet to the total.)

6. The total qualifying area must be greater than or equal to 50% of the total hardscape area (T), as in **Equation 2**.

Option 2

1. Calculate the total number of parking spaces for the project.

2. Calculate the number of parking spaces that are under cover (including underground, under the building, and under shade structures. This number must equal at least 50% of the total number of parking spaces.

Exemplary Performance

Projects may be awarded an innovation point for exemplary performance by demonstrating that either, 1) a minimum of 100% of non-roof impervious surfaces have been constructed with high-albedo

materials and/or open grid paving and/or will be shaded within five years; OR, 2) 100% of the on-site parking spaces have been located under cover.

Precertification Submittal Documentation

Provide the LEED-CS Precertification Submittal Templates, which include the following:

❑ Narrative describing how the project intends to accomplish the credit requirements on the credit-specific Submittal Template signed by the appropriate design team member

❑ Confirmation of this intent from the owner/developer on the LEED-CS Precertification Submittal Template

Certification Submittal Documentation

This credit is submitted as part of the **Construction Submittal**.

Design and Construction Credit Compliance

The following project data and calculation information is required to document credit compliance using the LEED-CS v2.0 Submittal Templates:

Equation 1

$$Q = (O + R + S)$$

Equation 2

$$Q \geq T/2$$

❑ Provide project site drawings, high-lighting the location of specific paving materials, landscape shading, and/or underground or covered parking.

AND

Option 1

Provide the following data in the submittal template:

❑ The measured reflectance and emittance of each paving material installed on-site (to calculate the SRI OR the actual SRI for each paving material installed on-site OR the default SRI value for typical materials from Table 1

❑ Total area of site hardscape

❑ Total area of hardscape to be shaded within 5 years

❑ Total area of installed SRI compliant hardscape materials

❑ Total area of open grid pavement

OR

Option 2

❑ Total number of parking spaces provided on-site

❑ Total number of covered parking spaces on-site

AND (For Either Compliance Option)

❑ Provide an optional narrative to describe any special circumstances or non-standard compliance paths taken by the project.

Tenant Sales or Lease Agreement Credit Compliance

This compliance method is not available for this credit.

Considerations

Environmental Issues

As the built environment grows and replaces natural settings, it also relinquishes associated ecological services. Vegetation cools the area surrounding it via shade and evapotranspiration. The use of dark, non-reflective surfaces for parking, roofs, walkways and other surfaces contributes to heat island effects created when radiation from the sun is absorbed and transferred through convection and conduction back to surrounding areas. As a result of heat island effects, ambient temperatures in urban areas can be artificially elevated by more than 10°F when compared with surrounding suburban and undeveloped areas. This results in increased cooling loads in the summer, requiring larger HVAC equipment and electrical demand resulting in more greenhouse gas and pollution generation, and increased energy consumption for building operations. Heat island effects can be mitigated through the application of shading and the use of materials that reflect the sun's heat instead of absorbing it.

Heat island effects are detrimental to site habitat, wildlife and migration corridors. Plants and animals are sensitive to higher temperatures and may not thrive in areas that are increasingly hot. Reduction of heat island effect minimizes disturbance of local microclimates. This can reduce summer cooling loads that in turn reduce energy use, greenhouse gas and pollution generation, and infrastructure requirements.

Higher reflectance pavements do increase overall light levels and may allow the designer to use fewer fixtures. Designers should weigh the benefits of using highly reflective pavements to reduce heat island effect against possible energy savings from reduced site lighting requirements. Lighting evaluations should include the evaluation of the inter-reflected component, and reflections off of high reflectance materials, such as white concrete, which can result in glare and cause disabled vision and increased light pollution. Steps should be taken to minimize the amount of light that is directed from site lighting fixtures directly onto reflective paving surfaces.

Economic Issues

According to the EPA, about $40 billion is spent annually in the United States to air-condition buildings—one-sixth of all electricity generated in a year. Reduction in heat islands lowers the cost of cooling and HVAC equipment needs. Energy to cool buildings is a substantial cost over a building's lifetime. Higher initial costs may result from installation of additional trees and architectural shading devices. However, these items have an acceptable payback when integrated into a whole systems approach that maximizes energy savings.

Resources

Please see the USGBC website at www.usgbc.org/resources for more specific resources on materials sources and other technical information.

Websites

American Concrete Pavement Association

www.pavement.com

(847) 966-2272

National association representing concrete pavement contractors, cement companies, equipment and material manufacturers, and suppliers. See the R&T Update #3.05, June 2002, "Albedo: A Measure of Pavement Surface Reflectance" (www.pavement.com/techserv/RT3.05.pdf).

Heat Island Group

Lawrence Berkeley National Laboratory

http://eetd.lbl.gov/HeatIsland/

LBL conducts heat island research to find, analyze and implement solutions to minimizing heat island effect, with current research efforts focusing on the study and development of more reflective surfaces for roadways and buildings.

Heat Island Effect

U.S. Environmental Protection Agency

www.epa.gov/heatisland

(202) 343-9299

Basic information about heat island effect, its social and environmental costs, and strategies to minimize its prevalence.

Definitions

Albedo is synonymous with solar reflectance (see below).

Emissivity is the ratio of the radiation emitted by a surface to the radiation emitted by a black body at the same temperature.

Heat Island Effects occur when warmer temperatures are experienced in urban landscapes compared to adjacent rural areas as a result of solar energy retention on constructed surfaces. Principal surfaces that contribute to the heat island effect include streets, sidewalks, parking lots and buildings.

Infrared or Thermal Emittance is a parameter between 0 and 1 (or 0% to 100%) that indicates the ability of a material to shed infrared radiation (heat). The wavelength range of this radiant energy is roughly 4 to 40 micrometers. Most building materials (including glass) are opaque in this part of the spectrum, and have an emittance of roughly 0.9. Materials such as clean, bare metals are the most important exceptions to the 0.9 rule. Thus clean, untarnished galvanized steel has low emittance, and aluminum roof coatings have intermediate emittance levels.

Non-Roof Impervious Surfaces include all surfaces on the site with a perviousness of less than 50%, not including the roof of the building. Examples of typically impervious surfaces include parking lots, roads, sidewalks and plazas.

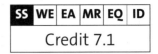

SS | WE | EA | MR | EQ | ID
Credit 7.1

Open-Grid Pavement is defined for LEED purposes as pavement that is less than 50% impervious and contains vegetation in the open cells.

Perviousness is the percent of the surface area of a paving material that is open and allows moisture to pass through the material and soak into the earth below the paving system.

Solar Reflectance (Albedo) is the ratio of the reflected solar energy to the incoming solar energy over wavelengths of approximately 0.3 to 2.5 micrometers. A reflectance of 100% means that all of the energy striking a reflecting surface is reflected back into the atmosphere and none of the energy is absorbed by the surface. The best standard technique for its determination uses spectro-photometric measurements with an integrating sphere to determine the reflectance at each different wavelength. An averaging process using a standard solar spectrum then determines the average reflectance (see ASTM Standard E903).

Solar Reflectance Index (SRI) is a measure of a material's ability to reject solar heat, as shown by a small temperature rise. It is defined so that a standard black (reflectance 0.05, emittance 0.90) is 0 and a standard white (reflectance 0.80, emittance 0.90) is 100. For example, a standard black surface has a temperature rise of 90°F (50°C) in full sun, and a standard white surface has a temperature rise of 14.6°F (8.1°C). Once the maximum temperature rise of a given material has been computed, the SRI can be computed by interpolating between the values for white and black.

Materials with the highest SRI values are the coolest choices for paving. Due to the way SRI is defined, particularly hot materials can even take slightly negative values, and particularly cool materials can even exceed 100. (Lawrence Berkeley National Laboratory Cool Roofing Materials Database)

Underground Parking is a "tuck-under" or stacked parking structure that reduces the exposed parking surface area.

Heat Island Effect

Roof

Intent

Reduce heat islands (thermal gradient differences between developed and undeveloped areas) to minimize impact on microclimate and human and wildlife habitat.

Requirements

OPTION 1

Use roofing materials having a Solar Reflectance Index (SRI)[3] equal to or greater than the values in the table below for a minimum of 75% of the roof surface.

OR

OPTION 2

Install a vegetated roof for at least 50% of the roof area.

OR

OPTION 3

Install high albedo and vegetated roof surfaces that, in combination, meet the following criteria:

(Area of SRI Roof / 0.75) + (Area of Vegetated Roof / 0.5) >/= Total Roof Area

Roof Type	Slope	SRI
Low-Sloped Roof	≤ 2:12	78
Steep-Sloped Roof	≥ 2:12	29

Potential Technologies & Strategies

Consider installing high-albedo and vegetated roofs to reduce heat absorption. SRI is calculated according to ASTM E 1980. Reflectance is measured according to ASTM E 903, ASTM E 1918, or ASTM C 1549. Emittance is measured according to ASTM E 408 or ASTM C 1371. Default values will be available in the LEED-CS v2.0 Reference Guide. Product information is available from the Cool Roof Rating Council website, at www.coolroofs.org.

---

3   The Solar Reflectance Index (SRI) is a measure of the constructed surface's ability to reflect solar heat, as shown by a small temperature rise. It is defined so that a standard black (reflectance 0.05, emittance 0.90) is 0 and a standard white (reflectance 0.80, emittance 0.90) is 100. To calculate the SRI for a given material, obtain the reflectance value and emittance value for the material. SRI is calculated according to ASTM E 1980. Reflectance is measured according to ASTM E 903, ASTM E 1918, or ASTM C 1549. Emittance is measured according to ASTM E 408 or ASTM C 1371. Default values for some materials will be available in this LEED-CS v2.0 Reference Guide.

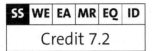
Summary of Referenced Standards

ASTM Standard E1980-01—Standard Practice for Calculating Solar Reflectance Index of Horizontal and Low-Sloped Opaque Surfaces.

This standard describes how surface reflectivity and emissivity are combined to calculate a Solar Reflectance Index (SRI) for a roofing material or other surface. The standard also describes a laboratory and field testing protocol that can be used to determine SRI.

ASTM E408-71(1996)e1—Standard Test Methods for Total Normal Emittance of Surfaces Using Inspection-Meter Techniques

www.astm.org

(610) 832-9585

This standard describes how to measure total normal emittance of surfaces using a portable inspection-meter instrument. The test methods are intended for large surfaces where non-destructive testing is required. See the standard for testing steps and a discussion of thermal emittance theory.

ASTM E903-96—Standard Test Method for Solar Absorptance, Reflectance, and Transmittance of Materials Using Integrating Spheres

www.astm.org

(610) 832-9585

Referenced in the ENERGY STAR® roofing standard, this test method uses spectrophotometers and need only be applied for initial reflectance measurement. Methods of computing solar-weighted properties from the measured spectral values are specified. This test method is applicable to materials having both specular and diffuse optical properties. Except for transmitting sheet materials that are inhomogeneous, patterned, or corrugated, this test method is preferred over Test Method E1084. The ENERGY STAR roofing standard also allows the use of reflectometers to measure solar reflectance of roofing materials. See the roofing standard for more details.

ASTM E1918-97—Standard Test Method for Measuring Solar Reflectance of Horizontal

And Low-Sloped Surfaces in the Field

www.astm.org

(610) 832-9585

This test method covers the measurements of solar reflectance of various horizontal and low-sloped surfaces and materials in the field, using a pyranometer. The test method is intended for use when the sun angle to the normal from a surface is less than 45 degrees.

ASTM C1371-04—Standard Test Method for Determination of Emittance of Materials Near Room Temperature Using Portable Emissometers

www.astm.org

(610) 832-9585

This test method covers a technique for determination of the emittance of typical materials using a portable differential thermopile emissometer. The purpose of the test method is to provide a comparative means of quantifying the emittance of opaque, highly thermally conductive materials near room temperature as a parameter in evaluating temperatures, heat flow, and derived thermal resistances of materials.

ASTM C1549-04—Standard Test Method for Determination of Solar Reflectance Near Ambient Temperature Using a Portable Solar Reflectometer

www.astm.org

(610) 832-9585

This test method covers a technique for determining the solar reflectance of flat opaque materials in a laboratory or in the field using a commercial portable solar reflectometer. The purpose of the test method is to provide solar reflectance data required to evaluate temperature and heat flows across surfaces exposed to solar radiation.

Approach and Implementation

To maximize energy savings and minimize heat island effects, materials must exhibit a high reflectivity and a high emissivity over the life of the product. Since multiple testing methods are available for measuring emissivity and reflectance, check manufacturer literature carefully to ensure use of appropriate data. For example, some manufacturers measure visible reflectance, which differs from the solar reflectance measurement referenced in this credit. Visible reflectance correlates to solar reflectance but the two quantities are not equal because solar gain covers a wider range of wavelengths than visible light. A material that exhibits a high visible reflectance usually has a lower solar reflectance. Typically, white roof products exhibit higher performance characteristics than non-white products. Performance

varies by roofing materials as well as brand. Check with roofing manufacturers and the Lawrence Berkeley National Laboratory's Cool Roofing Materials Database (http://eetd.lbl.gov/CoolRoofs) for specific information. **Table 1** provides example SRI values for typical roof surfaces.

Green roofs are vegetated surfaces that reduce heat island effect by replacing heat-absorbing surfaces with plants, shrubs and small trees that cool the air through evapotranspiration (or evaporation of water from leaves). Green roofs provide insulating benefits, aesthetic appeal and lower maintenance than standard roofs. Some green roofs require plant maintenance and are considered active gardens, while other gardens have grasses and plants that require no maintenance or watering. All types of green roofs require semiannual inspection but have longer lifetimes than conventional roofs.

Calculations

1. Calculate the total roof surface area of the project. Deduct areas with equipment, solar energy panels, and appurtenances.

Table 1: Solar Reflectance Index (SRI) for Typical Roofing Materials

Example SRI Values for Generic Roofing Materials	Solar Reflectance	Infrared Emittance	Temperature Rise	Solar Reflectance Index (SRI)
Gray EPDM	0.23	0.87	68F	21
Gray Asphalt Shingle	0.22	0.91	67F	22
Unpainted Cement Tile	0.25	0.9	65F	25
White Granular Surface Bitumen	0.26	0.92	63F	28
Red Clay Tile	0.33	0.9	58F	36
Light Gravel on Built-Up Roof	0.34	0.9	57F	37
Aluminum	0.61	0.25	48F	56
White-Coated Gravel on Built-Up Roof	0.65	0.9	28F	79
White Coating on Metal Roof	0.67	0.85	28F	82
White EPDM	0.69	0.87	25F	84
White Cement Tile	0.73	0.9	21F	90
White Coating - 1 Coat, 8 mils	0.8	0.91	14F	100
PVC White	0.83	0.92	11F	104
White Coating - 2 Coats, 20 mils	0.85	0.91	9F	107

Source: LBNL Cool Roofing Materials Database. These values are for reference only and are not for use as substitutes for actual manufacturer data.

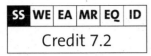

SS | WE | EA | MR | EQ | ID

Credit 7.2

2. Determine the roof surface area that meets the applicable SRI criteria and/or the area that is covered by green roof.

3. Determine whether the areas of cool roof and green roof meet the credit requirement, using **Equation 1**.

Note: a weighted average calculation may be performed for buildings with multiple roof surfaces to demonstrate that the total roof area has an average SRI equal to or greater than a theoretical roof with 75% at an SRI of 78 and 25% at an SRI of 30.

Exemplary Performance

This credit may be eligible for exemplary performance under the Innovation & Design section if 100% of the project's roof area (excluding mechanical equipment, photovoltaic panels and skylights) is comprised of a green roof system.

Precertification Submittal Documentation

Provide the LEED-CS Precertification Submittal Templates, which include the following:

❑ Narrative describing how the project intends to accomplish the credit requirements on the credit-specific Submittal Template signed by the appropriate design team member

❑ Confirmation of this intent from the owner/developer on the LEED-CS Precertification Submittal Template

Certification Submittal Documentation

This credit is submitted as part of the **Design Submittal**.

Design and Construction Credit Compliance

The following project data and calculation information is required to document credit compliance using the LEED-CS v2.0 Submittal Templates:

❑ Provide copies of the project's roof drawings to highlight the location of specific roof materials and/or green roof systems.

AND

Option 1

❑ Total area of installed SRI compliant roofing materials

❑ Provide a listing of installed roofing materials and their SRI values

OR

Option 2

❑ Total area of installed green roof systems

OR

Option 3

❑ Total area of installed green roof systems

❑ Total area of installed SRI compliant roofing materials

❑ Provide a listing of installed roofing materials and their SRI values

AND

❑ Provide an optional narrative to describe any special circumstances or non-standard compliance paths taken by the project.

Tenant Sales or Lease Agreement Credit Compliance

This compliance method is not available for this credit.

Equation 1

(Area of SRI Roof / 0.75) + (Area of vegetated roof / 0.5) >= Total Roof Area

Considerations

Environmental Issues

The heat island effect raises the localized temperature, impacting local microclimate. Plants and animals that are sensitive to large fluctuations in daytime and nighttime temperatures may not thrive in areas affected by heat islands. Heat islands also exacerbate air pollution for two reasons. First, smog is produced faster at higher temperatures. Secondly, rising temperatures lead to increased cooling requirements, requiring energy and causing associated emissions.

Garden roofs reduce stormwater volumes that may be collected and used for nonpotable purposes. Stormwater runoff volumes from garden roofs depend on the local climate, depth of soil, plant types, and other variables. However, all garden roofs decrease runoff volumes substantially.

Economic Issues

Green roofs or roofs with high Solar Reflectance Indexes reduce costs associated with cooling and HVAC equipment. Green roofs typically require an additional up-front investment, while cool roofs may or may not cost more than other roofs. However, any up-front investment is likely to result in energy cost savings throughout the lifecycle of the project. In addition, an increasing number of localities are beginning to require the use of cool roofs on new building projects.

Buildings in very cold climates may not experience year-round energy benefits from reflective roofing due to high emittance and low absorption, which may increase heating costs. However, increasing the reflectance of a roof reduces annual cooling energy use in almost all climates.

Resources

Websites

Cool Roof Rating Council

www.coolroofs.org

A nonprofit organization dedicated to implementing and communicating fair, accurate, and credible radiative energy performance rating systems for roof surfaces, supporting research into energy-related radiative properties of roofing surfaces, including durability of those properties, and providing education and objective support to parties interested in understanding and comparing various roofing options.

EPA ENERGY STAR® Roofing Products

www.energystar.gov/index.cfm?c=roof_prods.pr_roof_products

This site provides solar reflectance levels required to meet ENERGY STAR labeling requirements.

Extensive Green Roofs

www.wbdg.org/design/greenroofs.php

This Whole Building Design Guide article by Charlie Miller, PE details the features and benefits of constructing green roofs.

Greenroofs.com

www.greenroofs.com

The green roof industry resource portal offers basic information, product and service directory, and research links.

Lawrence Berkeley National Laboratory Heat Island Group–Cool Roofs

http://eetd.lbl.gov/HeatIsland/CoolRoofs/

This site offers a wealth of information about cool roof research and technology, including links to the Cool Roofing Materials Database.

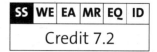

Penn State Center for Green Roof Research

http://hortweb.cas.psu.edu/research/greenroofcenter/

The Center has the mission of demonstrating and promoting green roof research, education and technology transfer in the Northeastern United States.

Definitions

Albedo is synonymous with solar reflectance (see below).

Heat Island Effects occur when warmer temperatures are experienced in urban landscapes compared to adjacent rural areas as a result of solar energy retention on constructed surfaces. Principal surfaces that contribute to the heat island effect include streets, sidewalks, parking lots and buildings.

Infrared or Thermal Emittance is a parameter between 0 and 1 (or 0% and 100%) that indicates the ability of a material to shed infrared radiation (heat). The wavelength range for this radiant energy is roughly 4 to 40 micrometers. Most building materials (including glass) are opaque in this part of the spectrum, and have an emittance of roughly 0.9. Materials such as clean, bare metals are the most important exceptions to the 0.9 rule. Thus clean, untarnished galvanized steel has low emittance, and aluminum roof coatings have intermediate emittance levels.

Solar Reflectance (Albedo) is the ratio of the reflected solar energy to the incoming solar energy over wavelengths of approximately 0.3 to 2.5 micrometers. A reflectance of 100% means that all of the energy striking a reflecting surface is reflected back into the atmosphere and none of the energy is absorbed by the surface. The best standard technique for its determination uses spectro-photometric measurements with an integrating sphere to determine the reflectance at each different wavelength. An averaging process using a standard solar spectrum then determines the average reflectance (see ASTM Standard E903).

Solar Reflectance Index (SRI) is a measure of a material's ability to reject solar heat, as shown by a small temperature rise. It is defined so that a standard black (reflectance 0.05, emittance 0.90) is 0 and a standard white (reflectance 0.80, emittance 0.90) is 100. For example, a standard black surface has a temperature rise of 90°F (50°C) in full sun, and a standard white surface has a temperature rise of 14.6°F (8.1°C). Once the maximum temperature rise of a given material has been computed, the SRI can be computed by interpolating between the values for white and black.

Materials with the highest SRI values are the coolest choices for roofing. Due to the way SRI is defined, particularly hot materials can even take slightly negative values, and particularly cool materials can even exceed 100. (Lawrence Berkeley National Laboratory Cool Roofing Materials Database)

Light Pollution Reduction

Intent

Minimize light trespass from the building and site, reduce sky-glow to increase night sky access, improve nighttime visibility through glare reduction, and reduce development impact on nocturnal environments.

Requirements

FOR INTERIOR LIGHTING

All non-emergency interior lighting, with a direct line of sight to any openings in the envelope (translucent or transparent), shall have its input power reduced (by automatic device) by at least 50% between the hours of 11:00 p.m. and 5:00 a.m. After hours override may be provided by a manual or occupant-sensing device, provided that the override last no more than 30 minutes.

OR

All openings in the envelope (translucent or transparent) with a direct line of sight to any non-emergency lighting shall have shielding (for a resultant transmittance of less than 10%) that will be controlled/closed by automatic device between the hours of 11:00 p.m. and 5:00 a.m.

AND

FOR EXTERIOR LIGHTING

Only light areas as required for safety and comfort. Do not exceed 80% of the lighting power densities for exterior areas and 50% for building facades and landscape features as defined in ASHRAE/IESNA Standard 90.1-2004, Exterior Lighting Section, without amendments.

All projects shall be classified under one of the following zones, as defined in IESNA RP-33, and shall follow all of the requirements for that specific zone:

LZ1 — Dark (Park and Rural Settings)

Design exterior lighting so that all site and building mounted luminaires produce a maximum initial illuminance value no greater than 0.01 horizontal and vertical footcandles at the site boundary and beyond. Document that 0% of the total initial designed fixture lumens are emitted at an angle of 90 degrees or higher from nadir (straight down).

LZ2 — Low (Residential Areas)

Design exterior lighting so that all site and building mounted luminaires produce a maximum initial illuminance value no greater than 0.10 horizontal and vertical footcandles at the site boundary and no greater than 0.01 horizontal footcandles 10 feet beyond the site boundary. Document that no more than 2% of the total initial designed fixture lumens are emitted at an angle of 90 degrees or higher from nadir (straight down). For site boundaries that abut public rights-of-way, light trespass requirements may be met relative to the curb line instead of the site boundary.

LZ3 — Medium (Commercial/Industrial, High-Density Residential)

Design exterior lighting so that all site and building mounted luminaires produce a maximum initial illuminance value no greater than 0.20 horizontal and vertical footcandles at the site boundary and no greater than 0.01 horizontal footcandles 15 feet beyond the site. Document that no more than 5% of the total initial designed fixture lumens are emitted at an angle of 90 degrees or higher from nadir (straight down). For site boundaries that abut public rights-of-way, light trespass requirements may be met relative to the curb line instead of the site boundary.

LZ4 — High (Major City Centers, Entertainment Districts)

Design exterior lighting so that all site and building mounted luminaires produce a maximum initial illuminance value no greater than 0.60 horizontal and vertical footcandles at the site boundary and no greater than 0.01 horizontal footcandles 15 feet beyond the site. Document that no more than 10% of the total initial designed site lumens are emitted at an angle of 90 degrees or higher from nadir (straight down). For site boundaries that abut public rights-of-way, light trespass requirements may be met relative to the curb line instead of the site boundary.

Potential Technologies & Strategies

Adopt site lighting criteria to maintain safe light levels while avoiding off-site lighting and night sky pollution. Minimize site lighting where possible and model the site lighting using a computer model. Technologies to reduce light pollution include full cutoff luminaires, low-reflectance surfaces and low-angle spotlights.

Summary of Referenced Standards

ASHRAE/IESNA Standard 90.1-2004, Energy Standard for Buildings Except Low-Rise Residential - Lighting, Section 9 (without amendments)

American Society of Heating Refrigeration and Air-Conditioning Engineers

www.ashrae.org

(800) 527-4723

Standard 90.1-2004 was formulated by the American Society of Heating, Refrigerating and Air-Conditioning Engineers, Inc. (ASHRAE), under an American National Standards Institute (ANSI) consensus process. The Illuminating Engineering Society of North America (IESNA) is a joint sponsor of the standard. Standard 90.1 establishes minimum requirements for the energy-efficient design of buildings, except low-rise residential buildings. The provisions of this standard do not apply to single-family houses, multifamily structures of three habitable stories or fewer above grade, manufactured houses (mobile and modular homes), buildings that do not use either electricity or fossil fuel, or equipment and portions of building systems that use energy primarily for industrial, manufacturing or commercial processes. The standard provides criteria in the following general categories: building envelope (section 5); heating, ventilating and air-conditioning (section 6); service water heating (section 7); power (section 8); lighting (section 9); and other equipment (section 10). Within each section, there are mandatory provisions that must always be complied with, as well as additional prescriptive requirements. Some sections also contain a performance alternate. The Energy Cost Budget option (section 11) allows the user to exceed some of the prescriptive requirements provided energy cost savings are made in other prescribed areas. However, in all cases, the mandatory provisions must still be met.

Section 9 of the Standard provides requirements for the lighting of buildings. Only the exterior lighting requirements (exterior site lighting & exterior building feature/façade lighting) apply to this credit. **Table 1** lists the ASHRAE 90.1-2004 allowable building exterior lighting power densities.

IESNA RP-33, Lighting for Exterior Environments

The Illuminating Engineering Society of North America

www.iesna.org

(212) 248-5000

The IESNA RP-33 addresses the challenges of lighting for the outdoor environment. The document addresses visual issues such as glare, luminance, visual activity and illuminance. Considerations regarding community responsive design are addressed as well as light pollution, regulatory ordinances, energy conservation, and technical considerations in various lighting environments.

Approach and Implementation

The credit is comprised of three main compliance requirements that deal with light pollution through the control of; 1) interior building lighting; 2) exterior lighting power density; and 3) exterior light distribution.

Interior Building Lighting

Option 1

This compliance path requires that all non-emergency interior lighting fixtures be automatically controlled and programmed to turn off following regular business hours. Controls may be automatic sweep timers, occupancy sensors, or programmed master lighting control panels. Manual override capabilities that enable lights to be turned on for after-hours use must be included in the design.

Table 1: ASHRAE 90.1-2004 Lighting Power Densities for Building Exteriors (Table 9.4.5)

	Applications	Lighting Power Densities
Tradable Surfaces (Lighting power densities for uncovered parking areas, building grounds, building entrances and exits, canopies and overhangs and outdoor sales areas may be traded.)	**Uncovered Parking Areas**	
	Parking Lots and drives	**0.15**W/ft2
	Building Grounds	
	Walkways less than 10 feet wide	**1.0**W/linear foot
	Walkways 10 feet wide or greater Plaza areas Special Feature Areas	**0.2**W/ft2
	Stairways	**1.0**W/ft2
	Building Entrances and Exits	
	Main entries	**30**W/linear foot of door width
	Other doors	**20**W/linear foot of door width
	Canopies and Overhangs	
	Canopies (free standing and attached and overhangs)	**1.25**W/ft2
	Outdoor Sales	
	Open areas (including vehicle sales lots)	**0.5**W/ft2
	Street frontage for vehicle sales lots in addition to "open area" allowance	**20**W/linear foot
Non-Tradable Surfaces (Lighting power density calculations for the following applications can be used only for the specific application and cannot be traded between surfaces or with other exterior lighting. The following allowances are in addition to any allowance otherwise permitted in the "Tradable Surfaces" section of this table.)	**Building Facades**	**0.2**W/ft2 for each illuminated wall or surface or **5.0**W/linear foot for each illuminated wall or surface length
	Automated teller machines and night depositories	**270**W per location plus 90W per additional ATM per location
	Entrances and gatehouse inspection stations at guarded facilities	**1.25**W/ft2 of uncovered area (covered areas are included in the "Canopies and Overhangs" section of "Tradable Surfaces")
	Loading areas for law enforcement, fire, ambulance and other emergency service vehicles	**0.5**W/ft2 of uncovered area (covered areas are included in the "Canopies and Overhangs" section of "Tradable Surfaces")
	Drive-up windows at fast food restaurants	**400**W per drive-through
	Parking near 24-hour retail entrances	**800**W per main entry

Option 2

This compliance path requires that all exterior openings such as windows have shielding that can be automatically controlled and programmed to close from 11:00 p.m. until 5:00 a.m. Shielding options include automatic shades that have less than 10% transmittance.

An example of this might include an automated rolling shade with the appropriate light transmittance that is controlled by a timer.

For core and shell buildings, these requirements are limited to the core and shell lighting. Typically this includes lobby and core circulation spaces. Tenant spaces for which no lighting is provided as part of the core and shell development are exempt from these requirements. Core and shell projects that do not install any interior lighting as part of the project scope have met this requirement.

Exterior Lighting Power Density

Design the project's exterior lighting to achieve lighting power densities that are less than the requirements set forth in ASHRAE 90.1-2004, Section 9, Table 9.4.5. Lighting for exterior areas, such as parking lots, building grounds and plazas, should be designed to achieve an overall lighting power density that is 20% below the referenced standard. Building façade and landscape feature lighting should be designed to achieve an overall lighting power density that is 50% below the referenced standard. Projects should consider selecting efficient fixtures using efficacious sources to reduce lighting power and illumination intensity.

Exterior Light Distribution

Design the project's exterior lighting to comply with the light pollution requirements for the specific project zone. The lighting requirements address the overall site illumination level and the luminaire distribution. The exterior lighting must meet the light distribution requirements under pre-curfew conditions (prior to 10 p.m. or business closing). Curfew timers and controls can be effective components of the overall lighting strategy, and may be used to mitigate specific, extenuating circumstances; but controls cannot be used to make otherwise non-compliant exterior areas comply with the credit.

Projects should consider the use of low intensity, shielded fixtures as well as curfew controllers to turn off non-essential site lighting after 10:00 p.m. or immediately after closing (whichever is later) to further reduce the effects of light pollution. Projects should minimize the lighting of architectural and landscape

features. Where lighting is required for safety, security, egress or identification, utilize down-lighting techniques rather than up-lighting.

For example, in environments that are primarily dark (Zone LZ1), no landscape features should be illuminated, and architectural lighting should be designed only as a last resort when other strategies cannot provide the minimum amount of required lighting. In areas of high ambient brightness (Zones LZ3 & 4), some low level (subtle) lighting of features, facades or landscape areas may be appropriate in pedestrian environments or for identification and way-finding in other areas where light trespass is not likely to be an issue. However, even in areas of high ambient brightness, all non-essential lighting, including landscape and architectural lighting, should be minimized or turned off after hours. If shielded, low brightness sources are used to selectively light features, they should be properly aimed so that light from the luminaires cannot be measured across project boundaries. In all cases, controls should be used wherever possible to turn off non-essential lighting after normal operating hours or in post-curfew periods. Consider at least the following strategies when designing the exterior lighted environment:

1. Employ a lighting professional to assess the project's lighting needs and provide recommendations based specifically on lighting for a sustainable design environment.

2. Carefully review and respond to any applicable lighting ordinances or by-laws that might impact the lighting design for the project site.

3. Determine the type of environmental zone that the project falls under from Wilderness Area (Zone LZ1) to High-Population City Centers (Zone LZ4). Understand the design implications of the environmental zone that best fits the project and study neighboring

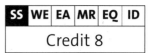

areas to identify potential light trespass problems.

4. Use the least amount of lighting equipment possible to achieve the goals of the project, but balance the quantity of equipment used with the need to provide for glare control and uniform lighting. In most cases, it is better to have two luminaires with lower light output and good glare control than one higher output luminaire.

5. Select all lighting equipment carefully. Any type of luminaire, whether it is full cut-off, semi-cutoff or non-cutoff, can produce excessive brightness in the form of glare. For example, horizontal lamp positions in full cutoff luminaires tend to produce much less glare than vertical lamps. Selecting high-performance equipment of good quality is not only essential in maintaining visual quality and providing sustainable lighting, but also will quickly pay for itself in reduced maintenance costs.

6. Design exterior lighting to produce minimal upward illumination from reflected light sources. Select luminaire locations carefully to control glare and contain light within the design area. Pay special attention to luminaires that are located near the property line to ensure that minimal measurable light from these luminaires crosses the project boundary.

7. Use the minimum amount of light necessary and only light areas that require it. Design and develop a control scheme to minimize, or turn lighting off, after hours or during post-curfew periods.

8. Create a computer model of the proposed electric lighting design and simulate system performance. Use this tool to provide point by point horizontal illuminance information or an iso-footcandle contour map demonstrating that illuminance values are as required at the project boundary. Where luminaires are within 2.5 times their mounting height from the project boundary and the light levels are not zero at the boundary, light trespass is more likely to be a problem.

9. After the lighting system is constructed, it should be commissioned to ensure

Table 2: Sample Fixture Candela Table

Angle	0	22.5	45	67.5	90
0	862	862	862	862	862
5	848	847	869	860	862
10	838	837	858	848	850
15	814	815	845	840	844
20	785	790	819	818	824
25	747	754	785	786	792
30	693	704	738	751	759
35	636	652	695	712	723
40	566	589	642	669	682
45	492	524	586	622	636
50	409	454	525	566	580
55	331	385	465	509	523
60	257	315	398	439	438
65	189	247	328	327	323
70	135	188	235	224	210
75	85	127	142	119	106
80	44	64	61	40	33
85	15	15	11	13	13
90	0	0	0	0	0

that it is installed and operating properly. Maintenance should be performed on the system on a regular basis to ensure that it continues to operate correctly, and that light pollution is minimized.

Calculations

Interior Building Lighting

There are no calculations associated with this portion of the credit.

Exterior Lighting Power Density

Calculate the lighting power density (LPD) for the project's exterior lighting fixtures using the fixture wattage (lamp & ballast) provided by the manufacturer. Separate the exterior fixtures into two categories: 1) Exterior Areas—includes parking, walkway, plaza, and other outdoor area lighting; and 2) Facades/Landscape Areas—includes any vertical surface illumination (façade/signage) and any accent or landscape lighting. **Calculation 1** provides an example of the calculation methodology.

After calculating the LPDs for the project, determine if the lighting design complies with the requirements for LPD reduction.

Exterior Light Trespass

In order to measure compliance with the light trespass requirements, projects should utilize lighting design software to develop a site illumination model. The model should show the full extent of the site and all installed exterior lighting fixtures. A horizontal calculation grid should be set up to measure the site illumination at the ground plane and a vertical calculation grid should be set at the property boundary and at the extent of the LZ requirements (10 feet beyond the site boundary for LZ2 and 15 feet beyond the site boundary for LZ3/LZ4) to measure vertical illumination. The calculation grid spacing should be a maximum of 10' x 10' and should exclude building interior areas. Additionally, teams should utilize the model to determine maximum and minimum illumination levels and the overall site uniformity (max/min ratio).

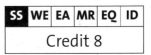

Calculation 1: Sample Exterior Lighting Power Density Calculation

Site Lighting Power Density Calculation						
Site Lighting Fixture	**Fixture Power (Watts)**	**Total Fixtures (Qty)**	**Total Fixture Power (Watts)**	**Site Location**	**Site Area (SF)**	**LPD (W/SF)**
Pole Fixture 1	250	14	3,500	Parking 1	32,000	0.11
Pole Fixture 1	250	8	2,000	Parking 2	18,000	0.11
Pole Fixture 2	115	1	115	Walkways 1	875	0.13
Bollard Fixture 1	40	4	160	Walkways 1	875	0.18
Bollard Fixture 1	40	6	240	Courtyard 1	1,500	0.16
Wall Washer 1	50	5	250	Building Facade N	2,500	0.10

Site Areas						
Identification	**Area (SF)**	**ASHRAE 90.1.2004 Allowable LPD (W/SF)**	**Actual LPD (From Site Lighting Table)**	**Actual LPD Reduction (%)**	**Required LPD Reduction (%)**	**Complies (Yes/No)**
Parking 1	32,000	0.25	0.11	27%	20%	YES
Parking 2	18,000	0.15	0.11	26%	20%	YES
Walkways 1 (10' wide)	875	0.2	0.16	21%	20%	YES
Courtyard 1	1,500	0.2	0.16	20%	20%	YES
Building Facade N	2,500	0.2	0.10	50%	50%	YES

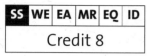

Utilizing manufacturers' fixture data, determine the initial lamp lumens for each luminaire. Additionally, from photometric data, determine the number of initial lamp lumens that are emitted at or above 90 degrees from nadir. Enter this data into **Table 3** to determine the percentage of lumens at or above 90 degrees. This number must be less than or equal to the value referenced for the selected site LZ.

Note: luminaires without photometric distribution shall be assumed to have 100% of its initial lamp lumens at or above 90 degrees. Luminaires with limited adjustability shall be assumed to have maximum tilt applied and lumens at or above 90 degrees shall be calculated from maximum tilted orientation. Luminaires with full range of adjustability (those that can be aimed above 90 degrees from nadir) shall be assumed to have 100% of the emitted fixture lumens at or above 90 degrees.

Exemplary Performance

This credit is not eligible for exemplary performance under the Innovation & Design section.

Precertification Submittal Documentation

Provide the LEED-CS Precertification Submittal Templates, which include the following:

- ❑ Narrative describing how the project intends to accomplish the credit requirements on the credit-specific Submittal Template signed by the appropriate design team member

- ❑ Confirmation of this intent from the owner/developer on the LEED-CS Precertification Submittal Template

Certification Submittal Documentation

This credit is submitted as part of the **Design Submittal**.

Design and Construction Credit Compliance

The following project data and calculation information is required to document credit compliance using the LEED-CS v2.0 Submittal Templates:

- ❑ Provide copies of the project lighting drawings (interior and site) to document the location and type of fixtures installed.

- ❑ Provide confirmation that automatic controls have been installed to turn off interior lighting during non-occupied hours OR, automatically controlled shielding devices have been provided for all openings in the envelope (translucent or transparent) with a direct line of sight to any non-emergency lighting. If automatic controls have been provided, include a narrative for the

Table 3: Lamp Lumen Calculation

Luminaire Type	Quantity of Installed Luminaires	Initial Fixture Lumens per Luminaire	Total Fixture Lumens (column 2 x column 3)	Initial Fixture Lumens from Luminaire above 90 Degrees (from nadir-straight down)	Total Fixture Lumens above 90 Degrees (column 2 x column 5)
A	10	4,600	46,000	100	1,000
B	20	11,900	238,000	0	0
C	5	2,000	10,000	2,000	10,000
Total			294,000		11,000

lighting control system and cut-sheets for the installed equipment. If shielding has been provided, include a narrative that describes the shielding system and cut-sheets for the equipment.

AND

For Projects With No Exterior Lighting

❑ Confirm that no exterior lighting has been installed.

For Projects With Exterior Lighting

❑ Complete the Lighting Power Density tables on the Submittal Template for both exterior site lighting and façade/landscape lighting. The following data will be required to complete the template: location and ID of each installed exterior luminaire; site area (sq.ft.) to be illuminated by the luminaire(s); installed LPD; and ASHRAE-allowable LPD.

❑ Document the site zone classification for the project.

❑ Complete the Site Lumen Calculation on the submittal template. The following data will be required to complete the template: luminaire type/ID; quantity installed; initial lamp lumens per luminaire; initial lamp lumens above 90 degrees from nadir.

❑ For multiple building projects where the LEED Project Boundary is not the project site area, provide an overall site plan with project boundaries indicated for each development parcel. The exterior lighting requirements must be met for the LEED Project Boundary.

AND

❑ Verify light trespass requirements are met by providing a site plan showing initial vertical footcandles at the site boundary on a 5-foot horizontal and 5 foot vertical grid. Calculate initial vertical footcandles perpendicular to the site boundary facing the site at 0 feet to the maximum luminaire mounting height above the grade level.

❑ Provide any additional comments or notes regarding special circumstances or considerations regarding the project's credit approach.

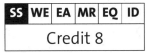

Considerations

Environmental Issues

Outdoor lighting is necessary for illuminating connections between buildings and support facilities such as sidewalks, parking lots, roadways and community gathering places. However, light trespass from poorly designed outdoor lighting systems can affect the nocturnal ecosystem on the site, and light pollution limits night sky access. Through thoughtful design and careful maintenance, outdoor lighting can address night sky visibility issues and site illumination requirements, while minimizing the negative impact on the environment.

Sensitively designed outdoor lighting can extend access and use of many areas into the nighttime hours. We can gain a unique appreciation for a place at night because of sensitively and creatively designed lighting systems. But any time lighting is added to an exterior environment, the potential of light pollution exists. Even with the best full cutoff luminaires and the lowest wattage lamp packages, the added light will be reflected off surfaces and into the atmosphere. Using the minimum amount of lighting equipment, limiting or eliminating all landscape lighting, and avoiding light pollution through the careful selection of lighting equipment and controls allows nocturnal life to thrive while still providing for nighttime activity.

Economic Issues

Carefully designed exterior lighting solutions can reduce infrastructure costs and energy use when compared to common practice solutions. Energy and maintenance savings over the lifetime of the project can be substantial.

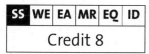

Credit 8

Community Issues

Minimizing light pollution allows for night sky access by the surrounding community. Another key benefit is better visual comfort and improved visibility. Sensitively designed lighting systems that minimize glare and provide more uniform light at lower levels will help create aesthetically pleasing environments that are safer and more secure. A carefully designed and maintained outdoor lighting system can help a project be a non-intrusive member of the community.

Resources

Please see the USGBC website at www. usgbc.org/resources for more specific resources on materials sources and other technical information.

Websites

American Society of Heating Refrigeration and Air-Conditioning Engineers

www.ashrae.org

ASHRAE/IESNA Standard 90.1-2004: Energy Standard for Buildings Except Low-Rise Residential

Illuminating Engineering Society of North America

www.iesna.org

This organization provides general exterior lighting design guidance and acts as a link to other IESNA outdoor lighting

California Energy Commission (CEC) - 2005 California Energy Efficiency Building Standards – Lighting Zones

www.energy.ca.gov/title24/ 2005standards/outdoor_lighting/ 2004-09-30_LIGHTING_ZONES. PDF

Provides a description of the outdoor lighting zones developed for use in the 2005 California Energy Efficiency Building Standards (Title 24).

International Dark-Sky Association

www.darksky.org/ida/ida_2/index.html

A nonprofit agency dedicated to educating and providing solutions to light pollution.

New England Light Pollution Advisory Group

http://cfa-www.harvard.edu/cfa/ps/ nelpag.html

A volunteer group to educate the public on the virtues of efficient, glare-free outdoor night lighting as well as the benefits of no lighting for many outdoor applications.

Sky & Telescope

http://skyandtelescope.com/resources/ darksky/default.asp

Includes facts on light pollution and its impact on astronomy, and information about purchasing light fixtures that minimize light pollution.

Print Media

Concepts in Practice Lighting: Lighting Design in Architecture by Torquil Barker, B.T. Batsford Ltd., 1997.

The Design of Lighting by Peter Tregenza and David Loe, E & FN Spon, 1998.

Definitions

Angle of Maximum Candela is the direction in which the luminaire emits the greatest luminous intensity.

Curfew Hours are locally determined times when greater lighting restrictions are imposed. When no local or regional restrictions are in place, 10:00 p.m. is regarded as a default curfew time.

Footcandle (fc) is a unit of illuminance and is equal to one lumen of light falling on a one-square foot area from a one candela light source at a distance of one foot.

Light Pollution is waste light from building sites that produces glare, is directed upward to the sky or is directed off the site.

Outdoor Lighting Zone Definitions (Developed by IDA for the Model Lighting Ordinance) provide a general description of the site environment/context and basic site lighting criteria.

Outdoor Lighting Zone Definitions

Zone	Ambient Illumination	Criteria
LZ1	Dark	For population densities of less than 200 people per square mile according the last U.S. census. Also for developed areas in state and national parks, areas near astronomical observatories, zoos, and ANY area where residents have expressed a desire to maintain a natural nighttime environment.
LZ2	Low	For population densities of 200-3,000 people per square mile, according the last U.S. census. This would include most areas zoned "residential" and is the default zone for residential areas.
LZ3	Medium	For population densities greater than 3,000 people per square mile according the last U.S. Census. This lighting zone is intended for high density urban neighborhoods, shopping and commercial districts and industrial parks. This is the default zone for commercial and industrial areas.
LZ4	High	This is for major city centers (with population densities greater than 100,000 according to the last U.S. Census), thematic attractions, entertainment districts, and major auto sale districts.

Tenant Design & Construction Guidelines

Intent

Provide tenants with a descriptive tool that both educates and helps them implement sustainable design and constructions features in their tenant improvement build-out.

Tenant Design and Construction Guidelines benefit the Core and Shell certified project for two important reasons: First, the Guidelines will help tenants design and build sustainable interiors and adopt green building practices; second, the Guidelines will help in coordinating LEED-CI and LEED-CS certifications.

Requirements

Publish an illustrated document that provides tenants with design and construction information that details the following:

❑ Provides a description of the sustainable design and construction features incorporated in the core and shell project and delineates the project intent with respect to sustainability goals and objectives including those for tenant spaces.

❑ Provides information that enables a tenant to coordinate their space design and construction with the core and shell's building systems. Specific building LEED-CS credits to be addressed when applicable include—

- Water Use Reduction
- Optimize Energy Performance, Lighting Power
- Optimize Energy Performance, Lighting Controls
- Optimize Energy Performance, HVAC
- Energy Use and Metering
- Measurement & Verification
- Ventilation and Outdoor Air Delivery
- Construction IAQ Management
- Indoor Chemical and Pollutant Source Control
- Controllability of Systems
- Thermal Comfort
- Daylighting and Views
- Commissioning
- The Elimination or Control of Environmental Tobacco Smoke
- Recommendations, including examples, of Sustainable Strategies, Products, Materials, and Service Suggestions

❑ Provides information on the LEED Green Building Rating System for Commercial Interiors (LEED-CI) and how the core and shell building contributes to achieving these credits.

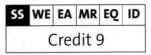

Credit 9

Potential Technologies & Strategies

Provide a copy of the Tenant Design & Construction Guidelines to tenants.

Summary of Referenced Standard

There is no standard referenced for this credit.

Approach and Implementation

This credit has two complementary goals, both aim at enabling a tenant design and construction team to understand and utilize the sustainable features of the core and shell building: 1) to communicate core and shell sustainable design and construction features so a tenant's design team has knowledge of the building systems and design features; 2) to provide information regarding the LEED-CI Rating System.

Develop a written scope summary of sustainable design features early in the core and shell project inception. This is particularly useful for tenant design and construction teams to have in the early phases of the tenant design work. This will continue to be developed as the project's design moves forward. Updated, current Guidelines should be made available to tenants as part of the lease negotiations.

The intent of the Tenant Design & Construction Guidelines is to provide building-specific best practice guidelines. The guidelines are not meant to be requirements by which the tenant must design. Some projects may elect to adopt portions, or all, of the Guidelines as tenant requirements, however this is not necessary to meet the requirements of this credit.

Core and Shell Sustainable Design and Construction Features

This portion of the Tenant Design and Construction Guidelines is intended to enable the tenant design team to understand and efficiently utilize the base building systems and design features. Technical information, building features, and base building policy should be clearly communicated. As appropriate for the project, this will include the following:

Water Use Reduction: Specify the core and shell water use goals. Provide information regarding installed base building water use fixtures and systems and how these assist in reaching these goals. Fixtures and systems recommendations should be included. This can be presented in narrative form with product cut sheets.

Optimize Energy Performance: This information should outline the energy optimization features of the core and shell and provide information and recommendations regarding how the tenant can further reduce energy use through their design. Specific features to be highlighted are—

Lighting Power: the greatest opportunity for tenants to optimize energy consumption is in the area of lighting. Core and shell building design can affect lighting power use dramatically by providing a base building design that allows for a reduction in lighting power without compromising light quality. A core and shell commercial office building design that allows for tenants to reduce lighting power through daylight harvesting should consider floor to ceiling heights, the bay size and depth of occupied spaces. Daylight shelves and glare control devices should be considered. Building orientation and site issues such as shading from surrounding buildings may also impact the opportunities available for tenants. The selection of glass and visible light transmittance critically impact the ability to reduce lighting power in the tenant space. An opportunity that should be considered for retail or manufacturing core and shell buildings is the use of skylights for top lighting and the reduction of lighting power.

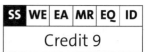

SS | WE | EA | MR | EQ | ID

Credit 9

To assist in a tenant's understanding and implementation of strategies aimed at reducing lighting power, information on technical and design decisions regarding the base building should be included in the Tenant Design & Construction Guidelines. Recommendations regarding base building lighting fixtures installed may also be appropriate.

Lighting Controls: Integrally linked with lighting power are tenant space lighting controls. Daylighting strategies that have been designed into the core and shell will be optimal if coupled with tenant space layout and lighting control implementation. Base building design information, potential tenant space layouts and technical recommendations are all valuable considerations.

HVAC: The choices that the core and shell design team makes, relative to the HVAC system, have a considerable affect on the tenant build-out. Information provided should include a description of the HVAC system including any energy efficiency features. This description should provide the benefits that this system brings to the tenants and how they can best be utilized.

Energy Use and Metering: Provide information regarding the building's expected energy use. Give an explanation on how the building's energy use is metered. Provide instructions on how the tenants can sub-meter their space. Explain how sub-metering can help foster tenant energy conservation.

Measurement & Verification: Describe the building's measurement and verification plan. This should include what M&V option is being used and how the core and shell M&V plan will be carried out. Information should also be provided on measurement and verification protocols that the tenant can use to create their own M&V plan.

Ventilation and Outdoor Air Delivery: Provide design and operational information for the ventilation system. This should include how the air is provided to the space (underfloor, overhead, displacement, natural ventilation, etc.).Include the amount of outside air that each system is capable of providing, and will allow the tenants to determine how much outside air is available to them. This document should describe the control system and identify opportunities that the tenant has to utilize the control system, by installing monitoring devices such as CO_2 sensors.

Construction IAQ Management: The Tenant Design and Construction Guidelines should highlight areas of the core and shell construction's Indoor Air Quality Management Plan that are applicable to the tenant build-out, since tenant work may be sequenced at the same time. This may include multiple tenant construction teams.

Indoor Chemical and Pollutant Source Control: Strategies utilized to accomplish this credit should be illustrated. Because it is possible for multiple tenants to share air return and supply systems, information regarding the benefits of isolating hazardous gases or chemicals should be included.

Controllability of Systems: Describe the building's HVAC control systems . If the building incorporates natural ventilation, describe how it can be used, and how it works with the building's other systems. For a completely mechanical system, provide details on how the tenants can use the control system to better regulate the thermal comfort in their spaces.

Thermal Comfort: Explain how the building's HVAC system will help maintain the thermal comfort in the building. Provide the design criteria of the system including indoor and outdoor conditions. Document any other assumptions made for the thermal comfort calculations including space internal loads, clothing and metabolic rate of the people in the space.

Daylighting and Views: Many of the issues related to daylighting are discussed earlier relative to energy optimization, however views should also be considered. For commercial office buildings, projects should consider supplying a tenant layout early in the project development, so that potential tenants can consider the benefits of views within their space layout.

Employees in retail or manufacturing core and shell buildings can also benefit from views to the outdoors. Building siting and envelope design should be considered.

Core and shell developments that have designed with this potential should describe this and provide illustrations in the Tenant Design & Construction Guidelines. The advantages of views to tenants can be part of the building marketing and lease negotiation process.

Commissioning: Building commissioning can help assure that a building is operating as intended. Provide details on the core and shell commissioning process. This may include the commissioning plan or report. Provide information on the building's Design Intent. This will allow the tenant to evaluate if their space is functioning as designed. This can also serve as a model for tenants to use in their own commissioning activities.

The Elimination or Control of Environmental Tobacco Smoke: Building policy regarding environmental tobacco smoke should be clearly stated. If Option 1 of prerequisite EQp 2 is utilized this policy should be part of the Tenant Design & Construction Guidelines and communicated to potential tenants during the lease negotiation. If Option 2 of prerequisite EQp 2 is utilized, separation, exhaust and pressurization requirements will need to be clearly communicated so that they can be included in the tenant's scope of construction.

Mixed use buildings that include a residential component should also describe methods utilized to comply with Option 3 of prerequisite EQp 2.

Recommendations Including Examples of Sustainable Strategies, Products, Materials and Service Suggestions: This section of the Tenant Design and Construction Guidelines should describe the sustainable materials, products, and strategies utilized by the core and shell. Tenant design teams will be able to use this information for material and product selection for their space. If the base building has specified low-emitting materials (EQc 4), specific adhesives and sealants, paints and coatings, carpet systems, and composite wood and agrifiber products used should be included. Other materials that have contributed to materials reuse, recycled content, regional materials and certified wood should be included in the Guidelines. Materials that have specific potential for the tenant space build-out should be highlighted.

Information Regarding the LEED-CI Rating System

This section of the Tenant Design and Construction Guidelines is intended to assist the tenant with a LEED-CI pursuit. General information about the LEED-CI Rating System should be provided with building-specific examples of the advantages of choosing to pursue LEED-CI.

This Reference Guide has included a keying tool in its margin indicating which LEED-CS credits bring synergies or direct benefits to a LEED-CI certification. In some instances, a core and shell building will allow a tenant to achieve LEED-CI credit with no additional effort. For example, three points toward LEED-CI certification may be achieved for 1) moving into a LEED certified building; 2) the development density of the building; and 3) alternative transportation options available at the building.

SS	WE	EA	MR	EQ	ID
Credit 9					

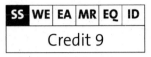

Calculations

There are no calculations associated with this credit.

Exemplary Performance

This credit is not eligible for exemplary performance under the Innovation & Design section. Core and shell projects that elect to mandate specific design and construction initiatives—above and beyond the "guidelines" intent of this credit—as tenant requirements may use this to achieve credit compliance through the alternative credit compliance method outlined in the Credit Compliance section of the introduction.

Precertification Submittal Documentation

Provide the LEED-CS Precertification Submittal Templates, which include the following:

❑ Narrative describing how the project intends to accomplish the credit requirements on the credit-specific Submittal Template signed by the appropriate design team member

❑ Confirmation of this intent from the owner/developer on the LEED-CS Precertification Submittal Template

Certification Submittal Documentation

This credit is submitted as part of the **Design Submittal**.

Design and Construction Credit Compliance

The following project data is required to document credit compliance using the LEED-CS v2.0 Submittal Templates:

❑ Provide the complete Tenant Design and Construction Guidelines. Technical back-up information such as construction documents and/or specifications is not required.

Tenant Sales or Lease Agreement Credit Compliance

This compliance method is not available for this credit.

Considerations

Environmental Issues

Due to the nature of the speculative market—with the building core and shell and the interior tenant spaces controlled by completely different entities—responsibility for environmental concerns is weighted differently for the owner/developer and the tenant. For example, the core and shell energy usage of a commercial office building is generally 15–25% of the total energy used in the building. The tenants' potential to reduce energy usage through efficient lighting design is significant. And, a tenant's ability to effectively utilize daylighting strategies is dependent on the core and shell construction. Also the base building automation system, or mechanical system, will directly influence the tenants' ability to optimize the occupants indoor environmental quality.

Because of this, the environmental benefits of a core and shell building are an essential first step toward a complete building that fosters further environmental stewardship in its tenants.

Economic Issues

Carefully designed core and shell will provide base building systems that enable cost effective tenant design and construction. Many base building systems are considerably more cost effective to install during initial construction, than to retrofit based on unanticipated tenant needs.

Lease agreements that require the tenant to meter and pay for their own energy costs provide market incentives to reduce energy and resource use.

Community Issues

Actively educating and marketing the advantages of sustainable core and shell buildings, and tenant build-outs, are an integral part of the market transformation goals of the USGBC toward sustainable design and construction practices.

Case Study

National Business Park 304
Annapolis Junction, Maryland

National Business Park 304 (NBP 304) is a five-story, 162,498-sq.ft. office building, which was fully leased during construction and earned LEED-CS Pilot Silver Certification. NBP 304 is located in a 285-acre business community and is the first building in a three building business campus arranged around a central sculpture plaza that allows for pedestrian connectivity.

Photo courtesy of: Jeffery Sauers

The precast panels and reflective glass exterior of the building is complementary to other buildings in the park, and sunshades are featured to reduce heat gain and glare. Some of the project's attributes include: highly filtered air; extremely efficient mechanical systems; water usage reduction of 40% compared to a typical office building; solar shading; and an extensive green housekeeping program. Sustainable features include: reduced site disturbance; heat island reduction through the use of a white roof; reduced light pollution with exterior lighting designed to prevent spillage beyond the site; alternative transportation opportunities with bicycle storage and changing rooms to encourage tenant employees to bike to work; and tenant design and construction guidelines to promote green practices by tenants.

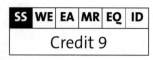

Water Efficiency

In the United States, approximately 340 billion gallons of fresh water are withdrawn per day from rivers, streams and reservoirs to support residential, commercial, industrial, agricultural and recreational activities. This accounts for about one-fourth of the nation's total supply of renewable fresh water. Almost 65% of this water is discharged to rivers, streams and other water bodies after use and, in some cases, treatment.

Additionally, water is withdrawn from underground aquifers. In some parts of the United States, water levels in these aquifers have dropped more than 100 feet since the 1940s. On an annual basis, the water deficit in the United States is currently estimated at about 3,700 billion gallons. In other words, Americans extract 3,700 billion gallons per year more than they return to the natural water system to recharge aquifers and other water sources.

On a positive note, U.S. industries today use 36% less water than they did in 1950 although industrial output has increased significantly. This reduction in water use is largely due to the rigorous water reuse strategies in industrial processes. In addition, the Energy Policy Act of 1992 (and as amended) mandated the use of water-conserving plumbing fixtures to reduce water use in residential, commercial and institutional buildings.

Using large volumes of water increases maintenance and lifecycle costs for building operations and increases consumer costs for additional municipal supply and treatment facilities. Conversely, facilities that use water efficiently can reduce costs through lower water use fees, lower sewage volumes to treat energy and chemical use reductions, and lower capacity charges and limits. Many water conservation strategies involve either no additional cost or rapid paybacks. Other water conservation strategies such as biological wastewater treatment, rainwater harvesting and graywater plumbing systems often involve more substantial investment.

Water efficiency measures in commercial buildings can easily reduce water usage by 30% or more. In a typical 100,000-square-foot office building, low-flow fixtures coupled with sensors and automatic controls can save a minimum of 1 million gallons of water per year, based on 650 building occupants each using an average of 20 gallons per day. Non-potable water volumes can be used for landscape irrigation, toilet and urinal flushing, custodial purposes and building systems. Utility savings, though dependent on the local water costs, can save thousands of dollars per year, resulting in rapid payback on water conservation infrastructure.

Water Efficiency Credit Characteristics

Table 1 shows which credits were substantially revised from LEED-NC Version 2.2, which credits are eligible to be submitted in the Design Phase Submittal, and which project team members are likely to carry decision-making responsibility for each credit. The decision-making responsibility matrix is not intended to exclude any party, rather to emphasize those credits that are most likely to require strong participation by a particular team member.

Overview of LEED® Prerequisites and Credits

WE Credit 1.1
Water Efficient Landscaping—Reduce by 50%

WE Credit 1.2
Water Efficient Landscaping—No Potable Water Use or No Irrigation

WE Credit 2
Innovative Wastewater Technologies

WE Credit 3.1
Water Use Reduction —20%

WE Credit 3.2
Water Use Reduction —30%

Table 1: WE Credit Characteristics

Credit	Significant Change from LEED-NC v2.2	Design Submittal	Construction Submittal	Owner Decision-Making	Design Team Decision-Making	Contractor Decision-Making
WEc1.1: Water Efficient Landscaping: Reduce by 50%		*			*	
WEc1.2: Water Efficient Landscaping: No Potable Water Use or No Irrigation		*		*	*	
WEc2: Innovative Wastewater Technologies	*	*			*	
WEc3.1: Water Use Reduction, 20%		*			*	
WEc3.2: Water Use Reduction, 30%		*			*	

Water Efficient Landscaping

Reduce by 50%

Intent

Limit or eliminate the use of potable water, or other natural surface or subsurface water resources available on or near the project site, for landscape irrigation.

Requirements

Reduce potable water consumption for irrigation by 50% from a calculated mid-summer baseline case.

Reductions shall be attributed to any combination of the following items:

❑ Plant species factor

❑ Irrigation efficiency

❑ Use of captured rainwater

❑ Use of recycled wastewater

❑ Use of water treated and conveyed by a public agency specifically for non-potable uses

Potential Technologies & Strategies

Perform a soil/climate analysis to determine appropriate plant material and design the landscape with native or adapted plants to reduce or eliminate irrigation requirements. Where irrigation is required, use high-efficiency equipment and/or climate-based controllers.

1 Point
in addition to
WE Credit 1.1

Water Efficient Landscaping

No Potable Water Use or No Irrigation

Intent

Eliminate the use of potable water, or other natural surface or subsurface water resources available on or near the project site, for landscape irrigation.

Requirements

Achieve WE Credit 1.1 and

Use only captured rainwater, recycled wastewater, recycled graywater, or water treated and conveyed by a public agency specifically for non-potable uses for irrigation.

OR

Install landscaping that does not require permanent irrigation systems. Temporary irrigation systems used for plant establishment are allowed only if removed within one year of installation.

Potential Technologies & Strategies

Perform a soil/climate analysis to determine appropriate landscape types and design the landscape with indigenous plants to reduce or eliminate irrigation requirements. Consider using stormwater, graywater, and/or condensate water for irrigation.

Summary of Referenced Standard

There is no standard referenced for this credit.

Approach and Implementation

Design landscaping with climate-tolerant plants that can survive on natural rainfall quantities after initial establishment. Contour the land to direct rainwater runoff through the site to give vegetation an additional water supply. Minimize the amount of site area covered with turf, and use techniques such as mulching, alternative mowing and composting to maintain plant health. These practices conserve water and help foster optimal soil conditions.

Recommended design principals

1. Planning and design
   - ❑ Develop a site map showing existing or planned structures, topography, orientation, sun and wind exposure, use of space and existing vegetation.
   - ❑ Perform shadow profiles of landscape areas for each season, based on middle of the day conditions and illustrate the plant selection within the profiles.
   - ❑ Reduce heat island effect by providing adequate shade from trees and buildings; plant hard wood trees to increase shade canopy as necessary.
   - ❑ Plan water use zones:

     High – regular watering

     Moderate – occasional watering

     Low – natural rain fall

2. Practical turf areas

   Plant turf grasses only for functional benefits such as recreational areas, pedestrian use, or specifically for soil conservation.

3. Soil analysis and preparation
   - ❑ Analyze soil in each zone.
   - ❑ Amend soil accordingly.

4. Appropriate use of plant materials
   - ❑ Choose plants that will easily adapt to the site.
     - A. Consider the mature size and form when choosing plant material for the location and intended purpose.
     - B. Consider growth rate.
     - C. Determine that texture and color combine with surrounding plantings and building background.
     - D. Use no mono-species or excessive multi-species selections.
     - E. Diversify species to prevent elimination of a species from diseases or pest infestation.

5. Effective and efficient watering practices
   - ❑ Regularly check irrigation systems for efficient and effective operation; verify watering schedules and duration on a monthly basis.
   - ❑ Use drip, micro misters, and sub-surface irrigation systems where applicable, and smart irrigation controllers throughout. Provide computer interface for monitoring and schedule modifications from a central location.
   - ❑ No irrigation of plants and turf in the months of November to April.
   - ❑ No irrigation of shrubs from September to June.

6. Use of mulch on trees, shrubs and flower beds
   - ❑ Keep landscape areas mulched to conserve moisture and prevent evaporative water loss from the soil surface to reduce the need for

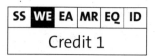

supplemental irrigation during periods of limited rainfall.

A number of factors, including owner preference, event uses, and maintenance expertise may also impact plant selection, but the intent of this credit is to create a landscape that maximizes the use of on-site natural resources to limit or eliminate the use of potable water for irrigation. This goal can be achieved by selecting native or adapted plants that require little or no irrigation after initial establishment. This goal also can be achieved by using high-efficiency irrigation equipment, captured rainwater, recycled graywater or treated wastewater to reduce the consumption of potable water. Often times, it is appropriate to use a combination of these strategies to first reduce potable water demand and then meet the irrigation demand in the most sustainable manner.

The use of native or adapted plants is an excellent approach because water conservation is built-in and is not reliant on high-tech equipment and controls. In some climates, it is possible to eliminate the need for permanent irrigation with this strategy. In other climates, irrigation requirements can be cut by 50% or greater compared to conventional building land-scapes simply by plant selection.

Technologies

The use of irrigation technology, rainwater capture, and/or advanced wastewater treatment is another excellent approach to achieving this credit because it allows for a broader plant species palette, while still conserving potable water supplies. High-efficiency irrigation strategies include micro-irrigation systems, moisture sensors, rain shut-offs, and weather-based evapotranspiration controllers. Drip systems apply water slowly and directly to the roots of plants, using 30 to 50%

less water than sprinkler irrigation[1]. Moisture and rain sensors save water by ensuring that plants only receive water when necessary.

A rainwater collection system (e.g., cisterns, underground tanks, ponds) can significantly reduce or completely eliminate the amount of potable water used for irrigation. Rainwater can be collected from roofs, plazas and paved areas and then filtered by a combination of graded screens and paper filters to pre-pare it for use in irrigation. Metal, clay or concrete-based roofing materials are ideal for rainwater harvest, as asphalt or lead-containing materials will contaminate the water. Rainwater with high mineral content or acidity may damage systems or plantings, but pollutants can be fil-tered out by soil or mechanical systems prior to being applied to plantings. It is important to check local rainfall quantity and quality, as collection systems may be inappropriate in areas with rainfall of poor quality or low quantity.

Wastewater recovery can be accomplished either on-site or at the municipal level. On-site systems include graywater and/or wastewater treatment. Graywater consists of wastewater from sinks, showers and washing machines; cooling tower bleed down water; condensation from air con-ditioning systems; and other building activities that do not involve human waste or food processing. In addition, many municipalities treat sewage to tertiary standards in central treatment plants and re-distribute that water regionally for ir-rigation use.

Calculations

To calculate the percent reduction in potable use for this credit, establish a base-line water use rate for your project and

---

1 Bilderback, T.E., and M.A. Powell. Efficient Irrigation. North Carolina Cooperative Extension Service, Publication Number AG-508-6, March 1996. 21 January 2005. www.bae.ncsu.edu/programs/extension/publicat/wqwm/ag508_6.html

then calculate the as-designed water use rate according to the steps listed below.

Standard Assumptions & Variables

❏ All calculations are based on irrigation during the month of July.

❏ The **Landscape Coefficient** (KL) indicates the volume of water lost via evapotranspiration and is dependent on the landscape species, the microclimate and the planting density. The formula for determining the landscape coefficient is given in **Equation 1**.

❏ The **Species Factor** (ks) accounts for variation of water needs by different plant species. The species factor can be divided into three categories (high, average and low) depending on the plant species considered. To determine the appropriate category for a plant species, use plant manuals and professional experience. This factor is somewhat subjective but landscape professionals should have a general idea of the water needs of particular plant species. Landscapes can be maintained in acceptable condition at about 50% of the reference evapotranspiration (ET0) value and thus, the average value of ks is 0.5. (Note: If a species does not require irrigation once it is established, then the effective ks = 0 and the resulting KL = 0.)

❏ The **Density Factor** (kd) accounts for the number of plants and the total leaf area of a landscape. Sparsely planted areas will have lower evapotranspiration rates than densely planted areas. An average kd is applied to areas where ground shading from trees is in the range of 60% to 100%. This is also equivalent to shrubs and ground cover shading 90% to 100% of the landscape area. Low kd values are found where ground shading from trees is less

than 60% or shrub and groundcover is less than 90%. For instance, a 25% ground shading from trees results in a kd value of 0.5. In mixed landscape plantings where trees cover understory groundcover and shrubs, evapotranspiration increases. This represents the highest level of landscape density and the kd value should be between 1.0 and 1.3.

❏ The **Microclimate Factor** (kmc) accounts for environmental conditions specific to the landscape, including temperature, wind and humidity. For instance, parking lot areas increase wind and temperature effects on adjacent landscapes. The average kmc is 1.0 and this refers to conditions where the landscape evapotranspiration rate is unaffected by buildings, pavements, reflective surfaces and slopes. Higher kmc conditions occur where evaporative potential is increased due to landscapes surrounded by heat-absorbing and reflective surfaces or are exposed to particularly windy conditions. Examples of high kmc areas include parking lots, west sides of buildings, west and south sides of slopes, medians, and areas experiencing wind tunnel effects. Low microclimate areas include shaded areas and areas protected from wind. North sides of buildings, courtyards, areas under wide building overhangs, and north sides of slopes are low microclimate areas.

Step 1 — Create Design Case

Determine the landscape area for the project. This number must represent the as-designed landscape area and must use the same project boundary as is used in all other LEED credits. Sort the total landscape area into the major vegetation types (trees, shrubs, groundcover, mixed and turfgrass), listing the area for each.

Equation 1

$$K_L = k_s \times k_d \times k_{mc}$$

Determine the following characteristics for each landscape area: Species Factor (ks), Density Factor (kd), and Microclimate Factor (kmc). Recommended values for each of these factors are provided in **Table 1**. Select the "low," "average," or "high" value for each parameter as appropriate for your design. Any variance from these recommended values should be explained in the credit narrative.

Calculate the Landscape Coefficient (KL) by multiplying the three area characteristics as shown in **Equation 1**.

Determine the reference evapotranspiration rate (ET0) for your region. The **evapotranspiration rate** is a measurement of the total amount of water needed to grow a certain reference plant (such as grass or alfalfa) expressed in millimeters or inches. The values for ET0 in various regions throughout the United States can be found in regional agricultural data (see Resources section). The ET0 for July is used in the LEED calculation because this is typically the month with the greatest evapotranspiration effects and, therefore, the greatest irrigation demands.

Calculate your project-specific evapotranspiration rate (ETL) for each landscape area by multiplying the (ET0) by your KL, as shown in **Equation 2**.

Determine your **Irrigation Efficiency** (IE) by listing the type of irrigation used for each landscape area and the corresponding efficiency. **Table 2** lists irrigation efficiencies for different irrigation systems.

Determine, if applicable, the Controller Efficiency (CE). CE is the percent reduction in water use from any weather-based controllers or moisture sensor-based systems. This number must be supported by either manufacturer documentation or detailed calculations by the landscape designer.

Determine, if applicable, the volume of reuse water (captured rainwater, recycled graywater or treated wastewater) available in the month of July. Reuse water volumes may depend on rainfall volume/frequency, building-generated graywater/wastewater, and on-site storage capacity. On-site reuse systems should be modeled to predict volumes generated on a monthly basis as well as optimal storage capacity. For captured rainwater calculations, project teams may use either the collected rainwater total for July based on historical average precipitation, or the historical data for each month in order to model collection and reuse throughout the year. The latter method allows the project team to determine what volume of water is expected to be in the storage

Table 2: Irrigation Types

Irrigation Type	IE
Sprinkler	0.625
Drip	0.90

Table 1: Landscape Factors

Vegetation Type	Species Factor (k_s) low	average	high	Density Factor (k_d) low	average	high	Microclimate Factor (k_{mc}) low	average	high
Trees	0.2	0.5	0.9	0.5	1.0	1.3	0.5	1.0	1.4
Shrubs	0.2	0.5	0.7	0.5	1.0	1.1	0.5	1.0	1.3
Groundcovers	0.2	0.5	0.7	0.5	1.0	1.1	0.5	1.0	1.2
Mixed: trees, shrubs, groundcovers	0.2	0.5	0.9	0.6	1.1	1.3	0.5	1.0	1.4
Turfgrass	0.6	0.7	0.8	0.6	1.0	1.0	0.8	1.0	1.2

Equation 2

$$ET_L [in] = ET_0 \times K_L$$

cistern at the beginning of July and add it to the expected rainwater volume collected during the month. This approach also allows the project team to determine the optimal size of the rainwater cistern.

Now you are ready to calculate your Total Water Applied (TWA) and Total Potable Water Applied (TPWA) for each landscape area and the Design Case. **Equations 3 and 4** show how to calculate these values.

Step 2 — Create Baseline Case

The Baseline Case is calculated by setting the Species Factor (ks), Density Factor (kd), and Irrigation Efficiency (IE) to average values representative of conventional equipment and design practices. The same Microclimate Factors (kMC), and the reference Evapotranspiration Rate (ET0) are used in both the Design and Baseline cases. If the design of the project included substitutions of low water-using landscape types (such as shrubs) for high water-using types (such as turfgrass), the landscape areas can be re-allocated in the baseline case, but the total landscape area must remain the same in the two cases. Also, it is unreasonable to assume that the baseline is 100% turfgrass if the project includes substantial areas of trees, shrubs and planting beds.

Calculate your TWA for the Baseline Case using **Equation 5**.

Step 3 — Calculate Percent Reduction in Total Irrigation Water Use (Potable and Reuse) AND Percent Reduction of Potable Water Use for Irrigation

Calculate your percent reduction of potable water use according to **Equation 6**.

If the Percent Reduction of Potable Water is equal to or greater than 50%, WE Credit 1.1 is earned.

If the Percent Reduction of Potable Water is 100%, you must also calculate the Percent Reduction of Total Water (Potable plus Reuse) according to **Equation 7**.

If the Percent Reduction of Potable Water is 100% AND the Percent Reduction of Total Water is equal to or greater than 50%, WE Credit 1.2 is earned in addition to WE Credit 1.1.

Example

An office building in Austin, Texas, has a total site area of 6,000 square feet. The site consists of three landscape types:

Equation 3

Design Case TWA [gal] = (Area [sf] x (ET$_L$ [in] / IE)) x CE x 0.6233 gal/sf/in

Equation 4

Design Case TPWA [gal] = TWA [gal] – Reuse Water [gal]

Equation 5

Baseline Case TWA [gal] = Area [sf] x (ET$_L$ [in] / IE) x 0.6233 gal/sf/in

Equation 6

Percent Reduction of Potable Water [%] = (1 – Design TPWA / Baseline TWA) x 100

Equation 7

Percent Reduction of Total Water [%] = (1 – Design TWA / Baseline TWA) x 100

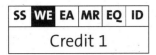
groundcover, mixed vegetation and turf grass. All of the site areas are irrigated with a combination of potable water and graywater harvested from the building. The reference evapotranspiration rate (ET0) for Austin in July was obtained from the local agricultural data service and is equal to 8.12. The high-efficiency landscape irrigation case utilizes drip irrigation with an efficiency of 90% and reuses an estimated 4,200 gallons of graywater during the month of July. **Table 3** shows the calculations to determine potable water use for the design case.

The baseline case uses the same reference evapotranspiration rate and total site area. However, the baseline case uses sprinklers for irrigation (IE = 0.625), does not take advantage of graywater harvesting, and uses only shrubs and turf grass. Calculations to determine potable water use for the baseline case are presented in **Table 4**.

The example illustrates that the design case has an irrigation water demand of 23,474 gallons. Graywater reuse provides 4,200 gallons towards the demand, and this volume is treated as a credit in the water calculation. Thus, the total potable water applied to the design case in July is 19,274 gallons. The baseline case has an irrigation demand of 62,518 gallons and reuses no graywater. The difference between the two cases results in potable water savings of 69% for the design case.

Exemplary Performance

There is no exemplary performance point available for this credit.

Precertification Submittal Documentation

Provide the LEED-CS Precertification Submittal Templates, which include the following:

❏ Narrative describing how the project intends to accomplish the credit requirements on the credit specific Submittal Template signed by the appropriate design team member

❏ Confirmation of this intent from the owner/developer on the LEED-CS Precertification Submittal Template

Table 3: Design Case (July)

Landscape Type [sf]	Area [sf]	Species Factor (k_s)	Density Factor (k_d)	Microclimate Factor (k_{mc})	KL	ETL	IE	TPWA [gal]
Shrubs	1,200	Low 0.2	Avg 1.0	High 1.3	**0.3**	2.11	Drip	2,815
Mixed	3,900	Low 0.2	Avg 1.1	High 1.4	**0.3**	2.50	Drip	10,837
Turfgrass	900	Avg 0.7	Avg 1.0	High 1.2	**0.8**	6.82	Sprinkler	9,822
							Subtotal [gal]	**23,474**
						July Rainwater and Graywater Harvest [gal]		(4,200)
							Net GPWA [gal]	**19,274**

Table 4: Base line Case (July)

Landscape Type [sf]	Area [sf]	Species Factor (k_s)	Density Factor (k_d)	Microclimate Factor (k_{mc})	KL	ETL	IE	TPWA [gal]
Shrubs	1,200	Avg 0.5	Avg 1.0	High 1.3	**0.7**	5.28	Sprinkler	10,134
Turfgrass	4,800	Avg 0.7	Avg 1.0	High 1.2	**0.8**	6.82	Sprinkler	52,384
							Net GPWA [gal]	**62,518**

Certification Submittal Documentation

Design and Construction Credit Compliance

This credit is submitted in the **Design Submittal**.

The following project data and calculation information is required to document credit compliance using the LEED-CS v2.0 Submittal Templates:

❏ The project's calculated baseline Total Water Applied (TWA [gal]). This data can be obtained using **Equation 5**.

❏ The project's calculated design case Total Water Applied (TWA [gal]). This data can be obtained using **Equation 5**.

❏ The total non-potable water supply (gal) available for irrigation purposes.

❏ Narrative describing the landscaping and irrigation design strategies employed by the project; description of the water use calculation methodology used to determine savings; and for projects using non-potable water, specific information regarding source and available quantity of non-potable supplies.

Tenant Sales or Lease Agreement Credit Compliance

This compliance method is not available for this credit.

Considerations

Landscape irrigation practices in the United States consume large quantities of potable water. Outdoor uses, primarily landscaping, account for 30% of the 26 billion gallons of water consumed daily in the United States[2]. Improved landscaping practices can dramatically reduce and even eliminate irrigation needs. Maintaining or reestablishing native or adapted plants on building sites fosters a self-sustaining landscape that requires minimal supplemental water and provides other environmental benefits. Improved irrigation systems can also reduce water consumption. Irrigation typically uses potable water, although non-potable water (e.g., rainwater, graywater or reclaimed water) is equally effective. Irrigation system efficiency varies widely, and high-efficiency irrigation systems can also reduce potable water consumption. For example, high-efficiency drip irrigation systems can be 95% efficient, while sprinkler or spray irrigation systems are only 60% to 70% efficient.[3]

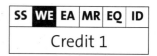

Environmental Issues

Reduction in the amount of potable water used for irrigation lessens demand on limited supplies. Since landscape irrigation uses large amounts of potable water, it is an important opportunity to reduce overall consumption. Native or adapted landscaping can reduce the amount of water needed for irrigation while also attracting native wildlife and creating a building site integrated with its natural surroundings. In addition, native or adapted plants tend to require less fertilizer and pesticides, and thus reduce water quality degradation and other environmental impacts.

Economic Issues

Currently, the most effective strategy to avoid escalating water costs for irrigation is to design landscaping adapted to the local climate and the site's microclimate.

---

2 United States Environmental Protection Agency, Office of Water. Water-Efficient Landscaping. EPA Publication 832-F-02-002, September 2002. 21 January 2005. www.epa.gov/owm/water-efficiency/final_final.pdf

3 Connellan, Goeff. Efficient Irrigation: A Reference Manual for Turf and Landscape. University of Melbourne. 2002. 21 January 2005. www.sewl.com.au/sewl/upload/document/WaterConManual.pdf

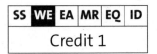

The cost can be reduced or eliminated through thoughtful planning and careful plant selection and layout. Native or adapted plants further reduce operating costs because they require less fertilizer and maintenance than turf grass. Although the additional design cost for a drip irrigation system may make it more expensive than a conventional system, a drip system usually costs less to install and has lower water use and maintenance requirements. This usually leads to a very short payback period. Many municipalities offer rebates or incentives for water-efficient irrigation systems, dedicated water meters and rain or moisture sensors.

Community Issues

Water-efficient landscaping helps to conserve local and regional potable water resources. Maintaining natural aquifer conditions is important to providing reliable water sources for future generations. Consideration of water issues during planning can encourage development when resources can support it, and prevent development if it exceeds the resource capacity.

Synergies and Trade-Offs

Successful water-efficient landscaping depends on site location and design. It is advantageous to couple landscape improvements with water use reduction strategies. The use of native or adapted plants can reduce site maintenance needs. Landscape plantings can mitigate climate conditions and reduce building energy consumption, for example by shading south-facing windows. Vegetation can aid passive solar design, serve as a windbreak, provide pleasant views for building occupants, and muffle off-site noise. Native plants can restore habitat for wildlife. In addition to reducing potable water consumption, rainwater capture systems can be used to manage rainwater runoff. Using graywater for irrigation reduces the amount of wastewater delivered to water treatment facilities.

Resources

Websites

America Rainwater Catchment Systems Association (ARCSA)

www.arcsa-usa.org

ARCSA was founded to promote rainwater catchment systems in the United States. Its website provides regional resources, publications, suppliers and membership information.

Graywater Systems, Compost Toilets & Rain Collection

www.rmi.org/sitepages/pid287.php

This web resource from the Rocky Mountain Institute provides general information and links to resources on rain collection and graywater systems.

The Irrigation Association

www.irrigation.org

This nonprofit organization focuses on promoting products that efficiently use water in irrigation applications.

Texas Evapotranspiration Network Website

http://texaset.tamu.edu

This website provides evapotranspiration data from the state of Texas with a discussion of crop water use and sprinkler efficiencies.

Texas Water Development Board Website

www.twdb.state.tx.us

This website provides data from the state of Texas regarding water resources and services, such as groundwater mapping and water availability modeling. The site also provides published brochures regarding indoor and outdoor water efficiency strategies.

Water-Efficient Landscaping

http://muextension.missouri.edu/xplor/agguides/hort/g06912.htm

This website has general descriptions and strategies for water efficiency in gardens and landscapes.

Water-Efficient Landscaping: Preventing Pollution and Using Resources Wisely

www.epa.gov/owm/water-efficiency/final_final.pdf

This manual from the Environmental Protection Agency provides information about reducing water consumption through creative landscaping techniques.

Water Wiser: The Water Efficiency Clearinghouse

www.awwa.org/waterwiser/

This clearinghouse provides articles, reference materials and papers on all forms of water efficiency.

Print Media

Landscape Irrigation: Design and Management by Stephen W. Smith, John Wiley and Sons, 1996. This text is comprehensive guide to landscape irrigation strategies, techniques, and hardware.

Turf Irrigation Manual, Fifth Edition by Richard B. Choate and Jim Watkins, Telsco Industries, 1994. This manual covers all aspects of turf and landscape irrigation.

Definitions

Conventional Irrigation refers to the most common irrigation system used in the region where the building is located. A common conventional irrigation system uses pressure to deliver water and distributes it through sprinkler heads above the ground.

Drip Irrigation is a high-efficiency irrigation method in which water is delivered at low pressure through buried mains and sub-mains. From the sub-mains, water is distributed to the soil from a network of perforated tubes or emitters. Drip irrigation is a type of micro-irrigation.

Graywater is defined by the Uniform Plumbing Code (UPC) in its Appendix G, titled "Graywater Systems for Single-Family Dwellings," as "untreated household wastewater which has not come into contact with toilet waste. Graywater includes used water from bathtubs, showers, bathroom wash basins, and water from clothes-washer and laundry tubs. It shall not include wastewater from kitchen sinks or dishwashers." The International Plumbing Code (IPC) defines graywater in its Appendix C, titled "Graywater Recycling Systems," as "wastewater discharged from lavatories, bathtubs, showers, clothes washers, and laundry sinks." Some states and local authorities allow kitchen sink wastewater to be included in graywater. Other differences with the UPC and IPC definitions can probably be found in state and local codes. Project teams should comply with graywater definitions as established by the authority having jurisdiction in their areas.

The **Landscape Area** of the site is equal to the total site area less the building footprint, paved surfaces, water bodies, patios, etc.

Micro-irrigation involves irrigation systems with small sprinklers and micro-jets or drippers designed to apply small volumes of water. The sprinklers and micro-jets are installed within a few centimeters of the ground, while drippers are laid on or below grade.

Potable Water is water suitable for drinking and supplied from wells or municipal water systems.

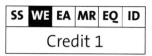

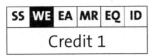

SS **WE** EA MR EQ ID

Credit 1

Case Study

Abercorn Commons
Savannah, Georgia

Photo courtesy of Jim Holmes

Abercorn Commons is a 177,000-sq.ft. all-retail core and shell project featuring renovation and over 70,000 sq.ft. of new construction. The project scope features a combination of boutique shops, big-box stores and restaurants, and encompasses a number of sustainable site attributes. The development decreased the amount of stormwater leaving the site by 25% due to an acre of porous pavement used in the parking. Storm drains are situated with the porous pavement fields, forcing water from impervious areas to sheet flow over the pervious pavement before reaching the storm drain. Abercorn Common also features a 500,000-gallon cistern that collects all rainwater from the roof. Rainwater is then stored and used to meet the irrigation needs of the landscaping. Native vegetation is located throughout the site, allowing water in these areas to infiltrate naturally and recharge local watersheds.

Alternative transportation features include the development location within a quarter-mile radius of three different bus lines, numerous bike racks throughout the site and locker-room/shower areas for tenant employees. A total of 35 preferred parking spaces are dedicated to hybrid vehicle parking. And, the project was able to obtain a variance to reduce the parking from the city requirement by 20%.

Innovative Wastewater Technologies

Intent

Reduce generation of wastewater and potable water demand, while increasing the local aquifer recharge.

Requirements

OPTION 1

Reduce potable water use for building sewage conveyance by 50% through the use of water-conserving fixtures (water closets, urinals) or non-potable water (captured rainwater, recycled graywater, and on-site or municipally treated wastewater).

OR

OPTION 2

Treat 50% of wastewater on-site to tertiary standards. Treated water must be infiltrated or used on-site.

Potential Technologies & Strategies

Specify high-efficiency fixtures and dry fixtures such as composting toilet systems and non-water-consuming urinals to reduce wastewater volumes. Consider reusing stormwater or graywater for sewage conveyance or on-site wastewater treatment systems (mechanical and/or natural). Options for on-site wastewater treatment include packaged biological nutrient removal systems, constructed wetlands, and high-efficiency filtration systems.

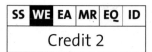
Summary of Referenced Standard

There is no standard referenced for this credit.

Approach and Implementation

Potable water is used for many functions that do not require high-quality water such as toilet and urinal flushing, and landscape irrigation. Rainwater and graywater systems can significantly reduce potable water demand. Graywater systems reuse the wastewater collected from sinks, showers and other sources for the flushing of toilets, landscape irrigation, and other functions that do not require potable water. Graywater treatment may be required prior to reuse according to end use and state jurisdiction. If it is likely that a graywater system will be used in the future, install dual plumbing lines during the initial construction to avoid the substantial costs and difficulty in adding them later. Rainwater systems provide non-potable water suitable for landscape irrigation, flushing toilets and urinals, and process water needs. Rainwater systems have significantly fewer code requirements than graywater systems and are often less expensive than graywater systems. Rainwater from roofs or site can also be collected and harvested to help displace potable water demand. Rainwater collected from impervious surfaces reduces rainwater runoff and control infrastructure requirements. Rainwater retention or detention systems can be designed with cisterns to hold rainwater runoff for non-potable usage.

The necessity and availability of wastewater reuse and treatment strategies is heavily influenced by the project's size and location. Very large projects or campus settings may provide sufficient economic reason to warrant on-site wastewater treatment. Close proximity to a municipal or private treatment facility can provide an opportunity to reuse treated wastewater to displace potable water demand. In remote locations, it may be more cost-effective to use an on-site wastewater treatment system than to extend existing infrastructure.

Conversely, a project located in a dense urban environment with little available site area may not be able to achieve this credit through development of on-site wastewater systems, graywater or rainwater systems, but may be able to utilize municipally provided recycled water to reduce potable water demand.

This credit has close ties to water efficiency efforts because a greater amount of potable water saved often results in less blackwater generated. For instance, water efficient water closets, urinals, showerheads and faucets not only reduce potable water demand but also reduce blackwater volumes created. Thus, performance results will often overlap with those of WE Credit 3.

Additional energy use may be needed for certain on-site treatment operations or for reuse strategies. These active systems also require commissioning and Measurement & Verification attention. Reuse of an existing building could hinder adoption of an on-site wastewater treatment facility.

When considering an on-site rainwater, graywater collection or blackwater treatment system it is important to first check with local government agencies for regulations governing the use of this water for irrigation and the permits required.

Each state has its own standards and requirements for the installation and operation of rainwater, graywater and water treatment systems. Texas and California, for example, have standards that encourage the use of graywater systems while other states have regulations that may limit or prohibit graywater use. In many areas, irrigation with graywater must be subsurface, although some regions allow above-ground irrigation.

Projects that plan to treat wastewater on-site should consider a treatment system such as constructed wetlands, a mechanical recirculating sand filter, or anaerobic biological treatment reactor.

In the case of any specialized system, is it imperative that key maintenance staff be trained in the operations and maintenance of the water systems.

Calculations

The following calculation methodology is used to support achievement of **Option 1**.

Occupancy

Calculate the **Full-Time Equivalent (FTE)** building occupants based on a standard 8-hour occupancy period. An 8-hour occupant has an FTE value of 1.0 while a part-time occupant has an FTE value based on their hours per day divided by 8. (Note that FTE calculations for the project must be used consistently for all LEED-CS credits.) In buildings with multiple shifts, use the number of FTEs from all shifts, since this credit is based on annual water consumption.

Core and shell building projects may not have identified the final occupancy count. Projects that do not know the occupancy count must utilize the default occupancy

SS **WE** EA MR EQ ID

Credit 2

Figure 1: An illustration of a Rain Harvesting System

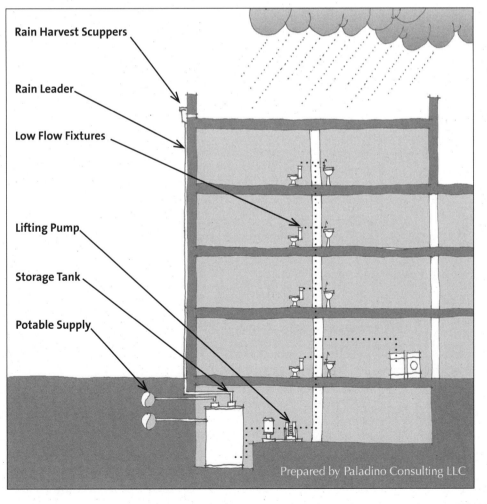

counts provided in Appendix 1 (see **Equation 2**). Projects that do know the tenant occupancy must use the tenant occupancy count as long as the gross square foot per employee is not greater than that in the default occupancy count table.

Estimate the **Transient** building occupants, such as visitors and customers. Since this credit is based on annual water consumption, use a transient occupancy number that is a representative daily average.

If the building has both FTE and Transient occupants, calculate the water use for each fixture separately for each occupancy type. This separation is necessary to represent the unique use patterns. For residential projects, the number of residents is used as the occupancy number.

Note: WE Credit 3, Table 2 provides default fixture use values for different occupancy types.

Design Case

Wastewater calculations are based on the annual generation of blackwater volumes from plumbing fixtures such as water closets and urinals. The calculations compare the design case with a baseline case. The steps to calculate the design case are as follows:

1. Create a spreadsheet listing each type of blackwater-generating fixture and frequency-of-use data. Frequency-of-use data includes the number of female and male daily uses, and the sewage generated per use. Use the daily use assumptions shown in **Table 1** as the basis for the calculations, unless alternate assumptions on daily use can be supported by specific back-up documentation. Using these values, calculate the total sewage generated for each fixture type and gender (see **Equation 1**).

2. Sum all of the sewage generation volumes used for each fixture type to obtain male and female daily sewage generation volumes.

3. Multiply the male and female sewage generation volumes by the number of male and female building occupants and sum these volumes to obtain the daily total sewage generation volume (see **Equation 2**).

4. Multiply the total daily sewage volume by the number of workdays in a typical year to obtain the total annual sewage generation volume for the building (see **Equation 3**).

5. If rainwater harvest or graywater reuse strategies are employed in the building, subtract these annual volumes from the annual sewage generation volume. The result shows how much potable water is used for sewage conveyance annually.

Table 1 shows example potable water calculations for sewage conveyance for a two-story office building with a capacity

Equation 1

$$\text{Sewage Volume [gal]} = \text{Uses} \times \text{Duration [mins or flushes]} \times \frac{\text{Water Volume [gal]}}{\text{Use [min or flush]}}$$

Equation 2

$$\text{Daily Sewage Generation [gal]} = \text{Male Occupants} \times \text{Male Sewage Generation [gal]} + \text{Female Occupants} \times \text{Female Sewage Generation [gal]}$$

Equation 3

$$\text{Annual Sewage Generation [gal]} = \text{Total Sewage Generation} \left[\frac{\text{gal}}{\text{day}}\right] \times \text{Workdays [days]}$$

Table 1: Design Case

Fixture Type	Daily Uses	Flowrate [GPF]	Occupants	Sewage Generation [gal]
Low-Flow Water Closet (Male)	0	1.1	150	0
Low-Flow Water Closet (Female)	3	1.1	150	495
Composting Toilet (Male)	1	0.0	150	0
Composting Toilet (Female)	0	0.0	150	0
Waterless Urinal (Male)	2	0.0	150	0
Waterless Urinal (Female)	0	0.0	150	0
Total Daily Volume [gal]				495
Annual Work Days				260
Annual Volume [gal]				128,700
Rainwater or Graywater Volume [gal]				(36,000)
TOTAL ANNUAL VOLUME [gal]				92,700

of 300 occupants. The calculations are based on a typical 8-hour workday. It is assumed that building occupants are 50% male and 50% female. Male occupants are assumed to use water closets once and urinals twice in a typical work day. Female occupants are assumed to use water closets three times.

When using graywater and rainwater volumes, calculations are required to demonstrate that these reuse volumes are sufficient to meet water closet demands. These quantities are then subtracted from the gross daily total because they reduce potable water usage. In the example in **Table 1**, 36,000 gallons of rainwater are harvested and directed to water closets for flushing.

Baseline Case

Repeat the above calculation methodology for the baseline case. Use Energy Policy Act of 1992 (and as amended) fixture flow rates for the baseline case (see **WE Credit 3, Table 1**). Do not change the number of building occupants, the number of workdays, or the frequency data. Do not include graywater or rainwater harvest volumes.

Table 2 provides a summary of baseline calculations. The baseline case estimates that 327,600 gallons of potable water per year are used for sewage conveyance.

Comparison of the baseline to the designed building indicates that a 72% reduction in potable water volumes used for sewage conveyance is realized (1 − 92,700/327,600). Thus, this strategy earns one point for this credit. When developing the baseline, only the fixtures, sewage generation rates and the water reuse credit are different from the designed building. Usage rates, occupancy

Table 2: Baseline Case

Fixture Type	Daily Uses	Flowrate [GPF]	Occupants	Sewage Generation [gal]
Water Closet (Male)	1	1.6	150	240
Water Closet (Female)	3	1.6	150	720
Urinal (Male)	2	1.0	150	300
Urinal (Female)	0	1.0	150	0
Total Daily Volume [gal]				1,260
Annual Work Days				260
TOTAL ANNUAL VOLUME [gal]				327,600

and number of workdays are identical for the design case and the baseline case. See **Table 3** for sample fixture flow rates.

When reusing graywater volumes from the building, it is necessary to model the system on an annual basis to determine graywater volumes, generated storage capacity of the system and any necessary treatment processes before reusing the water volumes. Graywater volumes may or may not be consistently available throughout the year because these volumes are dependent on building occupant activities. For instance, in a typical office building, graywater volumes will change slightly due to vacation schedules and holidays but should be relatively consistent over the year.

In contrast, graywater volumes in a school building will substantially decrease in summer months due to the school calendar, and therefore, graywater volumes may not be available for irrigation.

If the project uses rainwater volume as a substitute for potable volumes in water closets or urinals, it is necessary to calculate water savings over a time period of one year. Rain harvest volume depends on the amount of precipitation that the project

site experiences, the rainwater collection surface's area and efficiency, and storage tank capacity. See **Equation 4** and consult a rainwater harvesting guide for more detailed instruction. Rainfall data is available from the local weather service (see the Resources section). Rainwater volume depends on variations in precipitation, and thus, it is necessary to model the reuse strategy on an annual basis. A model of rainwater capture based on daily precipitation and occupant demand is helpful to determine the rainwater volumes captured and storage tank size. Subtract annual rainwater use for sewage conveyance in the design case calculations.

The following calculation methodology is used to support achievement of **Option 2**.

1. Create a spreadsheet listing each type of blackwater-generating fixture and frequency-of-use data. Frequency-of-use data includes the number of female and male daily uses, and the sewage generated per use. Use the daily use assumptions shown in **Table 1** as the basis for the calculations, unless alternate assumptions on daily use can be supported by specific back-up

Table 3: Sample Fixture Flow Rates

Flush Fixture Type	Water Use [gpf]
Conventional Low-Flow Toilet (Water Closet)	1.6
High-Efficiency Toilet (Water Closet)	Below 1.3*
Dual-Flush Toilet	0.8 to 1.1/1.6**
Composting Toilet	0.0
Conventional Low-Flow Urinal	1.0
High-Efficiency Urinal	0.5 or below***
Non-Water Consuming Urinal	0.0***

*High-efficiency toilets (HETs) include dual-flush toilets, 1.0-gpf pressure-assist toilets, and 1.28-gpf gravity-fed single-flush toilets.

** Dual flush toilets have an option of full flush (1.6 gal) or liquid-only flush (ranges between 0.8 gpf and 1.1 gpf, depend upon design). When calculating water use reductions from installation of these fixtures, use a composite (average) flush volume of 1.2 gal.

***High-efficiency urinals are currently available at 0.5 gpf and 0.0 gpf. Urinals at 0.25 gpf will be available in 2005.

Equation 4

Rainwater Volume [gal] = collection area [sf] x collection efficiency [%] x average rainfall [in] x 0.6233 gal/sf/in documentation. Using these values, calculate the total sewage generated for each fixture type and gender (see **Equation 1**).

2. Sum all of the sewage generation volumes used for each fixture type to obtain male and female daily sewage generation volumes.

3. Multiply the male and female sewage generation volumes by the number of male and female building occupants and sum these volumes to obtain the daily total sewage generation volume (see **Equation 2**).

4. Multiply the total daily sewage volume by the number of workdays in a typical year to obtain the total annual sewage generation volume for the building (see **Equation 3**).

5. Divide the annual volume of wastewater that is treated and reused and/or infiltrated on site by the calculated annual sewage generation volume for the building to determine the percent reduction of wastewater that is released into the municipal sewer system.

Exemplary Performance

Projects that demonstrate a 100% reduction in potable water use for sewage conveyance, OR, on-site treatment and re-use/infiltration of 100% of generated wastewater will be considered for one additional point under the Innovation in Design category.

Precertification Submittal Documentation

Provide the LEED-CS Precertification Submittal Templates, which include the following:

❏ Narrative describing how the project intends to accomplish the credit requirements on the credit specific Submittal Template signed by the appropriate design team member

❏ Confirmation of this intent from the owner/developer on the LEED-CS Precertification Submittal Template

Certification Submittal Documentation

Design and Construction Credit Compliance

This credit is submitted in the **Design Submittal**.

The following project data and calculation information is required to document credit compliance using the LEED-CS v2.0 Submittal Templates:

❏ Upload the applicable plumbing drawings from the construction documents that provide data regarding any on-site wastewater treatment facilities.

❏ The project's calculated occupants. The template will use a default one-to-one men to women ratio. Projects with special occupancy situations that result in an unbalanced ratio may enter project specific data for this credit.

❏ The project's calculated baseline water usage for sewage conveyance. This data is calculated using typical fixture types (provided in the template) and the project's mix of occupants.

❏ The project's calculated design case water usage for sewage conveyance. This data is calculated using project specified fixture types and the project's mix of occupants. Note: project teams must provide the following fixture information for each typical installed flush fixture type: fixture manufacturer, fixture model, flush rate in gallons per flush (gpf).

❏ For projects using non-potable water for sewage conveyance, provide the total non-potable water supply (gal) available for sewage conveyance purposes.

❏ For projects treating wastewater on-site, provide the annual quantity (gal)

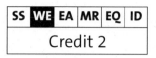
of water treated, the annual quantity (gal) of treated water that is infiltrated, and the annual quantity (gal) of treated water that is re-used on-site.

❏ Narrative describing the potable water reduction strategies employed by the project. For projects using non-potable water, include specific information regarding any reclaimed water usage (graywater reuse/rainwater reuse/on-site or municipally treated wastewater). If the project is treating wastewater on-site to tertiary standards, include specific information regarding the use(s) of the treated wastewater.

Tenant Sales or Lease Agreement Credit Compliance

This compliance method is available to core and shell projects that incorporate requirements into tenant sales or lease agreements for the use of water conserving fixtures or non-potable water as part of the tenant scope of work. Provide the LEED letter template for the credit pursued indicating the following:

❏ That 100% of leased square footage complies with credit requirements. Lease or sales agreements may be requested.

❏ That 100% of the unleased square footage shall comply with the credit requirements when leased. A statement signed by the owner/developer that all leases and/or sales agreements will comply may be requested.

❏ The project's calculated occupants. The template will use a default one-to-one men to women ratio. Projects with special occupancy situations that result in an unbalanced ratio may enter project specific data for this credit.

❏ The project's calculated baseline water usage for sewage conveyance. This data is calculated using typical fixture types (provided in the template) and the project's mix of occupants.

❏ The project's calculated design case water usage for sewage conveyance. This data is calculated using fixture performance specified in the tenant sales or lease agreement and the project's mix of occupants. Note: project teams must provide the flush rate in gallons per flush (gpf) for each flush fixture type.

Considerations

Cost Issues

Commercial and industrial facilities that generate large amounts of wastewater can realize considerable savings by recycling graywater. For example, car washes and truck maintenance facilities generate large volumes of graywater that can be effectively treated and reused. Often, a separate tank, filter and special emitters are necessary for a graywater irrigation system. Dual sanitary and graywater distribution piping doubles construction piping costs. In addition, local codes requiring filtration, disinfection treatment, overflow protection, etc., add to the cost of construction, operation, and maintenance; all of which should be considered by the owner when making a decision to collect graywater. Collection and use of rainwater for non-potable water applications has significantly fewer code requirements and associated costs. The highest cost in most rainwater systems is for water storage. Storage tanks and cisterns come in a variety of sizes and materials. Designers can lower construction costs by finding synergies such as adding a cistern to collect rainwater to a stormwater detention system. In some systems, pumps are required for distribution, incurring additional energy costs required for operation.

Water recovery systems are most cost-effective in areas where there is no municipal water supply, where the developed wells are unreliable, or if well water requires treatment. Collecting and using rainwater or other site water volumes reduces site runoff and the need for runoff devices. It also minimizes the need for utility-provided water, thus reducing some initial and operating costs. In some areas with a decentralized population, collection of rainwater offers a low-cost alternative to a central piped water supply.

A constructed wetland for wastewater treatment can add value to a development as a site enhancement. Wetlands are beneficial because they provide flood protection and stabilize soils on site. Currently, packaged biological wastewater systems have an initial high cost, relative to the overall building cost, due to the novelty of the technology.

Environmental Issues

On-site wastewater treatment systems transform perceived "wastes" into resources that can be used on the building site. These resources include treated water volumes for potable and non-potable use, as well as nutrients that can be applied to the site to improve soil conditions. Reducing wastewater treatment at the local wastewater treatment works minimizes public infrastructure, energy use and chemical use. In rural areas, on-site wastewater treatment systems avoid aquifer contamination problems prevalent in current septic system technology.

By reducing potable water use, the local aquifer is conserved as a water resource for future generations. In areas where aquifers cannot meet the needs of the population economically, rainwater and other recovered water is the least expensive alternative source of water.

Economic Issues

Wastewater treatment systems and water recovery systems involve an initial capital investment in addition to the maintenance requirements over the building's lifetime. These costs must balance with the anticipated savings in water and sewer bills. This savings can minimize the amount of potable water that a municipality must provide, thereby leading to more stable water rates and resources needed for economic growth.

Regional Issues

Local precipitation throughout the year should be factored into determining the feasibility of rainwater harvesting systems for use in the reduction of potable water for plumbing fixture flushing and landscape irrigation. Local building and health codes/ordinances vary with regards to allowance of graywater or harvested rainwater systems; and they are prohibited in some states. Additionally, codes differ in how alternative plumbing fixtures, such as dual-flush water closets, composting toilets and non-water using urinals are handled. It is critical to confirm acceptability of non-traditional approaches with code officials prior to commitment to specific water saving strategies.

Supply water quality from graywater and recycled water systems should also be considered in fixture selection. Project teams should identify if minimum supply water quality standards have been established for specific fixtures by manufacturers. When recycled graywater or collected rainwater is used with plumbing fixtures designed for use with municipally supplied potable water, it is good practice to verify that supply water quality is acceptable and will not compromise long-term fixture performance.

Resources

Please see the USGBC website at www.usgbc.org/resources for more specific resources on materials sources and other technical information.

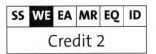
Websites

American Rainwater Catchment Systems Association

www.arcsa-usa.org

Includes a compilation of publications, such as the Texas Guide to Rainwater Harvesting.

Constructed Wetlands for Wastewater Treatment and Wildlife Habitat: 17 Case Studies

U.S. EPA

EPA Publication No. 832/B-93-005, 1993.

www.epa.gov/owow/wetlands/construc/

The case studies in this document provide brief descriptions of 17 wetland treatment systems that provide water quality benefits while also providing habitat. The projects described include systems involving constructed and natural wetlands, habitat creation and restoration, and the improvement of municipal effluent, urban stormwater and river water quality.

On-site Wastewater Treatment Systems Manual

U.S. EPA

www.epa.gov/owm/septic/pubs/septic_2002_osdm_all.pdf

This manual provides a focused and performance-based approach to on-site wastewater treatment and system management, including information on a variety of on-site sewage treatment options.

Print Media

Mechanical & Electrical Equipment for Buildings, Eighth Edition by Benjamin Stein and John Reynolds, John Wiley and Sons, 1992.

Sustainable Building Technical Manual, Public Technology, Inc., 1996. (www.pti.org)

Definitions

Aquatic Systems are ecologically designed treatment systems that utilize a diverse community of biological organisms (e.g., bacteria, plants and fish) to treat wastewater to advanced levels.

Blackwater does not have a single definition that is accepted nationwide. Wastewater from toilets and urinals is, however, always considered blackwater.

Wastewater from kitchen sinks (perhaps differentiated by the use of a garbage disposal), showers or bathtubs may be considered blackwater by state or local codes. Project teams should comply with the blackwater definition as established by the authority having jurisdiction in their areas.

Composting Toilet Systems are dry plumbing fixtures that contain and treat human waste via microbiological processes.

Graywater (also spelled greywater and gray water) is defined by the Uniform Plumbing Code (UPC) in its Appendix G, titled "Gray water Systems for Single-Family Dwellings," as "untreated household wastewater which has not come into contact with toilet waste. Grey water includes used water from bathtubs, showers, bathroom wash basins, and water from clothes-washer and laundry tubs. It shall not include wastewater from kitchen sinks or dishwashers."

The International Plumbing Code (IPC) defines graywater in its Appendix C, titled "Graywater Recycling Systems," as "wastewater discharged from lavatories, bathtubs, showers, clothes washers, and laundry sinks."

Some states and local authorities allow kitchen sink wastewater to be included in graywater. Other differences with the UPC and IPC definitions may be found in state and local codes. Project teams should comply with the graywater definitions as established by the authority having jurisdiction in their areas.

Non-potable Water is water that is not suitable for human consumption without treatment that meets or exceeds EPA drinking water standards.

Non-Water-Consuming Urinal (also know as a dry urinal) is a urinal that uses no water, but instead replaces the water flush with a specially designed trap that contains a layer of buoyant liquid that floats above the urine layer, blocking sewer gas and urine odors from the room. Other non-water technologies are also available for urinals.

On-site Wastewater Treatment uses localized treatment systems to transport, store, treat and dispose of wastewater volumes generated on the project site.

Potable Water is water that is suitable for drinking and is supplied from wells or municipal water systems.

Process Water is water used for industrial processes and building systems such as cooling towers, boilers and chillers.

Tertiary Treatment is the highest form of wastewater treatment that includes the removal of nutrients, organic and solid material, along with biological or chemical polishing (generally to effluent limits of 10 mg/L BOD5 and 10 mg/L TSS).

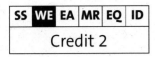

Water Use Reduction

20% Reduction

Intent

Maximize water efficiency within buildings to reduce the burden on municipal water supply and wastewater systems.

Requirements

Employ strategies that in aggregate use 20% less water than the water use baseline calculated for the building (not including irrigation) after meeting the Energy Policy Act of 1992 (and as amended) fixture performance requirements. Calculations are based on estimated occupant usage and shall include only the following fixtures (as applicable to the building): water closets, urinals, lavatory faucets, showers and kitchen sinks.

Potential Technologies & Strategies

Use high-efficiency fixtures, including dry fixtures such as composting toilet systems and non-water-consuming urinals, to reduce the potable water demand. Consider reuse of stormwater and treated graywater for non-potable applications such as toilet and urinal flushing, landscape irrigation, clothes washing, and custodial uses.

1 Point
in addition to
We Credit 3.1

Water Use Reduction

30% Reduction

Intent

Maximize water efficiency within buildings to reduce the burden on municipal water supply and wastewater systems.

Requirements

Employ strategies that in aggregate use 30% less water than the water use baseline calculated for the building (not including irrigation) after meeting the Energy Policy Act of 1992 (and as amended) fixture performance requirements. Calculations are based on estimated occupant usage and shall include only the following fixtures (as applicable to the building): water closets, urinals, lavatory faucets, showers and kitchen sinks.

Potential Technologies & Strategies

Use high-efficiency fixtures, including dry fixtures such as composting toilets and non- water-consuming urinals, to reduce the potable water demand. Consider reuse of stormwater and treated graywater for non-potable applications such as toilet and urinal flushing, landscape irrigation, clothes washing, mechanical systems, and custodial uses.

Summary of Referenced Standard

The Energy Policy Act (EPAct) of 1992 (and as amended)

This Act was promulgated by the U.S. government and addresses energy and water use in commercial, institutional and residential facilities. The water usage requirements of the Energy Policy Act of 1992 (and as amended) are provided in **Table 1**.

Approach and Implementation

Water use strategies depend on the site location and site design. Project sites with no access to municipal potable water service typically use groundwater wells to satisfy potable water demands. Site locations with significant precipitation volumes may determine that reuse of these volumes is more cost-effective than creating stormwater treatment facilities. Potable water use is significant for irrigation applications and is directly correlated with the amount of wastewater generated on-site.

Some water-saving technologies impact energy performance and require commissioning and Measurement & Verification (M&V) attention. Reuse of existing buildings may hinder water efficiency measures due to space constraints or characteristics of existing plumbing fixtures.

While graywater collection and storage may not be a water reduction method that many owners and designers have the opportunity to include in their projects, high-efficiency plumbing fixtures are. Early planning should focus on the code related issues (both plumbing code and health and safety code) associated with installation and use of water harvesting and collection systems, graywater recycling systems, and high-performance plumbing fixtures such as non-water-consuming urinals.

Effective methods to reduce potable water use include: reuse of roof runoff or collected graywater volumes for non-potable applications; installation and maintenance of fixture metering controls; installation of flow restrictors and/or reduced flow aerators on lavatory, sink, and shower fixtures; installation of high-efficiency toilets (HETs) such as dual-flush water closets and high-efficiency urinals (HEUs) such as 0.5-gallon, 0.2-gallon and non-water-consuming urinals; installation of dry fixtures such as composting toilet systems and non-water-consuming urinals.

Although water efficient dishwashers, clothes washers and other water consuming fixtures are not counted in the calculations for this credit they may be included in exemplary performance calculations. (See Exemplary Performance for this credit) A variety of high-efficiency plumbing fixtures and appliances are currently available in the marketplace and

Table 1: Energy Policy Act of 1992 (and as amended) Standards for Plumbing Fixture Water Usage

Fixture	Energy Policy Act of 1992 (and as amended) Standards for Plumbing Fixture Water Usage
Water Closets [gpf]	1.60
Urinals [gpf]	1.00
Showerheads [gpm]*	2.50
Faucets [gpm]**	2.20
Faucet Replacement Aerators [gpm]**	2.20
Metering Faucets [gal/cy]	0.25

When measured at a flowing water pressure of 80 pounds per square inch (PSI)

**When measured at a flowing water pressure of 60 pounds per square inch (PSI)*

can be installed in the same manner as conventional EPAct fixtures and non-efficient appliances.

To determine the most effective strategies for a particular condition, the project team should analyze the water conservation options available to the project based on location, code compliance (plumbing and life safety) and overall project function. Using the EPAct numbers as a baseline for plumbing fixtures, estimate the potable water needs for the project based on estimated occupant uses. Determine areas of high water usage and evaluate potential alternative water saving technologies. Using the same calculation method, examine the impacts of alternative fixture types and technologies. Compare the design case water usage to the calculated EPAct baseline to determine the optimal water savings for the project for plumbing fixtures.

In order to ensure continued water savings and owner/occupant satisfaction, it is imperative that key maintenance staff is trained in the operations and maintenance of any specialized equipment. For example, non-water-consuming urinals generally need to be cleaned according to manufacturer's specifications and their chemical traps appropriately maintained. Similarly, other HEUs, such as 0.5-gallon and 0.2-gallon flushing urinals, must likewise be maintained according to manufacturer's specifications.

Calculations

The following section describes the calculation methodology for determining water use savings under this credit. The calculated water use reduction for the project is the difference between the calculated design case and a baseline case. The credit percentage is determined by dividing the design case usage by the baseline usage.

The methodology differs from traditional plumbing design where the calculations are based on fixture counts; under this credit, the water use calculation is based on estimated occupant usage and fixture flow rates. Estimated occupant usage is determined by calculating Full-Time Equivalent (FTE) and transient occupants and applying appropriate fixture use rates to each type of occupant.

Occupancy

Calculate the **Full-Time Equivalent (FTE)** building occupants based on a standard 8-hour occupancy period. An 8-hour occupant has an FTE value of 1.0 while a part-time occupant has an FTE value based on their hours per day divided by 8. (Note that FTE calculations for the project must be used consistently for all LEED-CS credits.) In buildings with multiple shifts, use the number of FTEs from all shifts, since this credit is based on annual water consumption.

Core and shell building projects may not have identified the final occupancy count. Projects that do not know the occupancy count must utilize the default occupancy counts provided in Appendix 1 (see **Equation 2**). Projects that do know the tenant occupancy must use the tenant occupancy count as long as the gross square foot per employee is not greater than that in the default occupancy count table.

Estimate the **Transient** building occupants, such as visitors and customers. Since this credit is based on annual water consumption, use a transient occupancy number that is a representative daily average.

If the building has both FTE and Transient occupants, calculate the water use for each fixture separately for each occupancy type. This separation is necessary to represent the unique use patterns. For residential projects, the number of residents is used as the occupancy number.

Table 2 provides default fixture use values for different occupancy types. These values should be used in the calculations for this credit unless special circumstances exist

Table 2: Standard Fixture Uses by Occupancy Type

Water Closet					
female	3	0.5	0.2	5
male	1	0.1	0.1	5
Urinal					
female	0	0	0	n/a
male	2	0.4	0.1	n/a
Lavatory Faucet	3	0.5	0.2	5
(duration 15 sec; 12 sec with autocontrol)				
Shower	0.1	0	0	1
(duration 300 sec)				
Kitchen Sink, non-residential	1	0	0	n/a
(duration 15 sec)				
Kitchen Sink, residential	n/a	n/a	n/a	4
(duration 60 sec)				

within the project to require modification. The FTE uses are identical to those used in LEED-NC v2.1 and v2.2. The uses for the other occupancy types are provided as compromise default values based on v2.1 projects. Note that most buildings with Student/Visitor and Retail Customer occupants will also have FTE occupants. The Student/Visitor category is intended for college buildings, libraries, museums, and similar building types. 50% of all Student/Visitor occupants are assumed to use a flush fixture and a lavatory faucet in the building and are not expected to use a shower or kitchen sink. 20% of Retail Customer occupants are assumed to use a flush and a flow fixture in the building and no shower or kitchen sink. The default for Residential occupants is 5 uses per day of flush and flow fixtures, 1 shower, and 4 kitchen sink uses.

For consistency across LEED projects, the calculations require the use of a balanced, one-to-one gender ratio unless specific project conditions warrant an alternative. For these special situations, the project team will need to provide a narrative description to explain the unique circumstances.

The total fixture uses by all occupants must be consistent in the design and baseline cases.

Design Case

The design case annual water use is determined by totaling the annual volume of each fixture type and subtracting any reuse of stormwater/graywater. The design case must use the actual flow rates and flush volumes for installed fixtures. The flow and flush data should be obtained from manufacturer's published product literature.

In addition to the typical fixtures shown on the flush and flow fixture charts (**Table 3 and Table 4 respectively**), the project team may add others, as applicable.

Table 5 provides an example design case water use calculation. Note that flush fixtures, which include water closets and urinals, differentiate between females and males. The calculation should ensure that both the male and female occupants are appropriately represented. Zeros may be used when appropriate.

Where on-site collected graywater or rainwater is used for sewage conveyance, the project team should enter the estimated quantity in the calculation. The total annual graywater quantity is subtracted from the total annual design case water usage.

Table 3: Sample Flush Fixture Types

Flush Fixture Type	Water Use [gpf]
Conventional Low-Flow Toilet (Water Closet)	1.6
High-Efficiency Toilet (Water Closet)	Below 1.3*
Dual-Flush Toilet	0.8 to 1.1/1.6**
Composting Toilet	0.0
Conventional Low-Flow Urinal	1.0
High-Efficiency Urinal	0.5 or below***
Non-Water Consuming Urinal	0.0***

*High-efficiency toilets (HETs) include dual-flush toilets, 1.0-gpf pressure-assist toilets, and 1.28-gpf gravity-fed single-flush toilets.

** Dual flush toilets have an option of full flush (1.6 gal) or liquid-only flush (ranges between 0.8 gpf and 1.1 gpf, depend upon design). When calculating water use reductions from installation of these fixtures, use a composite (average) flush volume of 1.2 gal.

***High-efficiency urinals are currently available at 0.5 gpf and 0.0 gpf. Urinals at 0.25 gpf will be available in 2005.

Table 4: Sample flow Fixture Types

Flow Fixture Type	Water Use [gpm]
Conventional Low-Flow Lavatory Faucet	2.2
High-Efficiency Lavatory Faucet	1.8
Conventional Low-Flow Kitchen Sink Faucet	2.2
High-Efficiency Kitchen Sink Faucet	1.8
Conventional Low-Flow Showerhead	2.5
High-Efficiency Showerhead	2.0 and below
Low-Flow Janitor Sink Faucet	2.5
Low–Flow Hand Wash Fountain	0.5
Conventional Low Flow Self Closing Faucet	0.25 gals./cycle
High Efficiency Self Closing Faucet	0.2 gals./cycle and below

Baseline Case

The baseline case annual water use is determined by duplicating the Design Case table and then setting the fixture flush rates and flow rates to the EPAct default values (as opposed to actual installed values in the Design Case). **Table 6** provides an example baseline case water use calculation, based on the Design Case presented in **Table 5**.

Eligible Fixtures

This credit is limited to savings generated by water using fixtures regulated by the Energy Policy Act of 1992 (and as amended). EPAct covers the following fixture types: lavatories, kitchen sinks, showers, hand wash fountains, janitor sinks, water closets and urinals. Project teams are encouraged to apply for Innovation in Design credits for water use reduction in non-EPAct regulated and process water consuming fixtures. Examples of non-regulated and process water use include but are not limited to dishwashers, clothes washers and cooling towers.

Exemplary Performance

In addition to earning WE Credits 3.1 and 3.2, project teams that achieve a projected water savings of 40% are eligible for an exemplary performance ID credit.

Project teams may also achieve an ID credit for demonstrating potable water use reduction in process and non-regulated water consuming fixtures. The calculation methodology for demonstrating process and non-regulated water savings is similar to the calculation outlined above for regulated water use. Project teams define reasonable usage assumptions and calculate design and baseline water consumption based on high efficiency and standard water use fixtures. Process and non-regulated water use savings is then compared to regulated water use. If the process and non-regulated water use savings is at least 10% of the total design regulated water use, the project team is eligible for an Innovation in Design point.

Table 5: Sample Design Case Water Use Calculations

Flush Fixture	Daily Uses	Flow Rate [GFP]	Duration [flush]	Occupants	Water Use [gal]
Dual Flush Toilet (Male)	0	1.2	1	150	0
Dual Flush Toilet (Female)	3	1.2	1	150	540
Composting Toilet (Male)	1	0.0	1	150	0
Composting Toilet (Female)	0	0.0	1	150	0
Non-Water Consuming Urinal (Male)	2	0.0	1	150	0
Non-Water Consuming Urinal (Female)	2	0.0	1	150	0

Flow Fixture	Daily Uses	Flow Rate [GFM]	Duration [sec]	Occupants	Water Use [gal]
Conventional Low-Flow Lavatory Faucet	3	2.2	12	300	396
Conventional Low-Flow Kitchen Sink Faucet	1	2.2	12	300	132
Conventional Low-Flow Showerhead	0.1	2.5	300	300	375
				Total Daily Volume [gal]	1443
				Annual Work Days	260
				Annual Volume [gal]	375,180
				Graywater Reuse Volume [gal]	(36,000)
				TOTAL ANNUAL VOLUME	339,180

Table 6: Sample Baseline Case Water Use Calculations

Flush Fixture	Daily Uses	Flow Rate [GFP]	Duration [flush]	Occupants	Water Use [gal]
Conventional Low-Flow Toilet (Male)	1	1.6	1	150	240
Conventional Low-Flow Toilet Toilet (Female)	3	1.6	1	150	720
Conventional Low-Flow Urinal (Male)	2	1.0	1	150	300
Conventional Low-Flow Urinal (Female)	2	1.0	1	150	0

Flow Fixture	Daily Uses	Flow Rate [GFM]	Duration [sec]	Occupants	Water Use [gal]
Conventional Low-Flow Lavatory Faucet	3	2.2	15	300	495
Conventional Low-Flow Kitchen Sink Faucet	1	2.2	15	300	165
Conventional Low-Flow Showerhead	0.1	2.5	300	300	375
				Total Daily Volume [gal]	2295
				Annual Work Days	260
				TOTAL ANNUAL VOLUME	596,700

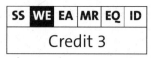

Precertification Submittal Documentation

Provide the LEED-CS Precertification Submittal Templates, which include the following:

❑ Narrative describing how the project intends to accomplish the credit requirements on the credit specific Submittal Template signed by the appropriate design team member

❑ Confirmation of this intent from the owner/developer on the LEED-CS Precertification Submittal Template

Certification Submittal Documentation

Design and Construction Credit Compliance

This credit is submitted as part of the **Design Submittal**.

The following project data and calculation information is required to document credit compliance using the LEED-CS v2.0 Submittal Templates:

❑ The project's calculated occupant(s). The template will use a default one-to-one men to women ratio. Projects with special occupancy situations that result in an unbalanced ratio may enter project specific data for this credit.

❑ The project's calculated design case water usage (flush and flow fixtures.) This data is calculated using project specified fixture types and the project's mix of occupants. Note: project teams must provide the following fixture information for each typical installed flush fixture type: fixture manufacturer, fixture model, rated flush rate in gallons per flush (gpf) or flow rate in gallons per minute (gpm).

❑ The project's calculated baseline water usage (flush and flow fixtures.) This data is calculated using typical fixture types (provided in the template) and the project's mix of occupants.

❑ For projects using non-potable water for sewage conveyance, provide the total non-potable water supply (gal) available for sewage conveyance purposes.

❑ Narrative describing the potable water reduction strategies employed by the project. For projects using non-potable water, include specific information regarding any reclaimed water usage (graywater reuse/rainwater reuse/onsite treated wastewater).

Tenant Sales or Lease Agreement Credit Compliance

This compliance method is available to core and shell projects that incorporate requirements into tenant sales or lease agreements for the installation of water reducing fixtures as part of the tenant scope of work. Provide the LEED letter template for the credit pursued indicating the following:

❑ That 100% of leased square footage complies with credit requirements. Lease or sales agreements may be requested.

❑ That 100% of the unleased square footage shall comply with the credit requirements when leased. A statement signed by the owner/developer that all leases and/or sales agreements will comply may be requested.

❑ The project's calculated occupant(s). The template will use a default one-to-one men to women ratio. Projects with special occupancy situations that result in an unbalanced ratio may enter project specific data for this credit.

❑ The project's calculated design case water usage (flush and flow fixtures.) This data is calculated using fixture performance specified in the tenant sales or lease agreement and the project's mix of occupants. Note: project teams must provide the flow rates required in gallons per minute (gpm).

❑ The project's calculated baseline water usage (flush and flow fixtures.) This data is calculated using typical fixture types (provided in the template) and the project's mix of occupants.

Considerations

Cost Issues

Water-efficient fixtures that use less water than requirements in the Energy Policy Act of 1992 (and as amended) may have higher initial costs, although such fixtures as high-efficiency toilets generally do not. Additionally, there may be a longer lead time for delivery because of their limited availability. However, installation of water-efficient fixtures and equipment can result in significant, long-term financial and environmental savings.

For example, the first cost of non-water-consuming urinals is marginally higher than conventional urinals and additional training of maintenance personnel is required to ensure that O&M staff follow the specific cleaning and maintenance procedures. Minor construction savings may be realized by eliminating the urinal water supply piping. Significant long-term operational savings can occur as a result of reduced sewage generation and elimination of potable water use. Significant additional operational costs may occur as a result of maintenance requirements, including maintenance supplies such as cartridge components, and cleaning and sealing fluids. A full benefit/cost life-cycle study should be undertaken before recommending such products.

Environmental Issues

The reduction of potable water use in buildings for toilets, showerheads and faucets reduces the total amount withdrawn from rivers, streams, underground aquifers and other water bodies. Another benefit of potable water conservation is reduced energy use and chemical inputs at municipal water treatment works.

Water use reductions, in aggregate, allow municipalities to reduce or defer the capital investment needed for water supply and wastewater treatment infrastructure. These strategies protect the natural water cycle and save water resources for future generations.

Economic Issues

Reductions in water consumption minimize overall building operating costs. In certain cases, these benefits may be partially or fully offset by increased operating costs associated with maintenance. Reductions can also lead to more stable municipal taxes and water rates. By reducing water use and resultant disposal to the sewer, water treatment facilities can delay expansion and maintain stable wastewater treatment prices.

Accelerated replacements of conventional non-efficient plumbing fixtures with high-efficiency fixtures through incentive programs has become a cost-effective way for some water and wastewater utilities to defer, reduce or avoid capital investments associated with water supply and wastewater facilities expansion.

Regional Issues

Local weather conditions should be factored into determining the feasibility of rainwater harvesting systems for use in reduction of potable water for flushing. Local building and health and safety codes/ordinances vary with regards to allowance of graywater or harvested rainwater for use in sewage conveyance. Additionally, codes differ in how alternative plumbing fixtures, such as composting toilets and non-water-consuming urinals are handled. It is critical to confirm acceptability of non-traditional approaches with code officials prior to commitment to specific water saving strategies.

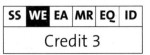

SS **WE** EA MR EQ ID

Credit 3

Supply water quality from graywater and recycled water systems should also be considered in fixture selection. Project teams should identify if minimum supply water quality standards have been established for specific fixtures by manufacturers. When recycled graywater or collected rainwater is used with plumbing fixtures designed for use with municipally supplied potable water, it is good practice to verify that supply water quality is acceptable and will not compromise long-term fixture performance or void product warranties.

Resources

Websites

Please see the USGBC website at www.usgbc.org/resources for more specific resources on materials sources and other technical information.

American Rainwater Catchment Systems Association

www.arcsa-usa.org

Includes a compilation of publications, such as the Texas Guide to Rainwater Harvesting.

Choosing a Toilet

www.taunton.com/finehomebuilding/pages/h00042.asp

An article in Fine Homebuilding that includes several varieties of water efficient toilets.

Composting Toilet Reviews

www.buildinggreen.com/features/mr/waste.html

(802) 257-7300

An Environmental Building News article on commercial composting toilets.

National Climatic Data Center

www.ncdc.noaa.gov/oa/climate/aasc.html

Useful site for researching local climate data, such as rainfall data for rainwater harvesting calculations. Includes links to state climate offices.

Rocky Mountain Institute

www.rmi.org/sitepages/pid15.php

This portion of RMI's website is devoted to water conservation and efficiency. The site contains information on commercial, industrial and institutional water use, watershed management, and articles on policy and implementation.

Smart Communities Network

This U.S. Department of Energy project provides information about water efficiency and national and regional water efficiency assistance programs, and links to additional resources.

Terry Love's Consumer Toilet Reports

www.terrylove.com/crtoilet.htm

This website offers a plumber's perspective on many of the major toilets used in commercial and residential applications.

Water Closet Performance Testing

www.cuwcc.org/MapTesting.lasso

This site provides the most comprehensive and up-to-date reports on toilet flush performance of over 200 different models, including HETs.

High-Efficiency Toilet Fixtures and Other Water-Efficient Products

www.cuwcc.org/products_tech.lasso

This site provides the latest listing of High-Efficiency Toilets (HETs) currently offered in the North American marketplace as well as much other technical information on water-efficient products, performance, and savings.

Water Efficiency Manual for Commercial, Industrial and Institutional Facilities

www.p2pays.org/ref/01/00692.pdf

A straightforward manual on water efficiency from a number of different North Carolina government departments.

Water Measurement Manual: A Water Resources Technical Publication

www.usbr.gov/pmts/hydraulics_lab/pubs/wmm/

This U.S. Department of the Interior publication is a guide to effective water measurement practices for better water management.

Water Use Efficiency Program

www.epa.gov/owm/water-efficiency

This website provides an overview of the U.S. EPA's Water Use Efficiency Program and information about using water more efficiently.

Water Wiser: The Water Efficiency Clearinghouse

www.awwa.org/waterwiser

(800) 926-7337

This web clearinghouse provides articles, reference materials and papers on all forms of water efficiency.

Definitions

Automatic Fixture Sensors are motion sensors that automatically turn on/off lavatories, sinks, water closets and urinals. Sensors may be hard wired or battery operated.

Blackwater does not have a single definition that is accepted nationwide. Wastewater from toilets and urinals is, however, always considered blackwater.

Wastewater from kitchen sinks (perhaps differentiated by the use of a garbage disposal), showers, or bathtubs may be considered blackwater by state or local codes. Project teams should comply with the blackwater definition as established by the authority having jurisdiction in their areas.

Composting Toilet Systems are dry plumbing fixtures that contain and treat human waste via microbiological processes.

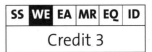

Graywater (also spelled greywater, gray water) is defined by the Uniform Plumbing Code (UPC) in its Appendix G, titled "Gray water Systems for Single-Family Dwellings" as "untreated household wastewater which has not come into contact with toilet waste. Gray water includes used water from bathtubs, showers, bathroom wash basins, and water from clothes-washer and laundry tubs. It shall not include wastewater from kitchen sinks or dishwashers."

The International Plumbing Code (IPC) defines graywater in its Appendix C, titled "Gray Water Recycling Systems" as "wastewater discharged from lavatories, bathtubs, showers, clothes washers, and laundry sinks."

Some states and local authorities allow kitchen sink wastewater to be included in graywater. Other differences with the UPC and IPC definitions may be found in state and local codes. Project teams should comply with the graywater definitions as established by the authority having jurisdiction in their areas.

Metering Controls are generally manual on/automatic off controls which are used to limit the flow time of water. These types of controls are most commonly installed on lavatory faucets and on showers.

Non-Water-Consuming Urinal (also known as a dry urinal) is a urinal that uses no water, but instead replaces the water flush with a specially designed trap that contains a layer of buoyant liquid that floats above the urine layer, blocking sewer gas and urine odors from the room. Other non-water technologies are also available for urinals.

Potable Water is water that is suitable for drinking and is supplied from wells or municipal water systems.

Process Water is water used for industrial processes and building systems such as cooling towers, boilers and chillers.

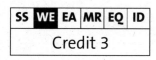

Energy and Atmosphere

Buildings consume approximately 37% of the energy and 68% of the electricity produced in the United States annually, according to the U.S. Department of Energy. Electricity generated from fossil fuels—oil and coal—impact the environment in a myriad of adverse ways, beginning with their extraction, transportation, refining and distribution. Coal mining disrupts habitats and can devastate landscapes. Acidic mine drainage further degrades regional ecosystems. Coal is rinsed with water, which results in billions of gallons of sludge stored in ponds. Mining is a dangerous occupation in which accidents and the long-term effects of breathing coal dust result in shortened life spans of coal miners.

Conventional fossil-based generation of electricity releases carbon dioxide, which contributes to global climate change. Coal-fired electric utilities emit almost one-third of the country's anthropogenic nitrogen oxide, the key element in smog, and two-thirds the sulfur dioxide, a key element in acid rain. They also emit more fine particulate material than any other activity in the United States. Because the human body is incapable of clearing these fine particles from the lungs, they are contributing factors in tens of thousands of cancer and respiratory illness-related deaths annually.

Natural gas, nuclear fission and hydroelectric generators all have adverse environmental impacts as well. Natural gas is a major source of nitrogen oxide and greenhouse gas emissions. Nuclear power increases the potential for catastrophic accidents and raises significant waste transportation and disposal issues. Hydroelectric generating plants disrupt natural water flows, resulting in disturbance of habitat and depletion of fish populations.

Green buildings address these issues in two primary ways: by reducing the amount of energy required, and by using more benign forms. The better the energy performance of a project, the lower the operations costs. As world competition for the available supply of fuels heightens, the rate of return on energy-efficiency measures improves. Electrical generation using sources other than fossil fuels reduces environmental impacts.

Energy & Atmosphere Credit Characteristics

Table 1 shows which credits were substantially revised for LEED-CS Version 2.0, which credits are eligible to be submitted in the Design Phase Submittal, and which project team members are likely to carry decision-making responsibility for each credit. The decision-making responsibility matrix is not intended to exclude any party, rather to emphasize those credits that are most likely to require strong participation by a particular team member.

Overview of LEED® Prerequisites and Credits

EA Prerequisite 1
Fundamental Commissioning of the Building Energy Systems

EA Prerequisite 2
Minimum Energy Performance

EA Prerequisite 3
Fundamental Refrigerant Management

EA Credit 1
Optimize Energy Performance

EA Credit 2
On-Site Renewable Energy

EA Credit 3
Enhanced Commissioning

EA Credit 4
Enhanced Refrigerant Management

EA Credit 5
Measurement & Verification

EA Credi 6
Green Power

Table 1: EA Credit Characteristics

Credit	Significant Change from LEED-NC v2.2	Design Submittal	Construction Submittal	Owner Decision-Making	Design Team Decision-Making	Contractor Decision-Making
EAp1: Fundamental Commissioning of the Building Energy Systems			*	*	*	*
EAp2: Minimum Energy Performance		*		*	*	*
EAp3: Fundamental Refrigerant Management		*		*		
EAc1: Optimize Energy Performance	*	*		*	*	*
EAc2: On-Site Renewable Energy	*	*		*	*	*
Eac3: Enhanced Commissioning			*	*	*	*
Eac4: Enhanced Refrigerant Management		*			*	
EAc5.1: M&V – Base Building	*	*			*	
EAc5.2: M&V – Tenant Submetering	*	*			*	
EAc6: Green Power	*		*	*		

Fundamental Commissioning of the Building Energy Systems

Intent

Verify that the building's energy related systems are installed, calibrated and perform according to the Owner's Project Requirements, Basis of Design, and construction documents.

Benefits of Commissioning

Benefits of commissioning include reduced energy use, lower operating costs, reduced contractor callbacks, better building documentation, improved occupant productivity, and verification that the systems perform in accordance with the Owner's Project Requirements.

Requirements

The following commissioning process activities shall be completed by the commissioning team, in accordance with this LEED-CS 2.0 Reference Guide.

1) Designate an individual as the Commissioning Authority (CxA) to lead, review and oversee the completion of the commissioning process activities.

   a) The CxA shall have documented commissioning authority experience in at least two building projects.

   b) The individual serving as the CxA shall be independent of the project's design and construction management, though they may be employees of the firms providing those services. The CxA may be a qualified employee or consultant of the Owner.

   c) The CxA shall report results, findings and recommendations directly to the Owner.

   d) For projects smaller than 50,000 square feet, the CxA may be a qualified person on the design or construction teams who has the required experience.

2) The Owner shall document the Owner's Project Requirements (OPR). The design team shall develop the Basis of Design (BOD). The CxA shall review these documents for clarity and completeness. The Owner and design team shall be responsible for updates to their respective documents.

3) Develop and incorporate commissioning requirements into the construction documents.

4) Develop and implement a commissioning plan.

5) Verify the installation and performance of the systems to be commissioned.

6) Complete a summary commissioning report.

Commissioned Systems

Commissioning process activities shall be completed, at a minimum, for the following energy-related systems if they are installed as part of the core and shell project:

❑ Heating, ventilating, air conditioning and refrigeration (HVAC&R) systems (mechanical and passive) and associated controls

❑ Lighting and daylighting controls

❑ Domestic hot water systems

❑ Renewable energy systems (wind, solar, etc.)

Potential Technologies & Strategies

In order to meet this prerequisite, Owners are required to use qualified individuals to lead the commissioning process. Qualified individuals are identified as those who possess a high level of experience in all of the following areas:

❑ Energy systems design, installation and operation

❑ Commissioning planning and process management

❑ Hands-on field experience with energy systems performance, interaction, start-up, balancing, testing, troubleshooting, operation, and maintenance procedures

❑ Energy systems automation control knowledge

Owners are encouraged to consider including water-using systems, building envelope systems, and other systems in the scope of the commissioning plan as appropriate. The building envelope is an important component of a facility which impacts energy consumption, occupant comfort and indoor air quality. While it is not required to be commissioned by LEED, an Owner can receive significant financial savings and reduced risk of poor indoor air quality by including building envelope commissioning.

This LEED-CS 2.0 Reference Guide provides guidance on the rigor expected for this prerequisite for the following:

❑ Owner's Project Requirements

❑ Basis of Design

❑ Commissioning Plan

❑ Commissioning Specification

❑ Performance Verification Documentation

❑ Commissioning Report

Summary of Referenced Standard

There is no standard referenced for this prerequisite.

Approach and Implementation

Relationship Between Fundamental and Enhanced Commissioning

LEED-CS addresses building commissioning in two places, EA Prerequisite 1 and EA Credit 3. For any given LEED project, the scope of services for the CxA and project team should be based on the Owner's Project Requirements (OPR). To meet the requirements of this prerequisite, the commissioning process activities must, at a minimum, address the commissioned systems noted in the prerequisite. Other systems, including the building envelope, stormwater management systems, water treatment systems, information technology systems, etc., may also be included in the commissioning process at the Owner's discretion.

Table 1 outlines the team members primarily responsible to perform each project requirement; and also which requirements are common to EA Prerequisite 1 and EA Credit 3. All individuals on the project team are encouraged to participate in the commissioning activities as part of a larger commissioning team.

Strategies

The commissioning process is a planned, systematic team-wide coordination/quality- assurance process that involves the owner, users, occupants, operations and maintenance staff, design professionals and contractors. It is most effective when implemented at project inception.

An explanation of the steps satisfying this LEED-CS prerequisite is summarized in the following sections.

Table 1: Primary Responsibilities Chart for EA Prerequisite 1 and EA Credit 3

Tasks	Responsibilities	
	If you are only meeting EAp1...	If you are meeting the EAp1 AND EAc3...
Designate Commissioning Authority (CxA)	Owner or Project Team	Owner or Project Team
Document Owner's Project Requirements (OPR)	Owner	Owner
Develop Basis of Design	Design Team	Design Team
Incorporate commissioning requirements into the construction documents	Project Team or CxA	Project Team or CxA
Conduct commissioning design review prior to mid-construction documents	N/A	CxA
Develop and implement a commissioning plan	Project Team or CxA	Project Team or CxA
Review contractor submittals applicable to systems being commissioned	N/A	CxA
Verify the installation and performance of commissioned systems	CxA	CxA
Develop a systems manual for the commissioned systems	N/A	Project Team and CxA
Verify that the requirements for training are completed	N/A	Project Team and CxA
Complete a summary commissioning report	CxA	CxA
Review building operation within 10 months after substantial completion	N/A	CxA

1. **Designate an individual as the Commissioning Authority (CxA) to lead, review and oversee the completion of the commissioning process activities.**

   It is recommend for the project to designate an individual as the CxA as early as possible in the project timeline, ideally during pre-design. The qualified individual designated as the CxA serves as an objective advocate for the Owner, and is responsible for 1) directing the commissioning team and process in the completion of the commissioning requirements, 2) coordinating, overseeing, and/or performing the commissioning testing and 3) reviewing the results of the systems performance verification.

   For LEED-CS projects a qualified CxA should have experience with two other projects of similar managerial and technical complexity. The Owner may want to develop additional experience or qualifications requirements in selecting the CxA, depending on the scope and nature of the commissioning. There are a number of CxA certification programs administered by various industry groups.

   For projects larger than 50,000 sq.ft. the individual serving as the CxA on a LEED-CS project shall be independent of the project's design and construction teams. The CxA may be a qualified staff member of the Owner, an Owner's consultant to the project, or an employee of one of the firms providing design and/or construction management services. The CxA shall not, however, have responsibility for design (e.g., engineer-of-record) or for construction. The CxA shall report results, findings and recommendations directly to the Owner.

   For projects smaller than 50,000 sq.ft. the CxA may be a qualified staff member of the Owner, an Owner's

consultant to the project, or an individual on the design or construction team, and may have additional project responsibilities beyond leading the commissioning services.

2. **The Owner shall document the Owner's Project Requirements (OPR). The design team shall develop the Basis of Design (BOD). The CxA shall review these documents for clarity and completeness. The Owner and design team shall be responsible for updates to their respective documents.**

   Clear and concise documentation of the Owner's Project Requirements and the Basis of Design is a valuable part of any successful project delivery and commissioning process. These documents are utilized throughout the Commissioning Process to provide an informed baseline and focus for validating systems' energy and environmental performance.

   ### Owner's Project Requirements (OPR)

   The OPR shall be completed by the Owner, Commissioning Agent, and Project Team prior to the approval of contractor submittals of any commissioned equipment or systems. Subsequent updates to the OPR during the design and construction process are the primary responsibility of the Owner.

   The OPR should detail the functional requirements of a project and the expectations of the building's use and operation as it relates to the systems to be commissioned. It is recommended that the OPR address the following issues, as applicable to the project:

   ❑ *Owner and User Requirements*—Describe the primary purpose, program, and use of the proposed project (e.g., office building with data center) and any pertinent project history. Provide any overarching goals relative to program needs, future expansion, flexibility, quality of materials, and construction and operational costs.

❑ *Environmental and Sustainability Goals*—Describe any specific environmental or sustainability goals (e.g., LEED-CS certification). Include preliminary LEED-CS assessment and Precertification information.

❑ *Energy Efficiency Goals*—Describe overall project energy efficiency goals relative to local energy code or ASHRAE Standard or LEED. Describe any goals or requirements for building siting, landscaping, façade, fenestration, envelope and roof features that will impact energy use.

❑ *Indoor Environmental Quality Requirements*—As applicable and appropriate, for each program/usage area describe the intended use; anticipated occupancy schedules; space environmental requirements (including lighting, space temperature, humidity, acoustical, air quality, ventilation and filtration criteria); desired user ability to adjust systems controls; desire for specific types of lighting; and accommodations for after-hours use.

❑ *Equipment and System Expectations*—As applicable and appropriate, describe the desired level of quality, reliability, type, automation, flexibility, and maintenance requirements for each of the systems to be commissioned. When known, provide specific efficiency targets, desired technologies, or preferred manufacturers for building systems.

❑ *Building Occupant and O&M Personnel Requirements*—Describe how the facility will be operated, and by whom. Describe the desired level of training and orientation required for the building occupants to understand and use the building systems.

Basis of Design

The design team must document the Basis of Design (BOD) for the systems to be commissioned prior to approval of contractor submittals of any commissioned equipment or systems. Subsequent updates to this document during the design and construction process are the responsibility of the design team. The Commissioning Agent shall review the BOD to ensure that it reflects the OPR.

The BOD shall provide a narrative describing the design of the systems to be commissioned and outlining any design assumptions that are not otherwise included in the design documents. The BOD should be updated with each subsequent design submission with increasing specificity as applicable.

The BOD shall, at a minimum, include the following as applicable:

❑ *Primary Design Assumptions*—including space use, redundancy, diversity, climatic design conditions, space zoning, occupancy, operations and space environmental requirements

❑ *Standards*—including applicable codes, guidelines, regulations, and other references that will be put into practice

❑ *Narrative Descriptions*—including performance criteria for the HVAC&R systems, lighting systems, hot water systems, on-site power systems, and other systems that are to be commissioned

SS	WE	EA	MR	EQ	ID
Prerequisite 1					

Table 2: Commissioning Requirements in Construction Documents

- ❑ Commissioning team involvement
- ❑ Contractors' responsibilities
- ❑ Submittals and submittal review procedures for Cx process/systems
- ❑ Operations and maintenance documentation, system manuals
- ❑ Meetings
- ❑ Construction verification procedures
- ❑ Start-up plan development and implementation
- ❑ Functional performance testing
- ❑ Acceptance and closeout
- ❑ Training
- ❑ Warranty review site visit

3. **Develop and incorporate commissioning requirements into the construction documents.**

   Typically the project specifications are used to inform the contractor(s) of their responsibilities in the commissioning process. These specifications may describe the components listed in **Table 2**.

   Often, all commissioning requirements are outlined in one section of the general conditions of the construction specifications. Placing all commissioning requirements in one location puts responsibility for commissioning work with the prime contractor, who can then appropriately assign responsibility to sub-contractors. It is also valuable to reference commissioning requirements on the drawings, in any bid forms, and in specification sections related to the systems to be commissioned.

4. **Develop and implement a Commissioning Plan.**

   Unique to a particular project, the Commissioning Plan is the reference document that identifies the strategies, aspects and responsibilities within the commissioning process for each phase of a project, for all of the project team members. This document outlines the overall process, schedule, organization and documentation requirements of the commissioning process.

The Commissioning Plan is developed at the start of the commissioning process, preferably during design development. The Commissioning Plan is updated during the course of a project to reflect changes in planning, schedule, or other supplemental information as warranted. The precertification information is suggested to be included as a section of this Plan.

The following outlines recommended components of the Commissioning Plan:

- ❑ Commissioning Program Overview
  - ▪ Goals and objectives
  - ▪ General project information
  - ▪ Systems to be commissioned
- ❑ Commissioning Team
  - ▪ Team members, roles and responsibilities
  - ▪ Communication protocol, coordination, meetings and management
- ❑ Description of Commissioning Process Activities
  - ▪ Documenting the Owner's Project Requirements
  - ▪ Preparing the Basis of Design
  - ▪ Developing systems functional test procedures
  - ▪ Verifying systems performance

- Reporting deficiencies and the resolution process

- Accepting the building systems

Project teams pursuing the enhanced commissioning credit (EA Credit 3) may need to expand the Commissioning Plan to include the following commissioning process activities:

❑ Documenting the commissioning review process

❑ Reviewing contractor submittals

❑ Developing the systems manual

❑ Verifying the training of operations personnel

❑ Reviewing building operation after final acceptance

5. **Verify the installation and performance of the systems to be commissioned.**

The purpose of commissioning is to verify the performance of commissioned systems as installed to meet the OPR, BOD and contract documents.

Verification of the installation and performance of commissioned systems typically includes the following steps for each commissioning system:

❑ Installation Inspection

❑ Systems Performance Testing

❑ Evaluation of Results Compared to OPR/BOD

Installation Inspections—(sometimes referred to as pre-functional inspections) are a systematic set of procedures intended to identify whether individual components of the systems to be commissioned have been installed properly. Often this process occurs at start-up of individual units of equipment and may use "pre-function checklists" or "start-up and check-out forms" to insure consistency in the inspections and to document the pro-

cess. Installation inspections may be performed by the CxA, the installing contractor, or by others, depending on the procedures outlined in the Commissioning Plan. Installation inspections provide quality control to insure that relatively minor issues (e.g., a mis-wired sensor, a control valve installed backwards) are discovered and corrected prior to systems performance testing.

Systems Performance Testing—(sometimes referred to as functional performance testing) occurs once all system components are installed, energized, programmed, balanced and otherwise ready for operation under part and full load conditions. Testing should include each sequence in the sequence of operations under central and packaged equipment control; including startup, shutdown, capacity modulation, emergency and failure modes, alarms and interlocks to other equipment. Systems performance testing typically relies on testing procedures developed by the CxA specifically for the system to be tested. Systems performance testing may use a wide variety of means and methods to simulate and evaluate that the system being tested performs as expected (per the OPR, BOD and contract documents) in all modes of operation. Systems performance testing may be performed by some combination of the CxA, the installing contractor, and others, depending on the procedures outlined in the commissioning specifications and the Commissioning Plan. Systems performance testing may yield minor or significant issues with the performance of the commissioned systems and may require significant follow-up and coordination between members of the project team to address and resolve these issues.

Evaluation of Results Compared to OPR/BOD—at each point in the process of Installation Inspections and Systems Performance Testing the CxA and the commissioning team should evaluate whether the installed systems meet the criteria for the project as set forth by the Owner in the OPR and the designers in the BOD. Any discrepancies or deficiencies should be reported to the Owner and the team should work collaboratively to find an appropriate resolution.

6. **Complete a summary commissioning report.**

   Upon completion of installation inspections and performance verification items, the results are tabulated and assembled into a summary commissioning report. The summary report should include confirmation from the CxA indicating whether individual systems meet the requirements of the OPR, BOD and Contract Documents. The summary commissioning report should include the following:

   ❏ Executive summary of the process and the results of the commissioning program —including observations, conclusions and any outstanding items

   ❏ A history of any system deficiencies identified and how they were resolved— including any outstanding issues or seasonal testing scheduled for a later date

   ❏ Systems performance test results and evaluation (Any other supporting information can be complied as a Cx record but is not required in the summary report.)

   In addition, for projects pursuing EA Credit 3, the commissioning report should include the following:

   ❏ A summary of the design review process

   ❏ A summary of the submittal review process

   ❏ A summary of the O&M documentation and training process

Core and Shell Concerns

Not all energy related systems are installed as part of the core and shell projects. Energy related systems include, but are not limited to, heating, ventilating, air conditioning and refrigeration (HVAC&R) systems, associated controls, lighting, daylighting controls, domestic hot water systems, and renewable energy systems (wind, solar, etc.). Commissioning is required for any of the above systems that are part of the core and shell project. Some commissioning activities will be limited due to the installed systems or components. Systems performance testing procedures are generally designed for complete system installations. Core and shell systems may not be complete. For example, a core and shell office VAV air-handling system may have the air handling unit installed, but not the VAV boxes and ductwork in the tenant spaces. Testing procedures may have to be changed or eliminated for systems that are incomplete. It is important to document all of the systems that will be installed as part of the core and shell project and to commission these systems.

Calculations

There are no calculations associated with this prerequisite.

Exemplary Performance

There is no exemplary performance point available for this prerequisite.

Precertification Submittal Documentation

Provide the LEED-CS Precertification Submittal Template, which includes the following:

❏ Narrative describing how the project intends to accomplish the credit requirements on the credit-specific Submittal Template signed by the appropriate design team member

❑ Confirmation of this intent from the owner/developer on the LEED-CS Precertification Submittal Template

Certification Submittal Documentation

This prerequisite is submitted as part of the **Construction Submittal**.

Design and Construction Credit Compliance

The following project data and calculation information is required to document prerequisite compliance using the LEED-CS v2.0 Submittal Templates:

❑ Provide the name and company information for the CxA.

❑ Confirm that the 6 required tasks have been completed.

❑ Provide a narrative description of the systems that were commissioned and the results of the commissioning process.

Tenant Sales or Lease Agreement Credit Compliance

This compliance method is not available for this credit.

Considerations

Economic Issues

Implementation of a commissioning process maintains the focus on quality control and high performance building principles from project inception through operation. Commissioning typically results in optimized mechanical, electrical and architectural systems—maximizing energy efficiency and thereby minimizing environmental impacts. A properly designed and executed Commissioning Plan may reduce errors and omissions in the design and installation process, improve coordination, reduce change orders, and generate substantial operational cost savings compared to systems that are not commissioned. Successful implementation of the commissioning process often yields improvements in energy efficiency of 5% to 10%.

In addition to improved energy performance, improved occupant well-being and productivity are potential benefits when commissioning results in building systems functioning as intended. Such benefits include avoiding employee illness, tenant turnover and vacant office space, liability related to indoor air quality and premature equipment replacement.

Researchers at Lawrence Berkeley National Lab (LBNL) completed a meta-analysis of 85 new construction commissioning projects in 2004. LBNL developed a detailed and uniform methodology for characterizing, analyzing and synthesizing the results. For new construction, this study found that median commissioning costs were $1.00/sq.ft. (0.6% of total construction costs), yielding a median payback time of 4.8 years from quantified energy savings alone (excluding savings from non-energy impacts and other benefits of commissioning). This study further concludes—

"Some view commissioning as a luxury and 'added' cost, yet it is only a barometer of the cost of errors promulgated by other parties involved in the design, construction, or operation of buildings. Commissioning agents are just the 'messengers'; they are only revealing and identifying the means to address pre-existing problems. We find that commissioning is one of the most cost-effective means of improving energy efficiency in commercial buildings."

Resources

Please see the USGBC website at www.usgbc.org/resources for more specific resources on materials sources and other technical information.

Websites

American Society of Heating, Refrigeration and Air-Conditioning Engineers (ASHRAE)

www.ashrae.org

(800) 527-4723

Building Commissioning Association (BCxA)

www.bcxa.org

(877) 666-BCXA (2292)

Promotes building commissioning practices that maintain high professional standards and fulfill building Owner's expectations. The association offers a five-day intensive course focusing on how to implement the commissioning process, intended for Commissioning Authorities with at least two years of experience.

California Commissioning Collaborative (CCC)

www.cacx.org

(503) 595-4432

The CCC is a nonprofit 501(c)3 organization committed to improving the performance of buildings and their systems. The CCC is made up of government, utility and building services organizations and professionals who have come together to create a viable market for building commissioning in California.

Cx Assistant Commissioning Tool

www.ctg-net.com/edr2002/cx/

This web-based tool provides project-specific building commissioning information to design teams and enables users to evaluate probable commissioning cost, identify an appropriate commissioning scope, and access sample commissioning specifications related to their construction project.

Portland Energy Conservation Inc. (PECI)

www.peci.org

PECI develops the field for commissioning services by helping building owners understand the value of commissioning, and producing process and technical information for commissioning providers. Their focus includes both private and public building owners, and a wide range of building types. PECI manages the annual National Conference on Building Commissioning.

Department of Engineering Professional Development University of Wisconsin, Madison

www.engr.wisc.edu

(800) 462-0876

Offers commissioning process training courses for building owners, architects, engineers, operations and maintenance staff, and other interested parties. The program also offers accreditation of commissioning process providers and managers.

Print Media

ASHRAE Guideline 0-2005: The Commissioning Process, American Society of Heating, Refrigerating and Air-Conditioning Engineers, 2005.

www.ashrae.org

(800) 527-4723

"The purpose of this Guideline is to describe the Commissioning Process capable of verifying that a facility and its systems meet the Owner's Project Requirements. The procedures, methods, and documentation requirements in this guideline describe each phase of the project delivery and the associated Commissioning Processes from pre-design through occupancy and operation, without regard to specific elements, assemblies, or systems, and provide the following: (a) overview of Commissioning Process activities, (b) description of each phase's processes, (c) requirements for acceptance of each phase, (d) requirements for documentation of each phase, and (e) requirements for training of operation and maintenance personnel. These Commissioning Process guideline procedures include the Total Building Commissioning Process (TB-CxP) as defined by National Institute of Building Sciences (NIBS) in its Commissioning Process Guideline 0."

ASHRAE Guideline 1-1996: The HVAC Commissioning Process, American Society of Heating, Refrigerating and Air-Conditioning Engineers, 1996.

www.ashrae.org

(800) 527-4723

"The purpose of this guideline is to describe the commissioning process to ensure that heating, ventilating and air-conditioning (HVAC) systems perform in conformity with design intent. The procedures, methods and documentation requirements in this guideline cover each phase of the commissioning process for all types and sizes of HVAC systems, from pre-design through final acceptance and post-occupancy, including changes in building and occupancy requirements after initial occupancy."

ASHRAE Guideline 4-1993: Preparation of Operations & Maintenance Documentation for Building Systems, American Society of Heating, Refrigerating and Air-Conditioning Engineers, 1993.

www.ashrae.org

(800) 527-4723

"The purpose of this guideline is to guide individuals responsible for the design, construction and commissioning of HVAC building systems in preparing and delivering O&M documentation."

Building Commissioning Guide, Office of Energy Efficiency and Renewable Energy Federal Energy Management Program, U.S. Department of Energy

www.eere.energy.gov

(800) DIAL-DOE

The Energy Policy Act of 1992 requires each federal agency to adopt procedures necessary to ensure that new federal buildings meet or exceed the federal building energy standards established by the U.S. Department of Energy (DOE). DOE's Federal Energy Management Program, in cooperation with the General Services Administration, developed the Building Commissioning Guide.

Commissioning for Better Buildings in Oregon, Oregon Office of Energy http://egov.oregon.gov/ENERGY/CONS/BUS/comm/bldgcx.shtml

(503) 378-4040

This document (and website of the same name) contains a comprehensive introduction to the commissioning process, including research, financial benefits and case studies.

The Cost-Effectiveness of Commercial Buildings Commissioning: A Meta-Analysis of Existing Buildings and New Construction in the United States, available at: http://eetd.lbl.gov/emills/PUBS/Cx-Costs-Benefits.html

PECI Model Building Commissioning Plan and Guide Specifications, Portland Energy Conservation Inc.

www.peci.org

(503) 248-4636

Details the commissioning process for new equipment during design and construction phases for larger projects. In addition to commissioning guidelines, the document provides boilerplate language, content, format and forms for specifying and executing commissioning. The document builds upon the HVAC Com-

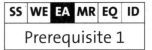

SS | WE | **EA** | MR | EQ | ID

Prerequisite 1

missioning Process, ASHRAE Guideline 1-1996, with significant additional detail, clarification and interpretation.

Commissioning Fact Sheets, Coalition For High Performance Schools (CHPS)

www.chps.net/manual/index.htm

These fact sheets explore how commissioning can help school districts ensure their schools are built as high performance facilities.

The Building Commissioning Handbook, Second Edition by John A. Heinz & Rick Casault, The Building Commissioning Association, 2004

www.bcxa.com

"This popular handbook has been revised by the original authors to include the most up-to-date information on all aspects of building commissioning. This is your guide to: Staying on Budget; Improving the Quality of your Buildings; Meeting your Schedule; Increasing Energy Efficiency. Chapters outline the commissioning process from pre-design to occupancy and explain the economics of commissioning and retro-commissioning."

Definitions

Basis of Design (BOD) includes design information necessary to accomplish the Owner's Project Requirements, including system descriptions, indoor environmental quality criteria, other pertinent design assumptions (such as weather data), and references to applicable codes, standards, regulations and guidelines.

Commissioning (Cx) is the process of verifying and documenting that the facility and all of its systems and assemblies are planned, designed, installed, tested, operated, and maintained to meet the Owner's Project Requirements.

Commissioning Plan is a document that outlines the organization, schedule, allocation of resources, and documenta-

tion requirements of the commissioning process.

Commissioning Report is the document that records the results of the commissioning process, including the as-built performance of the HVAC system and unresolved issues.

Commissioning Specification is the contract document that details the commissioning requirements of the construction contractors.

The **Commissioning Team** includes those people responsible for working together to carry out the commissioning process.

Installation Inspection is the process of inspecting components of the commissioned systems to determine if they are installed properly and ready for systems performance testing.

Owner's Project Requirements (OPR) is a written document that details the functional requirements of a project and the expectations of how it will be used and operated.

Systems Performance Testing is the process of determining the ability of the commissioned systems to perform in accordance with the Owner's Project Requirements, Basis of Design, and construction documents.

Minimum Energy Performance

Required

Intent

Establish the minimum level of energy efficiency for the proposed building and systems.

Requirements

Design the building project to comply with both—

❏ the mandatory provisions (Sections 5.4, 6.4, 7.4, 8.4, 9.4 and 10.4) of ASHRAE/IESNA Standard 90.1-2004 (without addenda); and

❏ the prescriptive requirements (Sections 5.5, 6.5, 7.5 and 9.5) or performance requirements (Section 11) of ASHRAE/IESNA Standard 90.1-2004 (without addenda).

Potential Technologies & Strategies

Design the building envelope, HVAC, lighting, and other systems to maximize energy performance. The ASHRAE 90.1-2004 User's Manual contains worksheets that can be used to document compliance with this prerequisite. For projects pursuing points under EA Credit 1, the computer simulation model may be used to confirm satisfaction of this prerequisite.

If a local code has demonstrated quantitative and textual equivalence following, at a minimum, the U.S. Department of Energy standard process for commercial energy code determination, then it may be used to satisfy this prerequisite in lieu of ASHRAE 90.1-2004. Details on the DOE process for commercial energy code determination can be found at www.energycodes.gov/implement/determinations_com.stm.

Summary of Referenced Standard

ASHRAE/IESNA 90.1-2004: Energy Standard for Buildings Except Low-Rise Residential

American Society of Heating, Refrigerating and Air-Conditioning Engineers

www.ashrae.org

(800) 527-4723

Standard 90.1-2004 was formulated by the American Society of Heating, Refrigerating and Air-Conditioning Engineers, Inc. (ASHRAE), under an American National Standards Institute (ANSI) consensus process. The Illuminating Engineering Society of North America (IESNA) is a joint sponsor of the standard.

Standard 90.1 establishes minimum requirements for the energy-efficient design of buildings, except low-rise residential buildings. The provisions of this standard do not apply to single-family houses, multi-family structures of three habitable stories or fewer above grade, manufactured houses (mobile and modular homes), or buildings that do not use either electricity or fossil fuel. Building envelope requirements are provided for semi-heated spaces, such as warehouses.

The standard provides criteria in the general categories shown in **Table 1**. Within each section, there are mandatory provisions that must always be complied with, as well as additional prescriptive requirements. Some sections also contain

a performance alternate. The Energy Cost Budget option (Section 11) allows the user to exceed some of the prescriptive requirements provided energy cost savings are made in other prescribed areas.

The Performance Rating Method option (Appendix G) provides a method for demonstrating performance beyond ASHRAE/IESNA 90.1-2004. In all cases, the mandatory provisions must still be met. See Design Strategies below for a more detailed summary of the requirements included in each section.

Approach and Implementation

LEED-CS addresses building energy efficiency in two places, EA Prerequisite 2 and EA Credit 1. EA Prerequisite 2 requires that the building comply with the mandatory provisions, and either the prescriptive or Energy Cost Budget Method performance requirements of ASHRAE/IESNA 90.1-2004 (Std. 90.1-2004). If energy simulations have been developed to document points earned for EA Credit 1, these energy simulations (based on Std. 90.1-2004 Appendix G) may be used rather than the Energy Cost Budget Method (Std. 90.1-2004 Section 11) to demonstrate compliance with the prerequisite.

Core and Shell Concerns

Core and shell buildings may not have all of the components addressed by

Table 1: Scope of Requirements Addressed by ASHRAE 90.1-2004

ASHRAE/IESNA 90.1-2004 Components	
Section 5	Building Envelope (including semi-heated spaces such as warehouses)
Section 6	Heating, Ventilating and Air-Conditioning (including parking garage ventilation, freeze protection, exhaust air energy recovery, and condenser heat recovery for service water heating)
Section 7	Service Water Heating (including swimming pools)
Section 8	Power (including all building power distribution systems)
Section 9	Lighting (including lighting for exit signs, building exterior, grounds, and parking garage)
Section 10	Other Equipment (including all permanently wired electrical motors)

ASHRAE/IESNA 90.1-2004 designed or defined. For these types of projects, it is necessary to show compliance for the scope of work that is controlled by the core and shell team. For example, if there is no lighting scope of work in the core and shell, the core and shell team need not demonstrate compliance with the lighting mandatory and prescriptive provision of the standard, but must show compliance with the other provisions.

Strategies

Each section of Std. 90.1-2004 describes the applicability of the provisions (e.g., definitions and the building elements of interest), lists the mandatory provisions, and lists the prescriptive requirements for complying with the standard.

Building Envelope Requirements (Std. 90.1-2004 Section 5) apply to enclosed spaces heated by a heating system whose output capacity is equal to or greater than 3.4 Btu/hour-square foot, or cooled by a cooling system whose sensible output capacity is equal to or greater than 5 Btu/hour-square foot.

Std. 90.1-2004 Section 6 lists minimum control schemes for thermostats (off-hours including setback and optimum start/stop), stair and elevator vents, outdoor air supply and exhaust vents, heat pump auxiliary heat, humidification and dehumidification, freeze protection, snow/ice melting systems, and ventilation for high occupancy areas.

Each county in the United States is assigned into one of eight representative climate zones (Std. 90.1-2004 Table B-1). Climate zone assignments for Canadian cities can be determined from Std. 90.1-2004 Table B-2, and climate zone assignments for other international cities can be determined from Std. 90.1-2004 Table B-3.

Prescriptive building envelope requirements are determined based on the building's climate zone classification (Std. 90.1-2004 Tables 5.5-1 to 5.5-8). For projects following the prescriptive compliance method, all building envelope components must meet the minimum insulation and maximum U-factor and SHGC requirements listed for the project's climate zone. Also, window area must be less than 50% of the gross wall area, and the skylight area must be less than 5% of the gross roof area.

For projects following the Energy Cost Budget Method in Section 11, the project may exceed the envelope prescriptive requirements, provided that the design energy cost for the project does not exceed the energy cost budget for the entire building; OR provided that the project uses energy simulation to document points earned for EA Credit 1.

Heating, Ventilation and Air Conditioning Requirements (Std. 90.1-2004 Section 6) apply for all building heating and air conditioning systems. Mandatory provisions for HVAC performance are documented in Std. 90.1-2004 Section 6.4, and include minimum system efficiency requirements (6.4.1); load calculation requirements (6.4.2); controls requirements (6.4.3); HVAC system construction and insulation requirements (6.4.4); and completion requirements (6.4.5).

The minimum system component efficiency requirements listed in Std. 90.1-2004 Tables 6.8.1A–G must be met even when using the Energy Cost Budget or Performance Rating methods.

Minimum control schemes are listed for thermostats (off-hours including setback and optimum stop/start), stair and elevator vents, outdoor air supply and exhaust vents, heat pump auxiliary heat, humidification and dehumidification, freeze protection and snow/ice melting systems, and ventilation for high occupancy areas.

Std. 90.1-2004 Part 6.5 provides a prescriptive compliance option. Prescriptive

SS	WE	**EA**	MR	EQ	ID
Prerequisite 2					

provisions are included for air and water economizers (6.5.1); simultaneous heating and cooling limitations (6.5.2); air system design and control including fan power limitation and variable speed drive control (6.5.3); hydronic system design and control including variable flow pumping (6.5.4); heat rejection equipment (6.5.5); energy recovery from exhaust air and service water heating systems (6.5.6); kitchen and fume exhaust hoods (6.5.7); radiant heating systems (6.5.8); and hot gas bypass limitations (6.5.9).

For projects served by existing HVAC systems, such as a central plant on a campus or district heating and cooling, the exception to Section 6.1.1.2 applies. The existing systems and existing equipment are not required to comply with the standard.

Service Water Heating Requirements (Std. 90.1-2004 Section 7) include mandatory provisions (7.4); and a choice of prescriptive (7.5) or performance based compliance (7.11). Mandatory provisions include requirements for load calculations (7.4.1); efficiency (7.4.2); piping insulation (7.4.3); controls (7.4.4); pool heaters and pool covers (7.4.5); and heat traps for storage tanks (7.4.6).

Power Requirements address mandatory provisions related to voltage drop (Std. 90.1-2004 Section 8.4.1).

Lighting Requirements (Std. 90.1-2004 Section 9) apply to all lighting installed on the building site including interior and exterior lighting. Mandatory provisions include minimum requirements for controls (9.4.1); tandem wiring (9.4.2); luminaire source efficacy for exit signs (9.4.3); exterior lighting power definitions (9.4.5); and luminaire source efficacy for exterior lighting fixtures (9.4.6). Per 9.4.1.2, occupancy controls are required in classrooms, conference rooms and employee lunch and break rooms. Interior lighting compliance must be documented using either the Building Area Method (9.5) or the Space-by-Space Method (9.6).

Lighting power calculations for Performance Methods must use the Building Area Method or the Space-by-Space Method. For both methods, the total installed interior lighting power is calculated by summing the luminaire wattages for all permanently installed general, task and furniture lighting, where the luminaire wattage includes lamps, ballasts, current regulators and control devices.

Building Area Method calculations can only be used in cases where the project involves the entire building, or a single independent occupancy within a multi-occupancy building. Allowable lighting power for this method is calculated by multiplying the allowable lighting power density for the given building type (found in Std. 90.1-2004 Table 9.5.1) by the interior building area.

Allowable lighting for the Space-by-Space Method is determined by summing the product of the allowable lighting power density for each space function in the building (found in Std. 90.1-2004 Table 9.6.1) by the corresponding area for each space function. If the total installed interior lighting power is lower than the interior lighting power allowance calculated using either the Building Area or Space-by-Space Method, the project complies.

The exterior lighting power allowance is calculated by summing the product of the allowable lighting power allowance for each exterior surface (found in Std. 90.1-2004 Table 9.4.5) by the total area or length associated with that surface, and then multiplying this number by 1.05. For non-tradable exterior lighting surfaces, the allowed lighting power can only be used for the specific application and cannot be traded between surfaces or with other exterior lighting.

Other Equipment Requirements including requirements for electric motors are addressed in Std. 90.1-2004 Section

10. This section only contains mandatory provisions (10.4).

The Energy Cost Budget Method is presented in Std. 90.1-2004 Section 11 and describes the process to set up and execute a building simulation to demonstrate compliance. This is the alternate to following the prescriptive provisions of this standard.

The Performance Rating Method is presented in Std. 90.1-2004 Appendix G, and is the required method for claiming credit under EA Credit 1: Optimize Energy Performance. If the project is using the Performance Rating Method to achieve points under EA Credit 1, the EA Credit 1 documentation can be used to prove compliance with the performance requirements (the second part) of this Prerequisite. The Performance Rating Method does not, however, exempt the project from also meeting the mandatory ASHRAE/IESNA Standard 90.1-2004 requirements listed for this prerequisite.

EA Credit 1 includes a more detailed discussion of the Performance Rating Method.

Calculations

Follow the calculation and documentation methodology as prescribed in Std. 90.1-2004. Record all calculations on the appropriate forms. These forms (see **Table 2**) and further information regarding the calculation methodology are available with the ASHRAE/IESNA Standard 90.1-2004 User's Guide.

Exemplary Performance

There is no exemplary performance point available for this prerequisite.

Precertification Submittal Documentation

Provide the LEED-CS Precertification Submittal Template, which includes the following:

❑ Narrative describing how the project intends to accomplish the credit requirements on the credit-specific Submittal Template signed by the appropriate design team member

❑ Confirmation of this intent from the owner/developer on the LEED-CS Precertification Submittal Template

Table 2: Forms for documenting compliance with ASHRAE Std. 90.1-2004

ASHRAE/IESNA 90.1-2004 Compliance Forms
Mandatory Measures – All Projects:
Building Envelope Compliance Documentation (Part I) – Mandatory Provisions Checklist
HVAC Compliance Documentation (Part II) – Mandatory Provisions Checklist
Service Water Heating Compliance Documentation (Part I) – Mandatory Provisions Checklist
Lighting Compliance Documentation (Part I) – Mandatory Provisions Checklist
Prescriptive Requirements – Projects Using Prescriptive Compliance Approach:
Building Envelope Compliance Documentation (Part II)
HVAC Compliance Documentation Part I (for small buildings < 25,000 square feet using the simplified approach), and Part III (for all other buildings)
Service Water Heating Compliance Documentation
Performance Requirements – Projects Using Performance Compliance Approach:
Energy Cost Budget Compliance Report (when credit is not being sought under EA Credit 1)
Performance Rating Report (when credit is being sought under EA Credit 1)
Table documenting energy-related features included in the design, and including all energy features that differ between the Baseline Design and Proposed Design models

Prerequisite 2

Certification Submittal Documentation

This prerequisite is submitted as part of the **Design Submittal**.

Design and Construction Credit Compliance

The following project data and calculation information is required to document prerequisite compliance using the LEED-CS v2.0 Submittal Templates:

❑ Confirm that the project meets the requirements of ASHRAE Std. 90.1-2004.

❑ Provide an optional narrative regarding special circumstances or considerations regarding the project's prerequisite approach.

Tenant Sales or Lease Agreement Credit Compliance

This compliance method is not available for this credit.

Resources

Please see the USGBC website at www.usgbc.org/resources for more specific resources on materials sources and other technical information.

Websites

Advanced Buildings

www.advancedbuildings.org

Hosted by a Canadian public/private consortium, this site provides explanations, costs, and information sources for 90 technologies and practices that improve the energy and resource efficiency of commercial and multi-unit residential buildings.

American Council for an Energy Efficient Economy

www.aceee.org

(202) 429-8873

ACEEE is a nonprofit organization dedicated to advancing energy efficiency as a means of promoting both economic prosperity and environmental protection.

Buildings Upgrade Manual
ENERGY STAR®

www.energystar.gov/index.cfm?c=business.bus_upgrade_manual

(888) 782-7937

This document from the EPA is a guide for ENERGY STAR Buildings Partners to use in planning and implementing profitable energy-efficiency upgrades in their facilities and can be used as a comprehensive framework for an energy strategy.

New Buildings Institute, Inc.

www.newbuildings.org

(509) 493-4468

The New Buildings Institute is a nonprofit, public-benefits corporation dedicated to making buildings better for people and the environment. Its mission is to promote energy efficiency in buildings through technology research, guidelines and codes.

Building Energy Codes Program
U.S. Department of Energy

www.energycodes.gov

(800) DIAL-DOE

The Building Energy Codes program provides comprehensive resources for states and code users, including news, compliance software, code comparisons and the Status of State Energy Codes database. The database includes state energy contacts, code status, code history, DOE grants awarded and construction data. The program is also updating the COM-*Check*EZ™ compliance tool to include ANSI/ASHRAE/IESNA 90.1-2004. This compliance tool includes the prescriptive path and trade-off compliance methods. The software generates appropriate compliance forms as well.

Print Media

ASHRAE 90.1 User's Manual

The 90.1 User's Manual was developed as a companion document to the ANSI/ASHRAE/IESNA Standard 90.1-2004 (Energy Standard for Buildings Except Low-Rise Residential Buildings). The User's Manual explains the new standard and includes sample calculations, useful reference material, and information on the intent and application of the standard. The User's Manual is abundantly illustrated and contains numerous examples and tables of reference data. The manual also includes a complete set of compliance forms and worksheets that can be used to document compliance with the standard. The User's Manual is helpful to architects and engineers applying the standard to the design of buildings; plan examiners and field inspectors who must enforce the standard in areas where it is adopted as code; and contractors who must construct buildings in compliance with the standard. A compact disc containing electronic versions of the compliance forms found in the User's Manual is included.

Case Study

Harborside Office Center
Port Huron, MI

Harborside Office Center is a 110,000-sq.ft. office building and is the first of several new facilities being constructed as part of a one-mile long riverfront reclamation project on former railway land and abandoned industrial sites. Harborside has earned LEED-CS Pilot Silver certification for its efforts. The building's HVAC system is comprised of a conventional heating and refrigeration cooling system augmented by numerous energy saving modifications. High efficiency (97%) hot water boilers with automatic temperature resets were selected along with an ef-

Photo courtesy of Albert Kahn Associates, Inc.
Photographer: Justin Maconochie

ficient air conditioning process where evaporatively-cooled condensers extract heat more efficiently than traditional air-cooled condensers. The attached 375-space parking garage includes a roof garden, light well and bioswale. Aesthetically, the light well allows daylight to be introduced into the structure. Functionally, this element provides an opportunity to treat stormwater on-site by collecting and treating first-flush rain events. Through the process of phytoremediation and filtering through three feet of sand, stormwater is detained, polished and released into the municipal storm system. The roof garden also helps to reduce heat island effect. The office building itself is roofed in white PVC and a large mechanical penthouse with a standing seam metal roof which was field painted with an acrylic/elastomeric coating, both complying with high emissivity requirements of the LEED program.

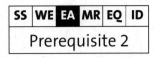

Fundamental Refrigerant Management

Required

Intent

Reduce ozone depletion.

Requirements

Zero use of CFC-based refrigerants in new base building HVAC&R systems. When reusing existing base building HVAC equipment, complete a comprehensive CFC phase-out conversion prior to project completion. Phase-out plans extending beyond the project completion date will be considered on their merits.

Potential Technologies & Strategies

When reusing existing HVAC systems, conduct an inventory to identify equipment that uses CFC refrigerants and provide a replacement schedule for these refrigerants. For new buildings, specify new HVAC equipment in the base building that uses no CFC refrigerants.

Summary of Referenced Standard

There is no standard referenced for this prerequisite.

Approach and Implementation

Replace or retrofit any CFC-based refrigerants in existing base building HVAC&R and fire suppression systems. If the building(s) is connected to an existing chilled water system, that system must be CFC-free; or a commitment to phasing out CFC-based refrigerants, with a firm timeline of five years from substantial completion of the project, must be in place. Prior to phase-out, reduce annual leakage of CFC-based refrigerants to 5% or less using EPA Clean Air Act, Title VI, Rule 608 procedures governing refrigerant management and reporting.

An alternative compliance path for buildings connected to a central chilled water system requires a third party (as defined in the LEED-EB Reference Guide) audit showing that system replacement or conversion is not economically feasible. Subsequent to the required economic analysis the replacement of a chiller(s) will be considered not economically feasible if the simple payback of the replacement is greater than 10 years. To determine the simple payback, divide the cost of implementing the replacement by the annual cost avoidance for energy that results from the replacement and any difference in maintenance costs, including make-up refrigerants. If CFC-based refrigerants are maintained in the central system, reduce annual leakage to 5% or less using EPA Clean Air Act, Title VI, Rule 608 procedures governing refrigerant management and reporting, and reduce the total leakage over the remaining life of the unit to less than 30% of its refrigerant charge.

Consider the characteristics of various CFC substitutes. Refrigerants have varying applications, lifetimes, ozone-depleting potentials (ODPs) and global-warming potentials (GWPs). **Table 1** provides examples of ODP values and GWP values for a variety of refrigerants. Refrigerants chosen should have short environmental lifetimes, small ODP values and small GWP values.

No "ideal" alternative for CFCs has been developed. See the EPA's List of Substitutes for Ozone-Depleting Substances (www.epa.gov/ozone/snap) for a current listing of alternatives to CFC refrigerants. Note that some alternatives are not suitable for retrofits.

Core and Shell Concerns

There are no additional core and shell particular issues regarding implementation.

Calculations

There are no calculations associated with this prerequisite.

Exemplary Performance

There is no exemplary performance point available for this prerequisite.

Precertification Submittal Documentation

Provide the LEED-CS Precertification Submittal Template, which includes the following:

❑ Narrative describing how the project intends to accomplish the credit requirements on the credit-specific Submittal Template signed by the appropriate design team member

❑ Confirmation of this intent from the owner/developer on the LEED-CS Precertification Submittal Template

Table 1: Ozone-depletion and global-warming potentials of refrigerants (100-yr values)

Refrigerant	ODP	GWP	Common Building Applications
Chlorofluorocarbons			
CFC-11	1.0	4,680	Centrifugal chillers
CFC-12	1.0	10,720	Refrigerators, chillers
CFC-114	0.94	9,800	Centrifugal chillers
CFC-500	0.605	7,900	Centrifugal chillers, humidifiers
CFC-502	0.221	4,600	Low-temperature refrigeration

Certification Submittal Documentation

This prerequisite is submitted as part of the **Design Submittal**.

Design and Construction Credit Compliance

The following project data and calculation information is required to document prerequisite compliance using the LEED-CS v2.0 Submittal Templates:

❑ Confirm that the project does not use CFC refrigerants.

OR

❑ Confirm that the project has a phase-out plan for any existing CFC-based equipment.

❑ Provide a narrative description of the phase-out plan, including dates and refrigerant quantities as a percentage of the overall project equipment.

Tenant Sales or Lease Agreement Credit Compliance

This compliance method is not available for this credit.

Considerations

Cost Issues

Renovations of some existing buildings will require additional first costs to convert or replace existing HVAC&R and fire suppression systems currently using CFCs. Replacement rather than conversion of HVAC systems may increase equipment efficiencies, minimize over-sizing, extend equipment life and/or enable projects to reap energy savings over the life of the building.

Environmental Issues

Older refrigeration equipment used chlorofluorocarbons (CFCs) in refrigerants. CFCs, when inevitably released to the atmosphere, cause significant damage to the protective ozone layer in the earth's upper atmosphere.

The reaction between a CFC and an ozone molecule in the earth's stratosphere destroys the ozone and reduces the stratosphere's ability to absorb a portion of the sun's ultraviolet (UV) radiation. Overexposure to UV rays can lead to skin cancer, cataracts and weakened immune systems. Increased UV can also lead to reduced crop yield and disruptions in the marine food chain.

CFCs fall into a larger category of ozone depleting substances (ODSs). Recognizing the profound human health risks associated with ozone depletion, 160 countries have agreed to follow the Montreal Protocol on Substances that Deplete the Ozone Layer since the late 1980s. This treaty includes a timetable for the phase-out of production and use of ODSs. In compliance with the Montreal Protocol, CFC production in the United States ended in 1995.

As part of the U.S. commitment to implementing the Montreal Protocol, Congress added new provisions to the Clean Air Act designed to help preserve and protect the stratospheric ozone layer.

These amendments require the U.S. Environmental Protection Agency (EPA) to develop and implement regulations for the responsible management of ozone depleting substances in the United States. EPA regulations include programs that ended the domestic production of ODSs, identified safe and effective alternatives to ODSs, and require manufacturers to label products either containing or made with chemicals that have a significant ozone depleting potential.

Banning the use of CFCs in refrigerants has slowed the depletion of the ozone layer. Specification of non-CFC building equipment is now standard and CFC-based refrigerants are no longer available in new equipment.

Resources

Please see the USGBC website at www.usgbc.org/resources for more specific resources on materials sources and other technical information.

Websites

Ozone Depletion

U.S. Environmental Protection Agency

www.epa.gov/ozone

Provides information about the science of ozone depletion, the regulatory approach to protecting the ozone layer (including phase-out schedules) and alternatives to ozone-depleting substances.

The Treatment by LEED of the Environmental Impact of HVAC Refrigerants

U.S. Green Building Council

www.usgbc.org/DisplayPage. aspx?CMSPageID=154

This report was prepared under the auspices of the U.S. Green Building Council's LEED Technical and Scientific Advisory Committee (TSAC), in response to a charge given TSAC by the LEED Steering Committee to review the atmospheric environmental impacts arising from the use of halocarbons as refrigerants in building heating, ventilating and air conditioning (HVAC) equipment.

Print Media

CFCs, HCFC and Halons: Professional and Practical Guidance on Substances that Deplete the Ozone Layer, ASHRAE, 2000.

The Refrigerant Manual: Managing The Phase-Out of CFCs, BOMA International, 1993.

Definitions

Chlorofluorocarbons (CFCs) are hydrocarbons that deplete the stratospheric ozone layer.

Hydrochlorofluorocarbons (HCFCs) are refrigerants that cause significantly less depletion of the stratospheric ozone layer compared to CFCs.

Refrigerants are the working fluids of refrigeration cycles. They absorb heat from a reservoir at low temperatures and reject heat at higher temperatures.

Optimize Energy Performance

Intent

Achieve increasing levels of energy performance above the baseline in the prerequisite standard to reduce environmental and economic impacts associated with excessive energy use.

Requirements

Select one of the three compliance path options described below. Project teams documenting achievement using any of the three options are assumed to be in compliance with EA Prerequisite 2.

OPTION 1 — WHOLE BUILDING ENERGY SIMULATION (1–8 Points)

Demonstrate a percentage improvement in the proposed building performance rating compared to the baseline building performance rating per ASHRAE/IESNA Standard 90.1-2004 (without addenda) by a whole building project simulation using the Building Performance Rating Method in Appendix G of the Standard. The minimum energy cost savings percentage for each point threshold is as follows:

New Buildings	Existing Building Renovations	Points
10.5%	3.5%	1
14%	7%	2
17.5%	10.5%	3
21%	14%	4
24.5%	17.5%	5
28%	21%	6
31.5%	24.5%	7
35%	28%	8

Appendix G of Standard 90.1-2004 requires that the energy analysis done for the Building Performance Rating Method include ALL of the energy costs within and associated with the building project. To achieve points using this credit, the proposed design—

❏ must comply with the mandatory provisions (Sections 5.4, 6.4, 7.4, 8.4, 9.4 and 10.4) in Standard 90.1-2004 (without amendments);

❏ must include all the energy costs within and associated with the building project; and

❏ must be compared against a baseline building that complies with Appendix G to Standard 90.1-2004 (without addenda). The default process energy cost is 25% of the total energy cost for the baseline building. For buildings where the process energy cost is less than 25% of the baseline building energy cost, the LEED submittal must include supporting documentation substantiating that process energy inputs are appropriate.

For the purpose of this analysis, process energy is considered to include, but is not limited to, office and general miscellaneous equipment, computers, elevators and escalators, kitchen cooking and refrigeration, laundry washing and drying, lighting exempt from the lighting power allowance (e.g., lighting integral to medical equipment) and other (e.g., waterfall pumps). Regulated (non-process) energy includes lighting (such as for the interior, parking garage, surface parking, façade, or building grounds, except as noted above), HVAC (such as for space heating, space cooling, fans, pumps, toilet exhaust, parking garage ventilation, kitchen hood exhaust, etc.), and service water heating for domestic or space heating purposes.

For EA Credit 1, process loads shall be identical for both the baseline building performance rating and for the proposed building performance rating. However, project teams may follow the Exceptional Calculation Method (ASHRAE 90.1-2004 G2.5) to document measures that reduce process loads. Documentation of process load energy savings shall include a list of the assumptions made for both the base and proposed design, and theoretical or empirical information supporting these assumptions.

OR

OPTION 2 — PRESCRIPTIVE COMPLIANCE PATH (1-3 Points)

Comply with the ASHRAE Advanced Energy Design Guide for Small Office Buildings recommendations.

Project teams must fully comply with all applicable criteria as established in the ASHRAE Advanced Energy Design Guide for Small Office Buildings for the climate zone in which the building is located. It should be noted that this compliance path may only be used for office buildings up to 20,000 sq.ft. (Note: the envelope, lighting and HVAC & SWH requirements vary by climate. For each climate there is a table that lists recommended levels for each "system.")

Envelope Performance: (1 point possible)

Install envelope systems which comply with all the envelope recommendations in the ASHRAE Advanced Energy Design Guide for Small Office Buildings table for the climate zone in which the building is located.

Lighting Systems: (1 additional point possible)

Install lighting systems which comply with all the lighting recommendations in the ASHRAE Advanced Energy Design Guide for Small Office Buildings table for the climate zone in which the building is located.

All such systems shall be included in systems commissioned under EA Prerequisite 1, Fundamental Commissioning of the Building Energy Systems.

HVAC and Service Water Heater Systems: (1 additional point possible)

Install HVAC and Service Water Heating (SWH) systems which comply with all the HVAC &

SWH recommendations in the ASHRAE Advanced Energy Design Guide for Small Office Buildings table for the climate zone in which the building is located.

All such systems shall be included in systems commissioned under EA Prerequisite 1, Fundamental Commissioning of the Building Energy Systems.

OR

OPTION 3 — PRESCRIPTIVE COMPLIANCE PATH (1 Point)

Comply with the Basic Criteria and Prescriptive Measures of the NBI Advanced Buildings Benchmark™ Version 1.1 with the exception of the following sections: 1.7 Monitoring and Trend-logging, 1.11 Indoor Air Quality, and 1.14 Networked Computer Monitor Control. The following restrictions apply:

❑ Project teams must fully comply with all applicable criteria as established in Advanced Buildings Benchmark for the climate zone in which the building is located.

❑ Project teams must show compliance with all applicable criteria for all systems that are part of the core and shell work.

Potential Technologies & Strategies

Design the building envelope and systems to maximize energy performance. Use a computer simulation model to assess the energy performance and identify the most cost-effective energy efficiency measures. Quantify energy performance as compared to a baseline building.

If a local code has demonstrated quantitative and textual equivalence following, at a minimum, the U.S. Department of Energy standard process for commercial energy code determination, then the results of that analysis may be used to correlate local code performance with ASHRAE 90.1-2004. Details on the DOE process for commercial energy code determination can be found at www.energycodes.gov/implement/determinations_com.stm.

Summary of Referenced Standard

OPTION 1—ASHRAE/IESNA 90.1-2004: Energy Standard for Buildings Except Low-Rise Residential, and Informative Appendix G – Performance Rating Method

American Society of Heating, Refrigerating and Air-Conditioning Engineers

www.ashrae.org

(800) 527-4723

Standard 90.1-2004 was formulated by the American Society of Heating, Refrigerating and Air-Conditioning Engineers, Inc. (ASHRAE), under an American National Standards Institute (ANSI) consensus process. The Illuminating Engineering Society of North America (IESNA) is a joint sponsor of the standard. ASHRAE 90.1 Standards form the basis for many of the commercial requirements in codes that states consider for adoption.

Standard 90.1 establishes minimum requirements for the energy-efficient design of buildings, except low-rise residential buildings. The provisions of this standard do not apply to single-family houses, multi-family structures of three habitable stories or fewer above grade, manufactured houses (mobile and modular homes), buildings that do not use either electricity or fossil fuel, or equipment and portions of building systems that use energy primarily for industrial, manufacturing or commercial processes. Building envelope requirements are provided for semi-heated spaces, such as warehouses.

Appendix G is an informative appendix for rating the energy efficiency of building designs. This appendix is NOT to be included as part of the minimum requirements to comply with code; instead, Appendix G is used to "quantify performance that substantially exceeds the requirements of Standard 90.1" (G1.1).

For EA Credit 1, LEED relies extensively on the Performance Rating Method explained in Appendix G. The method provides performance criteria for the components listed in **Table 1**.

The Performance Rating Method is intended to demonstrate performance beyond ASHRAE/IESNA 90.1-2004 through an interactive model that allows comparison of the total energy cost for the Proposed Design and a Baseline Design. To accomplish this efficiently, a number of restrictions on the modeling process are imposed by the method. Examples include simplified climate data, the fact that both buildings must have a mechanical system, and that process loads are to be included in both designs. Important restrictions that must be addressed to achieve compliance with the credit are highlighted in the Calculations section.

Table 1: Scope of Requirements Addressed by ASHRAE/IESNA 90.1-2004

ASHRAE/IESNA 90.1-2004 Components	
Section 5	Building Envelope (including semi-heated spaces such as warehouses)
Section 6	Heating, Ventilating and Air-Conditioning (including parking garage ventilation, freeze protection, exhaust air energy recovery, and condenser heat recovery for service water heating)
Section 7	Service Water Heating (including swimming pools)
Section 8	Power (including all building power distribution systems)
Section 9	Lighting (including lighting for exit signs, building exterior, grounds, and parking garage)
Section 10	Other Equipment (including all permanently wired electrical motors)

OPTION 2—ASHRAE Advanced Energy Design Guide for Small Office Buildings 2004

American Society of Heating, Refrigerating and Air-Conditioning Engineers

www.ashrae.org

(800) 527-4723

Advanced Energy Design Guide for Small Office Buildings 2004 was formulated by the American Society of Heating, Refrigerating and Air-Conditioning Engineers, Inc. (ASHRAE) to provide a simplified approach in small office buildings for exceeding ASHRAE 90.1-1999 standards. The guide provides climate-specific recommendations relative to the building envelope, interior lighting, and HVAC systems that will improve building energy performance beyond ASHRAE 90.1-1999 by approximately 30%.

OPTION 3—Advanced Buildings Benchmark™ Version 1.1

New Buildings Institute

Advanced Buildings Benchmark™ Version 1.1 was formulated by the New Buildings Institute to provide a method for exceeding national codes and standards, and to provide a standardized method for determining building performance.

For EA Credit 1—OPTION 3, LEED requires full compliance with all applicable criteria in the Sections of the Advanced Buildings Benchmark Version 1.1 shown in **Table 2**.

Approach and Implementation

OPTION 1—Whole Building Energy Simulation

The ASHRAE/IESNA Standards 90.1-2004 Informative Appendix G Performance Rating Method is an effective method for rating building energy performance, and for evaluating the relative costs and benefits of different energy efficiency strategies.

Table 2: Scope of Requirements Addressed by Advanced Buildings Benchmark™ Version 1.1 as pertaining to LEED Credit 1 Option 3

Advanced Buildings Benchmark™ Version 1.1 Criteria	
Section 5	
Required 1.1	Design Certification
Required 1.2	Construction Certification
Required 1.3	Operations Certification
Required 1.4	Energy Code Compliance
Required 1.5	Air Barrier Performance
Required 1.6	Window, Skylight and Door Certification
Required 1.8	Energy Efficient Transformers
Required 1.9	Lighting Controls
Required 1.10	Outdoor Lighting
Required 1.12	Below-Grade Exterior Insulation
Required 1.13	Refrigeration and Icemaker Efficiency Requirements
Section 6	
Required 2.1	Opaque Envelope Performance
Required 2.2	Fenestration Performance
Required 2.3	Cool Roofs and Ecoroofs
Required 2.4	Mechanical System Design
Required 2.5	Mechanical Equipment Efficiency Requirements
Required 2.6	Variable Speed Control
Required 2.7	Lighting Power Density

The terminology used by the Performance Rating Method is used in this LEED credit. The term "Proposed Building Performance" refers to the "the annual energy cost calculated for a proposed design." The term "Baseline Building Performance" refers to "the annual energy cost for a building design intended for use as a baseline for rating above standard design." The modeling methodology addressed in Appendix G of ASHRAE/IESNA 90.1-2004 describes procedures for establishing the Proposed Building Performance and the Baseline Building Performance in order to evaluate the Percentage Improvement in energy cost for the project.

The Performance Rating Method requires the development of an energy model for the Proposed Design, which is then used as the basis for generating the Baseline Design energy model. As the design progresses, any updates made to the Proposed Design energy model (such as changes to the building orientation, wall area, fenestration area, space function, HVAC system type, HVAC system sizing, etc.) should also be reflected in the Baseline Design energy model as dictated by Appendix G.

The Performance Rating Method described in Appendix G is a modification of the Energy Cost Budget (ECB) Method in Section 11 of ASHRAE 90.1-2004. A model using the Energy Cost Budget Method will NOT be accepted for credit under EA Credit 1.

The major differences between the ECB Method and the Performance Rating Method are as follows:

1. **Building Schedules** (Table G3.1.4):

    In the Performance Rating Method, building occupancy, lighting, and other schedules may be altered to model efficiency measures as long as these modifications are both reasonable and defensible. In the Energy Cost Budget Method, schedules may not be altered.

2. **Baseline Building Envelope** (Table G3.1.5):

    a. **Orientation:** The Performance Rating Method requires that the Baseline Building be simulated one time for each of four distinct building orientations, and that the results be averaged to calculate the Baseline Building Performance. The Energy Cost Budget requires that the Budget Building be modeled with an orientation identical to the Proposed Building.

    b. **Opaque Assemblies:** The Performance Rating Method specifies the type of assembly required for the Baseline Building wall, roof, and floor construction. The ECB method varies the construction assembly type modeled in the Budget Building Design based on the actual construction assembly type modeled in the Proposed Design.

    c. **Vertical Fenestration:** The Performance Rating Method limits the total fenestration modeled for the Baseline Building to 40% of the gross wall area or the actual fenestration percentage, whichever is less; and requires that this fenestration be uniformly distributed across all four orientations. The Energy Cost Budget Method limits the fenestration modeled to 50% of the gross wall area or the actual fenestration percentage, whichever is less; and requires that the fenestration be distributed similarly to the Proposed Design.

3. **Baseline Building HVAC System:**

    a. **HVAC System Type Selection** (Table G3.1.10, and Section G3.1.1, G3.1.2 and G3.1.3): Baseline Building system type selection using the Performance Rat-

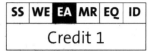

ing Method is determined based on building type, building area, quantity of floors and the heating fuel source for the proposed design. This method allows credit for selecting inherently efficient HVAC system types. In the Energy Cost Budget Method, Budget Building system type is determined based on the proposed design condenser cooling source, heating system classification, and single zone versus multi-zone classification. This method allows much less variation between the Proposed and Baseline Design Systems.

b. **Baseline Fan Power:** With the Performance Rating Method, total fan power for the Baseline System is fixed based on total supply air volume, and system classification as constant volume or variable volume. This method reflects the savings achieved through an improved duct design that reduces static pressure. With the Energy Cost Budget Method, the fan static pressure remains the same in the budget and the proposed case.

c. **Baseline System Sizing:** With the Performance Rating Method, the Baseline System is sized using default ratios. This allows credit for systems that are appropriately sized, and penalizes oversized systems. With the Energy Cost Budget Method, Budget Systems are sized with the same sizing factors as the Proposed Design.

Starting the energy modeling early in the project design can provide insights for design decisions and can provide an early indication of what it will take to achieve certain levels of energy cost reductions (and associated EA Credit 1 points) for a particular project.

The modeling methodology outlined in the Performance Rating Method enables the design team to identify the interactive effects of energy efficiency measures across all the building systems. For example, when the proposed lighting power is changed, this affects both the heating and cooling energy consumption. When building lighting power density is decreased in a hot climate with little or no heating, the model will indicate the quantity of additional cooling energy savings (due to lower internal loads) and how much the peak cooling equipment can be downsized (for first cost savings). For a cold climate, the model will reflect lower cooling energy savings, and an increase in heating energy (due to a lower internal load). In almost all cases, there will be savings beyond that of the lighting alone, with the greatest savings in the hottest climates and the least savings in the coldest climates.

The Performance Rating Method requires that annual energy cost expressed in dollars be used to calculate the percentage improvement in energy usage. Annual energy costs are determined using rates for purchased energy such as electricity, gas, oil, propane, steam and chilled water that are based on actual local utility rates, or that are based on the state average prices published annually by the U.S. Department of Energy's Energy Information Administration (EIA) at www.eia.doe.gov.

Core and Shell Energy Modeling Guidelines

1. These guidelines are intended to ensure that projects in different markets with different project teams are approaching the energy modeling requirements in a similar manner and that a minimum benchmark for energy optimization is established.**Create the ASHRAE 90.1-2004 Proposed Building Model and Baseline Building Model**

    1.1   Follow the ASHRAE 90.1-2004 Building Performance Rating Method. This is a whole building model inclusive of both core and shell , and tenant space scope. The following describes the prescriptive requirements for developing the whole building modeling of both the known core and shell work and unknown tenant space development.

1.2 Tenant spaces are defined as meeting all the following conditions:

1.2.1 Components exclusively serve the tenant space;

1.2.2 Components specifically designed for the tenant space;

1.2.3 Energy using components are metered and apportioned and/or billed to the tenant;

4.4.4 The tenant will pay for the components.

4.5 The core and shell building is designated as all parts of the building that are not tenant space.

2. Proposed Building Model

2.1 Core and Shell Building

2.1.1 HVAC Systems

2.1.1.1 Model the building system as described in the design documents.

❑ If the HVAC system is not yet designed, use the same HVAC system as the baseline model.

2.1.2 Building Envelope

2.1.2.1 Model the building envelope as shown on the architectural drawings.

2.1.3 Lighting

2.1.3.1 Model the lighting power as shown in the design documents for the core and shell spaces.

2.2 Tenant Spaces

2.2.1 Lighting

2.2.1.1 Model separate electric meters for the lighting in the core building and the tenant spaces.

2.2.1.2 Choose a space type classification for the building spaces. Use lighting levels shown in chart 9.3.1.2 of ASHRAE 90.1-2004 for the space type use classification.

❑ If the tenant lighting is designed and installed as part of the core and shell work, the project team may model the designed or installed lighting systems.

2.2.2 Plug Loads and Process Loads

2.2.2.1 Model separate meters for tenant plug loads and process loads.

2.2.2.2 Use the following values to model tenant plug loads or provide documentation for the modeled loads (see Process Energy in the Calculations section):

2.2.2.3 Computer intensive offices

❑ 2.0 W/sq.ft.

1.2.2.4 General office areas

❑ 1.5 W/sq.ft.

1.2.2.5 Large conference areas

❑ 1.0 W/sq.ft.

1.2.2.6 Corridors

❑ 0 W/sq.ft.

1.2.2.7 Server/computer rooms

❑ 50 W/sq.ft.

1.2.2.8 Other uses

❑ Use diversity in calculations

3. Baseline Building Model

3.1 Core and Shell Building

3.1.1 HVAC System

3.1.1.1 Model the baseline building HVAC system determined from Table G3.1.1A in ASHRAE 90.1-2004.

3.1.2 Building Envelope

3.1.2.1 Comply with the prescriptive requirements of ASHRAE 90.1-2004.

3.1.3 Lighting

3.1.3.1 Model the lighting power in the core and shell areas as determined by the space type classification in chart 9.6.1 of ASHRAE 90.1-2004.

3.2 Tenant Spaces

3.2.1 Lighting

3.2.1.1 Model separate electric meters for the lighting in the core building and the tenant spaces.

3.2.1.2 Use the same lighting power as modeled in the proposed building.

3.2.2 Receptacle and Other Loads

3.2.2.1 Model separate meters for tenant receptacle loads and process loads.

3.2.2.2 Use the same values for receptacle loads as used in the proposed building.

4. **Perform Energy Simulation of Proposed Building and Baseline Building**

   4.1 Simulate building performance for an entire year.

5. **Compare Annual Energy Costs of Proposed Building and Baseline Building**

   5.1 From the simulation, determine the annual energy costs of the budget building and design building.

   5.2 Verify that 25% of the overall energy cost is process load. Determine the percentage savings for annual energy costs

Strategies

Four fundamental strategies can increase energy performance: reduce demand, harvest free energy, increase efficiency, and recover waste energy.

❑ Accomplish demand reduction by optimizing building form and orientation, by reducing internal loads through shell and lighting improvements, and by shifting load to off-peak periods.

❑ Harvesting site energy includes using free resources such as daylight, ventilation cooling, solar heating and power, and wind energy to satisfy needs for space conditioning, service water heating and power generation.

❑ Increasing efficiency can be accomplished with more efficient envelope, lighting, and HVAC systems, and by appropriately sizing HVAC systems. More efficient systems reduce energy demand and energy use.

❑ Finally, waste energy can be recovered through exhaust air energy recovery systems, graywater heat recovery systems, and cogeneration. When applying these strategies, it is important to establish and document energy goals and expectations, and apply modeling techniques to reach these goals.

OPTION 2—Prescriptive Compliance Path

For small office buildings less than 20,000 sq.ft., the ASHRAE Advanced Energy Design Guide for Small Office Buildings 2004 provides an effective means of limiting building energy usage, and documenting improved building energy performance without the need for a building energy model. The climate-specific recommendations listed in the ASHRAE Advanced Energy Design Guide should be incorporated into the project early in the building design in order to optimize building performance with minimal impact on capital costs.

To comply with the prescriptive measures of the ASHRAE Advanced Energy Design Guide, the project team must first identify the climate zone where the building is located. Section 3 includes a United States map defining the eight climate zones by county borders.

The project team can then find the appropriate Climate Zone Recommendation table identifying all of the prescriptive criteria required for their project. These

SS | WE | **EA** | MR | EQ | ID

Credit 1

Diagram 1: Energy Modeling Decision Matrix

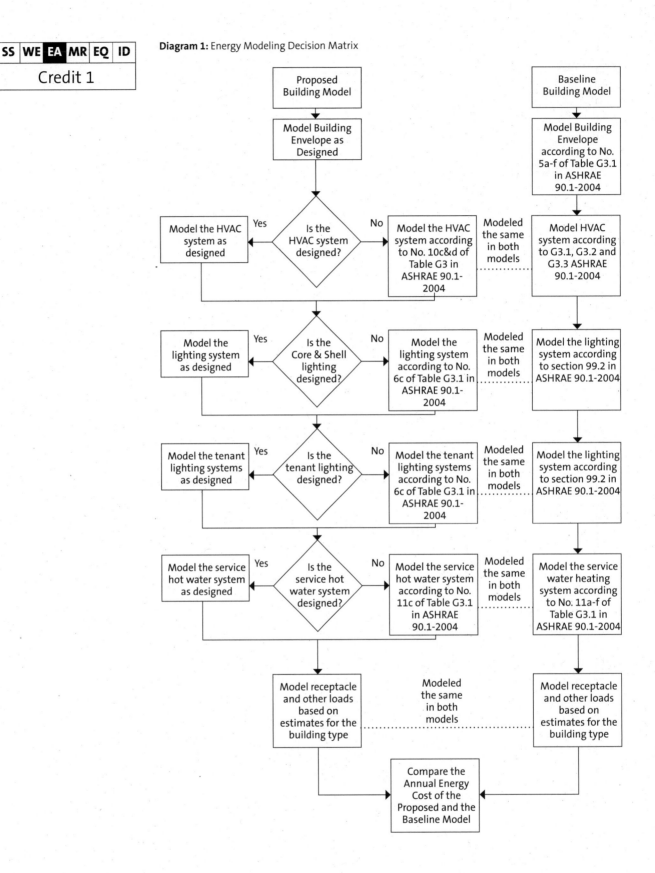

criteria include recommendations for roofs, walls, floors, slabs, doors, vertical glazing, skylights, interior lighting, ventilation, ducts, energy recovery, and service water heatingTo use this option, a core and shell project must first meet the applicable envelope criteria. All additional points awarded are dependant on this. There are 3 points available for this option.

❏ One point is available for projects that meet the envelope criteria for the climate zone in which the building is located.

❏ One point is available for meeting the HVAC criteria.

❏ One point is available for meeting the lighting criteria.

OPTION 3—Prescriptive Compliance Path

The Basic Criteria and Prescriptive Measures of the Advanced Buildings Benchmark™ Version 1.1 provide a prescriptive means of improving building energy performance. To comply with some of these measures, the project team must identify the climate zone where the building is located. The Advanced Buildings Benchmark™ Section 6.1 includes a United States map defining the eight climate zones by county borders. To achieve EA Credit 1, project teams must fully comply with all of the applicable Advanced Buildings Benchmark™ v1.1 Criteria listed in **Table 2** in the Summary of Referenced Standards. The criteria of this credit must be complied with for all of the components that are part of the core and shell project. However, components that are not part of the core and shell project are not considered for compliance. For example, a project that is not installing lighting in tenant spaces will not consider the lighting power density for those spaces.

Example

A core and shell project is an 800,000-sq.ft speculative office. The project is a 30-story building with a VAV air handling system with boilers and chillers. Spaces built as part of the core and shell project include the lobby and elevator lobbies on every floor. Items specified as part of the core and shell project include the following:

❏ Building envelope

❏ Building mechanical system including—

   ▪ Boilers, including piping

   ▪ Chillers, including piping

   ▪ Air-handling units, including medium pressure duct work

❏ Lobby lighting

❏ Elevator lobby lighting on all floors

Items not specified as part of the core and shell project include the following:

❏ Tenant space lighting

❏ Tenant space air distribution, including VAV boxes

This project must comply with the Basic Criteria and Prescriptive Measures of the Advanced Buildings Benchmark™ Version 1.1 for all of the items specified as part of the core and shell project. For this project, these criteria and measures include:

❏ Design Certification

❏ Construction Certification

❏ Operations Certification

❏ Energy Code Compliance

❏ Air Barrier Performance

❏ Window, Skylight and Door Certification

❏ Energy Efficient Transformers

❏ Outdoor Lighting

❏ Below-Grade Exterior Insulation

❏ Refrigeration and Icemaker Efficiency Requirements

❏ Opaque Envelope Performance

❑ Fenestration Performance

❑ Cool Roofs and Ecoroofs

❑ Mechanical System Design

❑ Mechanical Equipment Efficiency Requirements

❑ Variable Speed Control

The lighting installed in the lobby and elevator lobbies must also meet the requirements of:

❑ Lighting Controls

❑ Lighting Power Density

Core and Shell Concerns

Because core and shell buildings are by definition unfinished, some of the components and systems will be unknown. For Option 1, project teams will have to follow the procedure set forth in ASHRAE 90.1-2004 for components that have not yet been designed. These components will be the same in both the baseline and proposed cases. For Option 2 and Option 3 the project teams will need to meet the criteria for all applicable regulated components that are part of the core and shell. It will be helpful to define as clearly as possible, which components are part of the core and shell and which are not. The LEED-CS Project Scope Checklist, which is part of the submittal documentation, is a useful tool in determining core and shell project scope.

Calculations

Option 2 and Option 3 of EA Credit 1 use a prescriptive approach and do not require a software energy simulation of the project.

Option 1 relies entirely upon the ASHRAE 90.1-2004 Appendix G Performance Rating Method, and requires extensive calculations using an approved energy simulation program. The Performance Rating Method in 90.1 Appendix G is NOT equivalent to the Energy Cost Budget (ECB) Method in 90.1 Section 11, and the ECB Method will not be accepted for credit under LEED-CS v2.0 EA Credit 1.

A total of five energy simulation runs are required in order to demonstrate compliance using the Performance Rating Method. This includes one Proposed Design simulation which models the building as designed (with some minor exceptions), and four Baseline Design simulations. The four Baseline Design energy models are identical to each other, except that the building orientation for each is modified as described in ASHRAE Std. 90.1 Table G3.5.1(a): and the window SHGCs are revised to reflect the minimum ASHRAE Building Envelope Requirements for the revised building orientation.

The total annual energy cost projected by the Proposed Design simulation is called the "Proposed Building Performance." The average of the total projected annual energy costs for the four Baseline Design simulations is called the "Baseline Building Performance."

The basic method for demonstrating compliance is to first model and simulate the Proposed Design, and then revise the model parameters for the Baseline Design as described in Appendix G, and simulate the Baseline Design using each of the four prescribed orientations. A major difference between the Proposed Design and the Baseline Design is that the windows are distributed equally around the building in the Baseline Design.

Both the Baseline Building model and the Proposed Building model must include all building energy components including, but not limited to, interior and exterior lighting, cooling, heating, fan energy (including garage ventilation and exhaust fans), pumping, heat rejection, receptacle loads, freeze protection, elevators and escalators, swimming pool equipment, refrigeration and cooking equipment.

Schedules of Operation must be the same for the Proposed and Budget Building models unless schedule changes are necessary to model non-standard efficiency measures such as lighting controls, natural ventilation, demand control ventilation, or service water heating load reductions (ASHRAE Std. 90.1 Table G3.1.4). If there are schedule of operation differences between the Baseline Building model and the Proposed Building model these differences should be clearly and explicitly described in the EA Credit 1 submittal narrative.

Design Criteria, including both climate data and interior temperature and humidity setpoints, must be the same for the Proposed and Baseline Building models. Furthermore, both heating and cooling must be modeled in all conditioned spaces of both the Proposed and Baseline Building energy models, even if no heating or cooling system will be installed. Buildings that have no mechanical heating and/or cooling system, can achieve some credit by modeling fan systems as "cycling" in the Proposed Design versus continuously operated fans in the Baseline Design (ASHRAE Std. 90.1 Table G3.1 No. 4 – Fan Schedules).

Building Envelope (ASHRAE Std. 90.1 Table G3.1.5) will likely vary significantly between the Proposed and Baseline Design models. The Performance Rating Method requires that the Proposed Design be modeled as designed with a few minor exceptions. For the Baseline Design of new buildings, the above-grade walls, roof and floor assemblies must be modeled using light-weight assembly types (i.e., steel-framed walls, roofs with insulation entirely above deck, and steel-joist floors), with the ASHRAE Std. 90.1 prescriptive maximum U-factors for the building's climate. Even if the Proposed Design incorporates mass wall construction, the Baseline Design must be modeled using a steel-framed assembly.

The percentage of vertical fenestration modeled in the Budget Design should match that of the Proposed Design or 40% of the gross wall area, whichever is less. This fenestration must be equally distributed in horizontal bands across all four orientations.

"Cool roofs" (light colored roof finishes that have low heat absorption) can be modeled in the Proposed Design to show the impact of reduced heat gains. If the proposed roof is rated at a minimum initial solar reflectance of 0.70 and a minimum thermal emittance of 0.75, the Proposed Design can use a modeled reflectivity of 0.45 (accounting for degradation in actual reflectivity) versus the default reflectivity value of 0.30 which will be modeled for the Baseline Design.

Shading projections in the Proposed Design, which reduce the solar gains on the glazing, can also be modeled to demonstrate energy savings compared to the Baseline model, which will have fenestration flush to the exterior wall. Manually controlled interior shading devices such as blinds and curtains should not be modeled in either the Proposed or Baseline Design. However, automatically controlled interior shading devices can be modeled for credit in the Proposed Design, per ASHRAE Std. 90.1 Appendix G.

For existing buildings that are being renovated, the building envelope design parameters for the Baseline Design should be modeled using the existing (pre-retrofit) building envelope thermal parameters, rather than the ASHRAE Std. 90.1 prescriptive building envelope requirements for the specified climate. Any proposed changes to the building envelope (such as replacing windows or increasing roof insulation) should be modeled in the Proposed Design.

Lighting Systems for the Proposed Design should be modeled with the installed lighting power density, and

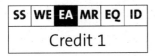
should account for all installed lighting on the site including interior ambient and task lighting, parking garage lighting and exterior lighting. Areas of core and shell buildings that do not have a lighting system specified must follow the ASHRAE Std. 90.1 method for modeling a lighting system in those areas. The lighting system power shall be determined according to the Building Area method for the appropriate building type. It must be identical to the system modeled in the Baseline Design.

Any daylight responsive lighting control systems can be directly modeled in the Proposed Design energy simulation. Credit can also be taken for occupant sensor lighting controls (ASHRAE Std. 90.1 Table G3.1, No.6); however, note that such controls are mandatory per 9.4.1.2 in classrooms, conference rooms and employee lunch and break rooms.

Lighting for the Baseline Design is modeled using the Building Area (9.5) or Space-by-Space (9.6) methods. The Baseline Design model should also include the Exterior Lighting Power Allowance (9.4.5).

Lighting excepted from the interior lighting power allowance should still be modeled in both the Proposed and Baseline Design; however, this lighting should be considered "Process" energy (ASHRAE Std. 90.1 Table G.3.1.6).

HVAC System Types will often vary between the Proposed Design and the Baseline Design models. The Proposed Design HVAC system type, quantities, capacities and efficiencies should reflect the actual design parameters except in cases where either a heating system or a cooling system has not been specified. Core and shell buildings that have not specified an HVAC system must follow the ASHRAE Std. 90.1 method for modeling an HVAC system. The system characteristics shall be identical to the system modeled in the Baseline Design.

If a heating system but no cooling system has been specified, the Proposed Design must include a cooling system modeled identically to the Baseline Design cooling system. If a cooling system, but no heating system has been specified, the Proposed Design must include a heating system modeled identically to the Baseline Design heating system. For areas of the project without heating or cooling systems (such as parking garages), there is no need to model heating or cooling systems in either the Proposed or Baseline Designs.

HVAC systems in green buildings are sometimes hybrid or experimental in nature. It may be necessary to approximate some or all of the functional aspects of Proposed Design experimental systems using the Exceptional Calculation Method (ASHRAE Std. 90.1 G2.5).

The Baseline HVAC System Type shall be determined using the actual building area, quantity of floors, occupancy (residential or non-residential), and heating fuel source per ASHRAE Std. 90.1 Tables G3.1.1A and G3.1.1B. The same Baseline HVAC system type should be used for the entire building except for mixed use occupancies, areas where occupancy or process loads differ significantly from the rest of the building, or areas with varying pressurization, cross-contamination or air circulation requirements (ASHRAE Std. 90.1 G3.1.1).

For projects served by existing HVAC systems, such as a central plant on a campus, Section 10(a) of Table G.3.1 states that when there is an existing HVAC system, the model shall reflect the actual system type using actual component capacities and efficiencies.

When the Baseline HVAC system type is defined as a single zone system, the Baseline Design should model exactly one single zone HVAC system per thermal block. Preheat coils should be modeled identically in the Proposed and Baseline cases whenever preheat can be modeled for the given Baseline system type (ASHRAE Std. 90.1 G3.1.2.3). Baseline System fan supply air volume should be based on a supply-air-to-room-air temperature difference of 20°F (ASHRAE Std. 90.1 G3.1.2.8). This supply air volume is used to calculate the total Baseline System brake horsepower (i.e., the sum of the supply, return, relief, and exhaust fan brake horsepower), which is used to calculate the total fan power for the Baseline System design (ASHRAE Std. 90.1 G3.1.2.9).

HVAC equipment capacities for the Baseline system should be oversized 15% for cooling, and 25% for heating (ASHRAE Std. 90.1 G3.1.2.2 and G3.1.2.2.1).

Economizers and exhaust air energy recovery systems should be modeled in the Baseline HVAC systems when required for the given climate zone and system parameters (ASHRAE Std. 90.1 G3.1.2.6 and G3.1.2.10).

Fan energy is separated from the cooling system in the Performance Rating Method. Thus, if the HVAC manufacturer provides an overall efficiency rating, such as an energy efficiency ratio (EER), it must be separated into the component energy using the coefficient of performance (COP) or other conversion (Equations G-A, G-B and G-C, Pages G-24 and G-26 of the ASHRAE 90.1-2004 User's Manual).

Unmet load hours (occupied periods where any zone is outside its temperature setpoints) may not exceed 300 hours for either the Baseline or Proposed Design. Also, the difference in unmet load hours between the Baseline and Proposed Design must be no greater than 50 (G3.1.2.2).

Other Systems regulated by ASHRAE/IESNA Standard 90.1-2004 include parking garage ventilation (ASHRAE Std. 90.1 6.4.3.3.5); freeze protection and snow/ice melting systems (6.4.3.7); exhaust air energy recovery, which applies to laboratory systems unless they comply with 6.5.7.2 (6.5.6.1); condenser heat recovery for service water heating, which applies primarily to high-rise residential occupancies, hotels, hospitals, and laundry facilities (6.5.6.2); kitchen hoods (6.5.7.1); laboratory fume hoods (6.5.7.2); swimming pools (7.4.2 and 7.4.5); all building power distribution systems (8.1); exit signs (9.4.3); exterior building grounds lighting (9.4.4); parking garage lighting (Table 9.5.1, 9.6.1); exterior lighting power (9.4.5); and all permanently wired electrical motors (10.4.1).

Where there are specific energy efficiency requirements for systems in ASHRAE Std. 90.1, the Baseline Design model shall reflect the lowest efficiency allowed by these requirements, and the Proposed Design shall reflect the actual installed efficiency.

Process Energy is considered to include, but is not limited to, office and general miscellaneous equipment, computers, elevators and escalators, kitchen cooking and refrigeration, laundry washing and drying, lighting exempt from the lighting power allowance (e.g., lighting integral to medical equipment) and other (e.g., waterfall pumps).

Process energy cost shall be equal to at least 25% of the Baseline Building Performance. For buildings where the process energy cost is less than 25% of the baseline building energy cost, the LEED submittal must include supporting documentation substantiating that process energy inputs are appropriate.

Table G-B of the ASHRAE 90.1-2004 User's Manual provides acceptable receptacle power densities per occupancy type, which can be incorporated into the building energy models. Other process energy inputs such as elevators, escalators, data center and telecom room com-

puting equipment, refrigeration, process lighting, and non-HVAC motors should be modeled based on actual power requirements, and assuming reasonable schedules of operation.

For EA Credit 1, process loads shall be identical for both the Baseline Building Performance rating and for the Proposed Building Performance rating. However, project teams may follow the Exceptional Calculation Method (ASHRAE Std. 90.1 G2.5) to document measures that reduce process loads. If credit is taken for process loads, the calculations must include reasonable assumptions for the baseline and proposed case.

Energy Rates are an important part of the Performance Rating Method. Rates from the local utility schedules are the default option to compute energy costs. The intent is to encourage simulations that provide Owners value, and help them minimize their energy costs. The modeler needs to use the same rates for both the budget and proposed building designs.

In the absence of a local utility rate schedule, or of energy rate schedules approved by the local ASHRAE/IESNA 90.1-2004 adopting authority, the applicant may use the energy rates listed in the state average prices published annually by the DOE Energy Information Administration (EIA) at www.eia.doe.gov. Regardless of the source of the rate schedule used, the same rate schedule must be used in both the baseline and proposed simulations.

On-Site Renewable Energy and Site-Recovered Energy costs are not included in the Proposed Building Performance (this is a LEED-CS exception to ASHRAE Std. 90.1 G2.4); therefore, these systems receive full credit using the Performance Rating Method.

Examples of on-site renewable energy systems include power generated by photovoltaics or wind turbines, and thermal energy collected by solar panels. Examples of site-recovered energy include heat recovered with chiller heat recovery systems or waste heat recovery units on distributed generation systems.

When the actual building design incorporates on-site renewable or site-recovered energy, the Baseline Design should be modeled based on the backup energy source for the actual building design, or electricity if no backup energy source is specified. Proposed Building Performance can be determined using one of the following two methods when on-site renewable energy or site-recovered energy is incorporated into the building project:

1. *Model the systems directly in the Proposed Design energy model.* If the building simulation program has the capability of modeling the on-site renewable or site-recovered energy systems, these systems can be modeled directly within the building energy model. The model should reflect the cost savings achieved through the on-site renewable or site-recovered energy systems.

2. *Model the systems using the Exceptional Calculation Method.* If the building simulation program does not have the capability of modeling the on-site renewable or site-recovered energy systems, the energy saved by these systems can be calculated using the Exceptional Calculation Method. The renewable or site-recovered energy cost can then be subtracted from the Proposed Building Performance.

The Exceptional Calculation Method (ASHRAE Std. 90.1 G2.5) shall be used to document any measures that cannot be adequately modeled in a simulation program. Documentation of energy savings using the exceptional calculation method shall include a list of the assumptions made for both the Baseline and Proposed Design, theoretical or empirical information supporting these assumptions, and the specific energy cost savings achieved based on the exceptional calculation. Examples of measures that may be modeled using the Exceptional Calculation Method include, but are not limited to, improvements to laboratory or kitchen exhaust systems, improved appliance efficiencies in high-rise residential buildings, graywater heat recovery, flat panel LCD computer monitors, improvements to refrigeration equipment efficiency, and zone VAV occupant sensor controls.

Common mistakes made using the Performance Rating Method. The following is a list of common mistakes to avoid when using the Performance Rating Method for developing EA Credit 1 calculations and submittals:

1. The Energy Cost Budget Method (Section 11) is incorrectly used rather than the Performance Rating Method (Appendix G) to obtain EA Credit 1 points.

2. Center-of-glass performance is incorrectly used rather than fenestration assembly U-factor and Solar Heat Gain Coefficient. The Building Envelope Requirements listed for each climate zone (ASHRAE Std. 90.1 Tables 5.5-1 through 5.5-8) refer to fenestration assembly maximum U-factors and SHGCs for glazing (also see ASHRAE Std. 90.1 Sections 5.2.8.4 and 5.2.8.5). The fenestration assembly performance accounts for the impacts of both the frame and the glazing. To determine the fenestration assembly U-factor and Solar Heat Gain Coefficient, Tables 8.1A and 8.2 should be used; OR the fenestration U-factors, SHGCs and visual light transmittance shall be certified and labeled in accordance with NFRC 100, 200 and 300 respectively (A8).

3. Baseline Design window area percentages are not calculated in accordance with the Performance Rating Method.

4. Baseline Design fenestration is not uniformly distributed across all four building orientations as required by the Performance Rating Method.

5. The Proposed Design does not account for portable (task) lighting.

6. Non-tradable surfaces (such as building facades) are incorrectly treated as tradable surfaces when determining the exterior lighting power allowance.

7. The Baseline HVAC System type is incorrectly determined.

8. The Baseline System Capacities, Design Supply Air Volume, or total fan power are incorrectly calculated.

9. Manufacturer's overall cooling energy efficiency ratings, (such as EERs) are not separated into the component energy using the coefficient of performance (COP) or other conversion factors in accordance with 90.1 requirements.

10. The quantities and/or types of chillers and boilers are not determined in accordance with the Performance Rating Method (ASHRAE Std. 90.1 G3.1.3.2, G3.1.3.7).

11. Insufficient information is provided for energy measures incorporating the Exceptional Calculation methodology.

12. Energy consumption is incorrectly used to calculate the Percentage Improvement rather than energy cost.

Calculating the Percentage Improvement requires the following steps:

First, the whole-building simulations are used to produce economic reports that show the total cost for electricity, gas and possibly other energy sources such as steam and chilled water. The total annual energy cost calculated for the Proposed Design simulation is the Proposed Building Performance. The average total energy cost for the four orientations simulated for

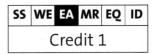

the Baseline Design is the Baseline Building Performance. ASHRAE Std. 90.1 also requires that the energy consumption and peak demand be reported for each building end-use. In DOE-2-based programs such as eQUEST or VisualDOE, this data can be found in the BEPS or BEPU and PS-E reports. In Trane® Trace™700, this information is reported in the Energy Consumption Summary. As with the Baseline Building Performance, the average of the four Baseline Building simulation results is used to calculate the energy consumption by end-use, and the peak demand by end-use.

=NOTE: separate point scales are provided for New and Existing Buildings in recognition of the constraints inherent in renovating an existing shell compared to new construction.

Example

The following example shows how the Performance Rating Method is applied to a 100,000-sq.ft. project. The design case uses a high performance envelope with 23% glazing, "Super T8" direct/indirect ambient lighting with supplemental task lighting, a VAV air system that receives chilled water from a 400-ton variable speed electric chiller, and 20 kW of photovoltaic panels installed on the roof. Using the Performance Rating Method system map, the budget HVAC system type is modeled as a Packaged VAV System with hot water reheat, variable speed fan control, and direct expansion cooling.

To determine the Proposed Building Performance, the energy modeler cre-

ates a design building energy simulation model using DOE-2, Trane Trace™700, EnergyPlus, Carrier HAP-E20 II or another hourly load and energy-modeling software tool. The model parameters for all loads, including receptacle and process loads and the expected building occupancy profile and schedule, are adjusted to determine central system capacities and energy use by system. Through parametric manipulation, the energy modeler working with the design team increases component efficiencies to exceed the referenced standard. The energy generated by the photovoltaic panels is calculated using PV Watts Version 1 software using the ASHRAE Std. 90.1 Exceptional Calculation Method.

The Proposed Building Performance is calculated as the total projected energy cost for the Proposed Design Energy Model minus the energy generated by the photovoltaic panels as calculated in PV Watts Version 1.

The Baseline Building Performance is then calculated by adjusting the model parameters to meet the requirements listed in ASHRAE/IESNA Standard 90.1-2004 Appendix G. The Baseline model includes the same plug and process loads and an identical building occupancy profile and schedule to the Proposed Design in order to accurately determine central system capacities and energy use by system.

For the Baseline Model, the energy modeler redistributes the glazing uniformly across all four building orientations, but

Figure 1: 3-D Rendering of Proposed Design

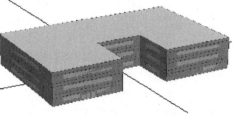

Figure 2: 3-D Rendering of Baseline Design

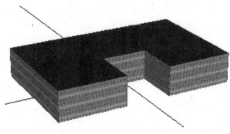

otherwise models the Baseline glazing percentage identically to the Proposed Design, since the ratio of window to wall area for the Proposed Design is less than 40%. The energy modeler adjusts the construction assembly types in accordance with ASHRAE Std. 90.1 Table G3.1.5, and to meet minimal Building Envelope Requirements for the building's climate zone. The Baseline HVAC System Type is modeled as a Packaged Variable Air Volume system with Hot Water Reheat (ASHRAE Std. 90.1 Table G3.1.1.A). The energy modeler uses minimum/prescriptive ASHRAE Std. 90.1 HVAC system component efficiencies and performs sizing runs to determine the fan supply air volume; and then uses this to calculate the total Baseline Design fan brake horsepower, and total Baseline Design fan power respectively.

The energy modeler performs the Baseline Design simulation first with the actual building orientation, and then rotating the building 90°, 180° and 270° respectively. For each of the four Baseline Building Design orientations, the energy modeler revises the window SHGC to reflect the minimum ASHRAE prescriptive requirements for the revised building orientations. The energy modeler takes the average of the total annual energy cost simulated for the four Baseline simulations to establish the Baseline Building Performance.

In the example, the General Building Energy Model Information is summarized in **Table 3,** the Baseline and Proposed Design input parameters are summarized in **Table 4,** the Baseline Performance is calculated in **Table 5,** and the Baseline Design and Proposed Design results, as well as the Percentage Improvement (**Equation 1**) are summarized in **Table 6.**

In **Tables 5 and 6**, energy is reported as site energy, not source energy. These four tables provide the format required for EA Credit 1 documentation submittal.

Exemplary Performance

There is no exemplary performance point available for this credit.

Precertification Submittal Documentation

Provide the LEED-CS Precertification Submittal Template, which includes the following:

❑ Narrative describing how the project intends to accomplish the credit requirements on the credit-specific Submittal Template signed by the appropriate design team member

❑ Confirmation of this intent from the owner/developer on the LEED-CS Precertification Submittal Template

Certification Submittal Documentation

This credit is submitted as part of the **Design Submittal**.

Design and Construction Credit Compliance

The LEED-CS v2.0 EA Credit 1 Submittal Template provides detailed tables and calculations to assist with the completion of this credit. Instructions are self-contained on the template and too lengthy to repeat here. Users are prompted for relevant project and model data, and the forms automatically generate percent savings and points achieved.

Equation 1

$$\text{Percentage Improvement} = 100 \times \left(1 - \frac{\text{Proposed Building Performance}}{\text{Baseline Building Performance}}\right)$$

Table 3: General Building Energy Model Information

Performance Rating Method Compliance Report				Page 1

Project Name:	Midrastleton Office Building			
Project Address:	2850 W. Washington Ave.	Date:	October 5, 2006	
Designer of Record:	Maddlestobum Architects	Telephone:	702-020-0400	
Contact Person:	Fenray Constrablik	Telephone:	702-014-9284	
City:	Las Vegas, NV	Principal Heating Source: ❑ Fossil Fuel ❑ Electricity ❑ Solar/Site Recovered ❑ Other		
Weather Data:	Las Vegas, NV (LAS-VENV.bin)			
Climate Zone:	3B			

Space Summary

Building Use	Conditioned Area (sf)	Unconditioned (sf)	Total (sf)
1. Office (Open Plan)	40,000		40,000
2. Office (Executive / Private)	30,000		30,000
3. Corridor	10,000		10,000
4. Lobby	5,000		5,000
5. Restrooms	5,000		5,000
6. Conference Room	4,000		4,000
7. Mechanical / Electrical Room	4,000		4,000
8. Copy Room	2,000		2,000
Total	100,000		100,000

Advisory Messages

	Proposed Building Design	Budget Building	Difference (Proposed Budget)
Number of hours heating loads not met (system / plant)	0	0	0
Number of hours cooling loads not met (system / plant)	0	0	0
Number of warnings	0	0	0
Number of errors	0	0	0
Number of defaults overridden	1	1	0

Description of differences between the budget building and proposed design not documented on other forms: ❑ Not Applicable ☒ Attached

Additional Building Information

Quantity of Floors	Three
Simulation Program	eQuest v. 3.55
Utility Rate: Electricity	Nevada Power Large General Service (average $0.0935/kWh)
Utility Rate: Natural Gas	Southwest Gas Medium General Service (average $1.04/therm)
Utility Rate: Steam or Hot Water	
Utility Rate: Chilled Water	
Utility Rate: Other	

| SS | WE | EA | MR | EQ | ID |

Credit 1

Performance Rating Method Compliance Report		Page 2
Comparison of Proposed Design versus Baseline Design Energy Model Inputs:		
Building Element	**Proposed Design Input**	**Baseline Design Input**
Envelope		
Above Grade Wall Construction(s)	1. Steel-frame Construction, R-19 insulation, 16 in. OC, 6" depth, U-factor = 0.109	Steel-frame Construction, R-13 insulation, U-factor = 0.124
Below Grade Wall Construction	Not applicable	Not Applicable
Roof Construction	Built-up Roof, Insulation entirely above deck, R-30 ci, U-factor = 0.032, Roof Reflectivity = 0.45 (cool roof)	Insulation entirely above deck, R-15ci, U-factor = 0.063, Roof Reflectivity = 0.30
Exterior Floor Construction	Not Applicable	Not Applicable
Slab-On-Grade Construction	Uninsulated, F-0.730	Uninsulated, F-0.730
Window-to-Gross Wall Ratio	23%	23%
Fenestration Type(s)	1. Dual-Pane Metal Frame tinted low-E glass doors with thermal break 2. Dual-Pane Metal-Frame low-E glass windows with thermal break	1. North Orientation 2. South, East, West Orientations
Fenestration Assembly U-factor	1. 0.61 2. 0.59	1. 0.57 2. 0.57
Fenestration Assembly SHGC	1. 0.25 2. 0.25	1. 0.39 2. 0.25
Fenestration Visual Light Transmittance	1. 0.44 2. 0.44	1. 0.44 2. 0.44
Fixed Shading Devices	1. None	1. None
Automated Movable Shading Devices	None	None
Electrical Systems & Process Loads		
Ambient Lighting Power Density, and Lighting Design Description	Building Area Method: 1.0 w/ft² Office	Building Area Method: 1.0 w/ft² Office
Process Lighting	None	None
Lighting Occupant Sensor Controls	Not installed	Not installed
Daylighting Controls	None	None
Exterior Lighting Power (Tradable Surfaces)	3.7 kW	4.2kW
Exterior Lighting Power (Non-Tradable Surfaces)	0.8kW	0.8kW
Receptacle Equipment	0.75 W/sf	0.75 W/sf
Elevators or Escalators	Two elevators operated intermittently (5kW per elevator with 490 equivalent full load hours of operation per elevator)	Two elevators operated intermittently (5kW per elevator with 490 equivalent full load hours of operation per elevator
Refrigeration Equipment	None	None
Other Process Loads	Telecom rooms, one per floor, 2.3kW peak wirh 3,680 equivalent full load hours of operation	Telecom rooms, one per floor, 2.3kW peak wirh 3,680 equivalent full load hours of operation

Table 4 continued: Baseline and Proposed Design Input Parameters

Performance Rating Method Compliance Report		Page 3
Comparison of Proposed Design versus Baseline Design Energy Model Inputs (Continued):		
Building Element	**Proposed Design Input**	**Baseline Design Input**
Mechanical & Plumbing Systems		
HVAC System Type(s)	1. Variable Air Volume with Reheat (one per floor) 2. Packaged single Zone systems with gas furnace (gas furnace not in actual design) serving telecom rooms and elevator equipment room	System Type 5: Packaged Rooftop Variable Air Volume with Reheat. Packaged Single Zone systems with gas furnace serving telecom rooms and elevator equipment room.
Design Supple Air Temperature Differential	23 deg. F	20 deg. F
Fan Control	VSD Control	VSD Control
Fan Power	1. AH-1: 14.0 bhp supply; 5.6 bhp return 2. AH-2: 14.5 bhp supply; 5.8 bhp return 3. AH-3: 14.4 bhp supply; 5.8 bhp return	94.8 total brake horsepower; 75.3kW total fan power (Supply Fans + Return Fans)
Economizer Control	Differential Temperature Economizers with maximum temperature of 70 deg. F	None
Demand Control Ventilation	Outside air quantity based on DCV zone sensors; Minimum Outside Air Sizing method set by critical zone	None
Unitary Equipment Cooling Efficiency	1. 2. 12 SEER for two small PSZ systems	1. 8.8 EER for Packaged Rooftop VAV units 2. 12 SEER for two small PSZ systems
Unitary Equipment Heating Efficiency	80% furnace efficiency for two small PSZ units	80% furnace efficiency for two small PSZ units
Chiller Type, Capacity, and Efficiency	one 300-ton VSD centrifugal chiller: 0.58kW/ton full load-efficiency, variable speed control for part-load operation	Not Applicable
Cooling Tower	one two-cell cooling tower; each cell has a 15 hp fan with variable speed control	Not Applicable
Boiler Efficiency	one 85% efficient boiler, 2.0 MBTUH	two boilers, 75% thermal efficiency; 1.25 MBTUH each
Chilled Water Loop and Pump Parameters	Variable primary flow with 25 hp variable speed pump; Chilled Water Temperature reset from 42 to 50 deg. F	Not Applicable
Condenser Water Loop and Pump Parameters	Constant flow with 25 hp variable speed pump; Condenser Water Temperature reset from 70 to 85 deg. F	Not Applicable
Hot Water Loop and Pump Parameters	Variable primary flow with 3 hp variable speed pump; Hot Water temperature reset based on load between 150 deg. and 180 deg. F	Variable primary flow with 3 hp constant speed pump; Hot water supply temperature reset based on outdoor dry-bulb temperature using the following schedule: 180 deg. F at 20 deg. F and below, 150 deg. F at 50 deg. F and above, and ramped linearly between 180 deg. F and 150 deg. F at temperatures between 20 deg. F and 50 deg. F
Domestic Hot Water System(s)	100 gallon storage gas water heater with 80% thermal efficiency, 175,000 btuh capacity, and 1,319 Btuh standby losses	100 gallon storage gas water heater with 80% thermal efficiency, 175,000 btuh capacity, and 1,319 Btuh standby losses

Table 5: Baseline Performance

Performance Rating Method Compliance Report	Page 4

Baseline Building Performance Table

Baseline Building Energy Summary by End Use

End Use	Process?	Energy Type	0° rotation Energy [10⁶ Btu]	0° rotation Peak [10⁶ Btuh]	90° rotation Energy [10⁶ Btu]	90° rotation Peak [10⁶ Btuh]	180° rotation Energy [10⁶ Btu]	180° rotation Peak [10⁶ Btuh]	270° rotation Energy [10⁶ Btu]	270° rotation Peak [10⁶ Btuh]	Average Energy [10⁶ Btu]	Average Peak [10⁶ Btuh]	Average Cost [$/yr]
Interior Lighting		Electricity	1,137.2	418.7	1,137.2	418.7	1,137.2	418.7	1,137.2	418.7	1,137.2	418.7	$31,990
Interior Lighting (Process)	X	Electricity											$0
Exterior Lighting		Electricity	54.4	17.1	54.4	17.1	54.4	17.1	54.4	17.1	54.4	17.1	$1,531
Space Heating (fuel 1)		Natural Gas	515.8	2,300.0	525.6	2,300.0	486.7	2,300.0	494.3	2,300.0	505.6	2,300.0	$4,916
Space Heating (fuel 2)		Electricity											$0
Space Cooling		Electricity	1,299.4	836.8	1,308.9	843.8	1,298.1	815.7	1,310.3	812.3	1,304.2	827.1	$36,687
Pumps		Electricity	3.2	3.1	3.3	3.1	2.9	3.1	2.9	3.1	3.1	3.1	$86
Heat Rejection		Electricity											$0
Fans - Interior		Electricity	222.5	106.9	228.1	108.6	223.8	106.8	223.5	106.5	224.5	107.2	$6,315
Fans - Parking Garage		Electricity											$0
Service Water Heating (fuel 1)		Natural Gas	57.3	10.4	57.3	10.4	57.3	10.4	57.3	10.4	57.3	10.4	$557
Service Water Heating (fuel 2)		Electricity											$0
Receptacle Equipment	X	Electricity	1,040.7	273.0	1,040.7	273.0	1,040.7	273.0	1,040.7	273.0	1,040.7	273.0	$29,276
Refrigeration (food, etc.)	X	Electricity											$0
Cooking (commercial, fuel 1)	X	Electricity											$0
Cooking (commercial, fuel 2)	X	Electricity											$0
Elevators and Escalators	X	Electricity	16.7	17.1	16.7	17.1	16.7	17.1	16.7	17.1	16.7	17.1	$470
Other Process	X	Electricity	28.9	7.8	28.9	7.8	28.9	7.8	28.9	7.8	28.9	7.8	$813
Total Building Consumption/Demand			4,376.1	3,990.9	4,401.2	3,999.6	4,346.7	3,969.7	4,366.3	3,965.9	4,372.6	3,981.5	$112,641
Total Process Energy			1,086.3	297.9	1,086.3	297.9	1,086.3	297.9	1,086.3	297.9	1,086.3	297.9	$30,559

Note: Energy Consumption is listed in units of site energy
10³ Btu = kWh x 3.413   10³ Btu = therms / 100

Baseline Building Energy Cost and Consumption by Fuel Type

Energy Type	0° rotation Energy Consumption [10³ Btu]	0° rotation Energy Cost [$/Yr]	90° rotation Energy Consumption [10³ Btu]	90° rotation Energy Cost [$/Yr]	180° rotation Energy Consumption [10³ Btu]	180° rotation Energy Cost [$/Yr]	270° rotation Energy Consumption [10³ Btu]	270° rotation Energy Cost [$/Yr]	Average Energy Consumption [10³ Btu]	Average Energy Cost [$/Yr]
Electricity	3,803.0	$107,174	3,818.3	$107.398	3,802.7	$107,021	3,814.7	$107,079	3,809.7	$107,168
Natural Gas	573.1	$5,563	582.9	$5,650	544.0	$5,305	551.6	$5,373	562.9	$5,473
Steam/Hot Water										
Other										
Total	4,376.1	$112,737	4,401.2	$113,048	4,346.7	$112,326	4,366.3	$112,452	4,372.6	$112,641

The process energy cost is 27% of the Baseline Building Performance. This meets the requirements of LEED EAc1.

Table 6: Percentage Improvement

Performance Rating Method Compliance Report						Page 5
Performance Rating Table				EAc1 Points:	**4**	
Energy Summary by End Use				EAc2 Points:	**1**	

End Use	Energy Type	Proposed Building Energy [10⁶ Btu]	Proposed Building Peak [10³ Btu/h]	Baseline Building Energy [10⁶ Btu]	Baseline Building Peak [10³ Btu/h]	Energy [%]
Interior Lighting (Ambient)	Electricity	1,137.2	418.7	1,137.2	418.7	0%
Interior Lighting (Process)	Electricity					
Exterior Lighting	Electricity	49.0	15.4	54.4	17.1	10%
Space Heating (fuel 1)	Natural Gas	360.2	1,600.0	505.6	2,300.0	29%
Space Heating (fuel 2)	Electricity					
Space Cooling	Electricity	452.0	331.1	1,304.2	827.1	65%
Pumps	Electricity	230.7	79.6	3.1	3.1	-7426%
Heat Rejection	Electricity	23.9	20.5			
Fans - Interior	Electricity	177.8	76.2	224.5	107.2	21%
Fans - Parking Garage	Electricity					
Service Water Heating (fuel 1)	Natural Gas	57.3	10.4	57.3	10.4	0%
Service Water Heating (fuel 2)	Electricity					
Receptacle Equipment	Electricity	1,040.7	273.0	1,040.7	273.0	0%
Refrigeration (food, etc.)	Electricity					
Cooking (commercial, fuel 1)	Natural Gas					
Cooking (commercial, fuel 2)	Electricity					
Elevators and Escalators	Electricity	16.7	17.1	16.7	17.1	0%
Other Process	Electricity	28.9	7.8	28.9	7.8	0%
Total Building Consumption		**3,573.9**	**2,849.8**	**4.372.6**	**3,981.5**	**22%**

Note: Energy Consumption is listed in units of site energy
10^3 Btu = kWh x 3.413 10^3 Btu = therms / 100

Type	Proposed Building Energy Use [10⁶ Btu]	Proposed Building Energy Cost [$/yr]	Baseline Building Energy Use [10⁶ Btu]	Baseline Building Energy Cost [$/yr]	Percentage Improvement Energy %	Percentage Improvement Cost %
Nonrenewable (Regulated & Unregulated)						
Electricity	3,156.4	$86,453	3,809.7	$107,168	17%	19%
Natural Gas	417.5	$4,184	562.9	$5,473	26%	24%
Steam or Hot Water						
Chilled Water						
Other						
Total Nonrenewable (Regulated & Unregulated)	**3,573.9**	**$90,638**	**4,372.6**	**$112,641**	**22%**	**24%**

Exceptional Calculation Method Savings (savings indicated as negative numbers)	Proposed Building Energy Use [10⁶ Btu]	Proposed Building Energy Cost [$/yr]	Baseline Building Energy Use [10⁶ Btu]	Baseline Building Energy Cost [$/yr]	Percentage Improvement Energy %	Percentage Improvement Cost %
Site-Generated Renewable (REC)	(96.4)	$ (2,639)			2%	2%
Site Recovered						
Exceptional Calculation #1 Savings						
Exceptional Calculation #2 Savings						
Exceptional Calculation #3 Savings						
Total including exceptional calculations	**3,477.5**	**$87,999**	**4,372.6**	**$112,641**	**25%**	**26%**

Percentage Improvement = 100 x [1 - (Proposed Building Performance / Baseline Building Performance)]	**21.88%**
Percent Renewable = REC / (Proposed Building Performance + REC)	**2.91%**

Tenant Sales or Lease Agreement Credit Compliance

This compliance method is not available for this credit.

Considerations

Cost Issues

Some energy-efficiency measures may not require additional first costs. Many measures that do result in higher capital costs may generate cost savings from lower energy use, smaller equipment, reduced space needs for mechanical and electrical equipment, and utility rebates. These savings may vastly exceed the incremental capital costs associated with the energy efficiency measures.

The importance of even small energy-efficiency measures is significant. For instance, replacing one incandescent lamp with a fluorescent lamp will result in $30 to $50 in energy cost savings over the operating lifetime of the lamp.

Environmental Issues

Commercial and residential buildings consume approximately 2/3 of the electricity and 1/3 of all energy in the United States. Conventional forms of energy production may have devastating environmental effects. Production of electricity from fossil fuels creates air and water pollution; hydroelectric generation plants can make waterways uninhabitable for indigenous fish; and nuclear power has safety concerns as well as problems with disposal of spent fuel.

Energy efficiency in buildings limits the harmful environmental side effects of energy generation, distribution and consumption. In an integrated design process, energy efficiency measures can be implemented in conjunction with indoor environmental quality measures to improve building comfort, while reducing facility operating costs.

Resources

Please see the USGBC website at www. usgbc.org/resources for more specific resources on materials sources and other technical information.

Websites

Advanced Buildings Technologies & Practices

Natural Resources Canada

www.advancedbuildings.org

This web resource supported by Natural Resources Canada presents energy efficient technologies and strategies for commercial buildings, along with pertinent case studies.

American Council for an Energy Efficient Economy (ACEEE)

www.aceee.org

(202) 429-8873

ACEEE is a nonprofit organization dedicated to advancing energy efficiency through technical and policy assessments; advising policymakers and program managers; collaborating with businesses, public interest groups, and other organizations; and providing education and outreach through conferences, workshops and publications.

American Society of Heating, Refrigeration and Air Conditioning Engineers (ASHRAE)

www.ashrae.org

(800) 527-4723

ASHRAE has developed a number of publications on energy use in existing buildings, including Standard 100-1995: Energy Conservation in Existing Buildings. This standard defines methods for energy surveys, provides guidance for operation and maintenance, and describes building and equipment modifications that result in energy conservation. Two publications referenced by this credit (ASHRAE 90.1-2004 and ASHRAE

Advanced Energy Design Guide for Small Office Buildings 2004) are available through ASHRAE.

Building Energy Codes Program

U.S. Department of Energy

www.energycodes.gov

(800) DIAL-DOE

The Building Energy Codes program is updating the COM*Check*EZ™ compliance tool to include ASHRAE/IESNA 90.1-2004. This compliance tool includes the prescriptive path and trade-off compliance methods. The software generates appropriate compliance forms as well.

Building Energy Use and Cost Analysis Software

www.doe2.com

Information and products from the developers of DOE-2 and DOE-2-based products including eQUEST, PowerDOE and COM*check*-Plus™.

ENERGY STAR®

www.energystar.gov

(888) 782-7937

ENERGY STAR is a government/industry partnership managed by the U.S. Environmental Protection Agency and the U.S. Department of Energy. The program's website offers energy management strategies, benchmarking software tools for buildings, product procurement guidelines and lists of ENERGY STAR-labeled products and buildings.

Building Upgrade Manual

www.energystar.gov/index. cfm?c=business.bus_upgrade_ manual&layout=print

This document is a guide for ENERGY STAR Buildings Partners to use in planning and implementing energy efficiency upgrades in their facilities, and can be used as a comprehensive framework for an energy strategy.

Energy-10TM Energy Simulation Software

National Renewable Energy Program (NREL)

www.nrel.gov/buildings/energy10>www. nrel.gov/buildings/energy10.html

(303) 275-3000

and

Sustainable Buildings Industry Council (SBIC)

www.Energy-10.com

(202) 628-7400 ext. 210

Energy-10TM is an award-winning software tool for designing low-energy buildings. Energy-10TM integrates daylighting, passive solar heating, and low-energy cooling strategies with energy-efficient shell design and mechanical equipment. The program is applicable to small commercial and residential buildings with up to two zones and simple HVAC equipment.

The Energy-10TM software was developed by the National Renewable Energy Laboratory under funding from the Office of Building Technologies, Energy Efficiency and Renewable Energy, U.S. Department of Energy. It is distributed by the Sustainable Buildings Industry Council under license to the Midwest Research Institute.

New Buildings Institute (NBI)

www.newbuildings.org

The mission of NBI is to encourage the efficient use of energy in buildings and to mitigate the adverse environmental impacts resulting from energy use. The site includes helpful information to plan building upgrades, such as the Advanced Lighting Guidelines that describe energy-efficient lighting strategies.

Office of Energy Efficiency and Renewable Energy

U.S. Department of Energy

www.eere.energy.gov/EE/buildings.html

(877) 337-3463

This extensive website for energy efficiency is linked to a number of DOE-funded sites that address buildings and energy. Of particular interest is the tools directory that includes the Commercial Buildings Energy Consumption Tool for estimating end-use consumption in commercial buildings. The tool allows the user to define a set of buildings by principal activity, size, vintage, region, climate zone and fuels (main heat, secondary heat, cooling and water heating), and to view the resulting energy consumption and expenditure estimates in tabular format.

Print Media

ASHRAE Publication 90.1-2004 User's Manual

The 90.1–2004 User's Manual was developed as a companion document to the ANSI/ASHRAE/IESNA Standard 90.1–2004 (Energy Standard for Buildings Except Low-Rise Residential Buildings). The User's Manual explains the new standard and includes sample calculations, useful reference material, and information on the intent and application of the standard.

ANSI/IESNA RP-1-04, American National Standard Practice for Office Lighting, ANSI

Daylight in Buildings: A Source Book on Daylighting Systems and Components, Lawrence Berkeley National Laboratory, Environmental Energy Technologies Division, Download at: http://gaia.lbl.gov/iea21/ (See Chapter 5 – Daylight-Responsive Controls)

Design Brief — Lighting Controls Energy Design Resources

www.energydesignresources.com

Developed by Southern California Edison.

Electricity Used by Office Equipment and Network Equipment in the U.S.: Detailed Report and Appendices, Kawamoto, et al, February 2001, Ernest Orlando, Lawrence Berkeley National Laboratory, University of California, Berkeley, CA.; Download at http://enduse.lbl.gov/Projects/InfoTech.html

Energy Information Agency's (EIA) Commercial Building Energy Consumption Survey (CBECS)

www.eia.doe.gov

IESNA Lighting Handbook, Ninth Edition, IESNA, 2000.

This handbook for industry professionals includes comprehensive information about lighting concepts, techniques, application, procedures and systems.

International Energy Agency Solar Heating and Cooling Programme

www.iea-shc.org

A report of the International Energy Agency (IEA) Solar Heating and Cooling Programme, Energy Conservation in Buildings and Community Systems (IEA SHC Task 21/ECBCS Annex 29, July 2000). Published by the Lawrence Berkeley National Laboratory with support from the Energy Design Resources. LBNL Report Number: LBNL-47493. *Advanced Lighting Guidelines: 2001 Edition*, Chapter 8 – Lighting Controls

Mechanical and Electrical Equipment for Buildings, 9th Edition by Benjamin Stein and John S. Reynolds, John Wiley and Sons, 2000. This reference resource details information on the relationship between mechanical and electrical systems in buildings.

New Buildings Institute, Inc, Published by New Buildings Inc. Available as a free download or purchased as a printed manual of 390 pages.

www.newbuildings.org/lighting.htm

Sustainable Building Technical Manual,
Public Technology Institute, 1996

www.pti.org

Definitions

Baseline Building Performance is the annual energy cost for a building design intended for use as a baseline for rating above standard design, as defined in ASHRAE 90.1-2004 Informative Appendix G.

Daylighting is the controlled admission of natural light into a space through glazing with the intent of reducing or eliminating electric lighting. By utilizing solar light, daylighting creates a stimulating and productive environment for building occupants.

An **ENERGY STAR**® rating is the rating a building earns using the ENERGY STAR Portfolio Manager to compare building energy performance to similar buildings in similar climates. A score of 50 represents average building performance.

Interior Lighting Power Allowance is the maximum light power in watts allowed for the interior of a building.

Lighting Power Density (LPD) is the installed lighting power, per unit area.

Percentage Improvement is the percent energy cost savings for the Proposed Building Performance versus the Baseline Building Performance.

Proposed Building Performance is the annual energy cost calculated for a proposed design, as defined in ASHRAE 90.1-2004 Informative Appendix G.

Rated Power is the nameplate power on a piece of equipment. It represents the capacity of the unit and is the maximum a unit will draw.

Receptacle Load refers to all equipment that is plugged into the electrical system, from office equipment to refrigerators.

On-Site Renewable Energy

Intent

Encourage and recognize increasing levels of on-site renewable energy self-supply in order to reduce environmental and economic impacts associated with fossil fuel energy use.

Requirements

Use on-site renewable energy systems to offset building energy cost. Calculate project performance by expressing the energy produced by the renewable systems as a percentage of the building annual energy cost.

Use the building annual energy cost calculated in EA Credit 1 or use the Department of Energy (DOE) Commercial Buildings Energy Consumption Survey (CBECS) database to determine the estimated electricity use. (See **Table 4** for the default energy consumption intensity for different building types.)

% Renewable Energy	Points
1%	1

Potential Technologies & Strategies

Assess the project for non-polluting and renewable energy potential including solar, wind, geothermal, low-impact hydro, biomass and bio-gas strategies. When applying these strategies, take advantage of net metering with the local utility.

Summary of Referenced Standard

ASHRAE/IESNA 90.1-2004: Energy Standard For Buildings Except Low-Rise

Residential

American Society of Heating, Refrigerating and Air-Conditioning Engineers

www.ashrae.org

(800) 527-4723

On-site renewable or site-recovered energy that might be used to capture EA Credit 2 is handled as a special case in the modeling process. If either renewable or recovered energy is produced at the site, the Performance Rating Method considers it free energy and it is not included in the Design Energy Cost. See the Calculations section for details.

Approach and Implementation

Renewable energy systems include technologies designed to capture solar, wind, geothermal, water, or bio-based energy to satisfy on-site electric power demand, or to directly offset space-heating, space-cooling, or water heating energy consumption. Renewable energy systems should be installed and commissioned to maximize useful contributions of renewable energy.

Eligible systems will produce either electric power and/or thermal energy for use on-site. Systems producing on-site renewable electrical power should be designed to facilitate net metering back to the grid for periods when renewable energy system output exceeds the site demand. Cost savings from renewable energy systems' shall be reported exclusive of energy costs associated with system operation (i.e., deduct energy costs of pumps, fans, and other auxiliary devices).

Renewable Energy Systems Eligible for EA Credit 2

❑ **Electrical Systems:** Photovoltaic (PV), wind, hydro, wave, tidal, and bio-fuel based electrical production systems deployed at the project site are renewable energy technologies and may be eligible for this credit.

❑ **Geothermal Energy Systems:** Geothermal energy systems using deep-earth water or steam sources (and not using vapor compression systems for heat transfer) may be eligible for this credit. These systems may either produce electric power or provide thermal energy for primary use at the building.

❑ **Solar Thermal Systems:** Active solar thermal energy systems that employ collection panels; heat transfer mechanical components, such as pumps or fans, and a defined heat storage system, such as a hot water tank are eligible for this credit. Thermo-siphon solar and storage tank "batch heaters" are also eligible.

Systems Not Eligible for EA Credit 2

❑ **Architectural Features:** Architectural passive solar and daylighting strategies provide significant energy savings that are chiefly efficiency related. Their contributions shall be documented in EA Prerequisite 2, and may be considered under EA Credit 1.

❑ **Geo-exchange Systems:** (a.k.a. geothermal or ground-source heat pumps) Earth-coupled HVAC applications which do not obtain significant quantities of deep-earth heat, and use vapor-compression systems for heat transfer are not eligible as renewable energy systems. These systems are adequately addressed in EA Prerequisite 2, and may be considered under EA Credit 1.

❏ **"Green Power":** Green power products (tradable renewable certificates, green TAGs, and renewable energy certificates [RECs]) that are purchased from qualified contractual sources and delivered to the site via electric transmission lines shall be accounted for in EA Credit 6.

Table 1: EA Credit 2 Eligible On-Site Renewable Energy Systems

- Photovoltaic systems
- Solar thermal systems
- Bio-fuel based electrical systems (subject to **Table 3**)
- Geothermal heating systems
- Geothermal electric systems
- Low-impact hydro electric power systems
- Wave and tidal power systems

Table 2: EA Credit 2 Ineligible On-Site Renewable Energy Systems

- Architectural features
- Passive solar strategies
- Daylighting strategies
- Geo-exchange systems (Ground Source Heat Pumps)
- Renewable or Green-power from off-site sources

Strategies

Design and specify the use of on-site non-polluting renewable technologies to contribute to the total energy requirements of the project. Consider and employ photovoltaic, solar thermal, geothermal, wind, biomass and bio-gas energy technologies. Make use of net metering arrangements with local utilities or electric service providers.

Core and Shell Concerns

The threshold for this credit was reduced to 1% and the total points available for this credit were reduced to 1. This reduction was made to tailor this credit to the core and shell market. This change still gives credit for providing renewable

Table 3: Eligible & Ineligible Bio-Fuels

For the purposes of EA Credit 2, electrical production using the following bio-fuels shall be considered renewable energy:
• Untreated wood waste including mill residues • Agricultural crops or waste • Animal waste and other organic waste • Landfill gas
Electrical production based on the following bio-fuels are excluded from eligibility for this credit:
• Combustion of municipal solid waste • Forestry biomass waste, other than mill residue • Wood that has been coated with paints, plastics, or plastic laminate • Wood that has been treated for preservation with materials containing halogens, chlorine compounds, halide compounds, chromated copper arsenate (CCA), or arsenic. If more than 1% of the wood fuel has been treated with these compounds, the energy system shall be considered ineligible for EA Credit 2.

energy systems at a level that is reasonable and achievable for the speculative development market.

Calculations

The fraction of energy cost supplied by the renewable energy systems is calculated against the Proposed Building Performance determined in EA Credit 1.

If no energy simulation was performed for EA Credit 1, then the fraction of energy cost shall be calculated based on the U.S. Department of Energy (DOE) Energy Information Administration (EIA) 2003 Commercial Sector Average Energy Costs by State (**Table 5**), in conjunction with the Commercial Buildings Energy Consumption Survey (CBECS) database of annual electricity and natural gas usage per square foot (see **Table 4**). This database provides electricity and fuel consumption factors in kWh/sq.ft. and kBtu/sq.ft. for various building types in the United States. Costs per square foot can be determined by multiplying the average electricity and natural gas costs

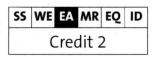

Table 4: Default Energy Consumption Intensity for Different Building Types (from EIA 1999 Commercial Building Energy Consumption Survey

Building Type	Median Electrical Intensity (kWh/sf-yr)	Median Non-Electrical Fuel Intensity (kBtu/sf-yr)
Education	6.6	52.5
Food Sales	58.9	143.3
Food Service	28.7	137.8
Health Care Inpatient	21.5	50.2
Health Care Outpatient	9.7	56.5
Lodging	12.6	39.2
Retail (Other than Mall)	8.0	18.0
Enclosed and Strip Malls	14.5	50.6
Office	11.7	58.5
Public Assembly	6.8	72.9
Public Order and Safety	4.1	23.7
Religious Worship	2.5	103.6
Service	6.1	33.8
Warehouse and Storage	3.0	96.9
Other	13.8	52.5

Table 5: Default Energy Costs by State (from EIA 2003 Commercial Sector Average Energy Costs by State)

State	Electricity ($/kWh)	Natural Gas ($/kBtu)	State	Electricity ($/kWh)	Natural Gas ($/kBtu)
Alabama	$0.0682	$0.00938	Missouri	$0.0505	$0.00796
Alaska	$0.1646	$0.00355	Montana	$0.0601	$0.00623
Arizona	$0.0670	$0.00758	Nebraska	$0.0500	$0.00698
Arkansas	$0.0526	$0.00668	Nevada	$0.0955	$0.00723
California	$0.1171	$0.00843	New Hampshire	$0.0973	$0.00917
Colorado	$0.0597	$0.00476	New Jersey	$0.0835	$0.00835
Connecticut	$0.0900	$0.01101	New Mexico	$0.0737	$0.00659
Delaware	$0.0693	$0.00840	New York	$0.1113	$0.00895
District of Columbia	$0.0645	$0.01266	North Carolina	$0.0641	$0.00863
			North Dakota	$0.0547	$0.00682
Florida	$0.0678	$0.001083	Ohio	$0.0723	$0.00789
Georgia	$0.0669	$0.00957	Oklahoma	$0.0571	$0.00755
Hawaii	$0.1502	$0.001926	Oregon	$0.0657	$0.00775
Idaho	$0.0601	$0.00612	Pennsylvania	$0.0819	$0.00898
Illinois	$0.0758	$0.00794	Rhode Island	$0.0834	$0.00964
Indiana	$0.0585	$0.00844	South Carolina	$0.0652	$0.00992
Iowa	$0.0602	$0.00750	South Dakota	$0.0605	$0.00693
Kansas	$0.0611	$0.00753	Tennessee	$0.0631	$0.00832
Kentucky	$0.0520	$0.00760	Texas	$0.0695	$0.00757
Louisiana	$0.0664	$0.00861	Utah	$0.0538	$0.00539
Maine	$0.1019	$0.01086	Vermont	$0.1087	$0.00778
Maryland	$0.0659	$0.00807	Virginia	$0.0572	$0.00920
Massachusetts	$0.0848	$0.01071	Washington	$0.0624	$0.00669
Michigan	$0.0701	$0.00631	West Virginia	$0.0545	$0.00734
Minnesota	$0.0546	$0.00778	Wisconsin	$0.0645	$0.00822
Mississippi	$0.0721	NA	Wyoming	$0.0548	$0.00469

by the electricity and fuel consumption factors respectively.

The quantity of energy generated by on-site renewable systems should be estimated (either using the same simulation tool employed for EA Credit 1 calculations or a separate calculation methodology). Performance of the renewable system may be predicted using a bin type calculation. This requires the applicant to account for the contribution of variables associated with the renewable source. For example, a BIPV design would include the effects of sunny, cloudy and overcast conditions, the orientation and attitude of the array, and system losses. The method used to predict the quantity of energy generated by on-site renewable systems should be clearly stated in the LEED submittal narrative.

The following example illustrates how to calculate the renewable energy cost contribution for EA Credit 2.

Calculation Based on EA Credit 1 Simulation

Once the amount of energy generated by the renewable system is calculated, an energy cost must be computed to establish the EA Credit 2 level of achievement. To assign a dollar value to the on-site energy, either use local utility rates or determine the "virtual" energy rate by dividing the annual energy cost for the specified fuel type by the annual energy consumption for that fuel type. Multiply the predicted on-site energy produced by the applicable energy rate for this fuel type.

When calculating the total energy cost of the Proposed Design using the Performance Rating Method, the contribution of any on-site renewable or recovered energy is accounted for by deducting the associated utility costs. In other words, the Renewable Energy Cost is excluded from the Proposed Building Performance. Core and shell buildings must use the total energy cost of the Proposed Design

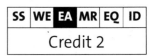
including all tenant energy costs modeled in EA Credit 1.

In the example project described in EA Credit 1, 20 kW of photovoltaics contribute 28,245 kWh (or 96.4 MBtu) of energy to meet building electric power requirements. The virtual electric rate for the project is used for this example and is calculated by dividing the annual electric energy cost simulated for the Proposed Design ($81,485) by the annual electric energy consumption simulated for the Proposed Design (2975.0 MBtu), resulting in a virtual electric rate of $0.094/kWh (or $27.39/MBtu). This virtual electric rate is then multiplied by the PV contribution of 28,245 kWh to calculate the Renewable Energy Cost (REC) contribution from the PV of $2,655.

The predicted Proposed Design building annual energy cost, prior to the energy cost offset by the PV, is $85,669. Dividing the REC by the building annual energy cost yields the Percent Renewable Energy (3.1%), which qualifies the project for one point under EA Credit 2.

Calculation Based on CBECS Data

If no energy performance calculation has been performed for the project, CBECS data can be used to determine the annual energy consumption intensities (kWh/sq.ft. and therms/sq.ft.) based on building type. The total estimated energy consumption for the project is then calculated by multiplying the energy consumption intensities by the total building area. Core and shell buildings must use the total square footage of the building including all tenant spaces. Building Annual Energy Cost is then calculated by summing the product of the energy consumption and average cost for electricity and natural gas, where the average electricity and natural gas costs are determined based on EIA 2003 commercial sector rates for the state the building is located in (see **Table 5**). The Renewable Energy Cost

(REC) is calculated by multiplying the renewable energy contribution by either the local utility rate or the EIA 2003 average energy cost for the renewable fuel type. Dividing the REC by the Building Annual energy cost yields the Percent Renewable Energy.

Example EA Credit 2 Calculation Based on CBECS Data

If a project is a 1,000,000-sq.ft. office building in New York, determine how much renewable energy is required to meet the requirements of EA Credit 2 by using **Tables 4 and 5** to find the default energy consumption intensity for office buildings and energy costs for New York State.

Default Annual Electrical Costs

1,000,000 sf x 11.7 kWh/sf-yr x $0.1113/kWh = $1,302,210/yr

Default Annual Fuel Costs

1,000,000 sf x 58.3kBtu/sf-yr x $0.00895/kWh = $521,785/yr

Default Total Annual Energy Costs

$1,302,210/yr + $521,785/yr = $1,823,995/yr

This project would need to meet 1% of its annual energy costs ($18,240) with renewable energy systems to earn one point under EA Credit 2. The project plans to install a 190-kW PV system that is predicted to produce 285,000 kWh/yr. Using the default cost of electricity for New York State in **Table 5** ($0.1113/kWh) this system will provide $31,720/yr of electricity or 1.7%—enough for one point under EA Credit 2.

Exemplary Performance

There is no exemplary performance point available for this credit.

Precertification Submittal Documentation

Provide the LEED-CS Precertification Submittal Template, which includes the following:

❑ Narrative describing how the project intends to accomplish the credit requirements on the credit-specific Submittal Template signed by the appropriate design team member

❑ Confirmation of this intent from the owner/developer on the LEED-CS Precertification Submittal Template

Certification Submittal Documentation

This credit is submitted as part of the **Design Submittal**.

Design and Construction Credit Compliance

The EA Credit 2 Submittal Template provides calculations to assist with the completion of this credit. The following project data and calculation information is required to document prerequisite compliance using the LEED-CS v2.0 Submittal Templates:

❑ Provide the on-site Renewable Energy Source(s) used, the annual energy generated from each source, and the backup fuel for each source (i.e., the fuel that is used when the renewable energy source is unavailable).

❑ Describe the source of the annual energy cost information (energy model or industry database), and provide the appropriate energy values and costs.

Tenant Sales or Lease Agreement Credit Compliance

This compliance method is not available for this credit.

Considerations

Renewable energy can be generated on a building site by using technologies that convert energy from the sun, wind and biomass into usable energy. On-site renewable energy is superior to conventional energy sources such as coal, nuclear, oil, natural gas and hydropower generation, because of its negligible transportation costs and impacts. In addition to preventing environmental degradation, on-site use of renewable power can improve power reliability and reduce reliance on the local power distribution grid.

Environmental Issues

Use of renewable energy reduces environmental impacts associated with utility energy production and use. These impacts include natural resource destruction, air pollution and water pollution. Utilization of biomass can divert an estimated 350 million tons of woody construction, demolition and land-clearing waste from landfills each year. Conversely, air pollution will occur due to incomplete combustion if these wastes are not processed properly.

Economic Issues

Use of on-site renewable energy technologies can result in energy cost savings, particularly if peak hour demand charges are high. Utility rebates are often available to reduce first costs of renewable energy equipment. In some states, first costs can be offset by net metering, where excess electricity is sold back to the utility. The reliability and lifetime of PV systems are also improving. Manufacturers typically guarantee their PV systems for up to 20 years.

Resources

Please see the USGBC website at www. usgbc.org/resources for more specific resources on materials sources and other technical information.

Websites

American Wind Energy Association (AWEA)

www.awea.org

(202) 383-2500

AWEA is a national trade association representing wind power plant developers, wind turbine manufacturers, utilities, consultants, insurers, financiers, researchers and others involved in the wind industry.

Database of State Incentives for Renewable Energy (DSIRE)

www.dsireusa.org

The North Carolina Solar Center developed this database to contain all available information on state financial and regulatory incentives (e.g., tax credits, grants and special utility rates) that are designed to promote the application of renewable energy technologies. DSIRE also offers additional features such as preparing and printing reports that detail the incentives on a state-by-state basis.

ENERGY Guide

www.energyguide.com

This website provides information on different power types, including green power, as well as general information on energy efficiency and tools for selecting power providers based on various economic, environmental and other criteria.

Green Power Network

U.S. Department of Energy

www.eere.energy.gov/greenpower

The Green Power Network provides news and information on green power markets and related activities and is maintained by the National Renewable Energy Laboratory for the U.S. Department of Energy.

National Center for Photovoltaics (NCPV)

www.nrel.gov/ncpv/

SS	WE	**EA**	MR	EQ	ID

Credit 2

NCPV provides clearinghouse information on all aspects of PV systems.

National Renewable Energy Laboratory

www.nrel.gov

The National Renewable Energy Laboratory (NREL) is a leader in the U.S. Department of Energy's effort to secure an energy future for the nation that is environmentally and economically sustainable.

Office of Energy Efficiency and Renewable Energy (EERE)

U.S. Department of Energy

www.eere.energy.gov

This website includes information on all types of renewable energy technologies and energy efficiency.

U.S. EPA Green Power Partnership

www.epa.gov/greenpower/index.htm

EPA's Green Power Partnership provides assistance and recognition to organizations that demonstrate environmental leadership by choosing green power. It includes a buyer's guide with listings of providers of green power in each state.

Print Media

Wind and Solar Power Systems by Mukund Patel, CRC Press, 1999. This text offers information about the fundamental elements of wind and solar power generation, conversion and storage, and detailed information about the design, operation and control methods of both stand-alone and grid-connected systems.

Wind Energy Comes of Age by Paul Gipe, John Wiley & Sons, 1995. This book provides extensive information on the wind power industry, and is one of several books by the author covering general and technical information about wind power.

Definitions

Biomass is plant material such as trees, grasses and crops that can be converted to heat energy to produce electricity.

The **Environmental Attributes of Green Power** include emission reduction benefits that result from green power being used instead of conventional power sources.

Net Metering is a metering and billing arrangement that allows on-site generators to send excess electricity flows to the regional power grid. These electricity flows offset a portion of the electricity flows drawn from the grid. For more information on net metering in individual states, visit the DOE's Green Power Network website at www.eere.energy.gov/greenpower/netmetering.

Renewable Energy Certificates (RECs) are a representation of the environmental attributes of green power, and are sold separately from the electrons that make up the electricity. RECs allow the purchase of green power even when the electrons are not purchased.

Enhanced Commissioning

1 point

Intent

Begin the commissioning process early during the design process and execute additional activities after systems performance verification is completed.

Requirements

Implement, or have a contract in place to implement, the following additional commissioning process activities in addition to the requirements of EA Prerequisite 1 and in accordance with this LEED-CS 2.0 Reference Guide:

1. Prior to the start of the construction documents phase, designate an independent Commissioning Authority (CxA) to lead, review, and oversee the completion of all commissioning process activities. The CxA shall, at a minimum, perform Tasks 2, 3 and 6. Other team members may perform Tasks 4 and 5.

   a. The CxA shall have documented commissioning authority experience in at least two building projects.

   b. The individual serving as the CxA shall be—

      i. independent of the work of design and construction;

      ii. not an employee of the design firm, though they may be contracted through them;

      iii. not an employee of, or contracted through, a contractor or construction manager holding construction contracts; and

      iv. (can be) a qualified employee or consultant of the Owner.

   c. The CxA shall report results, findings and recommendations directly to the Owner.

   d. This requirement has no deviation for project size.

2. The CxA shall conduct, at a minimum, one commissioning design review of the Owner's Project Requirements (OPR), Basis of Design (BOD), and design documents prior to the mid-construction documents phase and back-check the review comments in the subsequent design submission.

3. The CxA shall review contractor submittals applicable to systems being commissioned for compliance with the OPR and BOD. This review shall be concurrent with A/E reviews and submitted to the design team and the Owner.

4. Develop a systems manual that provides future operating staff the information needed to understand and optimally operate the commissioned systems.

5. Verify that the requirements for training operating personnel and building occupants are completed.

6. Assure the involvement by the CxA in reviewing building operation within 10 months after substantial completion with O&M staff and occupants. Include a plan for resolution of outstanding commissioning-related issues.

Potential Technologies & Strategies

Although it is preferable that the CxA be contracted by the Owner, for the enhanced commissioning credit, the CxA may also be contracted through the design firms or construction management firms not holding construction contracts.

This LEED-CS 2.0 Reference Guide provides detailed guidance on the rigor expected for following process activities:

❑ Commissioning design review

❑ Commissioning submittal review

❑ Systems manual

Summary of Referenced Standards

There is no standard referenced for this credit.

Approach and Implementation

Relationship Between Fundamental and Enhanced Commissioning

LEED-CS addresses building commissioning in two places, EA Prerequisite 1 and EA Credit 3. The exact scope of services for commissioning a LEED-CS project should be based on the Owner's Project Requirements. Other systems, including the building envelope, stormwater management systems, water treatment systems, information technology systems, etc., may be included in the commissioning process based on the Owner's Project Requirements.

Table 1 outlines the team members primarily responsible to perform each project requirement; and also which requirements are common to EA Prerequisite 1 and EA Credit 3. All individuals on the project team are encouraged to participate in the commissioning activities as part of a larger commissioning team.

Strategies

Commissioning is a planned, systematic quality-control process that involves the owner, users, occupants, operations and maintenance staff, design professionals and contractors. Commissioning often begins at project inception; provides ongoing verification of achievement of the Owner's Project Requirements; requires integration of contractor-com-

Table 1: Primary Responsibilities Chart for EA Prerequisite 1 and EA Credit 3

Tasks	Responsibilities	
	If you are only meeting EA Prerequisite 1...	If you are meeting the EAp1 AND EA credit 3...
Designate Commissioning Authority (CxA)	Owner or Project Team	Owner or Project Team
Document Owner's Project Requirements (OPR)	Owner	Owner
Develop Basis of Design	Design Team	Design Team
Incorporate commissioning requirements into the construction documents	Project Team or CxA	Project Team or CxA
Conduct commissioning design review prior to mid-construction documents	N/A	CxA
Develop and implement a commissioning plan	Project Team or CxA	Project Team or CxA
Review contractor submittals applicable to systems being commissioned	N/A	CxA
Verify the installation and performance of commissioned systems	CxA	CxA
Develop a systems manual for the commissioned systems	N/A	Project Team and CxA
Verify that the requirements for training are completed	N/A	Project Team and CxA
Complete a summary commissioning report	CxA	CxA
Review building operation within 10 months after substantial completion	N/A	CxA

pleted commissioning process activities into the construction documents; aids in the coordination of static and dynamic system testing; verifies staff training; and concludes with warranty verification and commissioning documentation.

The specific tasks satisfying this LEED-CS credit include the following:

1. **Prior to the start of the construction document phase, designate an independent Commissioning Authority (CxA) to lead, review, and oversee the completion of all commissioning process activities. The CxA shall, at a minimum, perform Tasks 2, 3 and 6 of the EA Credit 3 requirements. Other team members may perform Tasks 4 and 5.**

   The minimum defined experience for the designated CxA for EA Credit 3 is the same as described for EA Prerequisite 1. The design and submittal review activities called for in EA Credit 3 must be conducted by a third party CxA, independent of the firms responsible for design and construction, or a qualified member of the Owner's staff.

2. **The CxA shall conduct, at a minimum, one commissioning design review of the Owner's Project Requirements (OPR), Basis of Design (BOD), and design documents prior to the mid-construction documents phase, and back-check the review comments in the subsequent design submission.**

   The CxA shall review the OPR, BOD and design documents to provide the Owner and design team with an independent assessment of the state of the design for the commissioned systems. Typically the design review(s) performed by the CxA will focus on the following issues:

   ❑ Clarity, completeness and adequacy of OPR

   ❑ Verifying all issues discussed in OPR are addressed adequately in BOD

   ❑ Reviewing design documents for achieving the OPR and BOD and coordination of commissioned systems

   Additional reviews by the CxA, throughout the design and construction process may be advisable and appropriate depending on the project duration, phasing, complexity and the Owner's requirements.

3. **The CxA shall review contactor submittals applicable to systems being commissioned for compliance with the OPR and BOD. This review shall be concurrent with A/E reviews and submitted to the design team and the Owner.**

   The CxA shall provide a review of the contractor submittals to help identify any issues that might otherwise result in re-work and/or change orders. The CxA should specifically evaluate the submittals for the following:

   ❑ Meeting the OPR and BOD

   ❑ Operation and maintenance requirements

   ❑ Facilitating performance testing

   The CxA review of contractor submittals does not, typically, substitute or alter the scope or responsibility of the design team's obligations to approve or reject submittals.

4. **Develop a systems manual that provides future operating staff the information needed to understand and optimally operate the commissioned systems.**

   Provide a Systems Manual in addition to the O&M Manuals submitted by the Contractor. The Systems Manual generally focuses on operating, rather than maintaining, the equipment, and particularly on the interactions between equipment.

The Systems Manual shall include the following for each commissioned system:

❑ Final version of the BOD

❑ System single line diagrams

❑ As-built sequences of operations, control drawings and original set-points

❑ Operating instructions for integrated building systems

❑ Recommended schedule of maintenance requirements and frequency, if not already included in the project O&M manuals

❑ Recommended schedule for retesting of commissioned systems with blank test forms from the original Commissioning Plan

❑ Recommend schedule for calibrating sensors and actuators

5. **Verify that the requirements for training operating personnel and building occupants are completed.**

Based on the particular project, establish and document training expectations and needs with the Owner. Ensure that operations staff and occupants receive this training and orientation. Pay particular attention to new or uncommon sustainable design features that may have a potential to be over-ridden or removed because of a lack of understanding. Document that the training was completed according to the contract documents.

6. **Assure the involvement by the CxA in reviewing building operation within 10 months after substantial completion with O&M staff and occupants. Include a plan for resolution of outstanding commissioning-related issues.**

The CxA should coordinate with the Owner and the O&M staff to review the facility and its performance 8 to 10 months after handover of the facility. Any outstanding construction deficiencies or deficiencies identified in this post-occupancy review should be documented and corrected under manufacturer or contractor warranties.

The CxA review of the building operation with operations staff and occupants should identify any problems in operating the building as originally intended. Any significant issues identified by the CxA that will not be corrected should be recorded in the systems manual.

Core and Shell Concerns

Not all energy related systems are installed as part of core and shell projects. Energy related systems include, but are not limited to, heating, ventilating, air conditioning and refrigeration (HVAC&R) systems (mechanical and passive), associated controls, lighting, daylighting controls, domestic hot water systems, and renewable energy systems (wind, solar, etc.). Commissioning is required for any of the above systems that are part of the core and shell project. Some commissioning activities will be limited due to the installed systems or components. Systems performance testing may not include all of the activities generally required for systems that are incomplete. It is important to document all of the systems that will be installed as part of the core and shell project and to commission these systems.

Calculations

There are no calculations associated with this credit

Exemplary Performance

Projects that require the full scope of commissioning (both prerequisite and credit) for all the tenant spaces may be considered for an innovation point.

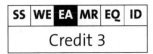
Core and shell projects that conduct comprehensive envelope commissioning may be considered for an innovation credit. These projects will need to demonstrate the standards and protocol by which the envelope was commissioned.

Precertification Submittal Documentation

Provide the LEED-CS Precertification Submittal Template, which includes the following:

❑ Narrative describing how the project intends to accomplish the credit requirements on the credit-specific Submittal Template signed by the appropriate design team member

❑ Confirmation of this intent from the owner/developer on the LEED-CS Precertification Submittal Template

Certification Submittal Documentation

This credit is submitted as part of the **Construction Submittal**.

Design and Construction Credit Compliance

The following project data and calculation information is required to document credit compliance using the LEED-CS v2.0 Submittal Templates:

❑ Provide the name, firm and experience information for the CxA

❑ Confirm that the 6 required tasks have been completed

❑ Provide a narrative description of the results of the commissioning design review, implementation of the systems manual and training, and the plan for the review of building operation at 8 to 10 months.

Tenant Sales or Lease Agreement Credit Compliance

This compliance method is not available for this credit.

Considerations

Cost Issues

An effective commissioning process will typically result in increased project soft costs and may require additional scheduling for commissioning activities. This investment is generally recouped in improved design and construction coordination, reduced change-orders, and reduced operating costs.

Facilities that do not perform as intended may consume significantly more resources over the useful life of the building. Commissioning can minimize the negative impacts buildings have on our environment by helping verify that buildings are designed, constructed and operated as intended and in accordance with the Owner's Project Requirements.

Building occupant comfort and indoor air quality may have tremendous impact on occupant productivity, health and well-being, as well as the cost of ownership. Commissioning can significantly reduce repairs, construction change orders, energy costs, and maintenance and operation costs.

Resources

Please see the USGBC website at www. usgbc.org/resources for more specific resources on materials sources and other technical information.

See the Resources section of EA Prerequisite 1 for a list of specific commissioning resources.

Definitions

Basis of Design includes all information necessary to accomplish the Owner's Project Requirements, including weather data, interior environmental criteria, other pertinent design assumptions, cost goals, and references to applicable codes, standards, regulations and guidelines.

Commissioning is the process of verifying and documenting that the facility and all of its systems and assemblies are planned, designed, installed, tested, operated, and maintained to meet the Owner's Project Requirements.

Commissioning Plan is a document that outlines the organization, schedule, allocation of resources, and documentation requirements of the Commissioning Process.

Commissioning Report is the document that records the results of the commissioning process, including the as-built performance of the HVAC system and unresolved issues.

Commissioning Specification is the contract document that details the commissioning requirements of the construction contractors.

Installation Inspection is the process of inspecting components of the commissioned systems to determine if they are installed properly and ready for systems performance testing.

Owner's Project Requirements is a written document that details the functional requirements of a project and the expectations of how it will be used and operated.

System Performance Testing is the process of determining the ability of the commissioned systems to perform in accordance with the Owner's Project Requirements, Basis Of Design and construction documents.

Enhanced Refrigerant Management

Intent

Reduce ozone depletion and support early compliance with the Montreal Protocol while minimizing direct contributions to global warming.

Requirements

OPTION 1

Do not use refrigerants.

OR

OPTION 2

Select refrigerants and HVAC&R that minimize or eliminate the emission of compounds that contribute to ozone depletion and global warming. The base building HVAC&R equipment shall comply with the following formula, which sets a maximum threshold for the combined contributions to ozone depletion and global warming potential:

$$LCGWP + LCODP \times 10^5 \leq 100$$

Where:

$LCODP = [ODP_r \times (Lr \times Life + Mr) \times Rc]/Life$

$LCGWP = [GWPr \times (Lr \times Life + Mr) \times Rc]/Life$

LCODP: Lifecycle Ozone Depletion Potential (lbCFC11/Ton-Year)

LCGWP: Lifecycle Direct Global Warming Potential (lbCO$_2$/Ton-Year)

GWPr: Global Warming Potential of Refrigerant (0 to 12,000 lbCO$_2$/lbr)

ODPr: Ozone Depletion Potential of Refrigerant (0 to 0.2 lbCFC11/lbr)

Lr: Refrigerant Leakage Rate (0.5% to 2.0%; default of 2% unless otherwise demonstrated)

Mr: End-of-life Refrigerant Loss (2% to 10%; default of 10% unless otherwise demonstrated)

Rc: Refrigerant Charge (0.5 to 5.0 lbs of refrigerant per ton of cooling capacity)

Life: Equipment Life (10 years; default based on equipment type, unless otherwise demonstrated)

For multiple types of equipment, a weighted average of all base building level HVAC&R equipment shall be applied using the following formula:

$$[\Sigma (LCGWP + LCODP \times 10^5) \times Qunit] / Qtotal \leq 100$$

Where:

Qunit = Cooling capacity of an individual HVAC or refrigeration unit (Tons)

Qtotal = Total cooling capacity of all HVAC or refrigeration

Small HVAC units (defined as containing less than 0.5 lbs of refrigerant), and other equipment such as standard refrigerators, small water coolers, and any other cooling equipment that contains less than 0.5 lbs of refrigerant, are not considered part of the "base building" system and are not subject to the requirements of this credit.

AND

Do not install fire suppression systems that contain ozone-depleting substances (CFCs, HCFCs or Halons).

Potential Technologies & Strategies

Design and operate the facility without mechanical cooling and refrigeration equipment. Where mechanical cooling is used, utilize base building HVAC and refrigeration systems for the refrigeration cycle that minimize direct impact on ozone depletion and global warming. Select HVAC&R equipment with reduced refrigerant charge and increased equipment life. Maintain equipment to prevent leakage of refrigerant to the atmosphere. Utilize fire suppression systems that do not contain CFCs, HCFCs or Halons.

Summary of Referenced Standard

There is no standard referenced for this credit.

Approach and Implementation

Most commonly used refrigerants contained in building HVAC and refrigeration equipment are stable chemical compounds that, when released to the environment, result in damage to the atmosphere by the following:

❑ Contributing to deterioration of the Earth's protective ozone layer (Ozone Depletion)

❑ Contributing greenhouse gases to the atmosphere (Global Warming)

Building HVAC&R systems also contribute to global warming through their associated energy consumption and power plant emissions of greenhouse gases. Over the life of the equipment, the "indirect" global warming impact of HVAC&R equipment may be much greater than the direct impact of releasing the refrigerant to the atmosphere. The indirect global warming impact of refrigerants in HVAC&R equipment is addressed by EA Credit 1, which credits the energy savings associated with more energy efficient equipment. EA Credit 4 addresses only the direct atmospheric impact of refrigerant selection and management decisions.

If the building(s) is (are) connected to an existing chilled water system, have the chilled water supplier perform the required calculations and submit a letter showing compliance with the requirements.

There are several strategies associated with reducing or eliminating the potential negative impact of refrigerant use on the environment.

Do Not Use Refrigerants

Green building designs that avoid the use of refrigerants by eliminating the use of vapor-compression HVAC&R equipment have no potential for atmospheric damage associated with refrigerant release. LEED projects that do not use refrigerants are awarded this LEED-CS credit with no calculations or analysis required. For example, a naturally ventilated building with no active cooling systems (and therefore no refrigerants) is awarded this credit.

"Natural refrigerants" including water, carbon dioxide and ammonia are used in some HVAC&R systems. These naturally occurring compounds generally have much lower potential for atmospheric damage than more common manufactured chemical refrigerants. Projects that employ natural refrigerants are eligible for this credit.

Select Refrigerants with Low ODP and GWP

Table 1 shows the Ozone Depleting Potential (ODP) and direct Global Warming Potential (GWP) of many common refrigerants.

The LEED Technical and Scientific Committee (TSAC) report that provides the basis of this LEED-CS credit notes the following:

"The ozone-depletion potential (ODP) of the HCFCs (e.g., HCFC-123, HCFC-22) is much smaller than the ODP of the CFCs, but is not negligible. In contrast, the HFCs (e.g., HFC-134a, HFC-410a) have an ODP that is essentially zero, but their global warming potential (GWP) is substantially greater than some of the HCFCs, leading to a direct global warming mechanism when the compound leaks into the atmosphere. Moreover, thermodynamic properties make the HFCs slightly less efficient refrigerants than the HCFCs given idealized equipment design, so the same amount of cooling

Table 1: Ozone-depletion and global-warming potentials of refrigerants (100-yr values)

Refrigerant	ODP	GWP	Common Building Applications
Chlorofluorocarbons			
CFC-11	1.0	4,680	Centrifugal chillers
CFC-12	1.0	10,720	Refrigerators, chillers
CFC-114	0.94	9,800	Centrifugal chillers
CFC-500	0.605	7,900	Centrifugal chillers, humidifiers
CFC-502	0.221	4,600	Low-temperature refrigeration
Hydrochlorofluorocarbons			
HCFC-22	0.04	1,780	Air conditioning, chillers,
HCFC-123	0.02	76	CFC-11 replacement
Hydrofluorocarbons			
HFC-23	~ 0	12,240	Ultra-low-temperature refrigeration
HFC-134a	~ 0	1,320	CFC-12 or HCFC-22 replacement
HFC-245fa	~ 0	1,020	Insulation agent, centrifugal chillers
HFC-404A	~ 0	3,900	Low-temperature refrigeration
HFC-407C	~ 0	1,700	HCFC-22 replacement
HFC-410A	~ 0	1,890	Air conditioning
HFC-507A	~ 0	3,900	Low-temperature refrigeration
Natural Refrigerants			
Carbon Dioxide (CO2)	0	1.0	
Ammonia (NH3)	0	0	
Propane	0	3	

may require more electricity and thereby causes the indirect release of more CO_2 in generating that electricity. The dilemma, therefore, is that some refrigerants cause more ozone depletion than others, but the most ozone-friendly refrigerants cause more global warming."

Refrigerants with non-zero ODP are being phased out according to an international agreement—the Montreal Protocol. In accordance with the Montreal Protocol, all chlorinated refrigerants including CFCs and HCFCs will be phased out by the year 2030.

In the meantime, selecting the appropriate refrigerant for any given project HVAC system may be impacted by available equipment, energy efficiency, budget and other factors. Where viable options are available, projects should select refrigerants with no or very little ODP and minimal GWP.

Minimize Refrigerant Leakage

Refrigerants cannot damage the atmosphere if they are contained and are never released to the environment. Unfortunately, in real world applications, some or all refrigerant provided for HVAC&R equipment is leaked to the environment during installation, operation, servicing, and/or decommissioning of the equipment.

Under Section 608 of the Clean Air Act of 1990, the EPA has established regulations that—

❏ Require service practices that maximize recycling of ozone-depleting compounds (both CFCs and HCFCs) during the servicing and disposal of air-conditioning and refrigeration equipment.

❏ Set certification requirements for recycling and recovery equipment, technicians, and reclaimers and restrict the sale of refrigerant to uncertified technicians.

❑ Require persons servicing or disposing of air-conditioning and refrigeration equipment to certify to EPA that they have acquired recycling or recovery equipment and are complying with the requirements of the rule.

❑ Require the repair of substantial leaks in air-conditioning and refrigeration equipment with a charge of greater than 50 pounds.

❑ Establish safe disposal requirements to ensure removal of refrigerants from goods that enter the waste stream with the charge intact (e.g., motor vehicle air conditioners, home refrigerators and room air conditioners).

❑ Prohibit individuals from knowingly venting ozone-depleting compounds (generally CFCs and HCFCs) used as refrigerants into the atmosphere while maintaining, servicing, repairing, or disposing of air-conditioning or refrigeration equipment (appliances).

Federal regulation and best practices for refrigerant management and equipment maintenance can minimize the loss of refrigerant to the atmosphere. Manufacturers may offer leakage rate guarantees for certain types of major HVAC&R equipment (such as chillers) as part of a long-term service contract.

Most refrigerant loss to the environment occurs due to undetected leaks in outdoor equipment and/or refrigerant loss during the installation, charging, servicing, or decommissioning of equipment.

Select Equipment with Efficient Refrigerant Charge

Refrigerant charge is the ratio of refrigerant required (lbs) to cooling capacity provided (tons) for a given piece of HVAC&R equipment. Equipment that uses refrigerant efficiently and therefore has low refrigerant charge has less potential to contribute to atmospheric damage.

Table 2 shows the maximum refrigerant charge for any single unit of equipment that would comply with this credit for various common refrigerants and types of equipment. Most projects have multiple units of base building HVAC&R equipment, but if each unit is compliant with Table 2, the project as a whole will comply with this credit. In Table 2 the calculations assume that refrigerant leakage default factors are used.

Select Equipment with Long Service Life

HVAC&R service equipment with long service life will generally reduce the potential amount of refrigerant leaked to the environment since a significant portion of refrigerant loss occurs during installation and decommissioning of equipment. The 2003 ASHRAE Applications Handbook provides general data on the typical

Table 2: Default Maximum Allowable Equipment Refrigerant Charge (lb/ton) for Compliance with EA Credit 4

Refrigerant	10 Year Life	15 Year Life	20 Year Life	23 Year Life
	(Room or Window AC & Heat Pumps)	(Unitary, split and packaged AC and heat pumps)	(Reciprocating compressors & chillers)	(Centrifugal, Screw & Absorption Chillers)
R-22	0.57	0.64	0.69	0.71
R-123	1.60	1.80	1.92	1.97
R-134a	2.52	2.80	3.03	3.10
R-245fa	3.26	3.60	3.92	4.02
R-407c	1.95	2.20	2.35	2.41
R-410a	1.76	1.98	2.11	2.17

service life of different types of HVAC equipment:

❑ Window air-conditioning units and heat pumps – 10 years

❑ Unitary, split and packaged air-conditioning units and heat pumps – 15 years

❑ Reciprocating compressors and reciprocating chillers – 20 years

❑ Centrifugal and absorption chillers – 23 years

Base Building HVAC&R Equipment

Base building HVAC&R equipment includes any equipment permanently installed in the building that contains more than 0.5 lbs of refrigerant. This includes chillers, unitary (split and packaged) HVAC equipment, room or window airconditioners, computer room air conditioning (CRAC) units, data and telecommunications room cooling units, and commercial refrigeration equipment. Portable cooling equipment (such as standard refrigerators), temporary cooling equipment, and equipment with less than 0.5 lbs of refrigerant (such as small water coolers) may be excluded from the calculations for this credit.

Core and Shell Concerns

There are no core and shell particular issues regarding implementation.

Calculations

To complete the calculations necessary to demonstrate compliance with this credit, the following information will be required for each unit of base building HVAC&R equipment:

❑ Refrigerant charge, (Rc) in lbs of refrigerant per ton of cooling capacity

❑ Refrigerant type (used to determine ODPr and GWPr)

❑ Equipment type (used to determine Life)

Table 1 includes ODPr and GWPr values for many common refrigerants. These values should be used in the calculations associated with this credit.

Equipment Life shall be assumed (as excerpted from 2003 ASHRAE Applications Handbook) to be the following:

❑ Window air-conditioning units and heat pumps – 10 years

❑ Unitary, split and packaged air-conditioning units and heat pumps – 15 years

❑ Reciprocating compressors and reciprocating chillers – 20 years

❑ Centrifugal and absorption chillers – 23 years

All other HVAC&R equipment will be assumed to have a life of 15 years. Applicants may use an alternate value for Equipment Life if they demonstrate and document information in support of their claim. For example if there is a manufacturer's guarantee and long-term service contract assuring a 30-year life for a chiller installation, this alternate value of equipment life could be used in the calculations for that unit of equipment.

Refrigerant Leakage Rate (Lr) is assumed to be 2% per year for all equipment types. End-of-life Refrigerant Loss (Mr) is assumed to be 10% for all equipment types. Applicants may use alternate values for Lr and Mr if they demonstrate and document information in support of their claim, such as—

❑ Manufacturers' test data for refrigerant leakage rates (%/yr);

❑ Refrigerant leak detection equipment in the room where the equipment is located;

❑ A preventative maintenance program for minimizing equipment refrigerant leakage; and

❑ A program for recovering and recycling refrigerant at the end of the equipment lifecycle.

Projects may not claim zero leakage over the lifecycle of the HVAC&R equipment installed in the project.

For each piece of HVAC&R equipment, the project should calculate the following values:

❏ Lifecycle Ozone Depletion Potential (LCODP) = [ODP_r x (Lr x Life + Mr) x Rc]/Life

❏ Lifecycle Direct Global Warming Potential (LCGWP) = [GWPr x (Lr x Life +Mr) x Rc]/Life

If there is only one piece of base building HVAC&R equipment, the following equation shall be used to demonstrate compliance with this LEED credit:

Refrigerant Atmospheric Impact = LCGWP + LCODP x $10^5 \leq 100$

If there are multiple pieces of base building HVAC&R equipment, the project should use a weighted average of all equipment, based on cooling capacity:

❏ Average Refrigerant Atmospheric Impact = [$\sum$ (LCGWP + LCODP x 10^5) x Qunit] / Qtotal ≤ 100

Where

❏ Qunit = Cooling capacity of an individual HVAC or refrigeration unit (tons)

❏ Qtotal = Total cooling capacity of all HVAC or refrigeration

Two examples of projects are shown below. In the office building example the overall project complies with EA Credit 4, although individual units of HVAC&R equipment have refrigerant atmospheric impact >100. The retail building, overall, does not comply with EA Credit 4.

Exemplary Performance

There is no exemplary performance point available for this credit.

Precertification Submittal Documentation

Provide the LEED-CS Precertification Submittal Template, which includes the following:

❏ Narrative describing how the project intends to accomplish the credit requirements on the credit-specific Submittal Template signed by the appropriate design team member

❏ Confirmation of this intent from the owner/developer on the LEED-CS Precertification Submittal Template

Example Calculation 1: Retail Building
❏ (12) 5-ton packaged HVAC units with HFC-410A for stores
❏ (1) 2-ton split system HVAC units with HCFC-22 for a storage area
❏ (1) 1-ton window HVAC unit with HCFC-22 for an office

		Inputs								Calculations			
N (Number of Units)	Qunit (Tons)	Refrigerant	GWPr	ODPr	Rc (lb/ ton)	Life (yrs)	Lr (%)	Mr (%)	Tr Total Leakage (Lr x Life + Mr)	LCGWP (GWPr x Tr x Rc)/ Life	LCODP x 10^5 100,000 x (ODPr x Tr x Rc)/ Life	Refrigerant Atmospheric Impact = LCGWP + LCODP x 10^5	(LCGWP + LCODP x 10^5) x N x Qunit
12	5	R410a	1,890	0	1.8	15	2%	10%	40%	90.72	0	90.7	5443
1	2	R22	1,780	0.04	3.3	15	2%	10%	40%	156.6	352	508.6	1017
1	1	R22	1,780	0.04	2.1	10	2%	10%	30%	112.1	252	364.1	364
Qtotal: 63 tons												Subtotal:	6825
Average Refrigerant Atmospheric Impact = [$\sum$ (LCGWP + LCODP x 105) x Qunit] / Qtotal :													108.3

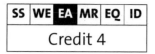

Certification Submittal Documentation

This credit is submitted as part of the **Design Submittal**.

Design and Construction Credit Compliance

The following project data and calculation information is required to document credit compliance using the LEED-CS v2.0 Submittal Templates:

❏ Enter into the template the HVAC&R equipment types, including number, size (tons), refrigerant, and refrigerant charge.

❏ Provide a narrative describing any special circumstances or calculation explanations.

Tenant Sales or Lease Agreement Credit Compliance

This compliance method is available to core and shell projects that incorporate into tenant sales or lease agreements language that requires compliance with the credit requirements as part of the tenant scope of work. Provide the LEED letter template for the credit pursued indicating the following:

❏ 100% of leased square footage is required to comply with credit requirements. Lease or sales agreements may be requested.

❏ 100% of the unleased square footage shall comply with the credit requirements when leased. A statement signed by the owner/developer that all leases and/or sales agreements will comply may be requested.

Considerations

LEED TSAC makes the following observation:

"An objective scientific analysis of trade-offs between global warming and ozone depletion is extremely complex, and will only come from a full understanding of all interacting pathways and the effects on economic activities, human health, and terrestrial and oceanic ecosystems. Any quantitative credit scheme addressing both must involve some subjectivity in the relative weight given to each issue."

Refrigerant management to minimize the negative impacts of refrigerant use on ozone depletion and global warming is dependant on several factors that include—

Example Calculation 2: Office Building

❏ (1) 500-ton centrifugal chiller with HFC-134a—provided with manufacturers data and service contract guaranteeing less than 1% per year leakage

❏ (1) 50-ton reciprocating "pony" chiller with HCFC-22

❏ (5) 10-ton computer room air conditioning units with HCFC-22

Inputs									Calculations			
N (Number of Units)	Qunit (Tons)	Refrigerant	GWPr	ODPr	Rc (lb/ton)	Life (yrs)	Lr (%)	Mr (%)	Tr Total Leakage (Lr x Life + Mr)	LCGWP (GWPr x Tr x Rc)/ Life	LCODP x 10⁵ 100,000 x (ODPr x Tr x Rc)/ Life	Refrigerant Atmospheric Impact = LCGWP + LCODP x 10⁵	(LCGWP + LCODP x 10⁵) x N x Qunit
1	500	R134a	1,320	0	2	23	1%	10%	33%	37.9	0	37.9	18939
1	50	R22	1,780	0.04	2.1	20	2%	10%	50%	93.5	210	303	15173
5	10	R22	1,780	0.04	2.4	15	2%	10%	40%	113.9	256	369.9	18496
Qtotal:	600 tons											Subtotal:	52608
Average Refrigerant Atmospheric Impact = [∑ (LCGWP + LCODP x 105) x Qunit] / Qtotal :													87.7

- Designing buildings that do not rely on chemical refrigerants;

- Designing HVAC&R equipment that uses energy efficiently;

- Selecting refrigerants with zero or low ODP and minimal direct GWP; and

- Maintaining HVAC&R equipment to reduce refrigerant leakage to the environment.

Resources

Please see the USGBC website at www. usgbc.org/resources for more specific resources on materials sources and other technical information.

Websites

EPA's Significant New Alternatives Policy (SNAP)

www.epa.gov/ozone/snap/index.html

SNAP is an EPA program to identify alternatives to ozone-depleting substances. The program maintains up-to-date lists of environmentally friendly substitutes for refrigeration and air conditioning equipment, solvents, fire suppression systems, adhesives, coatings and other substances.

Stratospheric Ozone Protection: Moving to Alternative Refrigerants

http://es.epa.gov/program/epaorgs/oar/altrefrg.html

This EPA document includes 10 case histories on buildings that have been converted to accommodate non-CFC refrigerants.

Print Media

The Treatment by LEED of the Environmental Impact of HVAC Refrigerants

U.S. Green Building Council

www.usgbc.org/DisplayPage.aspx?CMSPageID=154

(202) 82-USGBC

This report was prepared under the auspices of the U.S. Green Building Council's

LEED Technical and Scientific Advisory Committee (TSAC), in response to a charge given TSAC by the LEED Steering Committee to review the atmospheric environmental impacts arising from the use of halocarbons as refrigerants in building heating, ventilating and air conditioning (HVAC) equipment.

Building Systems Analysis & Retrofit Manual, SMACNA, 1995.

This manual provides an overview of a number of topics relating to HVAC retrofits, including energy management retrofits and CFC/HCFC retrofits.

CFCs, HCFC and Halons: Professional and Practical Guidance on Substances that Deplete the Ozone Layer, CIBSE, 2000.

This booklet provides background information on the environmental issues associated with CFCs, HCFCs and halons, design guidance, and strategies for refrigerant containment and leak detection.

The Refrigerant Manual: Managing the Phase-Out of CFCs, BOMA International, 1993.

This manual gives an overview of the phase-out of CFCs, including information on retaining existing equipment, retrofitting existing equipment, or replacing equipment.

Definitions

Chlorofluorocarbons (CFCs) are hydrocarbons that deplete the stratospheric ozone layer.

Halons are substances used in fire suppression systems and fire extinguishers in buildings. These substances deplete the stratospheric ozone layer.

Hydrochlorofluorocarbons (HCFCs) are refrigerants used in building equipment that deplete the stratospheric ozone layer, but to a lesser extent than CFCs.

Hydrofluorocarbons (HFCs) are refrigerants that do not deplete the stratospheric

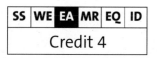
ozone layer. However, some HFCs have high global warming potential and, thus, are not environmentally benign.

Refrigerants are the working fluids of refrigeration cycles that absorb heat from a reservoir at low temperatures and reject heat at higher temperatures.

Measurement & Verification

Base Building

Intent

Provide for the ongoing accountability of building energy consumption over time.

Requirements

❑ Provide the necessary infrastructure within the base building design to facilitate metering building electricity and tenant electrical end-uses as appropriate

❑ Develop and implement a Measurement & Verification (M&V) Plan consistent with Option D: Calibrated Simulation (Savings Estimation Method 2), or Option B: Energy Conservation Measure Isolation, as specified in the *International Performance Measurement & Verification Protocol (IPMVP) Volume III: Concepts and Options for Determining Energy Savings in New Construction, April, 2003.*

Potential Technologies & Strategies

Develop an M&V Plan to evaluate building and/or energy system performance. Characterize the building and/or energy systems through energy simulation or engineering analysis. Install the necessary metering equipment to measure energy use. Track performance by comparing predicted performance to actual performance, broken down by component or system as appropriate. Evaluate energy efficiency by comparing actual performance to baseline performance.

While the IPMVP describes specific actions for verifying savings associated with energy conservation measures (ECMs) and strategies, this LEED credit expands upon typical IPMVP M&V objectives. M&V activities should not necessarily be confined to energy systems where ECMs or energy conservation strategies have been implemented. The IPMVP provides guidance on M&V strategies and their appropriate applications for various situations. These strategies should be used in conjunction with monitoring and trend logging of significant energy systems to provide for the ongoing accountability of building energy performance.

Summary of Referenced Standard

International Performance Measurement & Verification Protocol (IPMVP) Volume III: Concepts and Options for Determining Energy Savings in New Construction, April, 2003.

www.ipmvp.org

IPMVP Inc. is a nonprofit organization whose vision is a global marketplace that properly values energy and water efficiency.

IPMVP Volume III provides a concise description of best-practice techniques for verifying the energy performance of new construction projects. Chapter 2 describes the process for developing the theoretical Baseline for new construction projects and provides examples of relevant applications. Chapter 3 describes the basic concepts and structure of the M&V Plan. Chapter 4 describes specific M&V Methods for Energy Conservation Measure Isolation (Option B) and Whole Building Calibrated Simulation (Option D).

Approach and Implementation

The IPMVP Volume III presents four options for new construction M&V. Of these, Options B and D are deemed to be suitable for the purposes of LEED M&V (see **Table 1**).

Option B (ECM Isolation) addresses M&V at the system or ECM level. This approach is suitable for smaller and/or simpler buildings that may be appropriately monitored by isolating the main energy systems and applying Option B to each on an individual basis. Projects following Option B may also need to implement whole-building metering and tracking to satisfy the intent of this credit.

Option D (Whole Building Calibrated Simulation, Savings Estimation addresses M&V at the whole-building level. This approach is most suitable for buildings with a large number of ECMs or systems that are interactive, or where the building design is integrated and holistic, rendering isolation and M&V of individual ECMs impractical or inappropriate. It essentially requires comparing the actual energy use of the building and its systems with the performance predicted by a calibrated computer model (presumably created from the computer models used for EA Credit 1 Option 1). Calibration is achieved by adjusting the as-built simulation to reflect actual operating conditions and parameters. To

Table 1: Office Building

M&V Option	How Baseline is Determined	Typical Applications
B. ECM Isolation		
Savings are determined by full measurement of the energy use and operating parameters of the system(s) to which an ECM was applied, separate from the rest of the facility.	Projected baseline energy use is determined by calculating the hypothetical energy performance of the baseline system under measured post-construction operating conditions.	Variable speed control of a fan motor. Electricity use is measured on a continuous basis throughout the M&V period.
D. Whole Building Calibrated Simulation		
Savings are determined at the whole-building or system level by measuring energy use at main meters or sub-meters.	Projected baseline energy use is determined by energy simulation of the baseline under the post-construction operating conditions.	Savings determination for the purposes of a new building Performance Contract, with the local energy code defining the baseline.

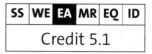

determine energy savings, similar calibrations or adjustments should be applied to the Baseline Building simulation.

Option D serves two purposes:

❏ Calibration of the as-built simulation model to actual energy use reveals ECM/design or operational underperformance.

❏ Adjusting the Baseline simulation allows meaningful performance comparisons and the determination of verified savings.

The IPMVP is not prescriptive regarding the application of M&V options, but instead defers to the professional judgment of the implementer(s) to apply the options in a manner that is appropriate to the project scale while still meeting the M&V objective (see Economic Issues section).

IPMVP Vol. III provides specific requirements for the M&V Plan. In general the plan identifies the M&V option(s) to be applied, defines the Baseline or how it will be determined, identifies metering requirements, and outlines specific methodologies associated with implementing the M&V Plan. Responsibility for the design, coordination, and implementation of the M&V Plan should reside with one entity of the design team. The person(s) responsible for energy engineering and analysis is usually best-suited for this role, although third-party verification may be appropriate in some cases. Since the pursuit of this credit is largely affected by the option selected to achieve EA Credit 1, the Baseline definition will vary. For EA Credit 1 Option 1 the baseline is defined by ASHRAE 90.1 Appendix G. The Baselines for EA Credit 1 Options 2 and 3 are defined by the respective prescriptive standards, which in some cases may be effectively the same as the Design. In that case the M&V Plan is reduced to addressing Design performance only. However, it is necessary in all cases to project the energy performance of the Design and/or

its systems. For Option B this can be accomplished through computer modeling or engineering analysis for simple buildings or systems.

The start of the M&V period should occur after the building has achieved a reasonable degree of occupancy and operational stability.

After the M&V period has been completed (after at least one year of stable and optimized operation) long term M&V can be economically implemented. Essentially, the one year of stable post-construction operation becomes the Base Year against which subsequent energy performance is compared by applying operational adjustments and regression analysis. Refer to IPMVP Volume I, which focuses on the pertinent methods of M&V, for further information.

Core and Shell Concerns

This credit is focused on the energy using systems, primarily the electrical energy using systems, of the core and shell building. This may include measuring electricity use in the tenant spaces. However, for the purposes of this credit, the electricity usage of the tenant spaces does not have to be broken out by tenant. The submetering of tenant spaces is addressed in EA Credit 5.2.

To achieve this credit, the electricity using systems in the core and shell building should be addressed in the M&V plan. Decisions must be made as to what electricity uses will be focused on and how this electricity use will be measured. Infrastructure, such as meters or a building management system, must be provided. If the building does not have any electricity using equipment, the project cannot achieve this credit. The project team may also want to consider measuring other energy use (i.e., natural gas) to get a complete picture of the energy use of the building.

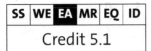
Calculations

IPMVP Volume III provides fundamental calculation formulae as well as quantitative guidelines for error estimation and tolerance for various M&V options.

Exemplary Performance

There is no exemplary performance point available for this credit.

Precertification Submittal Documentation

Provide the LEED-CS Precertification Submittal Template, which includes the following:

❑ Narrative describing how the project intends to accomplish the credit requirements on the credit-specific Submittal Template signed by the appropriate design team member

❑ Confirmation of this intent from the owner/developer on the LEED-CS Precertification Submittal Template

Certification Submittal Documentation

This credit is submitted as part of the Design Submittal.

Design and Construction Credit Compliance

The following project data and calculation information is required to document credit compliance using the LEED-CS v2.0 Submittal Templates:

❑ Confirm the IPMVP Option pursued by the project.

❑ Upload a copy of the M&V Plan.

❑ Provide a narrative describing any special circumstances or calculation explanations.

Section 3.2 of IPMVP Volume III provides specific content requirements for the M&V Plan.

Tenant Sales or Lease Agreement Credit Compliance

This compliance method is not available for this credit.

Considerations

The benefits of optimal building operation, especially in terms of energy performance, are substantial. The lifetime of many buildings is greater than 50 years. Even minor energy savings are significant when considered in aggregate. These long-term benefits often go unrealized due to maintenance personnel changes, aging of building equipment, and changing utility rate structures. Therefore, it is important to institute M&V procedures to achieve and maintain optimal performance over the lifetime of the building through continuous monitoring. The goal of M&V activities is to provide building Owners with the tools and data necessary to identify systems that are not functioning as expected, and to optimize building system performance.

Environmental Issues

Measurement & Verification of a building's ongoing energy use allows for optimization of related systems over the lifetime of the building. As a result, the cost and environmental impacts associated with energy can be minimized.

Economic Issues

The added cost to institute an M&V program in a new construction project is strongly tied to the complexity of the building systems. Costs can come from additional instrumentation and metering equipment, additional controls programming, and/or labor for the monitoring and processing of the data collected. The extent to which these costs are considered extraneous will depend on the level of instrumentation and controls in the Baseline Design. Often times, projects with sophisticated digital controls can support an effective M&V program without incurring significant additional costs. In other instances, projects with a series of chillers and air handlers and simple controls may need to install a significant amount of equipment to generate the necessary data for an effective M&V program. Smaller buildings with packaged HVAC equipment and fewer pieces of equipment may have lower costs because there are fewer systems to measure and verify. The cost of an M&V program must be balanced against the potential performance risk. A simple method of estimating performance risk can be based on the project value and technical uncertainty. An illustration is provided in **Table 2**.

A capital and operational budget for M&V may be established as a percentage of the project's performance risk over a suitable period of years. As illustrated, the smaller project consisting of predictable technologies has less performance risk (and thus a lower M&V budget) than the large project that includes less predictable technologies.

In general, higher M&V intensity and rigor means higher cost, both upfront and over time. The factors that typically affect M&V accuracy and costs are as follows (note that many are interrelated):

❑ Level of detail and effort associated with verifying post-construction conditions

❑ Number and types of metering points

❑ Duration and accuracy of metering activities

❑ Number and complexity of dependent and independent variables that must be measured or determined on an ongoing basis

❑ Availability of existing data collecting systems (e.g., energy management systems)

❑ Confidence and precision levels specified for the analyses

Resources

Please see the USGBC website at www.usgbc.org/resources for more specific resources on materials sources and other technical information.

Websites

International Performance Measurement & Verification Protocol (IP-MVP)

www.ipmvp.org

IPMVP Inc. is a nonprofit organization whose vision is a global marketplace that properly values energy and water efficiency.

Definitions

Energy Conservation Measures (ECMs) are installations of equipment or systems, or modifications of equipment or systems, for the purpose of reducing energy use and/or costs.

Table 2

Sample Project	Anticipated Annual Energy Costs	Estimated Savings	Estimated Uncertainty	Performance Risk
Small	$250,000	$50,000	20%	$10,000
Large	$2,000,000	$500,000	30%	$150,000

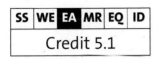

Measurement & Verification

Tenant Sub-metering

Intent

Provide for ongoing accountability of building electricity consumption performance over time.

Requirements

❏ Include a centrally monitored electronic metering network in the base building design that is capable of being expanded to accommodate the future tenant sub-metering as required by LEED for Commercial Interiors Rating System EA Credit 3.

❏ Develop a tenant M&V Plan that documents and advises future tenants of this opportunity and the means of their achievement.

Potential Technologies & Strategies

Install the necessary metering and sub-metering equipment to measure energy use. Develop and implement a Measurement & Verification Plan able to be utilized and expanded by the tenant, which compares predicted savings to actual energy performance.

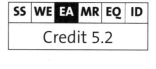

Can assist tenants in certification under LEED for Commercial Interiors

Summary of Referenced Standard

International Performance Measurement & Verification Protocol (IPMVP) Volume III: Concepts and Options for Determining Energy Savings in New Construction, April, 2003.

www.ipmvp.org

IPMVP Inc. is a nonprofit organization whose vision is a global marketplace that properly values energy and water efficiency.

IPMVP Volume III provides a concise description of best-practice techniques for verifying the energy performance of new construction projects. Chapter 2 describes the process for developing the theoretical Baseline for new construction projects and provides examples of relevant applications. Chapter 3 describes the basic concepts and structure of the M&V Plan. Chapter 4 describes specific M&V Methods for Energy Conservation Measure Isolation (Option B) and Whole Building Calibrated Simulation (Option D).

Approach and Implementation

This credit is designed to create the infrastructure that will allow any tenant that leases space in the building to be able to earn EA Credit 3 in LEED-CI. It is focused on providing the capability for tenants to sub-meter their leased space. Sub-metering is simply metering a utility for a designated portion of a building. The provision of utility meters for each tenant space is also considered sub-metering. In a commercial office building that has a master electric meter, sub-meters serve the purpose of advising individual tenants of their actual consumption. In tests of commercial and residential situations, individual tenant responsibility for utility charges has resulted in conservation. For electrical service, the equipment and installation of sub-meters is not a major expense.

To satisfy the credit requirement, the sub-metering need only be for the electricity to the space. The electricity used for lighting, plug loads and to run HVAC equipment may be measured on one meter and reported together.

Calculations

There are no calculations associated with this credit.

Exemplary Performance

There is no exemplary performance point available for this credit.

Submittal Documentation

This credit is submitted as part of the **Design Submittal**.

Design and Construction Credit Compliance

The following project data and calculation information is required to document credit compliance using the LEED-CS v2.0 Submittal Templates:

❏ Indicate how the utilities are apportioned to tenants. Describe the metering equipment installed for electricity. Provide cut-sheets for the meters that will be available for tenant use. Indicate the locations for the tenant sub-metering equipment on the tenant M&V Plan.

❏ Provide an M&V plan that details how the tenants can track their electrical use.

Tenant Sales or Lease Agreement Credit Compliance

This compliance method is not available for this credit.

Considerations

The goal of tenant sub-metering is to provide tenants with an incentive to save electricity. Sub-metering allows tenants a mechanism to account for their electricity consumption. This way the tenants can see a return on any energy saving investments that they make.

Some municipalities and/or utilities do not allow a second party to charge for electricity based on sub-metering. In this case, providing separate utility meters for each tenant may be the best option. Or for buildings that sub-meter, electricity cost can be apportioned to the tenants based on usage. It is recommended that the design team confirm strategies with both municipality and utility provider.

Environmental Issues

Tenant sub-metering is a mechanism to enable and encourage energy savings. Energy use must be measured in order to determine what the savings from conservation efforts will be. As a result of these efforts, the cost and environmental impacts associated with energy can be minimized.

Economic Issues

Sub-meters are not a major expense. By allowing tenants the opportunity to know what their electricity usage is, the tenants are given the opportunity to see savings by reducing their energy use.

Resources

Please see the USGBC website at www.usgbc.org/resources for more specific resources on materials sources and other technical information.

Websites

International Performance Measurement & Verification Protocol (IPMVP)

www.ipmvp.org

IPMVP Inc. is a nonprofit organization whose vision is a global marketplace that properly values energy and water efficiency.

Definitions

Energy Conservation Measures (ECMs) are installations of equipment or systems, or modifications of equipment or systems, for the purpose of reducing energy use and/or costs.

| SS | WE | **EA** | MR | EQ | ID |

Credit 5.2

Case Study

1180 Peachtree
Atlanta, Georgia

Photo courtesy of Joe F. Steed

1180 Peachtree is a 41-story, 670,000-sq.ft. mixed-use urban office tower located in Midtown Atlanta in close proximity to the future world-class Atlanta Symphony Center as well as numerous cultural arts venues. The building will house offices, retail merchant space and two restaurants. 1180 Peachtree incorporated state-of-the-art energy-efficient systems, such as high efficiency glazing, exterior shading fins, variable speed fan powered VAV boxes, high efficiency chillers, and heat recovery for preheating in the winter months. Water conservation measures include utilizing an underground stormwater storage vault for landscape irrigation and the use of low flow water use fixtures to lower the building's water use operation expenses. The building design team developed a comprehensive core and shell measurement and verification plan that included a tenant sub-metering plan. Detail regarding which tenant electrical sub-meters could be installed, equipment data, and information on how to gather and utilize the energy use data on a monthly basis was included. Glass selection and building design including a ten-foot floor to ceiling glass shell, allow tenants to design interior spaces that allow natural light to penetrate the building core and create a more spacious work environment with daylighting and views. A Tenant Design and Construction Guidelines manual was developed to assist tenants in optimizing their space design using the core and shell building features.

1180 Peachtree has been awarded LEED-CS Pilot Gold Certification and was the first high-rise office building in the world to earn pre-certified Silver status in the Leadership in Energy and Environmental Design Core and Shell Development program.

Green Power

Intent

Encourage the development and use of grid-source, renewable energy technologies on a net zero pollution basis.

Requirements

Provide at least 35% of the core and shell building's electricity from renewable sources by engaging in at least a two-year renewable energy contract. The core and shell building's electricity is defined as the electricity usage of the core and shell square footage as defined by BOMA calculations, but not less than 15% of the building's gross square footage. Renewable sources are as defined by the Center for Resource Solutions (CRS) Green-e products certification requirements.

DETERMINE THE BASELINE ELECTRICITY USE

Use the annual electricity consumption from the results of EA Credit 1.

OR

Use the Department of Energy (DOE) Commercial Buildings Energy Consumption Survey (CBECS) database to determine the estimated electricity use.

Potential Technologies & Strategies

Determine the energy needs of the building and investigate opportunities to engage in a green power contract. Green power is derived from solar, wind, geothermal, biomass or low-impact hydro sources. Visit www.green-e.org for details about the Green-e program. The power product purchased to comply with credit requirements need not be Green-e certified. Other sources of green power are eligible if they satisfy the Green-e program's technical requirements. Renewable energy certificates (RECs), tradable renewable certificates (TRCs), green tags and other forms of green power that comply with Green-e's technical requirements can be used to document compliance with EA Credit 6 requirements.

Summary of Referenced Standard

Center for Resource Solutions Green-e Product Certification Requirements

www.green-e.org

(888) 634-7336

The Green-e Program is a voluntary certification and verification program for green electricity products. Those products exhibiting the Green-e logo are greener and cleaner than the average retail electricity product sold in that particular region. To be eligible for the Green-e logo, companies must meet certain threshold criteria for their products. Criteria include qualified sources of renewable energy content such as solar electric, wind, geothermal, biomass and small or certified low-impact hydro facilities; "new" renewable energy content (to support new generation capacity); emissions criteria for the non-renewable portion of the energy product; absence of nuclear power; and other criteria regarding renewable portfolio standards and block products. Criteria are often specific per state or region of the United States. Refer to the standard for more details.

Approach and Implementation

There are three approaches for achieving this credit.

1. In a state with an open electrical market, building Owners may have the ability to select a Green-e certified power provider for their electricity purchases. In this scenario, the Owner secures a two-year contract for a minimum of 35% of their annual electrical power consumption from a Green-e certified provider.

2. In a state with a closed electrical market, the governing utility company may have a Green-e accredited utility program. In this case, the Owner sim-ply enrolls in the green power program for at least 35% of the provided electrical energy. In most cases, there is a premium added to the monthly utility billing.

3. If direct purchase of Green-e certified power is not available through the local utilities, the Owner and project team have the option of purchasing Green-e accredited Tradable Renewable Certificates (RECs). In this case, the team purchases a quantity of RECs equal to 35% of the predicted annual electrical consumption over a two year period (which is equivalent to 70% of predicted annual electrical consumption if all of the RECs are purchased at one time). These RECs or "green-tags" compensate Green-e generators for the premium of production over the market rate they sell to the grid. Purchasing Green-e certified RECs will have no impact for the project on the cost or procurement of the electricity from the local electrical utility. See the Calculations section for information on calculating electrical power consumption and determining the 35% threshold.

A separate campus facility that produces green power (to Green-e standards) may supply the building(s) on the same campus or be wheeled to a different campus through an internal campus agreement. Green power may be purchased or installed on a centralized basis and credit attributed to a specific project. This same green power may not be credited to another project.

Core and Shell Concerns

The requirement for this credit is to provide 35% of the core and shell electricity use through a two-year renewable energy purchase contract. This requires the calculation of the core and shell electricity use. Apportioning out the electricity usage of the core and shell part of the building can be challenging. Some core and shell projects do not have areas that may be considered exclusively core and shell. Determining the electricity purchase required for these projects can prove difficult. The goal is to create a uniform methodology for applying this credit across core and shell projects.

The first step is to determine the core and shell electricity usage utilizing BOMA area calculations. If there is no core and shell area or if the BOMA area calculation is less than 15%, use 15% as the default core and shell area. When the project uses the Design Energy Cost compliance path, the electricity use for the whole building should be apportioned out on a square footage basis. This kWh/sf-yr number can then be applied to the core and shell square footage to calculate the core and shell electricity use. For projects electing to use the default electricity consumption, the default kWh/sf-yr is multiplied by the calculated core and shell area.

Calculations

BOMA Area Calculation

The building's core and shell square footage is the gross square footage (GSF) minus the usable square footage (USF). GSF and USF are defined in ANSI/BOMA Standard Z65.1-1996.

To calculate the percentage of the building that is core and shell square footage, first calculate the building's GSF. Next calculate the building's USF. The percentage of the building that is Core and Shell Square footage is:

(GSF-USF)/GSF x 100

If this number is less than 15%, use 15% for the project's calculations.

Applicants have two compliance paths to calculate the amount of electrical energy that must be obtained from Green-e certified providers in order to achieve compliance with EA Credit 6.

1. Design Energy Cost (DEC)

The first compliance path is based on the design case annual electrical consumption that the project team may have calculated as part of compliance with EA Credit 1. The project Owner should contract with a Green-e certified power producer for that amount.

Example EA Credit 6 Calculation Based on Design Energy Cost

In the example of the Perfomance Rating Method for Option1 in EA Credit 1 above, the building's annual electricity use (including tenant use) was 843,422 kWh. From the BOMA calculation above it is determined that the core and shell square footage is 18% of the total building square footage. The core and shell electricity usage is defined as 18% of the total electricity usage. This would equal 151,816 kWh.

Required Green Power for EA Credit 6

151,816 kWh/yr x 35% x 2 yrs = 106,271 kWh

This project would need to purchase Green-e certified green power or RECs equal to 106,271 kWh/yr.

If, for example, the project obtained a quote from a RECs provider of $0.02/kWh, the total cost to the project to earn EA Credit 6 would be $2,125.

2. Default Electricity Consumption

If an energy model was not performed in EA Credit 1, use the Department of Energy (DOE) Commercial Buildings Energy Consumption Survey (CBECS) database to determine the estimated electricity use. This database provides electricity intensity factors (kWh/sf-yr) for various building types in the United States.

Table 1 presents a summary of median annual electrical intensities (kWh/sf-yr) for different building types, based on data from the latest CBECS. The energy intensity multiplied by the square footage

Table 1: Ozone-Depletion and Global-Warming Potentials of Refrigerants (100-yr values)

Building Type	Median Electrical Intensity (kWh/sf-yr)
Education	6.6
Food Sales	58.9
Food Service	28.7
Health Care Inpatient	21.5
Health Care Outpatient	9.7
Lodging	12.6
Retail (Other than Mall)	8.0
Enclosed and Strip Malls	14.5
Office	11.7
Public Assembly	6.8
Public Order and Safety	4.1
Religious Worship	2.5
Service	6.1
Warehouse and Storage	3.0
Other	13.8

of the project represents the total amount of green power (in kWh) that would need to be purchased over a two-year period to qualify for EA Credit 6 using this option.

Example EA Credit 6 Calculation Based on CBECS Data

The project is a 950,000-sq.ft. speculative office building. According to the BOMA calculation, the core and shell is 20% of the building total square footage or 190,000 sq.ft. The calculation for the renewable energy required is based on this 190,000 sq.ft. In order to determine how much renewable energy is needed to meet the requirements of EA Credit 6, use **Table 1** and the median electrical consumption intensity for offices.

Default Annual Electrical Consumption

190,000 sf x 11.7 kWh/sf-yr = 2,223,000 kWh/yr

Required Green Power for EA Credit 6

2,223,000 kWh/yr x 35% x 2 yrs = 1,556,100 kWh

This project would need to purchase Green-e certified green power or RECs equal to 1,556,100 kWh/yr. If, for example, the project obtained a quote from a RECs provider of $0.02/kWh, the total cost to the project to earn EA Credit 6 would be $31,122.

Exemplary Performance

Exemplary performance can be achieved by doubling the requirements of this credit, either by the amount of electricity or the length of contract.

Submittal Documentation

This credit is submitted as part of the **Construction Submittal**.

Design and Construction Credit Compliance

The following project data and calculation information is required to document credit compliance using the LEED-CS v2.0 Submittal Templates:

OPTION 1

❏ Provide the name of the green power provider and contract term

❏ Enter total annual electricity consumption (kWh) and total annual green power purchase (kWh)

OPTION 2

❑ Provide the name of the renewable energy certificate vendor

❑ Enter total annual electricity consumption (kWh)

❑ Enter the value of the green tags purchased (kWh)

Tenant Sales or Lease Agreement Credit Compliance

This compliance method is not available for this credit.

Considerations

Environmental Issues

Energy production is a significant contributor to air pollution in the United States. Air pollutants released from energy production include sulfur dioxide, nitrogen oxide and carbon dioxide. These pollutants are primary contributors to acid rain, smog and global warming. With other associated pollutants, they have widespread and adverse effects on human health in general, especially on human respiratory systems. The Green-e Program was established by the Center for Resource Solutions to promote green electricity products and provide consumers with a rigorous and nationally recognized method to identify green electricity products. These products reduce the air pollution impacts of electricity generation by relying on renewable energy sources such as solar, water, wind, biomass and geothermal sources. In addition, the use of ecologically responsive energy sources avoids reliance on nuclear power and large-scale hydropower. Deregulated energy markets have enabled hydroelectric generation activities to market their electricity in regions unaffected by the regional impacts that dams can have on endangered aquatic species. While green electricity is not environmentally benign, it greatly lessens the negative environmental impacts of power generation.

Costs for green power products may be somewhat greater than conventional energy products. However, green power products are derived, in part, from renewable energy sources with stable energy costs. As the green power market matures and impacts on the environment and human health are factored into power costs, green power products are expected to be less expensive than conventional power products.

Resources

Please see the USGBC website at www.usgbc.org/resources for more specific resources on materials sources and other technical information.

Websites

The Green Power Network

U.S. Department of Energy

www.eere.energy.gov/greenpower

Provides news on green power markets and utility pricing programs—both domestic and international. It contains up-to-date information on green power providers, product offerings, consumer issues and in-depth analyses of issues and policies affecting green power markets. The website is maintained by the National Renewable Energy Laboratory for the Department of Energy.

Green-e Program

www.green-e.org

(888) 634-7336

See the Summary of Referenced Standard for more information.

Clean Energy

Union of Concerned Scientists

www.ucsusa.org/clean_energy

(617) 547-5552

UCS is an independent nonprofit that analyzes and advocates energy solutions that are sustainable both environmen-

Credit 6

tally and economically. The site provides news and information on research and public policy.

Green Power Partnership

U.S. Environmental Protection Agency (EPA)

www.epa.gov/greenpower

EPA's Green Power Partnership is a new voluntary program designed to reduce the environmental impact of electricity generation by promoting renewable energy. The Partnership will demonstrate the advantages of choosing renewable energy, provide objective and current information about the green power market, and reduce the transaction costs of acquiring green power.

BOMA

www.boma.org

BOMA International was founded in 1907 as the National Association of Building Owners and Managers. The association assumed its present name in 1968 as it broadened its reach to include Canada and other affiliates around the globe.

BOMA publishes the BOMA *Standard*, which is the floor measurement method for commercial real estate approved by the American National Standards Institute (ANSI).

Definitions

No definitions for this section.

Materials and Resources

Building materials choices are important in sustainable design because of the extensive network of extraction, processing and transportation steps required to process them. Activities to create building materials may pollute the air and water, destroy natural habitats and deplete natural resources. Construction and demolition wastes constitute about 40% of the total solid waste stream in the United States.

Maintaining occupancy rates in existing buildings reduces redundant development and the associated environmental impact of producing and delivering all new materials. Reuse of existing buildings, versus building new structures, is one of the most effective strategies for minimizing environmental impacts. When rehabilitation of existing buildings components is included in the strategy, waste volumes can be reduced or diverted from landfills. Reuse results in less habitat disturbance and typically less infrastructure. An effective way to use salvaged interior components is to specify them in the construction documents. The actions of an increasing number of public and private waste management operations have reduced construction debris volumes by recycling these materials. Recovery activities typically begin with job-site separation into multiple bins or disposal areas. In some areas, regional recycling facilities are being constructed to accept commingled waste and separate the recyclable materials from those that must go to the landfill. These facilities are achieving waste diversion rates of 80% or greater in many areas.

When materials are selected for a project, it is important to evaluate new and different sources. Salvaged materials can be substituted for new materials, save costs and add character. Recycled-content materials reuse waste products that would otherwise be deposited in landfills. Use of local materials supports the local economy and reduces transportation. Use of rapidly renewable materials minimizes natural resource consumption and has the potential to better match the harvest cycle of the resource with the life of the material in buildings. Use of third-party certified wood improves the stewardship of forests and the related ecosystems.

Materials Cost

While projects are encouraged to determine the actual total materials cost (excluding labor and equipment) for calculation purposes, LEED-CS allows project teams to apply a 45% factor to total costs (including labor and equipment) to establish a default total materials cost for the project. Please reference **Table 2** for guidance regarding specification sections included in the cost calculation. The approach selected by the project team, (actual materials cost, or LEED default costs) must be consistent across all credits based on total materials cost. A project submittal may elect to include materials costs from Construction Specification Institute MasterFormat™ Division 12, furniture and furnishings, as long as this is utilized consistently. LEED-CS submittals that elect to utilize tenant sales or lease agreements to assist with credit compliance must also do so consistently.

Materials & Resources Credit Characteristics

Table 1 shows which credits were substantially revised from LEED-NC Version 2.2, which credits are eligible to be submitted in the Design Phase Submittal, and which project team members are likely to carry decision-making responsibility for each credit. The decision-making responsibility matrix is not intended to exclude any

Overview of LEED® Prerequisites and Credits

MR Prerequisite 1
Storage & Collection of Recyclables

MR Credit 1.1
Building Reuse—
Maintain 25% of Existing Walls, Floors & Roof

MR Credit 1.2
Building Reuse—
Maintain 50% of Existing Walls, Floors & Roof

MR Credit 1.3
Building Reuse—
Maintain 75% of Existing Walls, Floors & Roof

MR Credit 2.1
Construction Waste Management—
Divert 50% from Disposal

MR Credit 2.2
Construction Waste Management—
Divert 75% from Disposal

MR Credit 3
Materials Reuse—1%

MR Credit 4.1
Recycled Content—
10% (post-consumer + 1/2 pre-consumer)

MR Credit 4.2
Recycled Content—
20% (post-consumer + 1/2 pre-consumer)

MR Credit 5.1
Regional Materials—
10% Extracted, Processed & Manufactured Regionally

MR Credit 5.2
Regional Materials—
20% Extracted, Processed & Manufactured Regionally

MR Credit 6
Certified Wood

party, rather to emphasize those credits that are most likely to require strong participation by a particular team member.

The Materials & Resources credits are organized around several key parameters and categories. **Table 2** shows the metrics used to determine compliance with each credit, such as area, weight and cost. The table also shows which materials are included and excluded in the calculations. Materials that are blacked out in the table below are excluded from the corresponding credit calculations.

Special notes:

❑ Materials qualifying as reused for MR Credit 3.1 and 3.2 cannot be applied to MR Credits 1, 2, 4 or 6.

❑ Projects that are incorporating existing buildings but do not meet the requirements for MR Credit 1 may apply the reused portions of the existing buildings towards the achievement of MR Credit 2, Construction Waste Management.

Table 1: MR Credit Characteristics

Credit	Significant Change from LEED-NC v2.2	Design Submittal	Construction Submittal	Owner Decision-Making	Design Team Decision-Making	Contractor Decision-Making
MRp1: Storage & Collection of Recyclables		*		*	*	
MRc1.1: Building Reuse, Maintain 25% of Existing Walls, Floors & Roof	*		*	*	*	
MRc1.2: Building Reuse, Maintain 50% of Existing Walls, Floors & Roof	*		*	*	*	
MRc1.3: Building Reuse, Maintain 75% of Existing Walls, Floors & Roof	*		*	*	*	
MRc2.1: Construction Waste Management, Divert 50% from Disposal			*			*
MRc2.2: Construction Waste Management, Divert 75% from Disposal			*			*
MRc3: Materials Reuse, 1%	*		*		*	*
MRc4.1: Recycled Content, 10% (post-consumer + 1/2 pre-consumer)			*		*	*
MRc4.1: Recycled Content, 20% (post-consumer + 1/2 pre-consumer)			*		*	*
MRc5.1: Regional Materials, 10% Extracted, Processed & Manufactured Regionally			*		*	*
MRc5.1: Regional Materials, 20% Extracted, Processed & Manufactured Regionally			*		*	*
MRc6: Certified Wood			*		*	*

Table 2: MR Credit Metrics

Material	MRc1: Building Reuse	MRc2: Construction Waste Management	MRc3: Materials Reuse	MRc4: Recycled Content	MRc5: Regional Materials	MRc6: Certified Wood
CSI Divisions 2 thru 10	Based on area	Based on weight or volume. Include demolition and construction waste	Based on replacement value ($)	Based on cost of qualifying materials as a percent of overall materials cost for Divisions 2–10 ($)		Based on cost of FSC wood as a percentage of all new wood ($)
Mechanical						
Electrical						
Plumbing			May be included with Divisions 2–10, if done consistently for credits 3–7			
Furniture & Furnishings (CSI Division 12)			May be included with Divisions 2–10, if done consistently for credits 3–7			

Overview

Case Study

SBRI Building
Seattle, Washington

Photo courtesy of: Doug Scott Photography

The Seattle Biomedical Research Institute (SBRI) Building is a new five-story, 112,000-sq.ft., high performance biomedical research facility, sited just north of downtown Seattle. An innovative HVAC system reduces energy use by recovering both waste heat and cooling with custom air handlers and sprayed heat pipes. The system's design allowed both the boiler and chiller to be downsized, significantly reducing capital costs when compared to conventional laboratory systems. These and other strategies help reduce the core and shell modeled energy use by 35% beyond the ASHRAE 90.1-1999 base case. Reflective roofing, underground parking and the exterior lighting design help protect the local environment by minimizing nighttime light pollution and urban heat islands. Convenient bicycle storage, showers, and changing areas serve the needs of the facility's many bicycle-commuting researchers. Parking provides preferred spaces for carpools and vanpools. Tenants incorporated several of the core and shell's sustainable strategies into their tenant improvement scope of work including low-emitting building materials and furnishings, recycled content materials, energy-efficient fume hoods, and HVAC equipment with alternative refrigerants.

The Seattle Biomedical Research Institute was awarded LEED-CS Silver Rating making it one of the first laboratory buildings in the nation to qualify at this level.

Storage & Collection of Recyclables

Intent

Facilitate the reduction of waste generated by building occupants that is hauled to and disposed of in landfills.

Requirements

Provide an easily accessible area that serves the entire building and is dedicated to the collection and storage of non-hazardous materials for recycling, including (at a minimum) paper, corrugated cardboard, glass, plastics and metals.

Can assist tenants in certification under LEED for Commercial Interiors

Potential Technologies & Strategies

Coordinate the size and functionality of the recycling areas with the anticipated collection services for glass, plastic, office paper, newspaper, cardboard and organic wastes to maximize the effectiveness of the dedicated areas. Consider employing cardboard balers, aluminum can crushers, recycling chutes and collection bins at individual workstations to further enhance the recycling program.

Summary of Referenced Standard

There is no standard referenced for this credit.

Approach and Implementation

Dense urban areas typically have a recycling infrastructure in place while some less populated areas may still be developing this type of service. Building owners and designers must determine the most appropriate method for creating a dedicated recycling collection area that meets the project occupant's needs and also those of the collection infrastructure. It is possible that recyclable collection and storage space could increase the project footprint in some instances. It is important to address possible indoor environmental quality (IEQ) impacts on occupants due to recycling activities. Those activities that create odors, noise and air contaminants should be isolated or performed during non-occupant hours to maintain optimal IEQ. **Table 1** provides guidelines for the recycling storage area based on overall building square footage. The requirements of this prerequisite do not regulate the size of the recycling area. The intent is for the design team to size the facilities appropriate to the specific building operations, and the information provided below is intended as a resource for that exercise.

Designate well marked collection and storage areas for recyclables including office paper, cardboard, glass, plastic and metals. Locate a central collection and storage area in the basement or at the ground level that provides easy access for maintenance staff as well as collection vehicles. For projects with larger site areas, it may be possible to create a separate central collection area that is not located within the building footprint.

Design considerations for recycling areas should include signage to prevent con-

Table 1: Recycling Area Guidelines

Commercial Building Square Footage [sf]	Minimum Recycling Area [sf]
0 to 5,000	82
5,001 to 15,000	125
15,001 to 50,000	175
50,001 to 100,000	225
100,001 to 200,000	275
200,001 or greater	500

tamination, protection from the elements, and security for high value materials. Security of recyclable collection areas should also be designed to discourage illegal disposal. Allocate recycling space in common areas accessible to tenants as well as a centralized collection point. Common areas may be more easily maintained if recycling containers are no larger than 20–25 gallons. It may be beneficial to specify recycling bins that have wheeled carts to transport the recyclables from the common area to a centralized collection area. At the centralized collection point, it is useful to design enough space for a front-loader bin as well as a ramp up to the recycling area.

It may be helpful to research local recycling programs to find the best method of diverting recyclable materials from the waste stream for your particular building location. When allocating space for the centralized collection point of recyclables, it is beneficial to involve the local hauler who will be providing waste management services to the site. Space allocation needs can vary depending upon collection strategies used by the hauler; such as commingled or source-separated recyclables. For example, if the local hauler accepts commingled recyclables, then it may be possible to reduce the area that would be required if separate collection bins for each material were required. There is no requirement for projects to provide proof of contract for hauling services to achieve this prerequisite.

Where possible, provide instruction to tenants, building users, and maintenance personnel on recycling procedures. Encourage activities to reduce and reuse materials before recycling in order to reduce the amount of recyclable volumes handled. For instance, building tenants can be encouraged to reduce the solid waste stream by using reusable bottles, bags and other containers. Consider employing cardboard balers, aluminum can crushers, recycling chutes and other waste management technologies to further enhance the recycling program.

Core and Shell Concerns

Core and shell buildings will need to consider the maintenance and waste management practices for the entire building including tenant spaces. Dependant on the region, market, and business traits (or customs, or culture), core and shell building owners may approach these practices differently. Building owners who provide cleaning services for all tenants are able to control both the space needs and the procedures for removing, storing and hauling of recyclables. In these instances, the space needs should be evaluated based on the frequency the waste and recyclables are removed from the tenant spaces. In buildings where tenants contract their own cleaning services waste management should be addressed by providing adequate space for recyclable storage, and including specific instructions for use within tenant guidelines.

Larger buildings, and buildings where the cleaning services are contracted directly by the tenants, may want to consider a recycling approach that provides staged recyclable storage areas. For example, buildings with multiple tenant floors or large floor plates may want to provide storage spaces in the building core areas conveniently accessed by tenants. Recycla-bles can then be collected and removed as needed by the building owner's contracted recycling service.

Calculations

There are no calculations required to demonstrate compliance with this prerequisite. **Table 1** is provided as a guideline for sizing recycling areas. The values in this table were developed by the city of Seattle in support of an ordinance requiring minimum areas for recycling and storage of recyclables in commercial buildings. The ordinance is based on the total square footage of the building. Minimum areas for residential buildings were also specified in that reference document, but at not included in this guide.

Another potential source of guidelines for sizing recycling areas is the California Integrated Waste Management Board's (CIWMB) 1999 Statewide Waste Characterization Study, in which the waste disposal rates of 1,200 businesses were measured. See the References section of this prerequisite for details.

Precertification Submittal Documentation

Provide the LEED-CS Precertification Letter template, which includes the following:

❑ Narrative describing how the project intends to accomplish the credit requirements

❑ Confirmation of this intent from both the design professional and the owner/developer

Certification Submittal Documentation

This prerequisite is submitted as part of the **Design Submittal**.

Design and Construction Credit Compliance

The following project data and calculation information is required to document prerequisite compliance using the LEED-CS v2.0 Submittal Templates:

❏ Confirm that recycling collection areas have been provided, per requirements, to meet the needs of the project.

❏ Confirm the types of materials that are being collected for recycling.

❏ Provide an optional narrative describing any special circumstances or considerations regarding the project's prerequisite approach.

Tenant Sales or Lease Agreement Credit Compliance

This compliance method is not available for this prerequisite.

Considerations

Environmental Issues

By creating convenient recycling opportunities for building occupants, a significant portion of the solid waste stream can be diverted from landfills. Recycling of paper, metals, cardboard and plastics reduces the need to extract virgin natural resources. For example, recycling one ton of paper prevents the processing of 17 trees and saves three cubic yards of landfill space. Recycled aluminum requires only 5% of the energy required to produce virgin aluminum from bauxite, its raw material. Recycling also reduces environmental impacts of waste in landfills. Land, water and air pollution impacts can all be reduced by minimizing the volume of waste sent to landfills.

Economic Issues

Recycling requires minimal initial cost and offers significant savings in reduced landfill disposal costs or tipping fees. However, recycling activities use floor space that could be used otherwise. In larger projects, processing equipment such as can crushers and cardboard balers are effective at minimizing the space required for recycling activities. Some recyclables can generate revenue which can help to offset the cost of their collection and processing.

Resources

Please see the USGBC website at www. usgbc.org/resources for more specific resources on materials sources and other technical information.

Websites

California Integrated Waste Management Board

www.ciwmb.ca.gov/WasteChar/

Solid Waste Characterization Database, Estimated Solid Waste Generation Rates

California Statewide Solid Waste Characterization Study

www.ciwmb.ca.gov/Publications/default. asp?pubid=1097

Alternative Waste Calculations

California Integrated Waste Management Board's (CIWMB) Statewide Waste Characterization Study in which the waste disposal rates of businesses are measured.

Earth 911

www.earth911.org/master.asp

(480) 889-2650 or 877-EARTH911

Information and education programs on recycling as well as regional links to recyclers

Recycling at Work

U.S. Conference of Mayors

www.usmayors.org/USCM/recycle

(202) 293-7330

A program of the U.S. Conference of Mayors that provides information on workplace recycling efforts.

Waste at Work

Inform: Strategies for a Better Environment

www.informinc.org/wasteatwork.php

(212) 361-2400

An online document from Inform, Inc., and the Council on the Environment of New York City on strategies and case studies to reduce workplace waste generation.

Print Media

Composting and Recycling Municipal Solid Waste by Luis Diaz et al., CRC Press, 1993.

McGraw-Hill Recycling Handbook by Herbert F. Lund, McGraw-Hill, 2000.

Definitions

A **Landfill** is a waste disposal site for the deposit of solid waste from human activities.

Recycling is the collection, reprocessing, marketing and use of materials that were diverted or recovered from the solid waste stream.

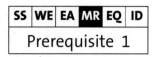

| SS | WE | EA | **MR** | EQ | ID |

Prerequisite 1

Building Reuse

Maintain 25% of Existing Walls, Floors & Roof

Can assist tenants in certification under LEED for Commercial Interiors

Intent

Extend the life cycle of existing building stock, conserve resources, retain cultural resources, reduce waste and reduce environmental impacts of new buildings as they relate to materials manufacturing and transport.

Requirements

Maintain at least 25% (based on surface area) of existing building structure (including structural floor and roof decking) and envelope (exterior skin and framing, excluding window assemblies and non-structural roofing material). Hazardous materials that are remediated as a part of the project scope shall be excluded from the calculation of the percentage maintained. If the project includes an addition to an existing building, this credit is not applicable if the square footage of the addition is more than 6 times the square footage of the existing building.

Potential Technologies & Strategies

Consider reuse of existing, previously occupied buildings, including structure, envelope and elements. Remove elements that pose contamination risk to building occupants and upgrade components that would improve energy and water efficiency such as windows, mechanical systems and plumbing fixtures. Quantify the extent of building reuse.

1 Point
in addition to
MR Credit 1.1

Can assist tenants in certification
under LEED for Commercial Interiors

Building Reuse

Maintain 50% of Existing Walls, Floors & Roof

Intent

Extend the life cycle of existing building stock, conserve resources, retain cultural resources, reduce waste and reduce environmental impacts of new buildings as they relate to materials manufacturing and transport.

Requirements

Maintain at least 50% (based on surface area) of existing building structure (including structural floor and roof decking) and envelope (exterior skin and framing, excluding window assemblies and non-structural roofing material). Hazardous materials that are remediated as a part of the project scope shall be excluded from the calculation of the percentage maintained. If the project includes an addition to an existing building, this credit is not applicable if the square footage of the addition is more than 6 times the square footage of the existing building.

Potential Technologies & Strategies

Consider reuse of existing, previously occupied buildings, including structure, envelope and elements. Remove elements that pose contamination risk to building occupants and upgrade components that would improve energy and water efficiency such as windows, mechanical systems and plumbing fixtures. Quantify the extent of building reuse.

Building Reuse
Maintain 75% of Interior Non-Structural Elements

Can assist tenants in certification under LEED for Commercial Interiors

Intent

Extend the life cycle of existing building stock, conserve resources, retain cultural resources, reduce waste and reduce environmental impacts of new buildings as they relate to materials manufacturing and transport.

Requirements

Maintain at least 75% (based on surface area) of existing building structure (including structural floor and roof decking) and envelope (exterior skin and framing, excluding window assemblies and non-structural roofing material). Hazardous materials that are remediated as a part of the project scope shall be excluded from the calculation of the percentage maintained. If the project includes an addition to an existing building, this credit is not applicable if the square footage of the addition is more than 6 times the square footage of the existing building.

Potential Technologies & Strategies

Consider reuse of existing, previously occupied buildings, including structure, envelope and interior non-structural elements. Remove elements that pose contamination risk to building occupants and upgrade components that would improve energy and water efficiency, such as mechanical systems and plumbing fixtures. Quantify the extent of building reuse.

Summary of Referenced Standard

There is no standard referenced for this credit.

Approach and Implementation

For any project that is reusing portions of an existing building, it is recommended that the project team inventory the existing conditions. Develop a floor plan showing the location of existing structural components, building core, and building envelope (exterior windows and doors). The drawings should provide the detail needed to determine the surface area of all these pre-existing elements.

Confirm that the items designated for reuse can be reused. Take the needed steps to retain them in the finished work. Fixed items, such as walls and doors that are found on-site are included in this credit and count toward the percentage of reuse when they perform the same function (i.e., doors reused as doors). If they are used for another purpose (i.e., doors made into tables) they contribute to earning MR Credits 3.1 and 3.2.

Projects that are incorporating existing buildings but do not meet the requirements for MR Credit 1 may apply the reused portions of the existing buildings toward the achievement of MR Credit 2, Construction Waste Management. To do so, project teams will be required to determine an approximate weight for existing building elements.

Calculations

This credit is based on surface areas of major existing building structural, core and envelope elements. Structural support elements, such as columns and beams, are considered to be a part of the larger surfaces they are supporting and are not required to be quantified separately. Pre-

pare a spreadsheet listing all envelope and structural elements within the building. Quantify each item, listing existing area (sq.ft.) and retained area (sq.ft.). Determine the percent of existing elements that are retained by dividing the total retained materials area (sq.ft.) by the total existing materials area (sq.ft.). Projects that retain a minimum of 25% of existing envelope and structural components will be awarded 1 point for MR Credit 1.1. Projects that retain a minimum of 50% of existing envelope and structural components will be awarded 2 points, and projects that retain a minimum of 75% of existing envelope and structural components will be awarded 3 points.

The area measurements are made in the same way as would be completed by a contractor preparing a bid for construction of a building. For structural floors and roof decking, calculate the square footage of each component. For existing exterior walls and existing walls adjoining other buildings or additions, calculate the exterior wall surface area (sq.ft.) only and subtract the area of exterior windows and exterior doors from both the existing and reused area tallies. For interior structural walls (i.e., shear walls), calculate the surface area (sq.ft.) of both sides of the existing wall element.

Table 1 provides an example of this calculation.

Project teams should exclude the following items from this calculation: non-structural roofing materials; window assemblies; structural and envelope materials that are deemed to be unsound from a structural perspective; structural and envelope materials that are considered hazardous and pose a contamination risk to building occupants.

Exemplary Performance

Exemplary performance may be achieved for this credit by maintaining 95% of existing walls, floors and roof.

Table 1: Example Building Structure / Envelope Reuse Calculation

Structure / Envelope Element	Existing Area (SF)	Reused Area (SF)	Percentage Reused (%)
Foundation / Slab on Grade	11,520	11,520	100%
2nd Floor Deck	11,520	10,000	87%
1st Floor Interior Structural Walls	240	240	100%
2nd Floor Interior Structural Walls	136	136	100%
Roof Deck	11,520	11,520	100%
North Exterior Wall (excl. windows)	8,235	7,150	87%
South Exterior Wall (excl. windows)	8,235	8,235	100%
East Exterior Wall (excl. windows)	6,535	6,535	100%
West Exterior Wall (excl. windows)	6,535	5,820	81%
TOTALS	**64,476**	**61,156**	**95%**

Precertification Submittal Documentation

Provide the LEED-CS Precertification Letter template, which includes the following:

❑ Narrative describing how the project intends to accomplish the credit requirements

❑ Confirmation of this intent from both the design professional and the owner/developer

Certification Submittal Documentation

These credits are submitted as part of the Construction Submittal.

Design and Construction Credit Compliance

The following project data and calculation information is required to document prerequisite compliance using the LEED-CS v2.0 Submittal Templates:

❑ Confirm whether the project is strictly a renovation of an existing building or a renovation with an addition. For projects with additions, confirm the square footage of the new addition(s).

❑ Provide a tabulation of the existing and reused areas (sq.ft.) of each structural/ envelope element.

❑ Provide an optional narrative describing any special circumstances or considerations regarding the project's prerequisite approach.

Tenant Sales or Lease Agreement Credit Compliance

This compliance method is not available for this prerequisite.

Considerations

Environmental Issues

Reusing existing buildings significantly reduces construction waste volumes. Reuse strategies also reduce environmental impacts associated with raw material extraction, manufacture and transportation.

Economic Issues

Reuse of existing components can reduce the cost of construction substantially. For instance, the Southern California Gas Company reused an existing building for its Energy Resource Center and estimated savings of approximately $3.2 million, based on typical first costs for a 44,000 square-foot building. The largest savings were realized in masonry (87% savings), site work (57% savings), concrete (49% savings) and carpentry (70% savings).

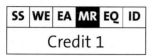

Resources

Please see the USGBC website at www. usgbc.org/resources for more specific resources on materials sources and other technical information.

Print Media

How Buildings Learn: What Happens After They're Built by Stewart Brand.

Definitions

Completed Design Area is the total area of building structure, core and envelope when the project is completed; exterior windows and exterior doors are not considered.

Existing Area is the total area of building structure, core and envelope that existed when the project area was selected; exterior windows and exterior doors are not considered.

Prior Condition is the state the project space was in at the time it was selected. Removing the demolition work from the project scope by making it the building owner's responsibility defeats the objective of this credit.

Reused Area is the total area of the building structure, core and envelope that existed in the prior condition that remained in the completed design.

Construction Waste Management

Divert 50% from Disposal

Intent

Divert construction, demolition and land-clearing debris from disposal in landfills and incinerators. Redirect recyclable recovered resources back to the manufacturing process. Redirect reusable materials to appropriate sites.

Requirements

Recycle and/or salvage at least 50% of non-hazardous construction and demolition debris. Develop and implement a construction waste management plan that, at a minimum, identifies the materials to be diverted from disposal and whether the materials will be sorted on-site or commingled. Excavated soil and land-clearing debris do not contribute to this credit. Calculations can be done by weight or volume, but must be consistent throughout.

Potential Technologies & Strategies

Establish goals for diversion from disposal in landfills and incinerators and adopt a construction waste management plan to achieve these goals. Consider recycling cardboard, metal, brick, acoustical tile, concrete, plastic, clean wood, glass, gypsum wallboard, carpet and insulation. Designate a specific area(s) on the construction site for segregated or commingled collection of recyclable materials, and track recycling efforts throughout the construction process. Identify construction haulers and recyclers to handle the designated materials. Note that diversion may include donation of materials to charitable organizations and salvage of materials on-site.

1 Point
in addition to
MR Credit 2.1

Construction Waste Management

Divert 75% from Disposal

Intent

Divert construction and demolition debris from disposal in landfills and incinerators. Redirect recyclable recovered resources back to the manufacturing process. Redirect reusable materials to appropriate sites.

Requirements

Recycle and/or salvage an additional 25% beyond MR Credit 2.1 (75% total) of non-hazardous construction and demolition debris. Excavated soil and land-clearing debris do not contribute to this credit. Calculations can be done by weight or volume, but must be consistent throughout.

Potential Technologies & Strategies

Establish goals for diversion from disposal in landfills and incinerators and adopt a construction waste management plan to achieve these goals. Consider recycling cardboard, metal, brick, acoustical tile, concrete, plastic, clean wood, glass, gypsum wallboard, carpet and insulation. Designate a specific area(s) on the construction site for segregated or commingled collection of recyclable materials, and track recycling efforts throughout the construction process. Identify construction haulers and recyclers to handle the designated materials. Note that diversion may include donation of materials to charitable organizations and salvage of materials on-site.

Summary of Referenced Standard

There is no standard referenced for this credit.

Approach and Implementation

MR Credits 2.1 and 2.2 address the extent to which waste material leaving the site is diverted from landfills. The percentage represents the amount diverted through recycling and salvage divided by the total waste generated.

Identify construction haulers and recyclers to handle the designated materials; they often serve as valuable partners in this effort. Make sure jobsite personnel understand and participate in the program, with updates throughout the construction process. Obtain and retain verification records (waste haul receipts, waste management reports, spreadsheets, etc.) to confirm the diverted materials have been recycled or salvaged as intended. Note that diversion may include donations to charitable organizations such as Habitat for Humanity®.

The availability of recycling opportunities tends to vary by region. In urban areas, recycling resources are typically more developed, and projects will have choices about whether to separate waste on-site or to hire a commingled waste recycler. Often, recycling construction waste can reduce project costs by significantly reducing landfill tipping fees. Commingled recycling may increase recycling costs but will simplify the waste management effort on-site and ensure that diversion rates will be high. This option is especially useful for projects with tight site constraints where there is no room for multiple collection bins. In more rural and remote areas, recyclers may be harder to find. The environmental benefits of recycling in these cases need to be balanced against the environmental impacts of transporting waste long distances to recycling centers.

Materials can be contaminated by other construction debris and food waste products. Beverages and other liquids can be particularly harmful to materials that may absorb these products, eliminating their ability to be recycled.

Projects that reuse existing buildings, but do not qualify for MR Credit 1, may apply the weight of the reused building materials towards achievement of this credit.

Calculations

Calculations for these credits are based on the amount of waste diverted from the landfill or incineration compared to the total amount of waste generated on-site. Convert all materials to either weight or volume in order to calculate the percentage. Hazardous waste should be excluded from calculations, and should be disposed of appropriately according to relevant regulations. Additionally, excavated soil and land clearing debris should be excluded from calculations. Projects that crush and reuse existing concrete, masonry or asphalt on-site should include the weight of these materials in the calculations for this credit. **Table 1** provides an example of a summary calculation for waste diversion.

If exact material weights are not available, project teams may use the conversion factors from **Table 2** to estimate the weight of construction waste.

For projects that use commingled recycling rather than on-site separation, summaries of diversion rates will be required from the recycler. Typically, the recycler should be required to provide monthly reports.

Exemplary Performance

Project teams may earn an Innovation in Design point for exemplary performance in Construction Waste Management when the percent of total waste diverted is 95% or greater.

Table 1: Sample Construction Waste Management Diversion Summary

Diverted / Recycled Materials Description	Diversion / Recycling Hauler or Location	Quantity of Diverted / Recycled Waste	Units (tons / cy)
Concrete	ABC Recycling	138.0	Tons
Wood	Z-Construction Reuse	10.2	Tons
Gypsum Wallboard	ABC Recycling	6.3	Tons
Steel	Re-Cycle Steel Collectors	1.1	Tons
Crushed Asphalt	On-Site Reuse	98.2	Tons
Masonry	ABC Recycling	6.8	Tons
Cardboard	ABC Recycling	1.6	Tons
TOTAL CONSTRUCTION WASTE DIVERTED		**262.2**	**Tons**

Landfill Materials Description	Landfill Hauler or Location	Quantity of Diverted / Recycled Waste	Units (tons / cy)
General Mixed Waste	XYZ Landfill	52.3	Tons
TOTAL CONSTRUCTION WASTE SENT TO LANDFILL		**52.3**	**Tons**
TOTAL OF ALL CONSTRUCTION WASTE		**314.5**	**Tons**
PERCENTAGE OF CONSTRUCTION WASTE DIVERTED FROM LANDFILL		**83.4%**	

Table 2: Solid Waste Conversion Factors

Material	Density [lbs/cy]
Cardboard	100
Gypsum Wallboard	500
Mixed Waste	350
Rubble	1,400
Steel	1,000
Wood	300

Precertification Submittal Documentation

Provide the LEED-CS Precertification Letter template, which includes the following:

❏ Narrative describing how the project intends to accomplish the credit requirements

❏ Confirmation of this intent from both the design professional and the owner/developer

Certification Submittal Documentation

These credits are submitted as part of the Construction Submittal.

Design and Construction Credit Compliance

The following project data and calculation information is required to document prerequisite compliance using the LEED-CS v2.0 Submittal Templates:

❏ Complete the construction waste calculation tables in the Submittal Template. The following information will be required to fill in these tables: general description of each type/category of waste generated; location of receiving agent (recycler/landfill) for waste; quantity of waste diverted (by category) in tons or cubic yards.

❏ Provide a narrative describing the project's construction waste management approach. The narrative should include the project's Construction Waste Management Plan. Please provide any additional comments or notes to describe special circumstances or considerations regarding the project's credit approach.

Tenant Sales or Lease Agreement Credit Compliance

This compliance method is not available for this credit.

Considerations

Environmental Issues

Construction and demolition (C&D) activities generate enormous quantities of solid waste. The U.S. EPA estimates that 136 million tons of C&D debris (versus 209.7 million tons of municipal solid waste) was generated in 1996—57% of it from non-residential construction, renovation and demolition activities. This equates to 2.8 pounds per capita per day. Commercial construction generates between 2 and 2.5 pounds of solid waste per square foot, and the majority of this waste can potentially be recycled.

The greatest environmental benefit is achieved by source control—reducing the total waste generated.

Recycling opportunities are expanding rapidly in many regions. Metal, vegetation, concrete and asphalt recycling opportunities have long been available and economical in most communities. Paper, corrugated cardboard, plastics and clean wood markets vary by regional and local recycling infrastructure, but are recycled in most communities. Some materials, such as gypsum wallboard, have recycling opportunities only in communities where reprocessing plants exist or where soil can handle the material as a stabilizing agent. The recyclability of a demolished material is often dependant on the amount of contamination attached to it. Demolished wood, for instance, is often not reusable or recyclable unless it is deconstructed and de-nailed.

Recycling of construction and demolition debris reduces demand for virgin resources and, in turn, reduces the environmental impacts associated with resource extraction, processing and, in many cases, transportation. Landfills contaminate groundwater and encroach upon valuable green space. Through effective construction waste management, it is possible to extend the lifetime of existing landfills, avoiding the need for expansion or new landfill sites.

Economic Issues

In the past, when landfill capacity was readily available and disposal fees were low, recycling or reuse of construction waste was not economically feasible. Construction materials were inexpensive compared to the cost of labor; thus, construction jobsite managers focused on worker productivity rather than on materials conservation. In addition, recycling infrastructure and a recycled materials marketplace that processes and resells construction debris did not exist. In recent years, particularly with the advent of international competition for both raw and recycled materials, the economics of recycling have improved. During this same period disposal costs have increased. Recognition for, and enactment of, more stringent waste disposal regulations coupled with ever decreasing landfill capacity have changed the waste management equation.

Waste management plans require time and money to draft and implement but they can also provide the guidance to achieve substantial savings throughout the construction process.

Recyclable materials have differing market values depending on the presence of local recycling facilities, reprocessing costs and the availability of virgin materials on the market. In general, it is economically beneficial to recycle metals, concrete, asphalt and cardboard. In most cases it is possible to receive revenue as well as avoid paying a landfill tipping fee. Market values normally fluctuate from month to month. When no revenue is received for materials, as is often the case for scrap wood and gypsum wallboard, it is still possible to benefit from potentially shorter hauling distances and by avoiding landfill tipping fees.

Resources

Please see the USGBC website at www.usgbc.org/resources for more specific resources on materials sources and other technical information.

Websites

Construction and Demolition Debris Recycling Information

California Integrated Waste Management Board

www.ciwmb.ca.gov/ConDemo

(916) 341-6499

A program by the California Integrated Waste Management Board including case studies, fact sheets and links.

Construction Materials Recycling Association

www.cdrecycling.org

(630) 585-7530

A nonprofit dedicated to information exchange within the North American construction waste and demolition debris processing and recycling industry

Construction Waste Management Handbook

Smart Growth Online

www.smartgrowth.org/library/articles.asp?art=15

(202) 962-3623

A report by the NAHB Research Center on residential construction waste management for a housing development in Homestead, Florida

Contractors' Guide to Preventing Waste and Recycling

Resource Venture

www.resourceventure.org/rv/issues/building/publications/index.php

(206) 343-8505

A guidebook on waste prevention in construction from the Business and Industry Resource Venture

Recycling and Waste Management During Construction

King County, WA

www.metrokc.gov/procure/green/wastemgt.htm

Specification language from the city of Seattle and Portland Metro projects on construction waste management

A Sourcebook for Green and Sustainable Building

www.greenbuilder.com/sourcebook/ConstructionWaste.html

A guide to construction waste management from the Sourcebook for Green and Sustainable Building

Environmental Specifications for Research Triangle Park

U.S. Environmental Protection Agency

www.epa.gov/rtp/new-bldg/environmental/specs.htm

Waste management and other specifications

Waste Spec: Model Specifications for Construction Waste Reduction, Reuse and Recycling

Triangle J Council of Governments

www.tjcog.dst.nc.us/regplan/wastespec.htm

(919) 549-0551

Model specifications developed by Triangle J Council of Governments in North Carolina; Ten case studies show results of using the specifications (downloadable PDF document)

Government Resources

Check with the solid waste and natural resources departments in your city or county. Many local governments provide information about regional recycling opportunities.

Definitions

Construction and Demolition (C&D) Debris includes waste and recyclables generated from construction, renovation, and demolition or deconstruction of pre-existing structures. Land clearing debris including soil, vegetation, rocks, etc. are not to be included.

Recycling is the collection, reprocessing, marketing and use of materials that were diverted or recovered from the solid waste stream.

Reuse is a strategy to return materials to active use in the same or a related capacity.

Tipping Fees are fees charged by a landfill for disposal of waste volumes. The fee is typically quoted for one ton of waste.

Intent

Reuse building materials and products in order to reduce demand for virgin materials and to reduce waste, thereby reducing impacts associated with the extraction and processing of virgin resources.

Case Study

One Crescent Drive
Philadelphia, Pennsylvania

Photo courtesy of: Vision Architecture

One Crescent Drive at Navy Yard covers more than 12 acres on what was formerly the Philadelphia Naval Base. The site is being redeveloped as a mixed-use, master-planned business campus and One Crescent Drive is the first office building completed. The project achieved LEED-CS Gold pre-certification, which was used to market the project to prospective tenants. The building will serve as a prototype for eight additional AA mid-sized office buildings.

A highly reflective inverted aggregate paving was used to reduce heat island effect. To promote alternative means of transportation, bicycle storage, on-site showers, and hybrid/AFV designated parking spaces are included. Daylighting of all regularly occupied areas including a central atrium core reduces lighting power needs. The modeled design measured a 35% greater energy efficiency than the ASHRAE 90.1-1999 base case. Over 30% of materials have recycled content, and over 40% of materials were produced locally. Over 95% of all construction waste was diverted from landfills through a strict on-site job waste management system. A green housekeeping program has been implemented throughout all common areas and tenant spaces to continue the healthy indoor environmental quality of the building.

One Crescent Drive achieved LEED-Gold Certification as well as the distinction of being the first LEED building in the City of Philadelphia.

Materials Reuse

1%

1 point

Requirements

Use salvaged, refurbished or reused materials such that the sum of these materials constitutes at least 1%, based on cost, of the total value of materials on the project.

Mechanical, electrical and plumbing components and specialty items such as elevators and equipment shall not be included in this calculation. Only include materials permanently installed in the project. Furniture may be included, providing it is included consistently in MR Credits 3–6.

Potential Technologies & Strategies

Identify opportunities to incorporate salvaged materials into building design and research potential material suppliers. Consider salvaged materials such as beams and posts, flooring, paneling, doors and frames, cabinetry and furniture, brick and decorative items.

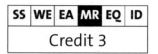

Summary of Referenced Standard

There is no standard referenced for this credit.

Approach and Implementation

Use of salvaged and refurbished materials in new building projects extends the life of materials and can reduce overall first costs of construction materials. Use of salvaged materials can also add character to the building and can be used effectively as architectural details. Some areas of the United States, such as New England, the Pacific Northwest and California, have well-developed markets for salvaged materials while other regions are just beginning to develop these markets.

For reused materials found on-site, there are two major groups. First are those items that were "fixed" components on-site before the project started. To qualify as reused for this credit, these fixed items must no longer be able to serve their original function, and must then have been reconditioned and installed for a different use or in a different location. An example would be a fire door removed and modified to serve as the counter top for the receptionist station. The remaining fixed items, such as walls, ceilings and flooring that remain as such in the new building are excluded from this credit, but are covered by MR Credits 1.2 and 1.3.

Another type of reused material found on-site is "finish" material that can be kept and refurbished. These reused components may continue to serve their original function, but have undergone refurbishment to become functional. An example would be refurbished door hardware.

Materials eligible for reuse are not limited to materials used in buildings. For reused materials obtained from off-site, the primary stipulation for qualifying as reused is simply that they must have been previously used. These materials may be purchased as salvaged, similar to any other project material, or they may be relocated from another facility (including one previously used by the occupant). The salvaged materials from both on-site and off-site can be applied to MR Credit 5, Regional Materials, if they comply with the requirements of that credit. Materials qualifying as reused for MR Credit 3.1 and 3.2 cannot be applied to MR Credits 1, 2, 4 or 6.

Furniture and furnishings (CSI Master-Format 1995 Division 12 components) are excluded from the calculations for this credit, unless they are included consistently across MR Credits 3–6. This credit applies primarily to CSI Divisions 2–10. Mechanical and electrical components, along with appliances and equipment cannot be included in this credit, as they are generally not appropriate and/or feasible. This exclusion is consistent with MR Credits 4 and 5.

Core and Shell Concerns

Generally core and shell buildings have limited opportunities to utilize materials that contribute to achievement of this credit. This is primarily due to the fact that core and shell buildings do not include much, if any, interior construction where most opportunities for achieving this credit are available. Core and shell materials that may be considered include brick, structural heavy timber, stone, or salvaged pavers.

Calculations

List the reused or salvaged materials used on the project. **Table 1** provides an example of a salvaged materials tracking log. Determine the cost of each material. This cost will either be the actual cost paid or the replacement value, if the material came from on-site. The replacement value can be determined by pricing a comparable

Table 1: Sample Salvaged Materials Tracking Log

Salvaged / Reused Material Description	Source for Salvaged / Reused Material	Value / Product Cost ($)
Salvaged Brick	ABC Salvage Suppliers	$62,500
Salvaged Wood Floor	Salvage Company Y	$24,200
Remanufactured Wood Doors (Used as Built-in Countertops)	On-Site Salvage / Remanufacture	$4,200
SUB-TOTAL SALVAGED / REUSED MATERIALS		**$90,900**
TOTAL CONSTRUCTION MATERIALS COST – OR 45% DEFAULT MATERIALS VALUE		**$1,665,498**
SALVAGED / REUSED MATERIALS AS A PERCENTAGE OF TOTAL MATERIALS COST		**5.5%**

material in the local market. When the actual cost paid for the reused or salvaged material is below the cost of an equivalent new item, use the higher value (or replacement cost) in the calculations. When the cost to reclaim an item found on-site is less than the cost of an equivalent new item, use the cost of the new item (or replacement cost) in the calculations.

Determine the Total Materials Cost for the project. The Total Materials Cost may be derived by multiplying the total construction cost (hard costs only in CSI MasterFormat 1995 Divisions 2–10) by 0.45. Alternately, the Total Materials Cost may be a tally of actual materials cost in CSI MasterFormat 1995 Divisions 2–10 from the project Schedule of Values or a similar document. The benefit of using actual materials costs, as opposed to the default 45%, is that projects with less than 45% materials cost would find it easier to achieve the 5% and 10% credit thresholds, since total materials cost is in the denominator of the equation below.

Calculate Percent Reuse Materials According to **Equation 1**.

Exemplary Performance

An Innovation in Design point for exemplary performance is available when a project documents that the value of salvaged or reused materials used on the project is equal to at least 15% of the total materials cost.

Precertification Submittal Documentation

Provide the LEED-CS Precertification Letter template, which includes the following:

❑ Narrative describing how the project intends to accomplish the credit requirements

❑ Confirmation of this intent from both the design professional and the owner/developer

Certification Submittal Documentation

These credits are submitted as part of the **Construction Submittal**.

Design and Construction Credit Compliance

The following project data and calculation information is required to document prerequisite compliance using the LEED-CS v2.0 Submittal Templates:

Equation 1

$$\text{Percent Reuse Materials} = \frac{\text{Cost of Reuse Materials (\$)}}{\text{Total Materials Cost (\$)}}$$

❑ Provide the total project materials cost (Divisions 2–10) or provide the total project cost for Divisions 2–10 to apply the 45% default materials value.

❑ Provide a tabulation of each salvaged/reused material used on the project. The tabulation must include a description of the material, the source/vendor for the material and the product cost.

❑ Provide a narrative describing the materials reuse strategy implemented by the project. Include specific information about reused/salvaged materials used on the project.

Tenant Sales or Lease Agreement Credit Compliance

Alternative compliance methods will be considered in cases where the developer can demonstrate the means of tenant compliance and the quantity of materials salvaged, refurbished or reused. This compliance method will need to illustrate the following:

❑ A sufficient amount of tenant scope is covered through tenant sales or lease agreement to comply with credit requirements. Provided that all requirements are met, a combination of core and shell scope and tenant scope may be utilized. Lease or sales agreements may be requested.

❑ Provide the total project materials cost (Divisions 2–10) or provide the total project cost for Divisions 2–10 to apply the 45% default materials value. The cost data provided must include project cost for the tenant square footage being addressed through sales or lease agreement requirements.

❑ Provide a tabulation of each salvaged/reused material that is required to be used in the tenant space. The tabulation must include a description of the material, the source/vendor for the material and the product cost.

❑ Provide a narrative describing the materials reuse strategy implemented by the project. Include specific information about reused/salvaged materials used on the project.

Considerations

Environmental Issues

Reuse strategies divert material from the construction waste stream, reducing the need for landfill space and diminishing the environmental impacts associated with water and air contamination. Use of salvaged materials also reduces the environmental impacts of producing new construction products and materials. These impacts are significant since buildings account for a large portion of our natural resources consumption, including 40% of raw stone, gravel and sand, and 25% of virgin wood.

Economic Issues

Some salvaged materials are more costly than new materials due to the high cost of labor involved in recovering and refurbishing processes. However, salvaged materials are often of higher quality and more durable than available new materials. Local demolition companies may be willing to sell materials recovered from existing buildings to avoid landfill tipping fees and to generate income. In some areas, municipalities and waste management companies have established facilities to sell salvaged building materials at landfill sites. Sometimes salvaged materials are offered at prices that appear to be cost-effective but may include hidden costs such as the need for reprocessing, exorbitant transportation costs or liabilities associated with toxic contamination. Conversely, certain salvaged materials may be impossible to duplicate (such as turn-of-the century lumber and casework) and may well be worth the higher cost compared to new but inferior materials.

Resources

Please see the USGBC website at www.usgbc.org/resources for more specific resources on materials sources and other technical information.

Websites

California Materials Exchange California Integrated Waste Management Board

www.ciwmb.ca.gov/CalMAX

(877) 520-9703

A program of the California Integrated Waste Management Board, this site allows users to exchange non-hazardous discarded materials online.

Guide to Resource-Efficient Building Elements

www.crbt.org/index.html

The Center for Resourceful Building Technology Directory of environmentally responsible building products. This resource provides introductory discussions per topic and contact information for specific products, including salvaged materials. (The CRBT project is no longer active, and the CRBT website is no longer updated. The National Center for Appropriate Technology is providing this website for archival purposes only).

Materials Exchanges on the Web

Industrial Materials Exchange (IMEX) Local Hazardous Waste Management Program in King County, OR

www.govlink.org/hazwaste

(206) 296-4899

A listing of materials exchanges on the Web.

Reuse Development Organization (ReDO)

www.redo.org

(410) 558-5625

A national nonprofit located in Indianapolis, Indiana, that promotes reuse as an environmentally sound, socially beneficial and economical means of managing surplus and discarded materials. See the List of ReDO Subscribers for contacts around the United States.

Salvaged Building Materials Exchange

Green Building Resource Guide

www.greenguide.com/exchange/search.html

A searchable database of salvaged building materials

Building Materials Reuse Association (formerly Used Building Materials Association)

www.ubma.org

(800) 990-BMRA (2672)

BMRA is a nonprofit, membership-based organization that represents companies and organizations involved in the acquisition and/or redistribution of used building materials.

Used Building Materials Exchange

www.build.recycle.net

(519) 767-2913

A free marketplace for buying and selling recyclables and salvaged materials

Old to New: Design Guide, Salvaged Building Materials in New Construction

The Greater Vancouver Regional District (GVRD)

www.gvrd.bc.ca/buildsmart

A useful and detailed guidebook, produced by the Greater Vancouver Regional District, to the use of salvaged materials, with real-life case studies.

Government Resources

Check with the solid waste authority and natural resources departments in your city or county. Many local governments provide information about regional materials exchanges and other sources.

Definitions

Chain-of-Custody is a tracking procedure to document the status of a product from the point of harvest or extraction to the ultimate consumer end use.

Salvaged or Reused Materials are construction materials recovered from existing buildings or construction sites and reused in other buildings. Common salvaged materials include structural beams and posts, flooring, doors, cabinetry, brick and decorative items.

Recycled Content

10% (post-consumer + 1/2 pre-consumer)

Intent

Increase demand for building products that incorporate recycled content materials, thereby reducing impacts resulting from extraction and processing of virgin materials.

Requirements

Use materials with recycled content such that the sum of post-consumer recycled content plus one-half of the pre-consumer content constitutes at least 10% (based on cost) of the total value of the materials in the project.

The recycled content value of a material assembly shall be determined by weight. The recycled fraction of the assembly is then multiplied by the cost of assembly to determine the recycled content value.

Mechanical, electrical and plumbing components and specialty items such as elevators shall not be included in this calculation. Only include materials permanently installed in the project. Furniture may be included, providing it is included consistently in MR Credits 3–6.

Recycled content shall be defined in accordance with the International Organization for Standardization document, *ISO 14021—Environmental labels and declarations—Self-declared environmental claims (Type II environmental labeling)*.

Post-consumer material is defined as waste material generated by households or by commercial, industrial and institutional facilities in their role as end-users of the product, which can no longer be used for its intended purpose.

Pre-consumer material is defined as material diverted from the waste stream during the manufacturing process. Excluded is reutilization of materials such as rework, re-grind or scrap generated in a process and capable of being reclaimed within the same process that generated it.

Potential Technologies & Strategies

Establish a project goal for recycled content materials and identify material suppliers that can achieve this goal. During construction, ensure that the specified recycled content materials are installed. Consider a range of environmental, economic and performance attributes when selecting products and materials.

1 Point
in addition to
MR Credit 4.1

Recycled Content

20% (post-consumer + 1/2 pre-consumer)

Intent

Increase demand for building products that incorporate recycled content materials, thereby reducing the impacts resulting from extraction and processing of virgin materials.

Requirements

Use materials with recycled content such that the sum of post-consumer recycled content plus one-half of the pre-consumer content constitutes an additional 10% beyond MR Credit 4.1 (total of 20%, based on cost) of the total value of the materials in the project.

The recycled content value of a material assembly shall be determined by weight. The recycled fraction of the assembly is then multiplied by the cost of assembly to determine the recycled content value.

Mechanical, electrical and plumbing components and specialty items such as elevators shall not be included in this calculation. Only include materials permanently installed in the project. Furniture may be included, providing it is included consistently in MR Credits 3–6.

Recycled content shall be defined in accordance with the International Organization for Standardization document, *ISO 14021—Environmental labels and declarations—Self-declared environmental claims (Type II environmental labeling)*.

Post-consumer material is defined as waste material generated by households or by commercial, industrial and institutional facilities in their role as end-users of the product, which can no longer be used for its intended purpose.

Pre-consumer material is defined as material diverted from the waste stream during the manufacturing process. Excluded is reutilization of materials such as rework, re-grind or scrap generated in a process and capable of being reclaimed within the same process that generated it.

Potential Technologies & Strategies

Establish a project goal for recycled content materials and identify material suppliers that can achieve this goal. During construction, ensure that the specified recycled content materials are installed. Consider a range of environmental, economic and performance attributes when selecting products and materials.

Summary of Referenced Standard

International Standard ISO 14021:1999 — Environmental Labels and Declarations — Self-Declared Environmental Claims (Type II Environmental Labeling)

International Organization for Standardization (ISO)

www.iso.org

This International Standard specifies requirements for self-declared environmental claims, including statements, symbols and graphics, regarding products. It further describes selected terms commonly used in environmental claims and gives qualifications for their use. This International Standard also describes a general evaluation and verification methodology for self-declared environmental claims and specific evaluation and verification methods for the selected claims in this standard.

Approach and Implementation

Recycled content goals should be established during the design phase. Careful research may be required to determine the percentages of recycled content that can realistically be expected in specific products and materials. Project teams are encouraged to run a preliminary calculation during the design phase as soon as a project budget is available in order to set appropriate recycled content targets. Many standard materials in the marketplace contain recycled content as a matter of course due to the nature and economics of their manufacture (examples include steel, gypsum board, and acoustical ceiling tile). Other materials may require research by design and construction teams to achieve higher levels of recycled content or to verify which models of a certain product line feature the desired recycled content (examples include carpet and ceramic tile).

The project team should work with subcontractors and suppliers to verify availability of materials that contain recycled content. The contractor should run preliminary calculations based on the construction budget or schedule of values during the preconstruction phase whenever possible. This will allow the construction team to focus, during the buy-out phase, on those materials with the greatest contribution to the project recycled content value.

The project team is typically responsible for documenting the amounts and values of recycled content of any given material used on the project. The project team must identify products which contain recycled content and pursue documentation from suppliers, manufacturers and vendors directly or through the subcontractors to confirm the actual recycled content for each product.

It is also important to distinguish between post-consumer and pre-consumer recycled content when tracking materials for the purpose of credit calculations. Detailed definitions of these terms are provided in the Definitions section of this guide.

Core and Shell Concerns

Because interior construction is not part of a core and shell project, it is recommended that projects should evaluate the major structural and envelope materials for opportunities to meet this credit.

Calculations

To calculate the percentage of recycled content materials used on a project, list all recycled content materials and products and their costs. For each product, identify the percentage of post-consumer and/or pre-consumer recycled content

SS	WE	EA	**MR**	EQ	ID

Credit 4

Equation 1

Recycled Content Value ($) = (% post-consumer recycled content x material cost) + 0.5 x (% pre-consumer recycled content x material cost)

by weight, and list the recycled content information source. Note that LEED requires that the information be from a reliable, verifiable source.

Calculate the Recycled Content Value of Each Material According to Equation 1.

Determine the Total Materials Cost for the project.

The Total Materials Cost may be derived by multiplying the total construction cost (hard costs for CSI MasterFormat 1995 Divisions 2–10 only) by 0.45. Alternately, the Total Materials Cost may be a tally of actual materials cost (CSI MasterFormat 1995 Divisions 2–10 only) from the project Schedule of Values or similar document. The benefit of using actual materials costs, as opposed to the default 45%, is that projects with less than 45% materials cost would find it easier to achieve the 10% and 20% credit thresholds, since total materials cost is the denominator of **Equation 2**. The purpose of the default value is to streamline the documentation process, as it can be challenging to separate the materials costs from labor and equipment costs for all materials on the project.

Calculate the Project Percent Recycled Content According to Equation 2.

Furniture and furnishings (CSI Master-Format 1995 Division 12 components) are excluded from the calculations for this credit, unless they are included consistently across MR Credits 3–6. This credit applies primarily to CSI Divisions 2–10. Mechanical, electrical and plumbing components, along with appliances and equipment cannot be included in this credit. These are excluded because, when compared with structural and finish materials, mechanical and electrical equipment tends to have a high dollar value relative to the amount of material it contains. That high dollar value would skew the results of the calculation, reducing the incentive to use recycled-content in high-mass materials.

Default Recycled Content

For steel products where no recycled content information is available, assume the recycled content to be 25% post-consumer. No other material has been recognized as having a similar consistent minimum recycled content. Note that many steel products will contain 90%, or higher, recycled content if manufactured by the electric arc furnace process, so it may be beneficial for a project to obtain actual information from the manufacturer rather than relying on the default value.

Calculating Assembly Recycled Content

Assemblies include all products that are composed of multiple materials, either in reaching a formulation for a material (i.e., composite wood panels), or of all the sub-components (i.e., a window system). For assembly recycled content values, consider the percents by weight of the post-consumer recycled content and the pre-consumer recycled content in the assembly. When there are sub-components, the final two percentages (post-consumer and pre-consumer) must be determined by using the weights of the smaller sub-

Equation 2

$$\text{Percent Recycled Content} = \frac{\text{Total Recycled Content Value (\$)}}{\text{Total Materials Cost (\$)}}$$

component elements. No consideration is given to relative costs of the materials or the sub-components, when calculating these percentages of recycled content. For example, a pound of steel in a window assembly is of equal significance in determining recycled content of an assembly as a pound of fabric on a movable wall panel.

Supplementary Cementitious Materials

In the case of supplementary cementitious materials (SCMs) used in concrete that are recycled from other operations, it is allowable to calculate the recycled content value based on the mass of the cementitious materials only, rather than on the entire concrete mix. For example, if 150 pounds of coal fly ash is used per yard of concrete, the fly ash would represent only a small fraction (5%) of the roughly 3,000 pounds of materials in that concrete. The project team can choose instead to calculate it as a fraction of the cementitious materials only. To accomplish this, the value of the cementitious materials will have to be obtained from the concrete supplier separately from the total cost of the concrete (see **Example 1**). Note: fly ash is a Pre-Consumer Recycled Content material.

Exemplary Performance

Project teams may earn an Innovation in Design point for exemplary performance when the requirements reach the next incremental step. For recycled content,

the total recycled value must be 30% or greater.

Precertification Submittal Documentation

Provide the LEED-CS Precertification Letter template, which includes the following:

❑ Narrative describing how the project intends to accomplish the credit requirements

❑ Confirmation of this intent from both the design professional and the owner/developer

Certification Submittal Documentation

These credits are submitted as part of the **Construction Submittal**.

Design and Construction Credit Compliance

The following project data and calculation information is required to document prerequisite compliance using the LEED-CS v2.0 Submittal Templates:

❑ Provide the total project materials cost (Divisions 2–10) or provide the total project cost for Divisions 2–10 to apply the 45% default materials value.

❑ Provide a tabulation of each material used on the project that is being tracked for recycled content. The tabulation must include a description of the material, the manufacturer of

Example 1: Sample Supplementary Cementitious Materials Calculation

Mix #	Mass of Portland cement* [lbs]	Mass of recycled SCMs [lbs]	Mass of total cementitious materials [lbs]	SCMs as a percentage of total cementitious materials [%]	Dollar value of all cementitious materials (from concrete supplier)	Recycled content value per yard [(SCM/2) x dollar value]
2	200	50	250	20%	$35	$3.50
3	300	100	400	25%	$45	$5.63

This column also includes any other cementitious ingredients that are not recycled.

the material, the product cost, the pre-consumer and/or post-consumer recycled content percentage, and the source of the recycled content data.

❑ Provide an optional narrative describing any special circumstances or considerations regarding the project's credit approach.

Tenant Sales or Lease Agreement Credit Compliance

This compliance method is available to core and shell projects that incorporate into tenant sales or lease agreements requirements for the use of materials with recycled content as part of the tenant scope of work. Provide the LEED letter template for the credit pursued indicating the following:

❑ A sufficient amount of tenant scope is covered through tenant sales or lease agreement to comply with credit requirements. Provided that all requirements are met, a combination of core and shell scope and tenant scope may be utilized. Lease or sales agreements may be requested.

❑ Provide the total project materials cost (Divisions 2–10) or provide the total project cost for Divisions 2–10 to apply the 45% default materials value. This must include materials costs for tenant spaces utilized for credit compliance.

❑ Provide a tabulation of each material that is required to be used on the project being tracked for recycled content. The tabulation must include a description of the material, the manufacturer of the material, the product cost, the pre-consumer and/or post-consumer recycled content percentage, and the source of the recycled content data.

❑ Provide an optional narrative describing any special circumstances or considerations regarding the project's credit approach.

Considerations

Environmental Issues

Building products with recycled content are beneficial to the environment because they reduce virgin material use and solid waste volumes. Success breeds future success: as the number of building products containing recycled content grows, the marketplace for recycled materials develops.

Economic Issues

Many commonly used products are now available with recycled content, including metals, concrete, masonry, acoustic tile, carpet, ceramic tile and insulation. Most recycled content products exhibit performance similar to products containing only virgin materials and can be incorporated into building projects with ease and minimal-to-no cost premium.

Resources

Please see the USGBC website at www. usgbc.org/resources for more specific resources on materials sources and other technical information.

Websites

Recycled Content Product Directory

California Integrated Waste Management Board

www.ciwmb.ca.gov/rcp

(916) 341-6606

A searchable database for recycled content products, developed by the California Integrated Waste Management Board.

GreenSpec

BuildingGreen, Inc.

www.buildinggreen.com/menus/index. cfm

(802) 257-7300

Detailed listings for more than 1,900 green building products, including environmental data, manufacturer information and links to additional resources

Guide to Resource-Efficient Building Elements

www.crbt.org/index.html

The Center for Resourceful Building Technology Directory of environmentally responsible building products. This resource provides introductory discussions per topic and contact information for specific products, including salvaged materials. (The CRBT project is no longer active, and the CRBT website is no longer updated. The National Center for Appropriate Technology is providing this website for archival purposes only).

Oikos

www.oikos.com

A searchable directory of resource-efficient building products and sustainable design educational resources

"Recycled Content: What is it and What is it Worth?"

Environmental Building News, February 2005.

www.buildinggreen.com/auth/article.cfm?filename=140201a.xml

U.S. EPA Comprehensive Procurement Guidelines Program

www.epa.gov/cpg/products.htm

Contains EPA information on recycled content materials with guidelines for recycled percentages. Includes a searchable database of suppliers.

Government Resources

Check with the solid waste and natural resources departments in your city or county. Many local governments provide information on recyclers and recycled content product manufacturers within their region.

Definitions

Assembly Recycled Content includes the percentages of post-consumer and pre-consumer content. The determination is made by dividing the weight of the recycled content by the overall weight of the assembly.

Post-Consumer Waste is material generated by households or by commercial, industrial and institutional facilities in their role as end-users of the product which can no longer be used for its intended purpose. This includes returns of materials from the distribution chain (source: ISO 14021). Examples of this category include construction and demolition debris, materials collected through curbside and drop-off recycling programs, broken pallets (if from a pallet refurbishing company, not a pallet making company), discarded products (e.g., furniture, cabinetry and decking) and urban maintenance waste (leaves, grass clippings, tree trimmings, etc.).

Pre-Consumer Content, previously referred to as Post-Industrial Content, is defined as material diverted from the waste stream during the manufacturing process. Excluded is reutilization of materials such as rework, regrind or scrap generated in a process and capable of being reclaimed within the same process that generated it (source ISO 14021). Examples in this category include planer shavings, plytrim, sawdust, chips, bagasse, sunflower seed hulls, walnut shells, culls, trimmed materials, print overruns, over-issue publications and obsolete inventories.

SS | WE | EA | **MR** | EQ | ID

Credit 4

Regional Materials

10% Extracted, Processed & Manufactured Regionally

Intent

Increase demand for building materials and products that are extracted and manufactured within the region, thereby supporting the use of indigenous resources and reducing the environmental impacts resulting from transportation.

Requirements

Use building materials or products that have been extracted, harvested or recovered, as well as manufactured, within 500 miles of the project site for a minimum of 10% (based on cost) of the total materials value. If only a fraction of a product or material is extracted/harvested/recovered and manufactured locally, then only that percentage (by weight) shall contribute to the regional value.

Mechanical, electrical and plumbing components and specialty items such as elevators and equipment shall not be included in this calculation. Only include materials permanently installed in the project. Furniture may be included, providing it is included consistently in MR Credits 3–6.

Potential Technologies & Strategies

Establish a project goal for locally sourced materials, and identify materials and material suppliers that can achieve this goal. During construction, ensure that the specified local materials are installed and quantify the total percentage of local materials installed. Consider a range of environmental, economic and performance attributes when selecting products and materials.

Regional Materials

20% Extracted, Processed & Manufactured Regionally

Intent

Increase demand for building materials and products that are extracted and manufactured within the region, thereby supporting the use of indigenous resources and reducing the environmental impacts resulting from transportation.

Requirements

Use building materials or products that have been extracted, harvested or recovered, as well as manufactured, within 500 miles of the project site for an additional 10% beyond MR Credit 5.1 (total of 20%, based on cost) of the total materials value. If only a fraction of the material is extracted/harvested/recovered and manufactured locally, then only that percentage (by weight) shall contribute to the regional value.

Potential Technologies & Strategies

Establish a project goal for locally sourced materials and identify materials and material suppliers that can achieve this goal. During construction, ensure that the specified local materials are installed. Consider a range of environmental, economic and performance attributes when selecting products and materials.

Summary of Referenced Standard

There is no standard referenced for this credit.

Approach and Implementation

Careful research may be required to determine what products can be sourced locally and can realistically be expected to be purchased for the project. As a result, it may be beneficial to evaluate this credit early in the design process, despite the appearance of it being exclusively a construction consideration. Project teams are encouraged to run a preliminary calculation during the design phase, as soon as a project budget is available, in order to set appropriate regional materials targets. For example, if the project has a $10 million budget, the materials cost (and subsequently the 10% of that materials cost) can be estimated using the 45% default rate. The team would calculate that the project would need to use at least $450,000 of materials meeting the requirements of this credit to achieve MR Credit 5.1 ($450,000 is 10% of $4.5 million, which is 45% of the $10 million project cost). This estimate will likely be high, since the final calculation is based on Divisions 2–10, but it is still useful as a conservative estimate.

The general contractor should work with subcontractors and suppliers to verify availability of materials which are extracted/harvested/recovered and manufactured locally (within 500 miles of the project site). The contractor should run preliminary calculations based on the construction budget or schedule of values during the preconstruction phase whenever possible. This will allow the construction team to focus on those materials with the greatest contribution to this credit during the buy-out phase.

The general contractor is typically responsible for documenting the amounts and values of regionally harvested and manufactured materials used on the project. The general contractor must track the materials cost of each locally harvested and manufactured product that will be applied to the LEED credit.

Calculations

List those products that are believed to be extracted/harvested/recovered and manufactured within 500 miles of the project site.

Indicate the name of the manufacturer, the product cost, the distance between the project site and the manufacturer, and the distance between the project site and the extraction site for each raw material contained within each product.

Determine the Total Materials Cost for the project.

The Total Materials Cost may be derived by multiplying the total construction cost (hard costs for CSI MasterFormat 1995 Divisions 2–10 only) by 0.45. Alternately, the Total Materials Cost may be a tally of actual materials cost (CSI Divisions 2–10 only) from the project Schedule of Values or similar document. The benefit to using actual materials costs, as opposed to the default 45%, is that projects with less than 45% materials cost would find it easier to achieve the 10% and 20% credit thresholds, since total materials cost is the denominator of **Equation 1**. The purpose of the default value is to streamline the documentation process, as it is often challenging to break out the materials costs from labor and equipment costs for all materials on the project.

Equation 1

$$\text{Percent Local Materials} = \frac{\text{Total Cost of Local Materials (\$)}}{\text{Total Materials Cost (\$)}}$$

Calculate the Percent Local Materials according to Equation 1.

Furniture and furnishings (CSI Division 12 components) are excluded from the calculations for this credit, unless they are considered consistently across MR Credits 3–6. This credit applies primarily to CSI Divisions 2–10. Mechanical, electrical and plumbing components, along with appliances and equipment cannot be included in this credit for reasons of fairness and simplification: limited manufacturing locations, skewed results due to relatively high cost compared to the actual mass of materials in the product, and the complexity of some systems is not conducive to gathering the data needed for LEED credits (the exclusion also applies to credits 3 and 4).

Reused and Salvaged Materials

Reused and salvaged materials that satisfy the requirements of MR Credits 3.1 and 3.2, may also contribute to MR Credits 5.1 and 5.2. The location from which they were salvaged may be used as the point of manufacture, and the location where they were originally manufactured may be used as the point of extraction. On-site salvaged materials automatically qualify.

For a material with more than one point of manufacture or extraction, all within the 500-mile radius, list a single item with the greatest distance. If a portion of the material was either manufactured or extracted beyond the 500-mile radius, list only that portion and associated cost satisfying the credit requirement.

For assemblies or products manufactured within the 500-mile radius but containing only some components that also were extracted within the 500-mile radius, use multiple lines in your list. Base the proportionality of such products' costs on the weight of their various components. (See the example for concrete shown in **Table 1** and **Table 2**.)

Exemplary Performance

An Innovation in Design point for exemplary performance may be available when the next incremental percentage threshold is achieved. For regionally harvested, extracted and manufactured materials, the credit calculation must be 40% or greater.

Precertification Submittal Documentation

Provide the LEED-CS Precertification Letter template, which includes the following:

❑ Narrative describing how the project intends to accomplish the credit requirements

Table 1: Sample Assembly Percent Regionally Extracted Calculation for Concrete

Components	Weight [lbs]	Distance between Project & Extraction Site [miles]	Weight Contributing to Regional Extraction [lbs]
Cement	282	1,250	0
Fly Ash	282	125	282
Water	275	1	275
Slag	750	370	750
Recycled Concrete & Aggregate	1,000	8	1,000
Sand	1,200	18	1,200
Component Totals	3,789		3,507
Percent Regionally Extracted Materials [3,507 / 3,789]			92.6%

Table 2: Sample MR Credit 5 Calculation

Product	Manufacturer	Distance Between Project & Manufacturer [mi]	Distance Between Project & Extraction/ Harvest [mi]	Product Cost [$]	Value Qualifying as Regional	Information Source
Plant material	Green's Landscape	5	5	$6,770	$6,770	contractor submittal
Concrete aggregate	Joe's Concrete	15	15	$21,000	$21,000	contractor submittal
Insulation	UR Warm	105	1,080	$9,250	-	product cut sheet
Gypsum board	Gypsum R Us	75	288	$8,550	$8,550	letter from manufacturer
Carpet	Fiber Good	355	721	$15,333	-	letter from manufacturer
Casework	Top Counter	18	320	$12,200	$12,200	contractor submittal
Lumber	My Mill	110	320	$38,990	$38,990	contractor submittal
Wood Doors	Closeby	71	320	$7,000	$7,000	contractor submittal

Total Cost of Regional Materials	**$94,510**
Total Materials Cost (Divisions 2–10)	**$751,000**
Percent Regional Materials	**13%**
Points Earned	**1**

❑ Confirmation of this intent from both the design professional and the owner/developer

Certification Submittal Documentation

These credits are submitted as part of the **Construction Submittal**.

The following project data and calculation information is required to document prerequisite compliance using the LEED-CS v2.0 Submittal Templates:

❑ Provide the project's total cost (for application of 45% default factor) or total materials cost. Note this reported value must be consistent across all MR credits.

❑ Complete the regional materials calculation table in the Submittal Template. The following information will be re-quired to complete this table: product name for each tracked material; material manufacturer; total product cost for each tracked material; percentage of product, by weight, that meets both the extraction and manufacture criteria; distance between the project site and extraction/harvest/recovery site; distance between the project site and the final manufacturing location.

❑ Provide an optional narrative describing any special circumstances or considerations regarding the project's credit approach.

Tenant Sales or Lease Agreement Credit Compliance

This compliance method is available to core and shell projects that incorporate into tenant sales or lease agreements requirements for the use of regional materials as part of the tenant scope of work.

Provide the LEED letter template for the credit pursued indicating the following:

❑ A sufficient amount of tenant scope is covered through tenant sales or lease agreement to comply with credit requirements. Provided that all requirements are met, a combination of core and shell scope and tenant scope may be utilized. Lease or sales agreements may be requested.

❑ Provide the project's total cost (for application of 45% default factor) or total materials cost. Note this reported value must be consistent across all MR credits. This must include materials costs for tenant spaces utilized for credit compliance.

❑ Complete the regional materials calculation table in the Submittal Template. The following information will be required to complete this table: product name for each material used and required to be used; material manufacturer; total product cost for each tracked material; percentage of product, by weight, that meets both the extraction and manufacture criteria; distance between the project site and extraction/harvest/recovery site; distance between the project site and the final manufacturing location.

❑ Provide an optional narrative describing any special circumstances or considerations regarding the project's credit approach.

Considerations

Environmental Issues

By purchasing regionally manufactured building materials, the local economy is supported, transportation costs and environmental impacts are reduced, and money paid for these materials is retained in the region, supporting the regional economy. The availability of regionally manufactured building materials is de-pendent on the project location. In some areas, the majority of products needed for the project can be obtained within a 500-mile radius. In other areas, only a small portion or none of the building materials can be sourced locally. It is also important to address the source of raw materials used to manufacture building products. Raw materials for some building products are harvested or extracted far from the point of manufacture, contributing to air and water pollution due to environmental impacts associated with transportation between point of extraction and point of manufacture.

The use of regional building materials reduces transportation activities and the accompanying pollution associated with delivering materials to the job site. Trucks, trains, ships and other vehicles deplete finite reserves of fossil fuels and generate air pollution. By selecting building materials that are produced from regional materials, transportation impacts are further reduced.

Economic Issues

Regional building materials are more cost effective for projects due to reduced transportation costs. Also, the support of regional manufacturers and labor forces retains capital for the community, contributing to a more stable tax base and a healthier local economy.

Resources

Please see the USGBC website at www. usgbc.org/resources for more specific resources on materials sources and other technical information.

Government Resources

Check with your local Chamber of Commerce and regional and state economic development agencies for building materials manufacturers in your area.

Definitions

Regionally Extracted Materials, for use in this credit, must have their source as a raw material from within a 500-mile radius of the project site.

Regionally Manufactured Materials, as defined for this credit, must be assembled as a finished product within a 500-mile radius of the project site. Assembly, as defined for this credit, does not include on-site assembly, erection or installation of finished components, as in structural steel, miscellaneous iron, curtainwall assemblies, or systems furniture.

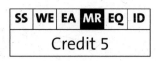

Certified Wood

1 point

Intent

Encourage environmentally responsible forest management.

Requirements

Use a minimum of 50% of wood-based materials and products, which are certified in accordance with the Forest Stewardship Council's (FSC) Principles and Criteria, for wood building components. These components include, but are not limited to, structural framing and general dimensional framing, flooring, sub-flooring, wood doors and finishes.

Include materials permanently installed in the project. Furniture may be included, providing it is included consistently in MR Credits 3–6. At the project's discretion, the calculation may include temporary wood materials purchased for the project. If any such materials are included, all such materials must be included in the calculation.

Potential Technologies & Strategies

Establish a project goal for FSC-certified wood products and identify suppliers that can achieve this goal. During construction, ensure that the FSC-certified wood products are installed and quantify the total percentage of FSC-certified wood products installed.

Summary of Referenced Standard

Forest Stewardship Council's Principles and Criteria

www.fscus.org

(877) 372-5646

Certification is a "seal of approval" awarded to forest managers who adopt environmentally and socially responsible forest management practices, and to companies that manufacture and sell products made from certified wood. This seal enables consumers, including architects and specifiers, to identify and procure wood products from well-managed sources and thereby use their purchasing power to influence and reward improved forest management activities around the world.

LEED accepts certification according to the comprehensive system established by the internationally recognized Forest Stewardship Council (FSC). FSC was created in 1993 to establish international forest management standards (known as the FSC Principles and Criteria) to assure that forestry practices are environmentally responsible, socially beneficial and economically viable. These Principles and Criteria have been established to ensure the long-term health and productivity of forests for timber production, wildlife habitat, clean air and water supplies, climate stabilization, spiritual renewal, and social benefit, such as lasting community employment derived from stable forestry operations. These global Principles and Criteria are translated into meaningful standards at a local level through region-specific standards setting processes.

FSC also accredits and monitors certification organizations. These "certifiers" are independent, third-party auditors that are qualified to annually evaluate compliance with FSC standards on the ground and to award certifications. There are two types of certification:

❏ **Chain-of-Custody (COC) Certification** is awarded to companies that process, manufacture and/or sell products made of certified wood after audits verify proper accounting of material flows and proper use of the FSC name and logo.

❏ **Forest Management Certification** is awarded to responsible forest managers after their operations successfully complete audits of forestry practices and plans.

Approach and Implementation

Establish a project goal for FSC-certified wood products and identify suppliers that can achieve this goal. Research the availability of the wood species and products that you wish to use to ensure that they are available from FSC-certified sources. Another method for lowering the impact of wood resources is to research and specify quality grades that are most readily available from well-managed forests. Using lower grades of wood can dramatically reduce pressure on forests, which produce only limited quantities of top-grade timber (i.e., Architectural Woodwork Institute [AWI] Grades 2 or 3 for lumber or veneer rather than Grade 1).

At the earliest opportunity make contact with local vendors, suppliers and manufacturers that provide FSC-certified products. Provide project bidders with a list of certified vendors and encourage them to make contact early in the project to establish product availability and pricing. See the Resources section for information on product databases and boilerplate forms. As the availability of certain certified wood products may vary over the life of a project, consider having the owner pre-purchase, store and supply particular items to the contractor ("Furnished by the Owner, Installed by the Contractor," or FOIC). Finding a storage location that best mimics the final ambient moisture of the space will ensure proper installation. Because of the typically high ambient moisture present during construction, a job site is not the best location to store wood if FOIC is being implemented.

Specify in contract documents that wood products shall come from forests that are certified as well-managed, according to the rules of the FSC, and require chain-of-custody documentation. Wherever possible, employ a line-item strategy based on current availability of specific products rather than a blanket approach.

Chain-of-Custody Requirements

COC certification is required to different extents based on two scenarios: products with and without the on-product FSC label. If a manufacturer places its FSC COC label on product packaging used for individual sale (generally applying to fabricated products), then subsequent entities in the supply chain are not required to have COC certification unless the product's packaging or form is changed before it reaches the end consumer. (Note: this instruction is meant for LEED compliance only; it varies from FSC rules). For example, a wholesaler or retailer does not need COC to market a packaged case good kit that is labeled with the manufacturer's COC number. A fabricator using a labeled product as a component of a larger assembly will need to have COC certification since it is altering the product's packaging, and possibly its form.

For products that are not individually packaged for sale to be sold as FSC-certified, all parties, from the vendor to the consumer, are required to have COC certification. Contractors and subcontractors are considered the end consumers; they can demonstrate with copies of invoices (if requested) the quantity purchased for the job and their suppliers' COC numbers. For example, a contractor or subcontractor that installs non-labeled FSC wood panels is not required to have COC certification; its supplier must have COC certification. A manufacturer that installs its own product (e.g., custom cabinetry) is not required to have COC certification.

Calculations

List all new wood on the project and identify which components are FSC-certified. Using **Equation 1**, tally both the new wood and the FSC-certified wood.

FSC wood products purchased for temporary use on the project may be included in the denominator at the project team's discretion. If any such materials are included, all such materials must be included in the calculation. Examples of these types of products used for temporary assemblies include formwork, bracing, scaffolding, sidewalk protection and guard rails. If such materials are purchased on multiple projects, the project team may include these materials on one—and only one—project at its discretion.

Assemblies

In the case of an assembly, only the percentage of FSC-certified wood can be applied toward the credit. Wood components that are labeled "FSC Pure" or "FSC Mixed" are 100% FSC (the latter is assured via volume credit accounting).

Determine the amount of new wood as a percent of the total weight, volume or cost

Equation 1

$$\text{Certified Wood Material Percentage} = \frac{\text{FSC-certified Wood Material Value (\$)}}{\text{Total New Wood Material Value (\$)}}$$

and the amount of FSC-certified wood as a percent of the total weight, volume or cost. The cost basis is expected to be useful for veneer. Enter these amounts in the MR Credit 6 Submittal Template along with the total value of the product. The template's spreadsheet will calculate all certified wood value as a percent of all new wood materials.

Project teams should develop a separate spreadsheet to calculate the amount of new wood and amount of FSC-certified wood for complicated assemblies and enter the summary data as one line item in the Submittal Template.

The calculations for certified wood shall include only new wood products. The value of any recycled wood fiber content of a product that qualifies as contributing to MR Credit 4, Recycled Content Materials, shall be excluded.

Exemplary Performance

Project teams may earn an Innovation in Design point for exemplary performance when the requirements reach the next incremental step. For FSC-certified wood, the credit calculation must be 95% FSC-certified wood or greater.

Precertification Submittal Documentation

Provide the LEED-CS Precertification Letter template, which includes the following:

❑ Narrative describing what wood based materials the project intends to utilize to accomplish the credit requirements

❑ Confirmation of this intent from both the design professional and the owner/developer

Certification Submittal Documentation

This credit is submitted as part of the **Construction Submittal**.

The following data and calculation information is required in order to complete the LEED-CS v2.0 Submittal Templates:

❑ A list of items (and/or components of products) claimed as FSC certified, including product type, manufacturer, and the appropriate entity's COC certification number.

Each product name can then be cross-referenced with the manufacturer or vendor COC number during the LEED certification review. An optional narrative can be submitted describing any special circumstances or considerations regarding the project's credit approach.

Tenant Sales or Lease Agreement Credit Compliance

This compliance method is available to core and shell projects that incorporate into tenant sales or lease agreements requirements for the use of FSC certified materials as part of the tenant scope of work. Provide the LEED letter template for the credit pursued indicating the following:

❑ 100% of leased square footage complies with credit requirements. Lease or sales agreements may be requested.

❑ 100% of the unleased square footage shall comply with the credit requirements when leased. A statement signed by the owner/developer that all leases and/or sales agreements will comply may be requested.

❑ A list of items (and/or components of products) claimed as FSC certified, including product type, manufacturer, and the appropriate entity's COC certification number.

Each product name can then be cross-referenced with the manufacturer or vendor COC number during the LEED certification review. For tenant agreement requirements, provide lease agreement with material and FSC requirement highlighted.

❑ An optional narrative can be submitted describing any special circumstances.

Considerations

Environmental Issues

The negative environmental impacts of irresponsible forest practices can include destruction of forests, loss of wildlife habitat, soil erosion and stream sedimentation, water and air pollution, and waste generation. The FSC Standard incorporates many criteria that contribute to the long-term health and integrity of forest ecosystems. From an environmental perspective, the elements of responsible FSC-certified forestry include sustainable timber harvesting (i.e., not removing more timber volume than replaces itself over the cutting interval or rotation); preserving wildlife habitat and biodiversity; maintaining soil and water quality; minimizing the use of harmful chemicals; and conserving high conservation value forests (e.g., endangered and old-growth forests).

Economic Issues

World trade in forest products has increased dramatically in the last 30 years, from $47 billion in 1970 to $139 billion in 1998. As more developing countries embrace world forest product markets and their growing economies encourage domestic consumption, the protection of forests will become a critical issue. Currently, the costs of FSC-certified wood products are equal to or higher than conventional wood products and availability varies by region. The price of FSC-certified wood products is expected to be more competitive with conven-

tional wood products in future years as the world's forest resources are depleted and the forest industry embraces more widespread adoption of sustainable business principles.

Irresponsible logging practices can have negative social impacts. Thus, the socioeconomic and political components to FSC certification include respecting indigenous people's rights and adhering to all applicable laws and treaties. Certification also involves forest workers and forest-dependent communities as stakeholders and beneficiaries of responsible forest management. Through the encouragement of responsible forest practices local timber economies are stabilized and forestland is preserved for future generations.

Resources

Websites

Forest Stewardship Council, United States

www.fscus.org/green_building

(202) 342-0413

For information and practical tools such as databases of certified product suppliers, referral service, specification language, and the "Designing & Building with FSC" guide and forms.

Print Media

Sustainable Forestry: Philosophy, Science, and Economics by Chris Maser, DelRay Beach, St. Lucie Press, 1994.

The Business of Sustainable Forestry: Strategies for an Industry in Transition by Michael B. Jenkins and Emily T. Smith, Island Press, 1999.

Definitions

Chain-of-Custody (COC) is the path taken by raw materials, processed materials, and products from the forest to the

SS | WE | EA | **MR** | EQ | ID

Credit 6

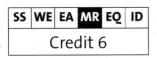
consumer, including all successive stages of processing, transformation, manufacturing and distribution. The COC certificate number is listed on invoices for non-labeled products to document that an entity has followed FSC guidelines for product accounting. COC is not required by distributors of a product that is individually labeled with the FSC logo and manufacturer's COC number.

Sustainable Forestry is the practice of managing forest resources to meet the long-term forest product needs of humans while maintaining the biodiversity of forested landscapes. The primary goal is to restore, enhance and sustain a full range of forest values—economic, social and ecological.

Vendor is defined as the company that supplies wood products to building project contractors or subcontractors for on-site installation. A vendor needs to have a chain-of-custody number only if it is selling FSC-certified products that are not individually labeled (e.g., most lumber).

Indoor Environmental Quality

Americans spend on average 90% of their time indoors where the U.S. Environmental Protection Agency reports that levels of pollutants may run two to five times—and occasionally more than 100 times—higher than outdoor levels[1]. Similarly, the World Health Organization reported in its Air Quality Guidelines for Europe, Second Edition[2] that most of an individual's exposure to many air pollutants comes through inhalation of indoor air. Many of these pollutants can cause health reactions in the estimated 17 million Americans who suffer from asthma and 40 million who have allergies, thus contributing to millions of days absent from school and work. Outbreaks of Legionnaires' disease and sick building syndrome confirm the relationship of indoor air quality to the occupant health.

Over the past twenty years, research and experience has improved our understanding of what is involved in attaining high Indoor Environmental Quality (IEQ), and revealed manufacturing and construction practices that can prevent many IEQ problems from arising. The use of better products and practices has reduced potential liability for design team members and building owners. The results are increased market value for buildings with exemplary IEQ and greater productivity for the occupants. In a case study included in the 1994 publication Greening the Building and the Bottom Line, the Rocky Mountain Institute cites how improved indoor environmental quality improved worker productivity by 16%, netting a rapid payback on the increased capital investment.

Preventing IEQ problems is generally much less expensive than identifying and solving them after they occur. One practical way to prevent IEQ problems from arising is to specify materials that release fewer and less harmful chemical compounds. Evaluation of the properties of the adhesives, paints, carpets, composite wood products and furniture, and specifying those materials with low levels of potentially irritating off-gassing, can reduce occupant exposure. Scheduling of deliveries and sequencing construction activities can reduce material exposure to moisture and absorption of off-gassed contaminants. Protection of air handling systems during construction and a building flush-out prior to occupancy further reduces potential for problems arising during the operational life of a building.

Using higher ratios of filtered outside air, increasing ventilation rates, managing moisture, and controlling the level of contaminants in the cleaning substances used can provide optimal air quality for building occupants. Installation of automatic sensors and controls to maintain proper temperature, humidity, and rates of outdoor air introduced to occupied spaces also plays a key role in maintaining optimal air quality. Use of sensors to alert building maintenance staff to potential Indoor Air Quality (IAQ) problems such as carbon dioxide (CO_2) build-up in an occupied space can also effectively balance energy and IEQ issues.

Occupant well-being can be improved by providing views to the exterior and by providing daylighting. In addition, providing occupants with the ability to

1 United States Environmental Protection Agency. *Healthy Buildings, Healthy People: A vision for the 21st Century*. October 2001. www.epa.gov/iaq/hbhp/hbhptoc.html

2 World Health Organization. *Air Quality Guidelines for Europe, Second Edition*. 2000. www.euro.who.int/document/e71922.pdf

---

Overview of LEED® Prerequisites and Credits

EQ Prerequisite 1
Minimum IAQ Performance

EQ Prerequisite 2
Environmental Tobacco Smoke (ETS) Control

EQ Credit 1
Outdoor Air Delivery Monitoring

EQ Credit 2
Increased Ventilation

EQ Credit 3
Construction IAQ Management Plan—During Construction

EQ Credit 4.1
Low-Emitting Materials—Adhesives & Sealants

EQ Credit 4.2
Low-Emitting Materials—Paints & Coatings

EQ Credit 4.3
Low-Emitting Materials—Carpet Systems

EQ Credit 4.4
Low-Emitting Materials—Composite Wood & Agrifiber Products

EQ Credit 4
Supplemental Information

EQ Credit 5
Indoor Chemical & Pollutant Source Control

EQ Credit 6
Controllability of Systems—Thermal Comfort

EQ Credit 7
Thermal Comfort—Design

EQ Credit 8.1
Daylight & Views—Daylight 75% of Spaces

EQ Credit 8.2
Daylight & Views—Views for 90% of Spaces

control their personal thermal environment can reduce hot/cold complaint calls and generally raise occupant satisfaction levels which can lead to increases in productivity.

The joint efforts of the owner, building design team, contractors, subcontractors and suppliers are integral to providing a quality indoor environment.

In their design and construction, core and shell projects can affect indoor air quality in two general manners. Most directly, the design and construction team is able to directly influence the quality of those spaces that they have control over. This might be lobby spaces, central circulation areas, and building cores. Second, but most importantly, the core and shell design and construction decisions can directly affect the indoor environmental quality of tenant spaces outside of the control of the core and shell submittal. Examples of this include ventilation design and careful design consideration for tenant ability to optimize daylight and views. Core and shell projects should consider how their decision could enable tenant fit-outs to deliver high Indoor Environmental Quality to the final occupants, the tenants.

Indoor Environmental Quality Credit Characteristics

Table 1 shows which credits were substantially revised from LEED-NC Version 2.2, which credits are eligible to be submitted in the Design Phase Submittal, and which project team members are likely to carry decision-making responsibility for each credit. The decision-making responsibility matrix is not intended to exclude any party, rather to emphasize those credits that are most likely to require strong participation by a particular team member.

Case Study

Collaborative Innovation Center Pittsburgh, Pennsylvania

Photo courtesy of: Massery Photography

Collaborative Innovation Center at Carnegie Mellon University contains 136,000-sq.ft. of tenant space above a 238-car parking garage in a building that fits into the visual context of the nearby older campus buildings. To reduce both solar gain and energy consumption for cooling, cantilevered concrete slabs provide shading from the sun on the appropriate elevations. A raised floor HVAC system and a daylight dimming system resulted in a building design energy model that measured at 23% better than the ASHRAE 90.1-1999 base case. Tenants are able to manually operate diffusers and thermostats. Operable windows also allow for individual comfort control. The building also features an 8,000-gallon cistern system that supplies all of the water to run a graywater system for the building. A 39.8% reduction in the use of potable water is achieved by gathering the stormwater and by selecting plants that do not need irrigation. Based on cost, 16.7% of the building materials contain recycled content, and more than 90% of the construction waste was diverted from landfills. 41% of the building materials were manufactured within the region and 52% of those materials were harvested locally. The Center was awarded a LEED-CS Gold Rating in December 2005.

Table 1: EQ Credit Characteristics

Credit	Significant Change from LEED-NC v2.2	Design Submittal	Construction Submittal	Owner Decision-Making	Design Team Decision-Making	Contractor Decision-Making
EQp1: Minimum IAQ Performance		*			*	
EQp2: Environmental Tobacco Smoke (ETS) Control		*		*	*	
EQc1: Outdoor Air Delivery Monitoring		*			*	
EQc2: Increased Ventilation		*			*	
EQc3: Construction IAQ Management Plan, During Construction			*			*
EQc4.1: Low-Emitting Materials, Adhesives & Sealants	*		*		*	*
EQc4.2: Low-Emitting Materials, Paints & Coatings	*		*		*	*
EQc4.3: Low-Emitting Materials, Carpet Systems	*		*		*	
EQc4.4: Low-Emitting Materials, Composite Wood & Agrifiber	*		*		*	*
EQc5: Indoor Chemical & Pollutant Source Control		*			*	
EQc6: Controllability of Systems, Thermal Comfort		*			*	
EQc7: Thermal Comfort, Design		*			*	
EQc8.1: Daylight & Views, Daylight 75% of Spaces		*			*	
EQc8.2: Daylight & Views, Views for 90% of Spaces		*			*	

Minimum IAQ Performance

Required

Can assist tenants in certification under LEED for Commercial Interiors

Intent

Establish minimum indoor air quality (IAQ) performance to enhance indoor air quality in buildings, thus contributing to the comfort and well-being of the occupants.

Requirements

Meet the minimum requirements of Sections 4 through 7 of ASHRAE 62.1-2004, Ventilation for Acceptable Indoor Air Quality. Mechanical ventilation systems shall be designed using the Ventilation Rate Procedure or the applicable local code, whichever is more stringent.

Naturally ventilated buildings shall comply with ASHRAE 62.1-2004, paragraph 5.1.

Mechanical ventilation systems installed during core and shell construction shall be capable of meeting projected ventilation levels based on anticipated future tenant requirements.

Potential Technologies & Strategies

Design ventilation systems to meet or exceed the minimum outdoor air ventilation rates as described in the ASHRAE standard. Balance the impacts of ventilation rates on energy use and indoor air quality to optimize for energy efficiency and occupant health. Use the ASHRAE 62 Users Manual for detailed guidance on meeting the referenced requirements.

Summary of Referenced Standard

ASHRAE Standard 62.1-2004: Ventilation For Acceptable Indoor Air Quality

American Society of Heating, Refrigerating and Air-Conditioning Engineers

www.ashrae.org

(800) 527-4723

"The purpose of this standard is to specify minimum ventilation rates and indoor air quality that will be acceptable to human occupants and are intended to minimize the potential for adverse health effects. This standard is intended for regulatory application to new buildings, additions to existing buildings and those changes to existing buildings that are identified in the body of the standard. This standard applies to all indoor or enclosed spaces that people may occupy, except where other applicable standards and requirements dictate larger amounts of ventilation than this standard. Release of moisture in residential kitchens and bathrooms, locker rooms, and swimming pools is included in the scope of this standard. Additional requirements for laboratory, industrial, and other spaces may be dictated by workplace and other standards, as well as by the processes occurring within the space. This standard considers chemical, physical, and biological contaminants that can affect air quality. Thermal comfort requirements are not included in this standard." (ASHRAE 62.1-2004)

Note that although ASHRAE Standard 62.1-2004 will be the relevant standard for the vast majority of LEED-CS projects, certain low-rise residential projects pursuing LEED-CS certification may use ASHRAE Standard 62.2-2004 Ventilation and Acceptable Indoor Air Quality in Low-Rise Residential Buildings to comply with this prerequisite.

Approach and Implementation

Building mechanical and passive ventilation systems seek to ensure that adequate fresh air is available for occupants in the space. Under-ventilated buildings may be stuffy, odorous, uncomfortable and/or unhealthy for occupants. ASHRAE Standard 62.1-2004 establishes minimum requirements for the ventilation air rates in various types of occupied zones and building ventilation systems. The standard takes into account the density of people within an area, the type of activity that is expected to occur in the space, and the nature of the ventilation air delivery system.

Core and Shell Considerations

Core and shell buildings may not have identified the final occupancy count. Projects that do not know the occupancy count must utilize the default occupancy counts provided in Appendix 1. Projects that do know the tenant occupancy must use these numbers as long as the gross square foot per employee is not greater than that in the default occupancy count table.

Often, not only is the occupancy of the building unknown, the distribution of that occupancy is also unknown. Occupancy distribution is necessary for portions of the calculations in ASHRAE 62.1-2004 that determine the percentage of outside air on a system level. For the core and shell project it typically is necessary to determine the system level outside air without the distribution of people. As an example, a typical office building has office and conference room space. The conference rooms require more outdoor air than the offices. If these spaces are all on the same system, the system level outside air must be increased to account for the outside air requirements of the conference rooms. A core and shell building will not know where conference rooms and other densely occupied spaces will be located. For the sake of the calculations, a distribution of people will have to be assumed.

Strategies

There are three basic methods for ventilating buildings:

❑ Active Ventilation (i.e., mechanical ventilation)

❑ Passive Ventilation (i.e., natural ventilation)

❑ Mixed-mode Ventilation (i.e., both mechanical and natural ventilation)

Mechanically Ventilated Spaces — Ventilation Rate Procedure

For mechanical ventilation systems, ASHRAE Standard 62.1-2004, Section 6, presents procedures for determining the minimum required ventilation rates for various applications, using either the Ventilation Rate Procedure or the Indoor Air Quality Procedure. The Ventilation Rate Procedure is more straightforward to apply and much more common in practice and is the prescribed approach required by EQ Prerequisite 1.

The Ventilation Rate Procedure methodology is found in Section 6.2 of ASHRAE 62.1-2004. The breathing zone outdoor airflow is equal to the sum of the outdoor airflow rate required per person times the zone population, plus the outdoor airflow rate required per unit area times the zone floor area. The standard's Table 6-1 "Minimum Ventilation Rates in Breathing Zone" provides information by occupancy category to determine both the amount of outdoor air needed to ventilate people-related source contaminants and area-related source contaminants. The people-related sources portion of the outdoor air rate addresses actual occupancy density and activity. The area-related sources portion accounts for background off-gassing from building materials, furniture and materials typically found in that particular occupancy. Finally, the required zone outdoor airflow is the breathing zone outdoor airflow adjusted to reflect the "zone air distribution effectiveness" using adjustment factors in Table 6-2 of the standard. For multiple-zone systems, outdoor air intake flow is adjusted to reflect the "system ventilation efficiency" of the air distribution configuration, using adjustment factors in Table 6-3 of the standard.

Core and Shell projects with multiple-zone systems will need to assume a "system ventilation efficiency." This must reflect the expected occupant distribution. A tenant fit test or sample plan can be used to approximate the occupant distribution and estimate the "system ventilation efficiency." **Table 1** is sample documentation

Table 1: Sample Summary Calculations Used to Determine Outdoor Air Ventilation Rates – Mechanically Ventilated

Zone Identification			Standard Case: ASHRAE Std 62.1-2004 Verification Rate Procedure									Design Case		
Zone	Occupancy Category	Area (sf)	People Outdoor Air Rate (cfm/person)	Area Outdoor Air Rate (cfm/sf)	Occupant Density (#/1000 sf)	Breathing Zone Outdoor Air Flow Vbz/(CFM)	Table 6-2 Zone Air Distribution Effectiveness Ez	Zone Outdoor Air Flow Voz/(CFM)	Table 6-3 System Ventilation Efficiency Ev	Outdoor Air Intake Flow Vot/(CFM)	Outdoor Air Intake Flow (CFM)	Zone Primary Air Flow Fraction Vpz/(CFM)	Primary Outdoor Air Fraction Zp = Voz/Vpz	Meets Standard?
General Office	Office Space	8000	5	0.06	5	680	1.0	680	1.0	680	800	8000	0.09	Y
Training Room	Lecture Classroom	750	7.5	0.06	65	411	1.2	342	0.9	360	400	1400	0.24	Y
Break Room	Conference Meeting	250	5	0.06	50	63	1.0	63	1.0	63	75	500	0.13	Y
Total		9000				1154		1085		1123	1275	9900		Y

Notes: For the general office space air distribution is overhead, hence Ez = 1. Outdoor air fraction, Zp, < 0.15, hence System Ventilation Efficiency is 1.0.
For the training room, air distribution is underfloor, hence Ez = 1.2. Outdoor air fraction, Zp < 0.25, hence System Ventilation Efficiency is 0.9.
For the break room, air distribution is overhead, hence Ez = 1. Outdoor air fraction, Zp, < 0.15, hence System Ventilation Efficiency is 1.0.

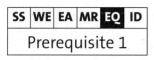
based on a reasonable breakdown of spaces in an office building. It is important for project teams to take this into account. Not accounting for spaces with a high occupant density can lead to undersized ventilation systems and can affect a tenant's ability to comply with ASHRAE Standard 62.1-2004 for their own projects.

This prerequisite requires that applicants demonstrate that the delivered minimum zone outdoor airflow for each zone and the outdoor air intake flow for the system meets or exceeds that required by ASHRAE Standard 62.1-2004 for each zone.

Naturally Ventilated Spaces

ASHRAE Standard 62.1-2004 Section 5.1 provides requirements on the location and size of ventilation openings for naturally ventilated buildings. The standard requires that all naturally ventilated spaces shall be permanently open to, and within 25 feet of, operable wall or roof openings and that the operable area be at least 4% of the net occupiable floor area. As appropriate, all other non-ventilation-related requirements (i.e., exhaust for combustion appliances, outdoor air assessment, and outdoor air intakes) in the standard must be met to comply with this prerequisite.

Mixed-Mode Ventilated Spaces

For mixed-mode ventilated spaces, project teams need to meet the minimum ventilation rates required by Chapter 6 of ASHRAE 62.1-2004 regardless of ventilation mode (natural ventilation, mechanical ventilation or both mechanical and natural ventilation).

Calculations

See **Table 1**.

Exemplary Performance

This prerequisite is not eligible for exemplary performance under the Innovation in Design section.

Precertification Submittal Documentation

Provide the LEED-CS Precertification Submittal Templates, which include the following:

❏ Narrative describing how the project intends to accomplish the credit requirements on the credit-specific Submittal Template signed by the appropriate design team member

❏ Confirmation of this intent from the owner/developer on the LEED-CS Precertification Submittal Template

Certification Submittal Documentation

This prerequisite is submitted as part of the **Design Submittal**.

Design and Construction Credit Compliance

The following project data and calculation information is required to document prerequisite compliance using the LEED-CS v2.0 Submittal Templates:

❏ Provide a design narrative describing the project's ventilation design. Include specific information regarding fresh air intake volumes and any special conditions that affected the project's ventilation design. The narrative should also address any assumptions made about occupant density and "system ventilation effectiveness."

AND

❏ For Mechanically Ventilated Buildings: confirmation that the project has been designed to meet the minimum requirements of ASHRAE Standard 62.1-2004, Ventilation for Acceptable Indoor Air Quality, using the Ventilation Rate Procedure. This should be provided in spreadsheet format similar to **Table 1**.

OR

❑ For Naturally Ventilated Buildings: confirmation that the project has been designed to comply with the requirements for location and size of window openings per ASHRAE Standard 62.1-2004, Section 5.1.

AND

❑ For Naturally Ventilated Buildings: provide applicable project drawings to show the naturally ventilated building zones and the operable window areas.

Tenant Sales or Lease Agreement Credit Compliance

This compliance method is available to core and shell projects that incorporate into tenant sales or lease agreements requirements for meeting this credit as part of the tenant scope of work. Provide the LEED letter template for the credit pursued indicating the following:

❑ 100% of leased square footage complies with credit requirements. Lease or sales agreements may be requested.

❑ 100% of the unleased square footage shall comply with the credit requirements when leased. A statement signed by the owner/developer that all leases and/or sales agreements will comply may be requested.

Considerations

Good indoor air quality in buildings may yield improved occupant comfort, well-being and productivity. A key component of maintaining indoor air quality in a green building is providing adequate ventilation. ASHRAE Standard 62.1-2004 describes procedures for avoiding the introduction of contaminants; the criterion includes location of air intakes as they relate to potential outdoor sources of contamination. The standard also outlines general ventilation rates for a variety of building types and occupancy categories.

Because ASHRAE Standard 62.1-2004 has become standard ventilation design practice for many areas, generally no additional design effort or capital cost will be required to meet this prerequisite. Its successful implementation reduces potential liability regarding indoor air quality issues for architects, builders, owners, building operators and occupants.

Resources

Please see the USGBC website at www. usgbc.org/resources for more specific resources on materials sources and other technical information.

Websites

American Society of Heating, Refrigerating and Air-Conditioning Engineers (ASHRAE)

www.ashrae.org

(404) 636-8400

ASHRAE advances the science of heating, ventilation, air conditioning and refrigeration for the public's benefit through research, standards writing, continuing education and publications.

U.S. Environmental Protection Agency's Indoor Air Quality Website

www.epa.gov/iaq

(800) 438-4318

This site includes a wide variety of tools, publications and links to address IAQ concerns in schools and large buildings.

Definitions

Indoor Air Quality is the nature of air inside the space that affects the health and well-being of building occupants.

Mechanical Ventilation is provided by mechanical powered equipment, such as motor-driven fans and blowers, but not by devices such as wind-driven turbine ventilators and mechanically operated windows (ASHRAE 62.1-2004).

SS | WE | EA | MR | **EQ** | ID

Prerequisite 1

Natural Ventilation is provided by thermal, wind or diffusion effects through doors, windows or other intentional openings in the building (ASHRAE 62.1-2004).

Ventilation is the process of supplying and removing air to and from a space for the purpose of controlling air contaminant levels, humidity or temperature within the space.

Mixed-mode Ventilation is a ventilation strategy that combines natural ventilation with mechanical ventilation allowing the building to be ventilated either mechanically or naturally and at times both mechanically and naturally simultaneously.

Environmental Tobacco Smoke (ETS) Control

Required

Can assist tenants in certification
under LEED for Commercial Interiors

Intent

Minimize exposure of building occupants, indoor surfaces, and ventilation air distribution systems to Environmental Tobacco Smoke (ETS).

Requirements

OPTION 1

❏ Prohibit smoking in the building.

❏ Locate any exterior designated smoking areas at least 25 feet away from entries, outdoor air intakes and operable windows.

OR

OPTION 2

❏ Prohibit smoking in the public areas of the building except in designated smoking areas. Public areas include all common areas that are part of the core and shell that are not tenant spaces. Locate any exterior designated smoking areas at least 25 feet away from entries, outdoor air intakes and operable windows.

❏ Locate designated smoking rooms to effectively contain, capture and remove ETS from the building. At a minimum, the smoking room must be directly exhausted to the outdoors with no re-circulation of ETS-containing air to the non-smoking area of the building, and enclosed with impermeable deck-to-deck partitions. With the doors to the smoking room closed, operate exhaust sufficient to create a negative pressure with respect to the adjacent spaces of at least an average of 5 Pa (0.02 inches of water gauge) and with a minimum of 1 Pa (0.004 inches of water gauge).

❏ Performance of the smoking room differential air pressures shall be verified by conducting 15 minutes of measurement, with a minimum of one measurement every 10 seconds, of the differential pressure in the smoking room with respect to each adjacent area and in each adjacent vertical chase with the doors to the smoking room closed. The testing will be conducted with each space configured for worst case conditions of transport of air from the smoking rooms to adjacent spaces with the smoking rooms' doors closed to the adjacent spaces.

OR

OPTION 3 (For residential buildings only)

❏ Prohibit smoking in all common areas of the building.

❏ Locate any exterior designated smoking areas at least 25 feet away from entries, outdoor air intakes and operable windows opening to common areas.

❏ Minimize uncontrolled pathways for ETS transfer between individual residential units by sealing penetrations in walls, ceilings and floors in the residential units, and by sealing vertical chases adjacent to the units.

❏ All doors in the residential units leading to common hallways shall be weatherstripped to minimize air leakage into the hallway.

❑ If the common hallways are pressurized with respect to the residential units then doors in the residential units leading to the common hallways need not be weather-stripped provided that the positive differential pressure is demonstrated as in Option 2, considering the residential unit as the smoking room. Acceptable sealing of residential units shall be demonstrated by a blower door test conducted in accordance with ANSI/ASTM-E779-03, Standard Test Method for Determining Air Leakage Rate By Fan Pressurization, AND use of the progressive sampling methodology defined in Chapter 4 (Building HVAC Requirements) of the Residential Manual for Compliance with California's 2005 Energy Efficiency Standards (www.energy. ca.gov/title24/residential_manual). Residential units must demonstrate less than 1.25 square inches leakage area per 100 square feet of enclosure area (i.e., sum of all wall, ceiling and floor areas).

Potential Technologies & Strategies

Prohibit smoking in commercial buildings or effectively control the ventilation air in smoking rooms. For residential buildings, prohibit smoking in common areas, design building envelope and systems to minimize ETS transfer among dwelling units.

Summary of Referenced Standards

ANSI/ASTM-E779-03, Standard Test Method for Determining Air Leakage Rate By Fan Pressurization

To purchase this standard go to: www.astm.org

"1.1 This test method covers a standardized technique for measuring air-leakage rates through a building envelope under controlled pressurization and de-pressurization…1.3 This test method is intended to produce a measure of airtightness of a building envelope…" (ASTM-E779-03)

Residential Manual for Compliance with California's 2005 Energy Efficiency Standards (For Low Rise Residential Buildings), Chapter 4

www.energy.ca.gov/2005publications/ CEC-400-2005-005/chapters_3q/4_ Building_HVAC.pdf

"The *Standards* require quality design and construction of HVAC systems and air distribution systems. They also offer compliance credit for the construction of less leaky building envelopes. With the 2005 *Standards*, testing of ducts, refrigerant charge, and airflow was added to the prescriptive requirements (Package D) and is assumed as part of the standard design in performance calculations. Many of the compliance credit options require installer diagnostic testing and certification, and independent diagnostic testing and field verification by a certified Home Energy Rater." (Residential Manual for Compliance with California's 2005 Energy Efficiency Standards [For Low Rise Residential Buildings] Chapter 4)

Approach and Implementation

Prohibit smoking in the building. Provide designated smoking areas outside of the building in locations where ETS will not enter the building or ventilation system. These designated areas should also be located away from concentrations of building occupants or pedestrian traffic. Post information regarding the building's non-smoking policy for all occupants to read.

If interior smoking areas are designed within the building, separate ventilation systems must be installed, and their effectiveness must be tested to ensure that they are isolated from other, non-smoking portions of the building.

The design criteria and instructions for Options 2 and 3 are detailed in the credit requirements and the referenced standard for Option 3.

Core and Shell Considerations

In many regions of North America, municipal regulations do not allow smoking. However, in areas where this is allowed and the owner does not make a building-wide policy prohibiting smoking in the building, careful consideration must be taken, if a core and shell building chooses to allow tenants the option of a smoking area in their space. Such an area must follow all of the requirements for smoking areas listed in this prerequisite. It is important to protect other tenants from the ETS and therefore extra care must be taken to ensure that the smoking area functions as intended. No air from the smoking area is allowed to return back to a common HVAC system. The building will have to accommodate a separate exhaust system from the smoking area. Providing for a separate exhaust system, that is not part of the original design can prove difficult. The space for mechanical equipment and chases in many buildings is so efficiently utilized that extra space for such systems will be at a premium.

Calculations

There are no calculations associated with this credit.

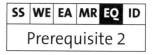

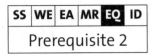

Exemplary Performance

This prerequisite is not eligible for exemplary performance under the Innovation in Design section.

Precertification Submittal Documentation

Provide the LEED-CS Precertification Submittal Templates, which include the following:

❑ Narrative describing how the project intends to accomplish the credit requirements on the credit-specific Submittal Template signed by the appropriate design team member

❑ Confirmation of this intent from the owner/developer on the LEED-CS Precertification Submittal Template

Certification Submittal Documentation

This prerequisite is submitted as part of the **Design Submittal**.

Design and Construction Credit Compliance

The following project data and information is required to document prerequisite compliance using the LEED-CS v2.0 Submittal Templates:

❑ Confirm that the project has met the requirements for the appropriate project category: Non-Smoking Building; Building with Designated Smoking Rooms; or Residential Project.

❑ For buildings with interior smoking rooms or for residential projects, provide appropriate copies of construction drawings to document the location of the smoking rooms, designed area separations, and dedicated ventilation systems.

❑ An optional narrative may be provided to further describe the testing proto-cols/results and compliance methods implemented by the project.

Tenant Sales or Lease Agreement Credit Compliance

This compliance method is not available for this credit.

Considerations

The relationship between smoking and various health risks, including lung disease, cancer and heart disease, has been well documented. A strong link between Environmental Tobacco Smoke (ETS) or "secondhand smoke" and health risks has also been demonstrated.

The most effective way to avoid health problems associated with ETS is to prohibit smoking indoors. If this cannot be accomplished, indoor smoking areas should be isolated from non-smoking areas and have separate ventilation systems to avoid the introduction of tobacco smoke contaminants to non-smoking areas.

Environmental Issues

Separate smoking areas occupy space in the building and may result in a larger building, additional material use and increased energy for ventilation. However, these environmental impacts can be offset by building occupants who are more comfortable, have higher productivity rates, and have lower absenteeism and illnesses.

Economic Issues

Separate smoking areas add to the design and construction costs of most projects. Maintenance of designated smoking areas also adds to lease and operating costs. Prohibition of indoor smoking can increase the useful life of interior fixtures and furnishings. Smoking within a building contaminates indoor air and can cause occupant reactions ranging from irritation and illness to decreased productivity. These problems increase expenses and liability for building owners, tenants, operators and insurance companies.

Core and shell buildings that choose to allow tenants to build smoking areas may need to oversize mechanical rooms and chases for this potential.

Community Issues

Air is a community natural resource, and promoting clean air benefits everyone. Strict no-smoking policies improve the health of the community as a whole, resulting in lower health care and insurance costs.

Resources

Please see the USGBC website at www. usgbc.org/resources for more specific resources on materials sources and other technical information.

Websites

ANSI/ASTM-E779-03, Standard Test Method for Determining Air Leakage Rate By Fan Pressurization

www.astm.org

Standard may be purchased at this website.

Home Energy Rating Systems (HERS) Required Verification And Diagnostic Testing, California Low Rise Residential Alternative Calculation Method Approval Manual

www.energy.ca.gov/2005publications/ CEC-400-2005-005/chapters_3q/4_ Building_HVAC.pdf

What You Can Do About Secondhand Smoke as Parents, Decision Makers, and Building Occupants

U.S. Environmental Protection Agency

www.epa.gov/smokefree/pubs/etsbro. html

(800) 438-4318

An EPA document on the effects of ETS and measures to reduce human exposure to it.

Setting the Record Straight: Secondhand Smoke Is a Preventable Health Risk

U.S. Environmental Protection Agency

www.epa.gov/smokefree/pubs/strsfs. html

An EPA document with a discussion of laboratory research on ETS and federal legislation aimed at curbing ETS problems.

Print Media

The Chemistry of Environmental Tobacco Smoke: Composition and Measurement, Second Edition by R.A. Jenkins, B.A. Tomkins, et al., CRC Press & Lewis Publishers, 2000.

The Smoke-Free Guide: How to Eliminate Tobacco Smoke from Your Environment by Arlene Galloway, Gordon Soules Book Publishers, 1988.

Definitions

Environmental Tobacco Smoke (ETS), or secondhand smoke, consists of airborne particles emitted from the burning end of cigarettes, pipes, and cigars, and exhaled by smokers. These particles contain about 4,000 different compounds, up to 40 of which are known to cause cancer.

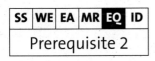

Outdoor Air Delivery Monitoring

Intent

Provide capacity for ventilation system monitoring to help sustain occupant comfort and well-being.

Requirements

Install permanent monitoring systems that provide feedback on ventilation system performance to ensure that ventilation systems maintain design minimum ventilation requirements. Configure all monitoring equipment to generate an alarm when the conditions vary by 10% or more from setpoint, via either a building automation system alarm to the building operator or via a visual or audible alert to the building occupants.

Can assist tenants in certification under LEED for Commercial Interiors

FOR MECHANICALLY VENTILATED SPACES

❏ For each mechanical ventilation system, provide a direct outdoor airflow measurement device capable of measuring the minimum outdoor airflow rate with an accuracy of plus or minus 15% of the design minimum outdoor air rate, as defined by ASHRAE 62.1-2004.

FOR NATURALLY VENTILATED SPACES

Monitor CO_2 concentrations within all naturally ventilated spaces. CO_2 monitoring shall be located within the room between 3 feet and 6 feet above the floor. One CO_2 sensor may be used to represent multiple spaces if the natural ventilation design uses passive stack(s) or other means to induce airflow through those spaces equally and simultaneously without intervention by building occupants.

Potential Technologies & Strategies

Install carbon dioxide and airflow measurement equipment and feed the information to the HVAC system and/or Building Automation System (BAS) to trigger corrective action, if applicable. If such automatic controls are not feasible with the building systems, use the measurement equipment to trigger alarms that inform building operators or occupants of a possible deficiency in outdoor air delivery.

Installation of CO_2 sensors in tenant spaces is not required during Core and Shell construction and tenants are not required to install CO_2 monitors, however they should be made aware of the capability of the core and shell system to monitor CO_2. The core and shell systems must be designed with the capacity for CO_2 monitoring. This entails a building automation system that can be expanded to include future tenant CO_2 points.

Summary of Referenced Standard

ASHRAE Standard 62.1-2004: Ventilation For Acceptable Indoor Air Quality

American Society of Heating, Refrigerating and Air-Conditioning Engineers

www.ashrae.org

(800) 527-4723

"The purpose of this standard is to specify minimum ventilation rates and indoor air quality that will be acceptable to human occupants and are intended to minimize the potential for adverse health effects. This standard is intended for regulatory application to new buildings, additions to existing buildings and those changes to existing buildings that are identified in the body of the standard. This standard applies to all indoor or enclosed spaces that people may occupy, except where other applicable standards and requirements dictate larger amounts of ventilation than this standard. Release of moisture in residential kitchens and bathrooms, locker rooms, and swimming pools is included in the scope of this standard. Additional requirements for laboratory, industrial, and other spaces may be dictated by workplace and other standards, as well as by the processes occurring within the space. This standard considers chemical, physical, and biological contaminants that can affect air quality. Thermal comfort requirements are not included in this standard." (ASHRAE 62.1-2004)

Note that although ASHRAE Standard 62.1-2004 will be the relevant standard for the vast majority of LEED-CS projects, certain low-rise residential projects pursuing LEED-CS certification may use ASHRAE Standard 62.2-2004 Ventilation and Acceptable Indoor Air Quality in Low-Rise Residential Buildings to comply with this prerequisite.

Approach and Implementation

Building HVAC systems are designed to flush out indoor airborne contaminants by exhausting old air and replacing it with fresh outdoor air. The rate of ventilation air exchange is generally determined in the design phase based on space density and type of occupancy. Many conventional ventilation systems do not directly measure the amount of outdoor air delivered. Implementation of the following strategies is recommended to achieve this credit.

Outdoor Air Flow Monitoring

Air flow monitoring of the outdoor air rate validates that the HVAC equipment is delivering the required ventilation rate. Air balance control methodologies, such as fan tracking and measuring building-pressurization based strategies, do not directly determine that appropriate ventilation air is being provided and do not satisfy the credit requirement. The ventilation rate can be measured at the outdoor air intake to an air distribution system using a variety of airflow devices including Pitot tubes, Venturi meters and rotating vane anemometers. Ventilation rate for a particular HVAC system can also be accurately determined from a mass balance calculation if both supply air flow and return air flow are directly measured with air flow monitoring devices. To satisfy the requirements of this credit, the measurement devices must detect when the system is 15% below the design minimum outdoor air rate. When the ventilation system fails to provide the required levels of fresh air, the monitoring system should be configured to deliver a visible or audible alert to the system operator. This alert will indicate to the system operator that operational adjustments may be necessary.

The minimum outdoor air rate may change based on the design and modes of the HVAC system. Constant volume systems, with steady-state design occupancy conditions usually have different outdoor air rates for weekdays and nighttime or off-peak conditions. In variable-air-volume (VAV) systems, the rate of outdoor air needs to stay above the design minimum even when the supply air flow is reduced due to reduced thermal load conditions.

CO_2 Monitoring

The effectiveness of the ventilation system to deliver the needed outdoor air can also be monitored using carbon dioxide (CO2) monitors. In demand controlled ventilation (DCV) systems, where the outdoor air rate supplied to an area is based on readings taken by one or more CO2 monitors located within the occupied spaces, the system-wide outdoor air rate will fluctuate. A DCV system is a typical energy conservation strategy for large spaces with variable occupancy, such as a large lecture hall where the number of people and times of use varies significantly. In this type of operation, the monitoring system confirms that the space—the lecture hall—is receiving adequate outdoor air for the current occupancy, and that the central system adjusts the ventilation rate to match the changing requirement.

CO2 sensors, when properly placed, are a practical means of confirming that a ventilation system is functioning properly. There are two typical system configurations that generally meet the requirements of this credit.

One approach utilizes CO2 sensors that use measured concentration to provide an alert. An indoor concentration of 1000 ppm has commonly been used in the past as the setpoint for the alarm, but a higher alarm concentration may be appropriate when the design complies with Standard 62.1-2004, since the effective ventilation rate per person has been reduced significantly for some zones.

ASHRAE 62.1-2004 Users Manual Appendix A provides a further discussion on CO2 sensors including demand control ventilation.

CO_2 monitoring locations should be selected so that they provide representative readings of the CO_2 concentrations in occupied spaces. Providing multiple CO_2 monitoring stations throughout occupied spaces will provide better information and control than providing a single CO_2 monitor for the entire system. A single CO_2 monitor, typically installed in the return air duct, is less expensive and more straightforward to implement than proving multiple sensors, but may not yield information that identifies areas within the building that are under-ventilated.

Ventilation Air Flow Monitoring

For mechanically-ventilated spaces this LEED-CS credit requires that the outdoor ventilation rate be directly measured and compared against the minimum required ventilation rate. Typically this will be provided by air flow monitoring stations located in the outdoor air intakes of each central HVAC air distribution system. The direct outdoor airflow measurement device must be capable of measuring the outdoor airflow rate at all expected system operating conditions within an accuracy of plus or minus 15% of the design minimum outdoor air rate.

CO_2 Monitoring in Naturally Ventilated Spaces

For naturally ventilated buildings, monitoring CO_2 levels in the occupied space provides feedback to building occupants and operators, so that they can make operational adjustments, such as opening windows, if the space becomes under ventilated. The CO_2 monitors in naturally ventilated spaces should be mounted in the vertical breathing zone between 3 and 6 feet above the floor.

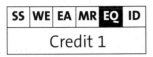

Operations & Maintenance

As part of the system commissioning, project teams should confirm that the outdoor air delivery monitoring system is calibrated, and that the appropriate setpoints and control sequences have been implemented. Provide the building owner, maintenance personnel and occupants with the information needed to understand, maintain and respond to the monitoring system. Maintenance personnel should make inspection of CO_2 monitors and airflow monitoring stations part of routine O&M and preventive maintenance activities. Sensors should be recalibrated based on the manufacturer's requirements. It is recommended to use CO_2 sensors that require recalibration no less than every 5 years. If a CO_2 monitor is allowed to fall out of calibration it may indicate that indoor CO_2 concentrations are lower or higher than they actually are, leading to under- or over-ventilation of the space.

A permanent ventilation monitoring system assists in detecting indoor air quality problems quickly so that corrective action can be taken. Under-ventilation of a space can lead to unsatisfactory indoor environmental conditions and occupant discomfort. Over-ventilation of a space may needlessly increase HVAC energy costs.

Building Type

Air flow and CO_2 monitoring systems can be applied to any building or HVAC system type—including both mechanically and naturally ventilated buildings. In addition to ventilation alarms, such monitors can provide building operators and automated control systems (i.e., demand control ventilation) with information that allows for operational adjustments, such as increasing or decreasing intake airflow rates.

For naturally ventilated buildings and spaces served by HVAC systems that do not allow for active control of ventilation rates, CO_2 monitors in the occupied spaces can provide building occupants and operators with useful information that allows for operational adjustments, such as opening windows or adjusting fixed ventilation rates, if the CO_2 monitors indicate that the space is under ventilated.

Core and Shell Considerations

Providing the required amount of outside air to tenant spaces is a very important consideration in core and shell buildings. Sufficient outside air must be provided at all times to the tenant spaces. Airflow monitoring stations allow the outdoor air quantities to be measured and tracked. This helps to ensure that proper ventilation is being provided.

Project teams may want to include measures to allow tenants to monitor the CO_2 in their spaces. The control system can be specified to include expansion capability, so that tenants can use CO_2 monitors. This gives tenants the opportunity to earn points in the LEED-CI rating system.

Calculations

There are no calculations required for this credit.

Exemplary Performance

This credit is not eligible for exemplary performance under the Innovation in Design section.

Precertification Submittal Documentation

Provide the LEED-CS Precertification Submittal Templates, which include the following:

❑ Narrative describing how the project intends to accomplish the credit requirements on the credit-specific Submittal Template signed by the appropriate design team member

□ Confirmation of this intent from the owner/developer on the LEED-CS Precertification Submittal Template

Certification Submittal Documentation

This credit is submitted as part of the **Design Submittal**.

Design and Construction Credit Compliance

The following project data and calculation information is required to document credit compliance using the LEED-CS v2.0 Submittal Templates:

□ Confirm the type of ventilation system and installed controls.

□ Provide a design narrative describing the project's ventilation design and CO_2 monitoring system (for naturally ventilated buildings). Include specific information regarding location and quantity of installed monitors, operational parameters and setpoints.

□ Provide copies of the applicable project drawings to document the location and type of installed sensors. Drawings should also show natural ventilation components (operable windows, air intakes, etc.) as applicable.

Tenant Sales or Lease Agreement Credit Compliance

This compliance method is available to core and shell projects that incorporate into tenant sales or lease agreements requirements for compliance with the credit as part of the tenant scope of work. Provide the LEED letter template for the credit pursued indicating the following:

□ 100% of leased square footage complies with credit requirements. Lease or sales agreements may be requested.

□ 100% of the unleased square footage shall comply with the credit requirements when leased. A statement signed by the owner/developer that all leases and/or sales agreements will comply may be requested.

Considerations

Cost Issues

CO_2 and ventilation rate monitoring systems increase initial construction costs compared to ventilation systems without such monitoring capabilities. Capital costs and annual costs for air flow monitoring equipment maintenance and calibration procedures may be offset by reduced absenteeism, increased occupant productivity and/or reduced HVAC energy use.

Regional Issues

Ambient outdoor CO_2 concentrations may fluctuate somewhat based on local and regional factors, between approximately 300 and 500 ppm. The time-of-day fluctuations near major congested highways and annual fluctuations, if any, should also be considered. High ambient CO_2 concentrations are typically an indicator of combustion or other contaminant sources. Lower ventilation rates may yield a sense of stuffiness or general dissatisfaction with IAQ.

Resources

Please see the USGBC website at **www. usgbc.org/resources** for more specific resources on materials sources and other technical information.

Websites

ASHRAE 62.1-2004 Users Manual Appendix A

www.ashrae.org

Provides information on CO_2 sensors including demand control ventilation.

SS | WE | EA | MR | EQ | ID

Credit 1

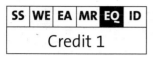

SS	WE	EA	MR	EQ	ID

Credit 1

American Society of Heating, Refrigerating and Air-Conditioning Engineers (ASHRAE)

www.ashrae.org

(404) 636-8400

ASHRAE advances the science of heating, ventilation, air conditioning and refrigeration for the public's benefit through research, standards writing, continuing education and publications.

Building Air Quality: A Guide for Building Owners and Facility Managers

www.epa.gov/iaq/largebldgs/baqtoc.html

(800) 438-4318

An EPA publication on IAQ sources in buildings and methods to prevent and resolve IAQ problems.

Print Media

Air Handling Systems Design by Tseng-Yao Sun, McGraw Hill, 1992.

ASHRAE Standard 55-2004: Thermal Environmental Conditions for Human Occupancy, ASHRAE, 2004

ASHRAE Standard 62.1-2004: Ventilation for Acceptable Indoor Air Quality, ASHRAE, 2004

ASHRAE Standard 62.2-2004: Ventilation for Acceptable Indoor Air Quality in Low-Rise Residential Buildings, ASHRAE, 2004

ASTM D 6245-1998: Standard Guide for Using Indoor Carbon Dioxide Concentrations to Valuate Indoor Air Quality and Ventilation, ASTM, 1998

Efficient Building Design Series, Volume 2: Heating, Ventilating, and Air Conditioning by J. Trost and Frederick Trost, Prentice Hall, 1998.

Definitions

CO$_2$ is carbon dioxide.

Mechanical Ventilation is ventilation provided by mechanically powered equipment, such as motor-driven fans and blowers, but not by devices such as wind-driven turbine ventilators and mechanically operated windows (ASHRAE 62.1-2004).

Natural Ventilation is ventilation provided by thermal, wind, or diffusion effects through doors, windows, or other intentional openings in the building (ASHRAE 62.1-2004).

ppm stands for parts per million

Ventilation is the process of supplying air to or removing air from a space for the purpose of controlling air contaminant levels, humidity or temperature within the space (ASHRAE 62.1-2004).

Increased Ventilation

Intent

Provide additional outdoor air ventilation to improve indoor air quality for improved occupant comfort, well-being and productivity.

Requirements

FOR MECHANICALLY VENTILATED SPACES

❑ Increase breathing zone outdoor air ventilation rates to all occupied spaces by at least 30% above the minimum rates required by ASHRAE Standard 62.1-2004 as determined by EQ Prerequisite 1.

FOR NATURALLY VENTILATED SPACES

Design natural ventilation systems for occupied spaces to meet the recommendations set forth in the Carbon Trust Good Practice Guide 237 [1998]. Determine that natural ventilation is an effective strategy for the project by following the flow diagram process shown in Figure 1.18 of the Chartered Institution of Building Services Engineers (CIBSE) Applications Manual 10: 2005, Natural ventilation in non-domestic buildings.

AND

❑ Use diagrams and calculations to show that the design of the natural ventilation systems meets the recommendations set forth in the CIBSE Applications Manual 10: 2005, Natural ventilation in non-domestic buildings.

OR

❑ Use a macroscopic, multi-zone, analytic model to predict that room-by-room airflows will effectively naturally ventilate, defined as providing the minimum ventilation rates required by ASHRAE 62.1-2004 Chapter 6, for at least 90% of occupied spaces.

❑ The core and shell buildings that are designed to be naturally ventilated must provide the capability for the tenant build-out to meet the requirements of this credit.

Can assist tenants in certification under LEED for Commercial Interiors

Potential Technologies & Strategies

For Mechanically Ventilated Spaces: use heat recovery, where appropriate, to minimize the additional energy consumption associated with higher ventilation rates.

For Naturally Ventilated Spaces: follow the eight design steps described in the Carbon Trust Good Practice Guide 237: 1) Develop design requirements, 2) Plan airflow paths, 3) Identify building uses and features that might require special attention, 4) Determine ventilation requirements, 5) Estimate external driving pressures, 6) Select types of ventilation devices, 7) Size ventilation devices, 8) Analyze the design. Use public domain software such as NIST's CONTAM, Multizone Modeling Software, along with LoopDA, Natural Ventilation Sizing Tool, to analytically predict room-by-room airflows.

Summary of Referenced Standards

ASHRAE Standard 62.1-2004: Ventilation For Acceptable Indoor Air Quality

American Society of Heating, Refrigerating and Air-Conditioning Engineers

www.ashrae.org

(800) 527-4723

"The purpose of this standard is to specify minimum ventilation rates and indoor air quality that will be acceptable to human occupants and are intended to minimize the potential for adverse health effects. This standard is intended for regulatory application to new buildings, additions to existing buildings, and those changes to existing buildings that are identified in the body of the standard. This standard applies to all indoor or enclosed spaces that people may occupy, except where other applicable standards and requirements dictate larger amounts of ventilation than this standard. Release of moisture in residential kitchens and bathrooms, locker rooms, and swimming pools is included in the scope of this standard. Additional requirements for laboratory, industrial, and other spaces may be dictated by workplace and other standards, as well as by the processes occurring within the space. This standard considers chemical, physical, and biological contaminants that can affect air quality. Thermal comfort requirements are not included in this standard." (ASHRAE 62.1-2004)

Note that although ASHRAE Standard 62.1-2004 will be the relevant standard for the vast majority of LEED-CS projects, certain low-rise residential projects pursuing LEED-CS certification may use ASHRAE Standard 62.2-2004 Ventilation and Acceptable Indoor Air Quality in Low-Rise Residential Buildings to comply with this credit.

The Carbon Trust Good Practice Guide 237—Natural ventilation in non-domestic buildings—a guide for designers; developers and owners (1998)

http://www.carbontrust.co.uk/Publications/publicationdetail.htm?productid=GPG237

"Carefully designed, naturally ventilated buildings can be cheaper to construct, maintain and operate than more heavily serviced equivalents. Occupants generally prefer windows that can be opened, and natural light, both of which are features of well designed, naturally ventilated buildings. The Guide summarizes the benefits of natural ventilation and considers the commercial implications, illustrating the issues by means of case studies." (The Carbon Trust)

CIBSE Applications Manual 10: 2005, Natural ventilation in non-domestic buildings.

www.cibse.org

"This publication is a major revision of the Applications Manual (AM) first published in 1997. At that time, there was a significant expansion of interest in the application of engineered natural ventilation to the design of non-domestic buildings. The original AM10 sought to capture the state of knowledge as it existed in the mid-90s and present it in a form suited to the needs of every member of the design team. Some 10 years on from the time when the initial manual was conceived, the state of knowledge has increased, and experience in the design and operation of naturally ventilated buildings has grown. This revision of AM10 is therefore a timely opportunity to update and enhance the guidance offered to designers and users of naturally ventilated buildings." (CIBSE)

Approach and Implementation

A green building should provide its occupants with superior indoor air quality to support their health, comfort and well-being. A key component for maintaining superior indoor air quality is providing adequate ventilation rates. Under-ventilated buildings may be stuffy, odorous, uncomfortable and/or unhealthy for occupants.

Building ventilation systems, including both active HVAC systems and natural ventilation systems, are designed and installed to introduce fresh outside air into the building while exhausting an equal amount of building air. HVAC systems typically serve other functions as well, including providing thermal comfort for occupants. Building conditioning systems that provide enhanced ventilation air, as efficiently and effectively as possible, will help to maintain a high standard of indoor air quality in the building.

The requirement for this credit is a 30% increase in ventilation rates beyond the amounts required by ASHRAE 62.1-2004 in office buildings at the breathing zone. The ASHRAE 62.1-2004 rates are approximately 15% to 20% lower than the ASHRAE 62.1-2001 rates. The threshold for this credit was developed based on documented research demonstrating indoor air quality benefits from ventilation rates in the 25 cfm/person range. To achieve 25 cfm/person, the increase would be closer to 50%. 30% was chosen as a compromise between indoor air quality and energy efficiency.

Core and Shell Considerations

Core and shell buildings may not know the final occupancy count. Core and shell projects must utilize the default occupancy counts provided in Appendix 1. Projects that do know the tenant occupancy must use these numbers as long as the gross square foot per employee is not greater than that in the default occupancy count table. Other numbers can be used if justification is provided.

Planning & Design Phase

Most projects decide early on whether to have a mechanical ventilation system, a passive ventilation system, or a combination of both. This decision may be influenced by the building size and type, as well as climatic, economic and organizational influences. **Figure 1** from CIBSE AM10 provides a decision diagram to aid in making a knowledgeable evaluation. In addition to these considerations, project teams considering natural ventilation should evaluate site conditions and building design. Potential IAQ problems might result from heavy traffic, nearby polluting industries and neighboring waste management sites.

For mechanical ventilation, the design and operating setpoints of the HVAC system will be the primary influence on ventilation rates in the building. Building owners and designers should determine if increasing ventilation rates beyond ASHRAE Standard 62.1-2004 requirements is a good idea for their facility. The HVAC design and sizing should account for increased ventilation rates if this strategy is applied.

Occupants generally take a primary role in managing ventilation conditions in naturally ventilated buildings by opening and closing windows as necessary and appropriate. Naturally ventilated buildings generally have somewhat more variable ventilation rates than actively conditioned buildings, whose systems are often designed to maintain no less than minimum ventilation requirements through all periods of occupancy.

Strategies

There are three basic methods for ventilating buildings:

❏ Active Ventilation (i.e., mechanical ventilation)

❏ Passive Ventilation (i.e., natural ventilation)

Figure 1: Selecting a Strategy, from CIBSE Applications Manual 10:2005, Natural ventilation in non-domestic buildings

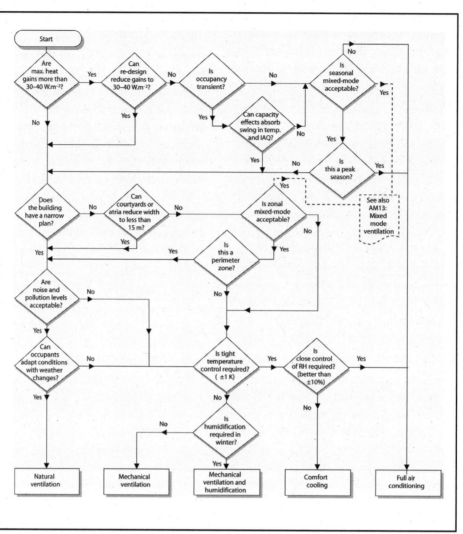

Reproduced with permission from The Chartered Institute of Building Services Engineers, London

❑ Mixed-mode Ventilation (i.e., both mechanical and natural ventilation)

Projects employing both mechanical and natural ventilation (i.e., mixed-mode ventilation) strategies will need to exceed minimum ventilation rates required by ASHRAE Standard 62.1-2004, Chapter 6 by at least 30%.

Mechanically Ventilated Spaces— Ventilation Rate Procedure

For mechanical ventilation systems, ASHRAE Standard 62.1-2004, Section 6, outlines procedures for determining ventilation rates for various applications,

using either the Ventilation Rate Procedure or the Indoor Air Quality Procedure. The Ventilation Rate Procedure is more straightforward to apply and much more common in practice—and it is the prescribed approach used in EQ Prerequisite 1, Minimum IAQ Performance.

The Ventilation Rate Procedure methodology is found in Section 6.2 of ASHRAE 62.1-2004. The breathing zone outdoor airflow is equal to the sum of the outdoor airflow rate required per person times the zone population, plus the outdoor airflow rate required per unit area times the zone floor area. The standard's Table

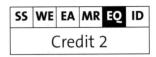
6-1 "Minimum Ventilation Rates in Breathing Zone" provides information by occupancy category to determine both the amount of outdoor air needed to ventilate people-related source contaminants and area-related source contaminants. The people-related sources portion of the outdoor air rate addresses actual occupancy density and activity. The area-related sources portion accounts for background off-gassing from building materials, furniture and materials typically found in that particular occupancy. Finally, the required zone outdoor airflow is the breathing zone outdoor airflow adjusted to reflect the "zone air distribution effectiveness" using adjustment factors in Table 6-2 of the Standard. For multiple-zone systems, outdoor air intake flow is adjusted to reflect the "system ventilation efficiency" for the air distribution configuration, using adjustment factors in Table 6-3 of the Standard.

Core and shell projects with multiple-zone systems will need to assume a "system ventilation efficiency." This must reflect the expected occupant distribution. A tenant fit test or sample plan can be used to approximate the occupant distribution and estimate the "system ventilation efficiency." It is important for project teams to take this into account. Not accounting for spaces with a high occupant density

can lead to undersized ventilation systems and can affect a tenant's ability to comply with ASHRAE Standard 62.1-2004 for their own projects.

This LEED-CS credit requires that applicants demonstrate that the delivered minimum zone outdoor airflow is at least 30% higher than the minimum airflow required by ASHRAE Standard 62.1-2004 for each zone. **Table 1** shows how the sample space used in EQ Prerequisite 1 has attained the 30% increase.

Naturally Ventilated Spaces

Project teams electing natural ventilation have two primary means of demonstrating credit compliance:

❏ The compliance path found in Chapter 2 of The CIBSE Applications Manual 10 (AM10)

OR

❏ Documentation using a macroscopic, multi-zone, analytic model that predicts room-by-room outdoor air flow rates

Those using the CIBSE AM10 (see **Figure 1**) begin by establishing the required flow rates through each space. There is an acceptable average rate needed for IAQ and thermal comfort; increasing this rate results in wasted energy during the heating seasons. There is also additional

Table 1: ASHRAE Std 62.1-2004 Ventilation Rate Procedure

Zone Identification			Standard Case: ASHRAE Std 62.1-2004 Verification Rate Procedure									Design Case		
Zone	Occupancy Category	Area (sf)	People Outdoor Air Rate (cfm/person)	Table 6-1 Area Outdoor Air Rate (cfm/sf)	Occupant Density (#/1000 sf)	Breathing Zone Outdoor Air Flow Vbz (CFM)	Table 6-2 Zone Air Distribution Effectiveness Ez	Zone Outdoor Air Flow Voz (CFM)	Table 6-3 System Ventilation Efficiency Ev	Outdoor Air Intake Flow Vot (CFM)	Outdoor Air Intake Flow (CFM)	Zone Primary Air Flow Faction Vpz (CFM)	Primary Outdoor Air Fraction Zp = Voz/Vpz	% Increase Over Standard
General Office	Office Space	8000	5	0.06	5	680	1.0	680	1.0	680	900	8000	0.09	32%
Training Room	Lecture Classroom	750	7.5	0.06	65	411	1.2	342	0.9	380	500	1400	0.24	32%
Break Room	Conference Meeting	250	5	0.06	50	63	1.0	63	1.0	63	85	500	0.13	36%
Total		**9000**				**1154**		**1085**		**1123**	**1485**	**9900**		**32%**

Notes: For the general office space air distrubution is overhead, hence Ez = 1. Outdoor air fraction, Zp, < 0.15, hence System Ventilation Efficiency is 1.0.

For the training room, air distrubution is underfloor, hence Ez = 1.2. Outdoor air fraction, Zp < 0.25, hence System Ventilation Efficiency is 0.9.

For the break room, air distrubution is overhead, hence Ez = 1. Outdoor air fraction, Zp, < 0.15, hence System Ventilation Efficiency is 1.0.

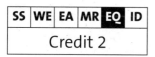
ventilation needed for the summer cooling requirements.

CIBSE AM10 lists several natural ventilation analysis methods, either using a separate manual or simulation software. Project teams should confirm their choice with justification. Submittals will need to include a narrative that provides information on the building, its orientation and the glazing ratios. Include a summary of the internal heat gains and weather conditions. Explain the ventilation strategy, including the airflow paths, the rates planned for different operational periods during the day and night, the peak internal temperatures, and means of shading for summer solar gains. Provide sample calculations on the determination of opening size for operable windows, trickle vents and louvers. Finally, include the calculations for the driving pressure showing the effects of both wind and stack-induced pressure differentials.

Project teams using a macroscopic, multi-zone, analytic model that predicts room-by-room air flow rates will need to provide a narrative including the same information listed above. They will also need to demonstrate that 90% of the occupied areas are effectively ventilated, that is to provide minimum ventilation rates required by ASHRAE 62.1-2004, Chapter 6, by natural ventilation. Room-by-room outdoor airflow rates predicted by the analysis should also be provided.

Calculations

For mechanical ventilation systems, project teams should prepare calculations to demonstrate that the design ventilation rates for each zone are at least 30% above the minimum rates required by the Ventilation Rate Procedure of ASHRAE 62.1-2004. This calculation should take the form of a table or spreadsheet similar to **Table 1**. The same calculation may be used to document both EQ Prerequisite 1 and EQ Credit 2.

If this credit is pursued, the design ventilation rates, at least 30% higher than standard ventilation rates, should be incorporated into the energy calculations in EA Credit 1. Depending on the system design and climatic factors, increased ventilation may reduce the calculated and actual energy performance of the building.

For naturally ventilated spaces, project teams should provide sample calculations demonstrating how opening size for operable windows, trickle vents and louvers were determined in accordance with CIBSE AM10 and The Carbon Trust Good Practice Guide 237 (see **Figure 1**).

For naturally ventilated spaces, project teams using a macroscopic, multi-zone, analytic model that predicts room-by-room air flow rates will need to provide the room-by-room outdoor airflow rates predicted by the analysis and a comparison to minimum ventilation rates required by ASHRAE Standard 62.1-2004, Chapter 6.

Exemplary Performance

This credit is not eligible for exemplary performance under the Innovation in Design section.

Precertification Submittal Documentation

Provide the LEED-CS Precertification Submittal Templates, which include the following:

❑ Narrative describing how the project intends to accomplish the credit requirements on the credit-specific Submittal Template signed by the appropriate design team member

❑ Confirmation of this intent from the owner/developer on the LEED-CS Precertification Submittal Template

Certification Submittal Documentation

This credit is submitted as part of the **Design Submittal**.

Design and Construction Credit Compliance

The following project data and calculation information is required to document credit compliance using the LEED-CS v2.0 Submittal Templates:

Mechanically Ventilated Buildings

❑ Confirm that the breathing zone ventilation rates in all occupied spaces have been designed to exceed the minimum rates required by ASHRAE Standard 62.1-2004 or the applicable local code, whichever is more stringent, by a minimum of 30%. This should be provided in a spreadsheet format similar to **Table 1**.

❑ Provide a design narrative describing the project's ventilation system design. Include specific information regarding the fresh air intake volume for each specific occupied zone to demonstrate that the design exceeds the referenced standard or the applicable local code, whichever is more stringent, by at least 30%. The narrative should also address any assumptions made about occupant density and "system ventilation effectiveness."

Naturally Ventilated Buildings

❑ Confirm that the natural ventilation system has been designed to meet the recommendations set forth in the Carbon Trust "Good Practice Guide 237" (1988).

❑ Provide a design narrative describing the design method (CIBSE Method/ Analytic Model) utilized in determining the natural ventilation design for the project. Provide specific information regarding calculation methodol-

ogy and/or model results to demonstrate that the ventilation design complies with the referenced standards.

Tenant Sales or Lease Agreement Credit Compliance

This compliance method is available to core and shell projects that incorporate into tenant sales or lease agreements language that requires compliance with this credit as part of the tenant scope of work. Provide the LEED letter template for the credit pursued indicating the following:

❑ 100% of leased square footage complies with credit requirements. Lease or sales agreements may be requested.

❑ 100% of the unleased square footage shall comply with the credit requirements when leased. A statement signed by the owner/developer that all leases and/or sales agreements will comply may be requested.

Considerations

Cost Issues

Increasing ventilation rates by 30% beyond ASHRAE Standard 62.1-2004 will yield higher HVAC energy costs and potentially greater HVAC capacity than associated with the ventilation rates established in the standard. This increase in HVAC capacity and energy use will be more pronounced in extreme climates than in mild, temperate climates. Some projects may choose to increase the outdoor air rate, and accept higher HVAC equipment and energy costs, because research indicates that the resulting indoor air quality is associated with improved employee health, welfare, well-being and productivity. For core and shell buildings this may result in improved tenant attraction and retention.

While a naturally ventilated building may have less equipment than a comparable mechanically ventilated building, natural ventilation designs may require additional

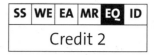

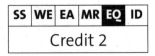

costs for operable windows, increased thermal mass, and other architectural elements which allow for passive ventilation and space conditioning. Energy and maintenance costs of naturally ventilated buildings tend to be lower than for comparable mechanically ventilated spaces.

Regional Issues

Additional ventilation is more practical for mild climates, where increasing ventilation rates beyond the ASHRAE 62.1-2004 minimum rates will not have as great an impact on HVAC systems capacity and energy consumption as in hot, humid or cold climates. Natural ventilation and passive conditioning approaches are also more typical in mild and temperate climates, although there are precedents for passively conditioned buildings in all climates. There may be variable conditions in naturally ventilated buildings, but occupants are satisfied because they control their environment.

Synergies and Trade-Offs

In addition to designing the HVAC systems properly and selecting appropriate building materials, increasing ventilation rates beyond standard practice may be one strategy to provide superior indoor air quality. Managing indoor air quality concerns during construction and operations is also appropriate for many green building projects.

For mechanically ventilated and air-conditioned buildings, increasing ventilation rates will require somewhat larger HVAC system capacity and greater energy use adding to both capital and operational costs. Natural ventilation systems can provide increased ventilation rates, good indoor air quality, and occupant control over thermal comfort and ventilation via operable windows while potentially reducing operating costs compared to mechanical ventilation systems.

Resources

Please see the USGBC website at www. usgbc.org/resources for more specific resources on materials sources and other technical information.

Websites

ASHRAE Standard 62.1-2004: Ventilation For Acceptable Indoor Air Quality

American Society of Heating, Refrigerating and Air-Conditioning Engineers

www.ashrae.org

(800) 527-4723

The Carbon Trust Good Practice Guide 237—Natural ventilation in non-domestic buildings—a guide for designers; developers and owners (1998)

www.thecarbontrust.co.uk

CIBSE Applications Manual 10: 2005, Natural ventilation in non-domestic buildings

www.cibse.org

"This publication is a major revision of the Applications Manual (AM) first published in 1997. At that time, there was a significant expansion of interest in the application of engineered natural ventilation to the design of non-domestic buildings. The original AM10 sought to capture the state of knowledge as it existed in the mid-90s and present it in a form suited to the needs of every member of the design team. Some 10 years on from the time when the initial manual was conceived, the state of knowledge has increased, and experience in the design and operation of naturally ventilated buildings has grown. This revision of AM10 is therefore a timely opportunity to update and enhance the guidance offered to designers and users of naturally ventilated buildings." (CIBSE)

American Society of Heating, Refrigerating and Air-Conditioning Engineers (ASHRAE)

www.ashrae.org

(404) 636-8400

ASHRAE advances the science of heating, ventilation, air conditioning and refrigeration for the public's benefit through research, standards writing, continuing education and publications. To purchase ASHRAE standards and guidelines, visit the bookstore on the ASHRAE website and search for the desired publication.

Building Assessment, Survey and Evaluation Study

U.S. Environmental Protection Agency

www.epa.gov/iaq/largebldgs/base_page.htm

Building Air Quality Action Plan

U.S. Environmental Protection Agency

www.epa.gov/iaq/largebldgs/actionpl.html

The Chartered Institution of Building Services Engineers (CIBSE)

www.cibse.org

This organization, located in London, on its own and in collaboration with other entities, publishes a full series of guides on the topic of ventilation, including natural ventilation.

Definitions

Air Conditioning is the process of treating air to meet the requirements of a conditioned space by controlling its temperature, humidity, cleanliness and distribution (ASHRAE 62.1-2004).

Breathing Zone is the region within an occupied space between planes 3 and 6 ft. above the floor and more than 2 ft. from the walls or fixed air-conditioning equipment.

Conditioned Space is that part of a building that is heated or cooled, or both, for the comfort of occupants (ASHRAE 62.1-2004).

Contaminant is an unwanted airborne constituent that may reduce acceptability of the air (ASHRAE 62.1-2004).

Exfiltration is uncontrolled outward air leakage from conditioned spaces through unintentional openings in ceiling, floors and walls to unconditioned spaces or the outdoors caused by pressure differences across these openings due to wind, inside-outside temperature differences (stack effect), and imbalances between supply and exhaust airflow rates (ASHRAE 62.1-2004).

Exhaust Air is the air removed from a space and discharged to outside the building by means of mechanical or natural ventilation systems.

Infiltration is uncontrolled inward air leakage to conditioned spaces through unintentional openings in ceilings, floors and walls from unconditioned spaces or the outdoors caused by the same pressure differences that induce exfiltration (ASHRAE 62.1-2004).

Makeup Air is any combination of outdoor and transfer air intended to replace exhaust air and exfiltration (ASHRAE 62.1-2004).

Mechanical Ventilation is ventilation provided by mechanically powered equipment, such as motor-driven fans and blowers, but not by devices such as wind-driven turbine ventilators and mechanically operated windows (ASHRAE 62.1-2004).

Natural Ventilation is ventilation provided by thermal, wind, or diffusion effects through doors, windows, or other intentional openings in the building (ASHRAE 62.1-2004).

Outdoor Air is the ambient air that enters a building through a ventilation system, through intentional openings for natural ventilation, or by infiltration (ASHRAE 62.1-2004).

Recirculated Air is the air removed from a space and reused as supply air (ASHRAE 62.1-2004).

Return Air is the air removed from a space to be then recirculated or exhausted (ASHRAE 62.1-2004).

Supply Air is the air delivered by mechanical or natural ventilation to a space, composed of any combination of outdoor air, recirculated air, or transfer air (ASHRAE 62.1-2004).

Construction IAQ Management Plan

During Construction

Intent

Reduce indoor air quality problems resulting from the construction/renovation process in order to help sustain the comfort and well-being of construction workers and building occupants.

Requirements

Develop and implement an Indoor Air Quality (IAQ) Management Plan for the construction and pre-occupancy phases of the building as follows:

❏ During construction meet or exceed the recommended Control Measures of the Sheet Metal and Air Conditioning Contractors National Association (SMACNA) IAQ Guidelines for Occupied Buildings under Construction, 1995, Chapter 3.

❏ Protect stored on-site or installed absorptive materials from moisture damage.

❏ If permanently installed air handlers are used during construction, filtration media with a Minimum Efficiency Reporting Value (MERV) of 8 shall be used at each return air grille, as determined by ASHRAE 52.2-1999. Replace all filtration media immediately prior to occupancy.

Potential Technologies & Strategies

Adopt an IAQ management plan to protect the HVAC system during construction, control pollutant sources and interrupt contamination pathways. Sequence the installation of materials to avoid contamination of absorptive materials such as insulation, carpeting, ceiling tile and gypsum wallboard. Coordinate with EQ Credit 5 to determine the appropriate specifications and schedules for filtration media.

If possible, avoid using permanently installed air handlers for temporary heating/cooling during construction. Consult this LEED-CS v2.0 Reference Guide for more detailed information on how to ensure the well-being of construction workers and building occupants if permanently installed air handlers must be used during construction.

Summary of Referenced Standards

IAQ Guidelines for Occupied Buildings Under Construction

Sheet Metal and Air Conditioning Contractors' National Association (SMAC-NA)

www.smacna.org

(703) 803-2980

This standard provides an overview of air pollutants associated with construction, control measures, construction process management, quality control, communications with occupants, and case studies. Consult the referenced standard for measures to protect the building HVAC system and maintain acceptable indoor air quality during construction and demolition activities.

ANSI/ASHRAE 52.2-1999: Method of Testing General Ventilation Air-Cleaning Devices for Removal Efficiency by Particle Size

American Society of Heating, Refrigerating and Air-Conditioning Engineers (ASHRAE)

www.ashrae.org

(800) 527-4723

This standard presents methods for testing air cleaners for two performance characteristics: the ability of the device to remove particles from the air stream and the device's resistance to airflow. The minimum efficiency reporting value (MERV) is based on three composite average particle size removal efficiency (PSE) points. Consult the standard for a complete explanation of MERV value calculations.

Approach and Implementation

Strategies

This credit hinges on performance by the general contractor. The IAQ Manage-ment Plan should be completed before construction begins and should include construction-related IAQ procedures in the pre-construction and construction progress meeting agendas. Education of subcontractors and all field personnel on the goals of the IAQ Management Plan and importance of following the plan's procedures ensures compliance and achievement. If warranted, select a member of the contractor's team to serve as the IAQ Manager who will have the responsibility to identify IAQ problems and their mitigation. The referenced SMACNA standard recommends control measures in five areas: HVAC protection, source control, pathway interruption, housekeeping and scheduling. For each project, review the applicability of each control measure and include those that apply in the final IAQ Management Plan. The control measures are as follows:

HVAC Protection

Ideally, permanently installed HVAC systems should not be used during the construction process as using this equipment can cause contamination of the HVAC system. In most cases, use of the HVAC system during construction activates the manufacturer's warranty, exposing the contractor to potential out-of-pocket costs if problems occur when the manufacturer's warranty has expired but the warranty for the building has not. Using temporary heaters is feasible, practical and generally not costly.

Protect all HVAC equipment from both dust and odors. Ideally, do not use the system during construction, particularly during demolition. Seal all duct and equipment openings with plastic. If the system must be operated to maintain service to other occupied portions of the building or to protect finished work be sure to protect the return/negative pressure side of the system. If the returns cannot be closed off, install and maintain temporary filters over grilles and openings. To

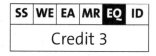

comply with the credit requirements the filtration medium must have a rating of MERV 8 or better. If an unducted plenum over the construction zone must be used, isolate it by having all ceiling tiles in place. Leaks in the return ducts and air handlers should be checked. Make needed repairs promptly. Avoid using the mechanical rooms for construction storage.

Replace all filtration media immediately prior to occupancy, installing only a single set of final filtration media. Note that the requirement for MERV 13 rated filters has been moved to EQ Credit 5. This credit does not regulate the efficiency of the filters used for the long-term operation of the building.

Source Control

Specify finish materials such as paints, carpet, composite wood, adhesives, and sealants that have low toxicity levels, or none at all. The selection of low-emitting materials is covered under EQ Credit 4. The IAQ Management Plan should specify the control measures for materials containing VOCs. Recover, isolate and ventilate containers housing toxic materials. Also, avoid exhaust fumes from idling vehicles and gasoline fueled tools.

Pathway Interruption

During construction, isolate areas of work to prevent contamination of clean or occupied spaces. Depending on the weather conditions, ventilate using 100% outside air to exhaust contaminated air directly to the outside during installation of VOC-emitting materials. Depressurize the work area allowing the air pressure differential between construction and clean areas to contain dust and odors. Provide temporary barriers that contain the construction area.

Housekeeping

Institute cleaning activities designed to control contaminants in building spaces during construction and prior to occu-

pancy. Porous building materials should be protected from exposure to moisture and stored in a clean area prior to installation. Some other strategies are using vacuum cleaners with high efficiency particulate filters, increasing the cleaning frequency and utilizing wetting agents for dust.

Scheduling

Coordinate construction activities to minimize or eliminate disruption of operations in the occupied portions of the building. Construction activities over the duration of the project should be sequenced carefully to minimize the impact on the indoor air quality. It may be necessary to conduct activities with high pollution potential during off-hours, such as on the weekends or in the evenings to allow time for new materials to air out. Plan adequate time to complete work so flush-out and IAQ test procedures can be completed prior to occupancy. Upon completion of construction, replace all filtration media immediately prior to occupancy. This activity should be coordinated with the activities and requirements addressed in EQ Credit 3.2 and 5.

Utilizing temporary ventilation units is one strategy to meet the SMACNA control measure for HVAC protection, but does not on its own satisfy all of the requirements of this credit.

Core and Shell Considerations

For some core and shell building types, there is generally a period where ongoing core and shell construction is happening at the same time as tenant space build-out. This is generally at the point in the project when the building is completely enclosed and major building systems are in place. Core and shell projects should give careful consideration to coordination of the Construction IAQ Management Plan with tenant construction. Ideally, a tenant IAQ management plan would be developed in coordination with the core and shell construction team's IAQ Plan.

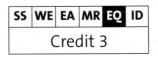
While future tenant fit-outs are not addressed through LEED-CS, minimizing cross contamination of tenant spaces as future tenants build out their spaces should also be considered. A tenant pursuing a LEED-CI certification will need to consider this for the tenant space. SMACNA's IAQ Guidelines for Occupied Buildings Under Construction details many measures to help improve the IAQ of occupied buildings under construction. One of these measures is sealing off the return air system from the construction site. Another measure is proving local exhaust to the construction area to directly exhaust any contaminants from the construction. A comprehensive building Construction IAQ Management Plan can help reduce the complaints from existing tenants during construction of new tenant space.

Calculations

There are no calculations to support this credit.

Exemplary Performance

Core and hell projects that require and enforce a Construction IAQ Management Plan for 100% of the tenant spaces are eligible for exemplary performance under the Innovation in Design section.

Precertification Submittal Documentation

Provide the LEED-CS Precertification Submittal Templates, which include the following:

❑ Narrative describing how the project intends to accomplish the credit requirements on the credit-specific Submittal Template signed by the appropriate design team member

❑ Confirmation of this intent from the owner/developer on the LEED-CS Precertification Submittal Template

Certification Submittal Documentation

This credit is submitted as part of the **Construction Submittal**.

Design and Construction Credit Compliance

The following project data and calculation information is required to document credit compliance using the LEED-CS v2.0 Submittal Templates:

❑ Provide a copy of the project's Indoor Air Quality (IAQ) Management Plan.

❑ Confirm if the permanently installed air handling equipment was used during construction.

❑ Provide photos to highlight the implemented construction IAQ practices.

❑ List all filtration media (manufacturer, model #, MERV rating, location of installed filter) installed during construction and confirm that each was replaced prior to final occupancy.

❑ Provide an optional narrative describing any special circumstances or non-standard approaches taken by the project.

Tenant Sales or Lease Agreement Credit Compliance

This compliance method is not available for this credit.

Considerations

Building construction invariably introduces contaminates into the building. If unaddressed, the contamination can result in poor indoor air quality extending over the lifetime of the building. Fortunately there are IAQ management strategies, if instituted during construction and before occupancy, that will minimize potential problems.

Environmental Issues

Contaminant reduction is beneficial to building occupants, resulting in greater comfort, lower absenteeism and greater productivity.

Economic Issues

Superior indoor air quality is likely to increase worker productivity translating to greater profitability for companies. Additional time and labor may be required during construction to protect and clean ventilation systems and building spaces. However, these actions can extend the lifetime of the ventilation system and improve ventilation system efficiency, resulting in reduced energy use. The sequencing of material installation may require additional time and could potentially delay the date of initial occupancy. Early coordination between the contractor and subcontractors can minimize or eliminate scheduling delays.

Resources

Please see the USGBC website at www. usgbc.org/resources for more specific resources on materials sources and other technical information.

Websites

Controlling Pollutants and Sources

U.S. Environmental Protection Agency

www.epa.gov/iaq/schooldesign/ controlling.html

Detailed information on exhaust or spot ventilation practices during construction activity can be found toward the end of the webpage at the abovementioned URL address.

The State of Washington (SOW) Program and IAQ Standards

http://www.aerias.org/DesktopModules/ ArticleDetail.aspx?articleId=85

This IAQ standard for the state of Washington was the first state-initiated program to ensure the design of buildings with acceptable indoor air quality.

Sheet Metal and Air Conditioning Contractors' National Association, Inc. (SMACNA)

www.smacna.org

(703) 803-2980

SMACNA is a professional trade association that publishes the referenced standard as well as *Indoor Air Quality: A Systems Approach*, a comprehensive discussion of the sources of pollutants, measurement, methods of control, and management techniques.

Print Media

Indoor Air Quality, Construction Technology Centre Atlantic. Written as a comprehensive review of indoor air quality issues and solutions, the report is available for purchase from http://ctca.unb.ca/CTCA/ communication/IAQ/Order_IAQ.htm or by calling (506) 453-5000.

Definitions

A **Construction IAQ Management Plan** is a document specific to a building project that outlines measures to minimize contamination in the building during construction and to flush the building of contaminants prior to occupancy.

HVAC Systems include heating, ventilating, and air-conditioning systems used to provide thermal comfort and ventilation for building interiors.

SS | WE | EA | MR | **EQ** | ID

Credit 3

Low-Emitting Materials

Adhesives & Sealants

Intent

Reduce the quantity of indoor air contaminants that are odorous, irritating and/or harmful to the comfort and well-being of installers and occupants.

Requirements

All adhesives and sealants used on the interior of the building (defined as inside of the weatherproofing system and applied on-site) shall comply with the requirements of the following reference standards:

❑ Adhesives, Sealants and Sealant Primers: South Coast Air Quality Management District (SCAQMD) Rule #1168. VOC limits are listed in the table below and correspond to an effective date of July 1, 2005 and rule amendment date of January 7, 2005.

Table 1: SCAQMD VOC Limits

Architectural Applications	VOC Limit [g/L less water]	Specialty Applications	VOC Limit [g/L less water]
Indoor Carpet Adhesives	50	PVC Welding	510
Carpet Pad Adhesives	50	CPVC Welding	490
Wood Flooring Adhesives	100	ABS Welding	325
Rubber Floor Adhesives	60	Plastic Cement Welding	250
Subfloor Adhesives	50	Adhesive Primer for Plastic	550
Ceramic Tile Adhesives	65	Contact Adhesive	80
VCT & Asphalt Adhesives	50	Special Purpose Contact Adhesive	250
Drywall & Panel Adhesives	50	Structural Wood Member Adhesive	140
Cove Base Adhesives	50	Sheet Applied Rubber Lining Operations	850
Multipurpose Construction Adhesives	70	Top & Trim Adhesive	250
Structural Glazing Adhesives	100		

Substrate Specific Applications	VOC Limit [g/L less water]	Sealants	VOC Limit [g/L less water]
Metal to Metal	30	Architectural	250
Plastic Foams	50	Nonmembrane Roof	300
Porous Material (except wood)	50	Roadway	250
Wood	30	Single-Ply Roof Membrane	450
Fiberglass	80	Other	420

Sealant Primers	VOC Limit [g/L less water]
Architectural Non Porous	250
Architectural Porous	775
Other	750

1 Point
for Achievement
of 2 Requirements
(4.1, 4.2, 4.3 or 4.4)

2 Points
for Achievement
of 3 Requirements
(4.1, 4.2, 4.3 or 4.4)

3 Points
for Achievement
of 4 Requirements
(4.1, 4.2, 4.3 or 4.4)

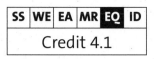
Table 2: Greenseal VOC Limits

Aerosol Adhesives	VOC Weight [g/L minus water]
General purpose mist spray	65% VOCs by weight
General purpose web spray	55% VOCs by weight
Special purpose aerosol adhesives (all types)	70% VOCs by weight

Potential Technologies & Strategies

Specify low-VOC materials in construction documents. Ensure that VOC limits are clearly stated in each section of the specifications where adhesives and sealants are addressed. Common products to evaluate include general construction adhesives, flooring adhesives, fire-stopping sealants, caulking, duct sealants, plumbing adhesives, and cove base adhesives.

Summary of Referenced Standards

South Coast Rule #1168 October 3, 2003 Amendment by the South Coast Air Quality Management District

South Coast Air Quality Management District

www.aqmd.gov/rules/reg/reg11/r1168.pdf

(909) 396-2000

The South Coast Air Quality Management District is a governmental organization in Southern California with the mission to maintain healthful air quality for its residents. The organization established source specific standards to reduce air quality impacts. The South Coast Rule #1168 VOC limits for adhesives are summarized in Table 1.

Green Seal Standard 36 (GS-36), Effective October 19, 2000

www.greenseal.org/standards/commercialadhesives.htm

Green Seal is an independent nonprofit organization that promotes the manufacture and sale of environmentally responsible consumer products. GS-36 is a standard that sets VOC limits for commercial adhesives.

Approach and Implementation

See the Supplemental Section at the end of this credit for all EQ Credit 4 instructions.

Calculations

There are no calculations associated with this credit.

Exemplary Performance

Core and shell projects that require and enforce compliance with the suite of EAc 4 credits for 100% of the tenant spaces are eligible for one exemplary performance point under the Innovation in Design section.

Precertification Submittal Documentation

Provide the LEED-CS Precertification Submittal Template, which includes the following:

❏ Narrative describing how the project intends to accomplish the credit requirements on the credit-specific Submittal Template signed by the appropriate design team member

❏ Confirmation of this intent from the owner/developer on the LEED-CS Precertification Submittal Template

Certification Submittal Documentation

This credit is submitted as part of the **Construction Submittal**.

Design and Construction Credit Compliance

The following project data and calculation information is required to document credit compliance using the LEED-CS v2.0 Submittal Templates:

❏ Provide a listing of each indoor adhesive, sealant and sealant primer product used on the project. Include the manufacturer's name, product name, specific VOC data (in g/L, less water) for each product, and the corresponding allowable VOC from the referenced standard.

❏ Provide a listing of each indoor aerosol adhesive product used on the project. Include the manufacturer's name, product name, specific VOC data (in g/L, less water) for each product, and the corresponding allowable VOC from the referenced standard.

❏ Provide a narrative to describe any special circumstances or non-stan-

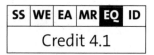

dard compliance paths taken by the project.

Tenant Sales or Lease Agreement Credit Compliance

This compliance method is not available for this credit.

Resources

Please see the USGBC website at www. usgbc.org/resources for more specific resources on materials sources and other technical information.

Websites

South Coast Rule #1168 by the South Coast Air Quality Management District

South Coast Air Quality Management District

www.aqmd.gov/rules/reg/reg11/r1168.pdf

(909) 396-2000

The South Coast Air Quality Management District is a governmental organization in Southern California with the mission to maintain healthful air quality for its residents. The organization established source specific standards to reduce air quality impacts. The South Coast Rule #1168 VOC limits for adhesives are summarized in Table 1.

Green Seal Standard 36 (GS-36)

www.greenseal.org/standards/commercialadhesives.htm

Green Seal is an independent nonprofit organization that promotes the manufacture and sale of environmentally responsible consumer products. GS-36 is a standard that sets VOC limits for commercial adhesives.

Definitions

Adhesive is any substance that is used to bond one surface to another surface by attachment. Adhesives include adhesive bonding primers, adhesive primers, adhesive primers for plastics, and any other primer.

Aerosol Adhesive is an adhesive packaged as an aerosol product in which the spray mechanism is permanently housed in a non-refillable can designed for hand-held application without the need for ancillary hoses or spray equipment. Aerosol adhesives include special purpose spray adhesives, mist spray adhesives and web spray adhesives.

Indoor Adhesive, Sealant and/or Sealant Primer product is defined as an adhesive or sealant product applied on-site, inside of the building's weatherproofing system.

Porous Sealant is a substance used as a sealant on porous materials. Porous materials have tiny openings, often microscopic, in which fluids may be absorbed or discharged. Such materials include, but are not limited to, wood, fabric, paper, corrugated paperboard and plastic foam.

Primer is a material applied to a substrate to improve adhesion of subsequently applied adhesive.

Non-porous Sealant is a substance used as a sealant on non-porous materials. Non-porous materials do not have openings in which fluids may be absorbed or discharged. Such materials include, but are not limited to, plastic and metal.

A **Sealant** is any material with adhesive properties that is formulated primarily to fill, seal, or waterproof gaps or joints between two surfaces. Sealants include sealant primers and caulks.

VOC (Volatile Organic Compounds) are carbon compounds that participate in atmospheric photochemical reactions (excluding carbon monoxide, carbon dioxide, carbonic acid, metallic carbides and carbonates, and ammonium carbonate). The compounds vaporize (become a gas) at normal room temperatures.

Low-Emitting Materials

Paints & Coatings

1 Point
for Achievement
of 2 Requirements
(4.1, 4.2, 4.3 or 4.4)

2 Points
for Achievement
of 3 Requirements
(4.1, 4.2, 4.3 or 4.4)

3 Points
for Achievement
of 4 Requirements
(4.1, 4.2, 4.3 or 4.4)

Intent

Reduce the quantity of indoor air contaminants that are odorous, irritating and/or harmful to the comfort and well-being of installers and occupants.

Requirements

Paints and coatings used on the interior of the building (defined as inside of the weatherproofing system and applied on-site) shall comply with the following criteria:

❑ Architectural paints, coatings and primers applied to interior walls and ceilings: Do not exceed the VOC content limits established in Green Seal Standard GS-11, Paints, First Edition, May 20, 1993.

- Flats: 50 g/L
- Non-Flats: 150 g/L

❑ Anti-corrosive and anti-rust paints applied to interior ferrous metal substrates: Do not exceed the VOC content limit of 250 g/L established in Green Seal Standard GC-03, Anti-Corrosive Paints, Second Edition, January 7, 1997.

❑ Clear wood finishes, floor coatings, stains, and shellacs applied to interior elements: Do not exceed the VOC content limits established in South Coast Air Quality Management District (SCAQMD) Rule 1113, Architectural Coatings, rules in effect on January 1, 2004.

- Clear wood finishes: varnish 350 g/L; lacquer 550 g/L
- Floor coatings: 100 g/L
- Shellacs: clear 730 g/L; pigmented 550 g/L
- Sealers: waterproofing sealers 250g/L; sanding sealers 275 g/L; all other sealers 200 g/L
- Stains: 250 g/L

Potential Technologies & Strategies

Specify low-VOC paints and coatings in construction documents. Ensure that VOC limits are clearly stated in each section of the specifications where paints and coatings are addressed. Track the VOC content of all interior paints and coatings during construction.

SS	WE	EA	MR	**EQ**	ID
		Credit 4.2			

Summary of Referenced Standards

Green Seal Standard GS-11

www.greenseal.org/standards/paints.htm

(202) 872-6400

Green Seal is an independent nonprofit organization that promotes the manufacture and sale of environmentally responsible consumer products. GS-11 is a standard that sets VOC limits for commercial flat and non-flat paints.

Green Seal Standard GS-03

www.greenseal.org/standards/anti-corrosivepaints.htm

(202) 872-6400

GS-03 is a Green Seal standard that sets VOC limits for anti-corrosive and anti-rust paints.

South Coast Air Quality Management District (SCAQMD) Rule 1113, Architectural Coatings

www.aqmd.gov/rules/reg/reg11/r1113.pdf

The South Coast Air Quality Management District is a governmental organization in Southern California with the mission to maintain healthful air quality for its residents. The organization established source specific standards to reduce air quality impacts.

Approach and Implementation

See the Supplemental Section at the end of this credit for all EQ Credit 4 instructions.

Calculations

There are no calculations associated with this credit.

Exemplary Performance

Core and shell projects that require and enforce compliance with the suite of EAc 4 credits for 100% of the tenant spaces are eligible for one exemplary performance point under the Innovation in Design section.

Precertification Submittal Documentation

Provide the LEED-CS Precertification Submittal Template, which includes the following:

❑ Narrative describing how the project intends to accomplish the credit requirements on the credit-specific Submittal Template signed by the appropriate design team member

❑ Confirmation of this intent from the owner/developer on the LEED-CS Precertification Submittal Template

Certification Submittal Documentation

This credit is submitted as part of the **Construction Submittal**.

Design and Construction Credit Compliance

The following project data and calculation information is required to document credit compliance using the LEED-CS v2.0 Submittal Templates:

❑ Provide a listing of each indoor paint and coating used on the project. Include the manufacturer's name, product name, specific VOC data (in g/L) for each product, and the corresponding allowable VOC from the referenced standard.

❑ Provide a narrative to describe any special circumstances or non-standard compliance paths taken by the project.

Tenant Sales or Lease Agreement Credit Compliance

This compliance method is not available for this credit.

Resources

Please see the USGBC website at www. usgbc.org/resources for more specific resources on materials sources and other technical information.

Websites

Green Seal

www.greenseal.org

South Coast Air Quality Management District

www.aqmd.gov

Definitions

Anti-corrosive Paints are coatings formulated and recommended for use in preventing the corrosion of ferrous metal substrates.

Paint is a liquid, liquefiable or mastic composition that is converted to a solid protective, decorative, or functional adherent film after application as a thin layer. These coatings are intended for on-site application to interior or exterior surfaces of residential, commercial, institutional or industrial buildings.

Indoor Paint or **Coating Product** is defined as a paint or coating product applied on-site inside of the building's weatherproofing system.

Flat Coatings are coatings that register a gloss of less than 15 on an 85-degree meter or less than 5 on a 60-degree meter.

Non-flat Coatings are coatings that register a gloss of 5 or greater on a 60-degree meter and a gloss of 15 or greater on an 85-degree meter.

Primer is a material applied to a substrate to improve adhesion of subsequently applied adhesive.

VOCs (Volatile Organic Compounds) are carbon compounds that participate in atmospheric photochemical reactions (excluding carbon monoxide, carbon dioxide, carbonic acid, metallic carbides and carbonates, and ammonium carbonate). The compounds vaporize (become a gas) at normal room temperatures.

Low-Emitting Materials

Carpet Systems

Intent

Reduce the quantity of indoor air contaminants that are odorous, irritating and/or harmful to the comfort and well-being of installers and occupants.

Requirements

All carpet installed in the building interior shall meet the testing and product requirements of the Carpet and Rug Institute's Green Label Plus™ program.

All carpet cushion installed in the building interior shall meet the requirements of the Carpet and Rug Institute Green Label program.

All carpet adhesive shall meet the requirements of EQ Credit 4.1: VOC limit of 50 g/L.

Potential Technologies & Strategies

Clearly specify requirements for product testing and/or certification in the construction documents. Select products that are either certified under the Green Label Plus program or for which testing has been done by qualified independent laboratories in accordance with the appropriate requirements.

The Green Label Plus program for carpets and its associated VOC emission criteria in micrograms per square meter per hour, along with information on testing method and sample collection developed by the Carpet & Rug Institute (CRI) in coordination with California's Sustainable Building Task Force and the California Department of Health Services (DHS), are described in Section 9, Acceptable Emissions Testing for Carpet, DHS Standard Practice CA/DHS/EHLB/R-174, dated 07/15/04. This document is available at: www.dhs.ca.gov/ps/deodc/ehlb/iaq/VOCS/Section01350_7_15_2004_FINAL_PLUS_ADDENDUM-2004-01.pdf. (also published as Section 01350 Section 9 [dated 2004] by the Collaborative for High Performance Schools [www.chps.net]).

1 Point
for Achievement
of 2 Requirements
(4.1, 4.2, 4.3 or 4.4)

2 Points
for Achievement
of 3 Requirements
(4.1, 4.2, 4.3 or 4.4)

3 Points
for Achievement
of 4 Requirements
(4.1, 4.2, 4.3 or 4.4)

Summary of Referenced Standard

Carpet and Rug Institute Green Label Plus Testing Program

Carpet and Rug Institute

www.carpet-rug.com

(800) 882-8846

The Carpet and Rug Institute is a trade organization representing the carpet and rug industry. Green Label Plus is an independent testing program that identifies carpets with very low emissions of volatile organic compounds (VOCs). The "Green Label Plus" program for carpets and its associated VOC emission criteria in micrograms per square meter per hour developed by the Carpet & Rug Institute (CRI) in coordination with California's Sustainable Building Task Force and the California Department of Health Services (DHS) are described on the CRI website. In the CRI Green Label Plus Program, emission rates must be verified by conducting annual testing. Valid/approved certification numbers can be reviewed on the CRI website under Indoor Air Quality/Green Label Plus/Approved companies. Approved products are listed under the company heading.

Testing Criteria

Carpet must not exceed the maximum target emission factors used in the CRI Green Label program and comply with the test protocol used by Green Label Plus. Test results submitted must be no more than 2 years old at the time of submission. Standard Practice for the Testing of Volatile Organic Emissions from Various Sources using Small-Scale Environmental Chambers (State of California Standard 1350), Section 9

www.dhs.ca.gov/ps/deodc/ehlb/iaq/VOCS/Section01350_7_15_2004_FINAL_PLUS_ADDENDUM-2004-01.pdf

This standard practice document specifies testing criteria for carpet emissions that will satisfy the credit requirements.

Approach and Implementation

See the Supplemental Section at the end of this credit for all EQ Credit 4 instructions.

Calculations

There are no calculations associated with this credit.

Exemplary Performance

Core and shell projects that require and enforce compliance with the suite of EAc 4 credits for 100% of the tenant spaces are eligible for one exemplary performance point under the Innovation in Design section.

Precertification Submittal Documentation

Provide the LEED-CS Precertification Submittal Template, which includes the following:

❑ Narrative describing how the project intends to accomplish the credit requirements on the credit-specific Submittal Template signed by the appropriate design team member

❑ Confirmation of this intent from the owner/developer on the LEED-CS Precertification Submittal Template

Certification Submittal Documentation

This credit is submitted as part of the **Construction Submittal**.

Design and Construction Credit Compliance

The following project data and calculation information is required to document credit compliance using the LEED-CS v2.0 Submittal Templates:

❑ Provide a listing of each carpet product installed in the building interior. Confirm that the product complies with the CRI Green Label Plus testing program.

❑ Provide a listing of each carpet cushion product installed in the building interior. Confirm that the product complies with the CRI Green Label testing program.

❑ Provide a narrative to describe any special circumstances or non-standard compliance paths taken by the project.

Tenant Sales or Lease Agreement Credit Compliance

This compliance method is not available for this credit.

Resources

Please see the USGBC website at www. usgbc.org/resources for more specific resources on materials sources and other technical information.

Websites

Carpet and Rug Institute

www.carpet-rug.org

Definitions

Indoor carpet systems are defined as carpet, carpet adhesive, or carpet cushion product installed on-site inside of the building's weatherproofing system.

VOCs (Volatile Organic Compounds) are carbon compounds that participate in atmospheric photochemical reactions (excluding carbon monoxide, carbon di-oxide, carbonic acid, metallic carbides and carbonates, and ammonium carbonate). The compounds vaporize (become a gas) at normal room temperatures.

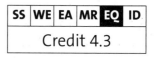

SS | WE | EA | MR | **EQ** | ID

Credit 4.3

Low-Emitting Materials

Composite Wood & Agrifiber Products

Intent

Reduce the quantity of indoor air contaminants that are odorous, irritating and/or harmful to the comfort and well-being of installers and occupants.

Requirements

Composite wood and agrifiber products used on the interior of the building (defined as inside of the weatherproofing system) shall contain no added urea-formaldehyde resins. Laminating adhesives used to fabricate on-site and shop-applied composite wood and agrifiber assemblies shall contain no added urea-formaldehyde resins.

Composite wood and agrifiber products are defined as: particleboard, medium density fiberboard (MDF), plywood, wheatboard, strawboard, panel substrates and door cores. Furniture and fixtures are not considered base building elements and are not included.

Potential Technologies & Strategies

Specify wood and agrifiber products that contain no added urea-formaldehyde resins. Specify laminating adhesives for field and shop applied assemblies that contain no added urea-formaldehyde resins.

1 Point
for Achievement
of 2 Requirements
(4.1, 4.2, 4.3 or 4.4)

2 Points
for Achievement
of 3 Requirements
(4.1, 4.2, 4.3 or 4.4)

3 Points
for Achievement
of 4 Requirements
(4.1, 4.2, 4.3 or 4.4)

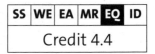
Summary of Referenced Standard

There is no standard referenced for this credit.

Approach and Implementation

See the Supplemental Section at the end of this credit for all EQ Credit 4 instructions.

Calculations

There are no calculations associated with this credit.

Exemplary Performance

Core and shell projects that require and enforce compliance with the suite of EAc 4 credits for 100% of the tenant spaces are eligible for one exemplary performance point under the Innovation in Design section.

Precertification Submittal Documentation

Provide the LEED-CS Precertification Submittal Template, which includes the following:

❏ Narrative describing how the project intends to accomplish the credit requirements on the credit-specific Submittal Template signed by the appropriate design team member

❏ Confirmation of this intent from the owner/developer on the LEED-CS Precertification Submittal Template

Certification Submittal Documentation

This credit is submitted as part of the **Construction Submittal**.

Design and Construction Credit Compliance

The following project data and calculation information is required to document credit compliance using the LEED-CS v2.0 Submittal Templates:

❏ Provide a listing of each composite wood and agrifiber product installed in the building interior. Confirm that each product does not contain any added urea-formaldehyde.

❏ Provide a narrative to describe any special circumstances or non-standard compliance paths taken by the project.

Tenant Sales or Lease Agreement Credit Compliance

This compliance method is not available for this credit.

Resources

Please see the USGBC website at www. usgbc.org/resources for more specific resources on materials sources and other technical information.

Websites

An Update on Formaldehyde

Consumer Product Safety Commission

www.cpsc.gov/CPSCPUB/PUBS/725. html

An informational document from the Consumer Product Safety Commission.

Definitions

Agrifiber Board is a composite panel product derived from recovered agricultural waste fiber from sources including, but not limited to, cereal straw, sugarcane bagasse, sunflower husk, walnut shells, coconut husks, and agricultural prunings. The raw fibers are processed and mixed with resins to produce panel products with characteristics similar to those derived from wood fiber. The following conditions describe which products must comply with the requirements:

1. The product is inside of the building's waterproofing system.

2. Composite components used in assemblies are to be included (e.g., door cores, panel substrates, etc.)

3. The product is part of the base building systems.

Composite Wood is a product consisting of wood or plant particles or fibers bonded together by a synthetic resin or binder. Examples: plywood, particle-board, OSB, MDF, composite door cores. For the purposes of this credit, the following conditions describe which products must comply with the requirements:

1. The product is inside of the building's waterproofing system.

2. Composite wood components used in assemblies are included (e.g., door cores, panel substrates, plywood sections of I-beams).

3. The product is part of the base building systems.

Formaldehyde is a naturally occurring VOC found in small amounts in animals and plants, but is carcinogenic and an irritant to most people when present in high concentrations—causing headaches, dizziness, mental impairment, and other symptoms. When present in the air at levels above 0.1 ppm parts of air, it can cause watery eyes, burning sensations in the eyes, nose and throat; nausea; coughing; chest tightness; wheezing; skin rashes; and asthmatic and allergic reactions.

Indoor Composite Wood or **Agrifiber product** is defined as a composite wood or agrifiber product installed on-site, inside of the building's weatherproofing system.

Laminate Adhesive is an adhesive used in wood/agrifiber products (veneered panels, composite wood products contained in engineered lumber, door assemblies, etc.).

Urea Formaldehyde is a combination of urea and formaldehyde that is used in some glues and may emit formaldehyde at room temperature.

Phenol Formaldehyde, which off-gasses only at high temperature, is used for exterior products, although many of those products are suitable for interior applications.

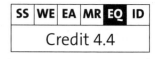

SS | WE | EA | MR | **EQ** | ID

Credit 4.4

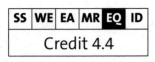

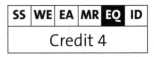

Supplemental Information

Approach and Implementation

The four parts of LEED-CS EQ Credit 4 apply to products and installation processes that have the potential to adversely affect the indoor air quality (IAQ) of a project space and, in turn, those exposed to the contaminants these materials may off-gas.

Because core and shell buildings do not have direct control over the tenant spaces, the owner/developer's ability to affect the building's overall indoor air quality through the selection of Low VOC materials and products is diminished. Core and shell buildings are encouraged to communicate the benefits of low VOC materials to their tenants through Tenant Design and Construction Guidelines. Projects may want to consider going beyond this and mandate specific materials with proven VOC off-gassing performance as requirements for the build-out of all tenant spaces.

Strategies

The requirements for products and activities covered in EQ Credit 4 should be noted in the project specifications and, ideally, within the specific section of the document applicable to a particular trade or supplier.

Design Phase

In order to achieve this goal, credit requirements should be clearly stated in project specifications. Reference the credit requirements in both Division 1 and in the technical divisions. Indicate what must be provided in the way of cut sheets, material safety data sheets (MSD sheets), certificates and test reports. Consider making submittal of this compliance documentation a condition of product approval.

Construction Phase

Meeting the requirements set forth in EQ Credit 4 may not be common practice for all construction teams and suppliers. Consider asking the project owner to stress the importance of meeting the LEED requirements during pre-bid meetings and again at the time of contract award. During these sessions, have LEED Accredited Professionals available and solicit questions from bidding contractors. Include requirements in subcontract and purchase order language.

Composition Limits

All materials that emit contaminants that have the potential to enter the indoor air will be considered as indoor sources of contaminants. Materials which have the potential to communicate their emissions to the indoor air include all indoor surfaces in contact with the indoor air including flooring; walls; ceilings; interior furnishings; suspended ceiling systems and the materials above those suspended ceilings; all ventilation system components in communication with the ventilation supply or return air; and all materials inside of wall cavities, ceiling cavities, floor cavities, or horizontal or vertical chases. These materials include the caulking materials for windows and insulation in ceilings or walls. An example of a material that has little or no potential for communicating with the indoor air is siding that is on the exterior side of the waterproofing membrane. In this approach the formulation of a product is controlled. Limits are set on the amount of volatile organic compounds (VOCs) permitted in a given volume of the product. The threshold limits and the content within a particular product are generally expressed in grams per liter (g/L). EQ Credits 4.1 and 4.2 use this approach for adhesives, sealants, paints and coatings. EQ Credit 4.4 also controls formulation by setting a limit of zero added urea-formaldehyde resins.

Emission Factors

This standard sets a limit on the rate that off-gassing may occur. The rate is stated as the mass of contaminant that may be off-gassed by a given unit quantity of the product in a set period of time. This approach is used in EQ Credit 4.3 for carpet where the rate is expressed as micrograms of contaminant per square meter of carpet per hour. These tests, which are now being done on an array of product types, place samples of precise size in test chambers.

Air samples are drawn off at set times, generally over several days, and analyzed. There are extensive protocols established to make the testing representative of actual conditions on a project site and consistent between similar products from multiple manufactures. The Carpet and Rug Institute (CRI) Green Label Plus program uses emission factor test results for its certifications.

VOC Budgets

This alternative compliance path allows for specialty applications for which there is no low-VOC product option. It may be used with adhesives and sealants covered in EQ Credit 4.1 and with paints and coatings covered in EQ Credit 4.2. The documentation must demonstrate that the overall low-VOC performance has been attained for paints and adhesives separately, not in combination. The calculation is a comparison between a baseline case and the design case. When the design (or actual) is less than the baseline, the credit requirement is satisfied. The values used in the comparison are the total VOCs contained in the products (i.e., paint) used on the project. The total VOCs is determined by multiplying the volume of the product used by the threshold VOC level for the baseline case and actual product VOC level for the design case. The baseline application rate should not be greater than that used in the design case. When submitting a VOC budget calculation, also provide the supporting documentation concerning the product—the name, application rate, class or use to confirm that the correct threshold VOC level has been used in determining the baseline case, and finally the actual VOC level of the product. As the term "budget" implies, this compliance path should be a decision planned in advance. Occasionally, honest mistakes occur—even on LEED projects. If realized in time, this approach may be used to determine if credit compliance can be attained. A narrative explaining the situation should accompany the project submittal, but project teams should never "paint" their way out of a mistake. Additional coats, even with products below the threshold limits, add to the overall level of off-gassed VOCs. It is not enough to meet the requirements; the intent also has to be met to earn the credit.

Considerations

A large number of building products contain compounds that have a negative impact on indoor air quality and the Earth's atmosphere. The most prominent of these compounds, volatile organic compounds (VOCs), contribute to smog generation and air pollution outdoors while having an adverse effect on the well-being of building occupants indoors. By selecting low-emitting materials, both outdoor and indoor air quality impacts can be reduced.

Environmental Issues

VOCs react with sunlight and nitrogen oxides in the atmosphere to form ground-level ozone, a chemical that has a detrimental effect on human health, agricultural crops, forests and ecosystems. Ozone damages lung tissue, reduces lung function, and sensitizes the lungs to other irritants. Ozone is also a major component of smog, which affects agricultural crops and forestland.

Economic Issues

Healthy occupants are more productive and have less illness-related absenteeism. Use of high-VOC content materials can cause illness and may decrease occupant productivity. These problems result in increased expenses and liability for building owners, operators and insurance companies. As a result, the construction market is driving product manufacturers to offer low-VOC alternatives to conventional building products. Costs for these low-VOC products are generally competitive with conventional materials. However, some low-VOC materials are more expensive than conventional materials, particularly when the products are first introduced to the marketplace. Low-VOC products may also be difficult to obtain for some product types. However, these problems will recede as application of low-VOC products become more commonplace.

Synergies and Trade-Offs

Selecting materials that are low in VOCs helps reduce sources of pollutants during the construction process and in the finished building. There are typically multiple products available that meet these criteria for a wide variety of applications. However, these criteria must be balanced against other green building considerations, such as location of manufacture, durability and performance.

Case Study

171 17th Street
Atlanta, Georgia

171 17th Street, the first commercial high-rise in the Atlantic Station® development, achieved a LEED-CS Pilot Silver Certification. The structure is a 21-story, 500,000-sq.ft. commercial office tower on a 138-acre mixed-use urban redevelopment of the former Atlantic Steel Mill. The office tower incorporates several sustainable elements, such as materials with recycled contents, carbon dioxide sensors and low VOC paints, sealants and adhesives. These features, along with

Photo courtesy of: The Epsten Group

Atlantic Station's central location, thoughtful site design and incorporation of alternative transportation, combine to create a higher quality indoor and outdoor environment for 171 17th Street occupants.

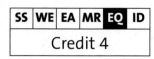

Indoor Chemical & Pollutant Source Control

1 point

Intent

Minimize exposure of building occupants to potentially hazardous particulates and chemical pollutants.

Requirements

Design to minimize and control pollutant entry into buildings and later cross-contamination of regularly occupied areas:

❑ Employ permanent entryway systems at least six feet long in the primary direction of travel to capture dirt and particulates from entering the building at all entryways that are directly connected to the outdoors. Acceptable entryway systems include permanently installed grates, grilles, or slotted systems that allow for cleaning underneath. Roll-out mats are only acceptable when maintained on a weekly basis by a contracted service organization. Qualifying entryways are those that serve as regular entry points for building users.

❑ Where hazardous gases or chemicals may be present or used (including garages, housekeeping/laundry areas and copying/printing rooms), exhaust each space sufficiently to create negative pressure with respect to adjacent spaces with the doors to the room closed. For each of these spaces, provide self-closing doors and deck to deck partitions or a hard lid ceiling. The exhaust rate shall be at least 0.50 cfm/sq.ft., with no air re-circulation. The pressure differential with the surrounding spaces shall be at least 5 Pa (0.02 inches of water gauge) on average and 1 Pa (0.004 inches of water) at a minimum when the doors to the rooms are closed.

❑ In mechanically ventilated buildings, provide regularly occupied areas of the building with air filtration media prior to occupancy that provides a Minimum Efficiency Reporting Value (MERV) of 13 or better. Filtration should be applied to process both return and outside air that is to be delivered as supply air.

Potential Technologies & Strategies

Design facility cleaning and maintenance areas with isolated exhaust systems for contaminants. Maintain physical isolation from the rest of the regularly occupied areas of the building. Install permanent architectural entryway systems such as grilles or grates to prevent occupant-borne contaminants from entering the building. Install high-level filtration systems in air handling units processing both return air and outside supply air. Ensure that air handling units can accommodate required filter sizes and pressure drops.

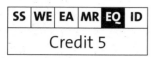

Summary of Referenced Standard

ANSI/ASHRAE 52.2-1999: Method of Testing General Ventilation Air-Cleaning Devices for Removal Efficiency by Particle Size

American Society of Heating, Refrigerating and Air-Conditioning Engineers (ASHRAE)

www.ashrae.org

(800) 527-4723

This standard presents methods for testing air cleaners for two performance characteristics: the ability of the device to remove particles from the air stream and the device's resistance to airflow. The minimum efficiency reporting value (MERV) is based on three composite average particle size removal efficiency (PSE) points. Consult the standard for a complete explanation of MERV value calculations. **Table 1** summarizes the requirements for a MERV value of 13.

Approach and Implementation

The indoor air quality of buildings is adversely affected by seemingly benign activities of daily occupancy and operations. Occupants and building visitors contribute to IAQ issues within buildings by tracking in contaminants on their shoes and clothing. Daily copier, fax and printer operations add contaminants to the building's interior environment. Additionally, the storage, mixing and disposal of housekeeping liquids may adversely affect the health and productivity of building occupants. This credit strives to improve indoor environmental conditions by mitigating the amount of particulate, chemical and biological contaminants that occupants are exposed to inside buildings.

Incorporate permanent entryway systems, which remove debris from shoes, at all high-traffic exterior access points to reduce the amount of contaminants tracked into the occupied space by people. The entryway systems should be designed to capture and remove particles from shoes without allowing build-up of contaminants. Open grates/grilles or other entryway systems that have a recessed collection area are generally thought to be most effective. (Carpeted systems are not regarded as providing the same effectiveness in particulate removal as open grid type systems and require continuous cleaning/maintenance to avoid build-up of dirt and debris.)

High traffic exterior access points will always include the main building entry, but may not be limited to this. Buildings that have entries from structured parking will have a high volume of use in these locations. In some instances these entry points are inside of a garage structure. While a covered garage does provide protection from the elements, as a source of possible contaminants, it functions as a direct connection to the outdoors. Likewise, buildings that may have distinct employee and visitor entry points should include permanent entryway systems in these locations as well. Projects should evaluate all building entry points to determine whether permanent entryway systems should be incorporated.

Retail or mixed-use core and shell buildings with tenant retail spaces that have access from the exterior should also provide a permanent entryway system or properly maintained walk-off mats in these loca-

Table 1: Requirements for a MERV Value 13

| Composite Average Particle Size Efficiency [%] | | | | Minimum Final Resistance | |
0.30 – 1.0 μm	1.0 – 3.0 μm	3.0 – 10.0 μm	[Pa]		[in. of water]
< 75%	≥90%	≥90%	350		1.4

tions. This should be provided in all areas that the core and shell owner/developer is able to control. In some instances the tenant, not the developer, will determine the location of the exterior entries. In such cases, properly maintained interior walk-off mats are a viable solution.

Locate high-volume copy, print and fax equipment away from occupant work spaces in enclosed rooms with self-closing doors. In order to effectively remove airborne contaminants generated by this type of equipment, the rooms must be physically separated from adjacent spaces. This may be accomplished through installation of deck to deck partitions or sealed gypsum board enclosures. Rooms with large openings but no doors will not be able to meet the credit requirement. To remove airborne contaminants, and prevent cross-contamination into occupied spaces, copy, print and/or fax rooms must be equipped with a dedicated exhaust system (no return air) that creates a negative pressure within the room meeting the requirements of this credit. Convenience (small) copier and printer use should be minimized where possible. Although encouraged, designing exhaust systems that account for convenience copier and printer use is not required for this credit.

Chemical storage and mixing areas, such as janitor's closets and photo labs should also be located away from occupant work areas. Additionally, these rooms must be physically separated from adjacent spaces via installation of deck-to-deck partitions or sealed gypsum board enclosures. Rooms must be equipped with a dedicated exhaust system (no return air) that creates the required negative pressurization to ensure that cross contamination into adjacent occupied spaces will not occur.

All building HVAC systems must be designed to accommodate filtration systems with a minimum MERV 13 rating.

Additional ventilation systems to mitigate contaminating space activities may affect building energy performance and require commissioning and Measurement & Verification attention. Ventilation system design will also be affected to ensure that installed systems are capable of accommodating filtration media required for credit compliance. This may be difficult to achieve for spaces with low capacity, packaged air handling systems, due to the size of these filters and their associated pressure drop. The selected space layout may prohibit deck-to-deck separation and separate ventilation systems for chemical use areas. Storage areas for recyclable materials may also be considered to be contaminant sources, depending on the items recycled. Janitorial supplies may impact indoor air quality if not wisely chosen.

Core and Shell Considerations

Many core and shell buildings include structured parking as an integrated part of the project. Projects that include parking levels or attached structured parking should consider these entry points as directly connected to the outdoors.

Another aspect of speculative core and shell buildings is the level of control the building owner/developer has over the different spaces in a multiple use building. For example, a commercial office building may have a retail component at the ground level. The final location of each of these tenant entries will be determined based on the needs and demands of the tenant, outside of the direct control of the core and shell owner. Entry points such as these are encouraged to install permanent entryway systems or properly maintained walk-off mats but, because the owner/developer does not directly control them, are not required to comply with this credit's requirements for a LEED-CS submission.

As is the case in all core and shell credits, the requirements of the credit exclude the

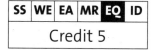

fit out of the tenant spaces. Tenant space activities such as copier, fax and printer use are not considered for the LEED-CS submission. Including this information in the Tenant Design and Construction Guidelines should be considered. Because the decisions of one tenant can impact the indoor environmental quality of the other tenants, LEED-CS projects should consider making these requirements of the tenants lease.

Calculations

There are no specific calculations associated with this credit.

Exemplary Performance

This credit is not eligible for exemplary performance under the Innovation in Design section.

Precertification Submittal Documentation

Provide the LEED-CS Precertification Submittal Template, which includes the following:

❏ Narrative describing how the project intends to accomplish the credit requirements on the credit-specific Submittal Template signed by the appropriate design team member

❏ Confirmation of this intent from the Owner/Developer on the LEED-CS Precertification Submittal Template

Certification Submittal Documentation

This credit is submitted as part of the **Design Submittal**.

Design and Construction Credit Compliance

The following project data and calculation information is required to document credit compliance using the LEED-CS v2.0 Submittal Templates:

❏ Provide confirmation that required entryway systems have been installed.

❏ Provide a listing of each entryway product installed in the building. For roll-up or carpeted systems, confirm that the required contracted maintenance will take place.

❏ Provide copies of the project's construction drawings to highlight the location of the installed entryway systems.

❏ Confirm that chemical use areas have been designed as separate rooms with dedicated exhaust systems and appropriate negative pressurization.

❏ Provide copies of the project's mechanical drawings to highlight the location of chemical usage areas, room separations, and the associated exhaust systems.

❏ If mechanically ventilated, confirm that the installed filters have a MERV rating of 13 or better.

❏ Provide a listing of the installed filters and their associated MERV ratings.

❏ Provide a narrative to describe any special circumstances or non-standard compliance paths taken by the project.

Tenant Sales or Lease Agreement Credit Compliance

This compliance method is available to core and shell projects that incorporate into tenant sales or lease agreements language that requires compliance with this credit as part of the tenant scope of work. Provide the LEED letter template for the credit pursued indicating the following:

❏ 100% of leased square footage is required to comply with credit requirements. Lease or sales agreements may be requested.

❑ 100% of the unleased square footage shall comply with the credit requirements when leased. A statement signed by the owner/developer that all leases and/or sales agreements will comply may be requested.

❑ Provide confirmation that entryway systems are required, including a description of the entryway system specified. For roll-up or carpeted systems, confirm that the required contracted maintenance will take place.

❑ Provide a drawing indicating the locations where the entryway systems will be installed.

❑ Provide confirmation that chemical use areas are required to be designed as separate rooms with dedicated exhaust systems and appropriate negative pressurization. Indicate the expected tenant spaces where this will be a requirement.

❑ Confirm that the required filters have a MERV rating of 13 or better.

❑ Provide a narrative to describe any special circumstances or non-standard compliance paths taken by the project.

Considerations

Cost Issues

Additional sinks, drains, room separations, and separate exhausts for copying and housekeeping areas can increase the project's overall initial cost. Also, dedicated ventilation and exhaust systems may require additional ductwork and associated installation costs. However, effective cleaning spaces and systems coupled with good human health initiatives should prove economically sound over the lifetime of the building. Clean air can help support worker productivity, and this translates into increased profitability for the company. Reducing the potential for spills can avoid costly environmental cleanups.

Community Issues

Good housekeeping benefits the community by reducing the potential for chemical spills that can impact neighboring properties. An environmentally sound building also supports the well-being of occupants, which may contribute to lowering health insurance rates and healthcare costs.

Regional Issues

Local weather conditions should be factored into determining the location and type of entryway systems. For example, in areas that are prone to large amounts of rain or snow, it may be prudent to locate entryway systems in an enclosed vestibule or inside the building. A floor drain beneath the grille may also be necessary to remove collected moisture.

Environmental Issues

Additional materials and energy may be required to provide entryway systems and isolated chemical use areas. This can increase natural resource consumption as well as air and water pollution. However, through proper management of hazardous chemicals used for building operations and maintenance, chemical spills and accidents can be avoided that would otherwise harm wildlife and ecosystems.

Resources

Please see the USGBC website at www.usgbc.org/resources for more specific resources on materials sources and other technical information.

Websites

Green Seal

www.greenseal.org/recommendations.htm

(202) 872-6400

Green Seal is an independent nonprofit organization that promotes the manufacture and sale of environmentally respon-

SS	WE	EA	MR	EQ	ID

Credit 5

Credit 5

sible consumer products. This website contains product recommendations for general purpose cleaning solutions.

Janitorial Products Pollution Prevention Project

www.westp2net.org/janitorial/jp4.htm

A governmental and nonprofit project that researches issues and provides fact sheets, tools and links.

EPA Environmentally Preferable Product Information

www.epa.gov/opptintr/epp/

This website includes links to cleaning product information and a database of environmental information on over 600 products, including janitorial and pest control products.

Print Media

Clean and Green: The Complete Guide to Non-Toxic and Environmentally Safe Housekeeping by Annie Berthold-Bond, Ceres Press, 1994.

Controllability of Systems

Thermal Comfort

1 point

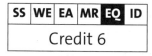

Can assist tenants in certification under LEED for Commercial Interiors

Intent

Provide a high level of thermal comfort system control by individual occupants or by specific groups in multi-occupant spaces (i.e., classrooms or conference areas) to promote the productivity, comfort and well-being of building occupants.

Requirements

Provide individual comfort controls for 50% (minimum) of the building occupants to enable adjustments to suit individual task needs and preferences. Operable windows can be used in lieu of comfort controls for occupants of areas that are 20 feet inside of and 10 feet to either side of the operable part of the window. The areas of operable window must meet the requirements of ASHRAE 62.1-2004, paragraph 5.1, Natural Ventilation.

AND

Provide comfort system controls for all shared multi-occupant spaces to enable adjustments to suit group needs and preferences.

Conditions for thermal comfort are described in ASHRAE Standard 55-2004 to include the primary factors of air temperature, radiant temperature, air speed and humidity. Comfort system control, for the purposes of this credit, is defined as the provision of control over at least one of these primary factors in the occupant's local environment.

Core and shell buildings that do not purchase and/or install the mechanical system or operable windows (or a combination of both) have not met the intent of this credit.

See Appendix 1 – Default Occupancy Counts for occupancy count requirements and guidance.

Potential Technologies & Strategies

Design the building and systems with comfort controls to allow adjustments to suit individual needs or those of groups in shared spaces. ASHRAE Standard 55-2004 identifies the factors of thermal comfort and a process for developing comfort criteria for building spaces that suit the needs of the occupants involved in their daily activities. Control strategies can be developed to expand on the comfort criteria to allow adjustments to suit individual needs and preferences. These may involve system designs incorporating operable windows, hybrid systems integrating operable windows and mechanical systems, or mechanical systems alone. Individual adjustments may involve individual thermostat controls, local diffusers at floor, desk or overhead levels, or control of individual radiant panels, or other means integrated into the overall building, thermal comfort systems, and energy systems design. In addition, designers should evaluate the closely tied interactions between thermal comfort (as required by ASHRAE Standard 55-2004) and acceptable indoor air quality (as required by ASHRAE Standard 62.1-2004, whether natural or mechanical ventilation).

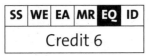

Summary of Referenced Standards

ANSI/ASHRAE Standard 62.1-2004: Ventilation for Acceptable Indoor Air Quality

American Society of Heating, Refrigerating and Air-Conditioning Engineers (ASHRAE)

www.ashrae.org

(800) 527-4723

Section 5.1 (Natural Ventilation) of the standard provides minimum requirements for operable openings. The portion of the window that can be opened must be 4% of the net occupiable floor area. The means to open the windows must be readily accessible to building occupants.

ANSI/ASHRAE Standard 55-2004: Thermal Environmental Conditions for Human Occupancy

American Society of Heating, Refrigerating and Air-Conditioning Engineers (ASHRAE)

www.ashrae.org

(800) 527-4723

Standard 55-2004 identifies the factors of thermal comfort and the process for developing comfort criteria for a building space and the occupants of that space. "This standard specifies the combinations of indoor space environment and personal factors that will produce thermal environmental conditions acceptable to 80% or more of the occupants within a space. The environmental factors addressed are temperature, thermal radiation, humidity, and air speed; the personal factors are those of activity and clothing." (ASHRAE)

Approach and Implementation

Conventional buildings too frequently are built as sealed space where the occupants have no control. A more desirable approach provides individuals the controls to adjust the thermal conditions for a more comfortable environment. The components of an individual's thermal comfort include air temperature and velocity, the amount of outside air and moisture content.

The design team should determine the level of individual control desired. Design the building with comfort controls to suit both individual needs and those of groups in shared spaces.

Strategies to consider include designs with operable windows, hybrid designs incorporating operable windows and mechanical systems, or mechanical systems alone. Individual control of comfort with mechanical systems may be integrated into the overall systems design by enabling individual adjustment of selected comfort parameters, such as individual thermostats, individual diffusers (located at floor, desk or overhead), and individual radiant panels. Occupancy sensors can also be integrated in the design to automatically turn down the thermostat and reduce airflow when occupants are away, helping reduce energy use.

Occupants must be educated on individual control of their office space environment. Additionally, key maintenance staff must be trained in the operations of the HVAC equipment and any installed controls.

Core and Shell Considerations

Core and shell HVAC system designs are typically incomplete; there are no occupants to design for. The intent of this credit in the core and shell rating system is to provide building HVAC systems that can be expanded to allow for a high degree of occupant control. Some system types make this credit easier to achieve and document than others. An underfloor air system that allows tenants to use individual diffusers is one of these system types. Buildings that use an overhead VAV system, will have to demonstrate that it is possible for the system to provide enough control points for 50% of the occupants.

Calculations

Individual Thermal Comfort

To determine if a project has met the requirements of this credit, the project team must first calculate the expected occupancy of the building. The default occupancy numbers in Appendix 1 may be used for this. The next step is to determine the number of controls that the HVAC system can support. This credit is achieved if the system can support enough controls for 50% of the occupants calculated above.

Operable windows may be used in lieu of individual controls for those occupants located within 20 ft. of the exterior wall and within 10 ft. of either side of the operable part of the window. The operable portion of the window will need to comply with the free-opening size criteria of ASHRAE Standard 62.1-2004 Section 5.1. The minimum area of the window opening may be 4% of the net occupiable area for the ventilation purposes, however larger opening areas may be required for thermal comfort over a wide range of outside conditions. Based on the limits used in this credit, for an area 20 ft. by 20 ft. per window, the opening size would need to be 16 sq.ft.

Shared Multi-Occupant Spaces

Buildings designed for shared multi-occupant spaces, such as retail complexes, must provide control to each space. To satisfy the requirement for these types of buildings, start by identifying those areas where transient groups share spaces, such as retail sales floors. Specific types or numbers of controls are not listed in the credit requirements to allow for flexibility in designing to the unique uses of each project. Confirm that there is at least one means of control over thermal comfort that is accessible to employees.

Exemplary Performance

This credit is not eligible for exemplary performance under the Innovation in Design section.

Precertification Submittal Documentation

Provide the LEED-CS Precertification Submittal Template, which includes the following:

❏ Narrative describing how the project intends to accomplish the credit requirements on the credit-specific Submittal Template signed by the appropriate design team member

❏ Confirmation of this intent from the owner/developer on the LEED-CS Precertification Submittal Template

Certification Submittal Documentation

This credit is submitted as part of the **Design Submittal**.

Design and Construction Credit Compliance

The following project data and calculation information is required to document credit compliance using the LEED-CS v2.0 Submittal Templates:

❏ Provide the number of expected occupants on a floor-by-floor basis. See Appendix 1 for the default occupancy counts. State which systems serve each floor.

❏ Provide a narrative describing the project's comfort control strategy. Include data regarding the type of controls available to tenants. State the maximum number of controls allowed for each system. Demonstrate that 50% of the occupants can be served by the controls (or one control per multi-occupant space). For buildings with operable windows, determine

the number of occupants that could be located within 20 ft. of the exterior wall and within 10 ft. of either side of the operable part of the window. The operable windows may count as the control for these occupants.

Tenant Sales or Lease Agreement Credit Compliance

This compliance method is available to core and shell projects that incorporate into tenant sales or lease agreements language that requires compliance with this credit as part of the tenant scope of work. Provide the LEED letter template for the credit pursued indicating the following:

❑ 100% of leased square footage is required to comply with credit requirements. Lease or sales agreements may be requested.

❑ 100% of the unleased square footage shall comply with the credit requirements when leased. A statement signed by the owner/developer that all leases and/or sales agreements will comply may be requested.

Considerations

Cost Issues

The most frequently reported occupant complaints involve thermal discomfort. Greater thermal comfort may increase occupant performance and attendance and, at least, will reduce complaints. According to the Rocky Mountain Institute's Green Developments: Integrating Ecology and Real Estate, office worker salaries are estimated to be 72 times higher than energy costs, and they account for 92% of the life-cycle costs of a building; with this in mind, thermal comfort can have a tremendous effect on overall costs. As noted in a report published by the Center for the Built Environment ("Giving Occupants What They Want: Guidelines for Implementing Personal Environmental Control in Your Building" by Fred S.

Bauman, PE – 1999) studies have shown that individual occupant controls can potentially increase the satisfaction and productivity of occupants. The financial implications of such improvements can be extremely large for building owners. Additional controllability may add to first costs of a project, however, these costs are generally offset by energy savings through lower conditioned temperatures, natural ventilation and less solar gain through proper use of shading devices. Conversely, abuse of personal controls such as setting thermostats too high or leaving windows open during non-working hours increases energy costs. Therefore, it is important to educate occupants on the design and function of system controls.

Alteration of the ventilation and temperature scheme may change the energy performance of the building and may require commissioning and Measurement & Verification attention. Controllability of systems may not be possible for occupants of existing buildings that are being rehabilitated, especially with regard to operable windows. The degree of occupant controls will affect the performance of the ventilation system. Daylighting and view strategies are affected by the controlling requirements of the operable windows in this credit.

Regional Issues

Local weather and ambient air conditions must be considered when determining the feasibility of operable windows for projects. For example, in areas that are prone to extreme temperatures for a majority of the year, or urban areas where traffic and air pollution are problematic, operable windows may not be an appropriate addition to a building.

Resources

Please see the USGBC website at www. usgbc.org/resources for more specific resources on materials sources and other technical information.

Websites

Center for the Built Environment

www.cbe.berkeley.edu

This University of California, Berkeley Center for Environmental Design Research provides information on underfloor air distribution technologies and other topics. See the publications page for articles such as "A Field Study of PEM (Personal Environmental Module) Performance in Bank of America's San Francisco Office Buildings."

"Do Green Buildings Enhance the Well-being of Workers? Yes"

Environmental Design + Construction

http://www.edcmag.com/CDA/Archives/fb077b7338697010VgnVCM100000f932a8c0

An article by Judith Heerwagen in the July/August 2000 edition, of Environmental Design + Construction quantifies the effects of green building environments on productivity.

Print Media

Controls and Automation for Facilities Managers: Applications Engineering by Viktor Boed, CRC Press, 1998.

Giving Occupants What They Want: Guidelines for Implementing Personal Environmental Control in Your Building by Fred S. Bauman, PE, Center for the Built Environment, 1999.

Using advanced office technology to increase productivity: the impact of environmentally responsive workstations (ERWs) on productivity and worker attitude by W. Kroner, J. Stark-Martin and T. Willemain. The Center for Architectural Research, Rensselaer Polytechnic Institute, Troy, New York, 1992.

Definitions

Shared (Group) Multi-Occupant Spaces include retail sales floors.

Individual Occupant Spaces are typically private offices and open office plans with workstations.

Non-Occupied Spaces include all rooms used by maintenance personnel that are not open for use by occupants. Included in this category are janitorial, storage and equipment rooms and closets.

Non-Regularly Occupied Spaces include corridors, hallways, lobbies, break rooms, copy rooms, storage rooms, kitchens, restrooms, stairwells, etc.

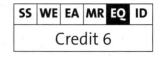

SS | WE | EA | MR | **EQ** | ID

Credit 6

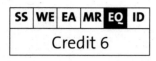

Thermal Comfort

Design

Intent

Provide a comfortable thermal environment that supports the productivity and well-being of building occupants.

Can assist tenants in certification under LEED for Commercial Interiors

Requirements

Design HVAC systems and the building envelope to meet the requirements of ASHRAE Standard 55-2004, Thermal Comfort Conditions for Human Occupancy. Demonstrate design compliance in accordance with the Section 6.1.1 Documentation.

See Appendix 1 – Default Occupancy Counts for occupancy count requirements and guidance.

The core and shell base building mechanical system must provide the capability for the tenant build-out to meet the requirements of this credit.

Core and shell buildings designed for mechanical ventilation that do not purchase and/or install the mechanical system can not achieve this credit.

Potential Technologies & Strategies

Establish comfort criteria per ASHRAE Standard 55-2004 that support the desired quality and occupant satisfaction with building performance. Design building envelope and systems with the capability to deliver performance to the comfort criteria under expected environmental and use conditions. Evaluate air temperature, radiant temperature, air speed, and relative humidity in an integrated fashion and coordinate these criteria with EQ Prerequisite 1, EQ Credit 1 and EQ Credit 2.

Summary of Referenced Standards

ASHRAE Standard 55-2004, Thermal Comfort Conditions for Human Occupancy

American Society of Heating, Refrigerating and Air-Conditioning Engineers

www.ashrae.com

(800) 527-4723

"This standard specifies the combinations of indoor space environment and personal factors that will produce thermal environmental conditions acceptable to 80% or more of the occupants within a space. The environmental factors addressed are temperature, thermal radiation, humidity, and air speed; the personal factors are those of activity and clothing." (ASHRAE)

Approach and Implementation

If properly designed, built and operated, a green building provides its occupants with comfortable indoor conditions that support their productivity and well-being. Although often associated only with air temperature, thermal comfort is a complex issue, impacted by environmental conditions (air temperature, radiant temperature, humidity and air speed) and personal factors (metabolic rate and clothing level) as well as personal preferences of occupants.

Strategies

There are three basic approaches to providing thermal comfort within a project space:

❑ Active Conditioning (e.g. mechanical HVAC systems)

❑ Passive Conditioning (e.g. natural ventilation)

❑ Mixed-mode conditioning—employing a combination of active and passive systems

The owner and project team should make a decision as to which of the conditioning approaches are appropriate for the building. ASHRAE Standard 55-2004 provides thermal comfort standards, with an optional alternate approach specifically for naturally ventilated spaces.

ASHRAE 55-2004 is based on the Predicted Mean Vote (PMV) comfort model which incorporates heat balance principles to relate the personal and environmental thermal comfort factors based on the thermal sensation scale that shows seven levels ranging from +3 (hot) to -3 (cold). The PMV model is applicable to air speeds not greater than 0.20 m/s (40 fpm).

For naturally ventilated spaces, the standard notes that field experiments have shown that occupants' thermal responses depend in part on the outdoor climate and may differ from thermal responses in buildings with centralized HVAC systems. This is primarily because of the different thermal experiences, changes in clothing, availability of control, and shifts in occupant expectations. The standard provides an optional method of compliance, intended for naturally ventilated spaces. This optional method (Section 5.3 of the standard) provides broad indoor temperature ranges as a function of mean monthly outdoor temperatures; assuming light, sedentary activity but independent of humidity, air speed and clothing considerations.

Planning & Design Phase

Using ASHRAE Standard 55-2004, the design team and the owner in collaboration should identify the environmental parameters required to maintain the desired thermal comfort in the project space and then identify the conditioning systems (whether active or passive) that can best provide these conditions. This decision may be influenced by the size, type, location, and climatic conditions of the proposed building as well as the nature of the operations that will occur in the building.

There are many well established HVAC load calculation methodologies to assist designers in sizing and selecting HVAC equipment in order to provide thermal comfort conditions. Lighting systems and other internal HVAC loads are integrated into the HVAC sizing calculations, to allow for adequate system capacity to meet thermal comfort criteria without over-sizing the HVAC systems.

A natural ventilation approach may be more difficult to evaluate in design and require more intensive analysis and/or reliance on experience and precedents. For naturally ventilated buildings CIBSE AM10 presents design strategies for comfortable and healthy naturally ventilated buildings.

Operation Phase

For mechanical conditioning, the operating setpoints and parameters of the HVAC system will be a primary influence on thermal comfort conditions in the project space. Many facility operators in mechanically air-conditioned spaces spend significant effort and time adjusting thermostat setpoints and other operational parameters in order to limit complaints associated with poor thermal comfort. Systems where individual occupants are provided some amount of direct control over temperature and/or air movement generally yield fewer thermal comfort complaints.

The maxim "passive buildings, active occupants" fits the natural ventilation model well. Occupants generally take a primary role in managing thermal comfort conditions in naturally ventilated buildings by opening and closing windows as necessary and appropriate. Thermal comfort in naturally conditioned buildings is also somewhat more variable and tied to the ambient conditions than in mechanically conditioned buildings where systems are often designed to maintain relatively consistent conditions throughout all periods of occupancy.

Core and Shell Considerations

Core and shell HVAC system designs are typically incomplete: there are no occupants to design for. The intent of this credit in the core and shell rating system is to furnish building HVAC systems that provide a thermally comfortable environment. To achieve this credit, projects must demonstrate that the core and shell systems are designed to maintain the tenant spaces at the thermal comfort conditions detailed in ASHRAE 55-2004.

Calculations

There are no calculations required for this LEED-CS credit. However, project teams should be able to describe how thermal comfort conditions were established for the project and how the design of conditioning systems addresses the thermal comfort design criteria.

Exemplary Performance

This credit is not eligible for exemplary performance under the Innovation in Design section.

Precertification Submittal Documentation

Provide the LEED-CS Precertification Submittal Template, which includes the following:

❏ Narrative describing how the project intends to accomplish the credit requirements on the credit-specific Submittal Template signed by the appropriate design team member

❏ Confirmation of this intent from the owner/developer on the LEED-CS Precertification Submittal Template

Certification Submittal Documentation

This credit is submitted as part of the **Design Submittal**.

Design and Construction Credit Compliance

The following project data and calculation information is required to document credit compliance using the LEED-CS v2.0 Submittal Templates:

❑ Provide data regarding seasonal temperature and humidity design criteria.

❑ Provide a narrative describing the method used to establish the thermal comfort conditions for the project and how the systems design addresses the design criteria. Include specific information regarding compliance with the referenced standard.

Tenant Sales or Lease Agreement Credit Compliance

This compliance method is available to core and shell projects that incorporate into tenant sales or lease agreements language that requires compliance with this credit as part of the tenant scope of work. Provide the LEED letter template for the credit pursued indicating the following:

❑ 100% of leased square footage is required to comply with credit requirements. Lease or sales agreements may be requested.

❑ 100% of the unleased square footage shall comply with the credit requirements when leased. A statement signed by the owner/developer that all leases and/or sales agreements will comply may be requested.

Considerations

Environmental Issues

Building conditioning systems, including both active HVAC systems and natural ventilation systems, are designed and installed in buildings to enhance thermal comfort for building occupants. These building conditioning systems may serve other functions as well, including providing ventilation air and providing thermal conditioning for equipment and processes. Designing and installing building conditioning systems to provide superior thermal comfort, ventilation, and indoor air quality as efficiently, and cost effectively as possible is a central challenge for many green building projects

Synergies and Trade-Offs

An active HVAC system generally will provide a higher degree of control over indoor thermal comfort conditions than a passive conditioning system. Capital, energy and lifecycle costs, however, are generally higher for an active HVAC system than for a naturally ventilated system.

Natural ventilation and other passive conditioning approaches are often dependent on occupants' managing the system (e.g. opening windows or closing blinds at appropriate times) to meet the comfort criteria. Active conditioning systems generally rely on central automation systems to comply with little or no direct occupant control.

Resources

Please see the USGBC website at www. usgbc.org/resources for more specific resources on materials sources and other technical information.

Websites

Enhance Indoor Environmental Quality (IEQ)

The Whole Building Design Guide

www.wbdg.org/design/ieq.php

The Indoor Environmental Quality section provides a wealth of resources including definitions, fundamentals, materials and tools.

Print Media

ASHRAE Standard 62.1-2004: Ventilation for Acceptable Indoor Air Quality, ASHRAE, 2004.

Humidity Control Design Guide by L. Harriman, G.W. Brundett and R. Kittler, ASHRAE, 2000.

The Impact of Part-Load Air-Conditioner Operation on Dehumidification Performance: Thermal Comfort by P.O. Fanger, Mc-Graw Hill, 1973.

Thermal Delight in Architecture by Lisa Heschong, MIT Press, 1979.

Definitions

Natural Ventilation is the ventilation provided by thermal, wind, or diffusion effects through doors, windows, or other intentional openings in the building (ASHRAE 62.1-2004).

Relative Humidity is the ratio of partial density of water vapor in the air to the saturation density of water vapor at the same temperature and the same total pressure (ASHRAE 55-2004).

Thermal Comfort is a condition of mind experienced by building occupants expressing satisfaction with the thermal environment.

Comfort Criteria is specific original design conditions that shall at minimum include temperature (air, radiant and surface), humidity and air speed as well as outdoor temperature design conditions, outdoor humidity design conditions, clothing (seasonal) and activity expected (ASHRAE 55-2004).

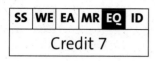

Daylight and Views

Daylight 75% of Spaces

Intent

Provide for the building occupants a connection between indoor spaces and the outdoors through the introduction of daylight and views into the regularly occupied areas of the building.

Can assist tenants in certification under LEED for Commercial Interiors

Requirements

OPTION 1 — GLAZING FACTOR CALCULATION

Achieve a minimum glazing factor of 2% in a minimum of 75% of all regularly occupied areas. The glazing factor is calculated as follows:

$$\text{Glazing Factor} = \frac{\text{Window Area [SF]}}{\text{Floor Area [SF]}} \times \text{Window Geometry Factor} \times \frac{\text{Actual } T_{vis}}{\text{Minimum } T_{vis}} \times \text{Window Height Factor}$$

OR

OPTION 2 — DAYLIGHT SIMULATION MODEL

Demonstrate, through computer simulation, that a minimum daylight illumination level of 25 footcandles has been achieved in a minimum of 75% of all regularly occupied areas. Modeling must demonstrate 25 horizontal footcandles under clear sky conditions, at noon, on the equinox, at 30" above the floor.

OR

OPTION 3 — DAYLIGHT MEASUREMENT

Demonstrate, through records of indoor light measurements, that a minimum daylight illumination level of 25 footcandles has been achieved in at least 75% of all regularly occupied areas. Measurements must be taken on a 10-foot grid for all occupied spaces and must be recorded on building floor plans.

OR

OPTION 4 — PRESCRIPTIVE

Use a combination of side-lighting and top-lighting to achieve a total Daylighting Zone (floor area meeting the following requirements) that is at least 75% of all the regularly occupied spaces.

Sidelighting Daylight Zone:

❑ Achieve a product of the visible light transmittance (VLT) and window to floor area ratio (WFR) of daylight zone between the values of 0.150 and 0.180. Window area included in the calculation must be of the portion of the window at least 2'-6" above the floor.

0.150 < VLT x WFR < 0.180

❑ In section, ceiling should not obstruct a line that joins the window-head to a line on the floor that is parallel to the plane of the window and is, in distance from the plane of the glass as measured perpendicular to the plane of the glass, two times the height of the window head above the floor. See **Figure 1**.

❑ Provide sunlight redirection and/or glare control devices to ensure daylight effectiveness.

Figure 1: Sidelighting Daylight Zone

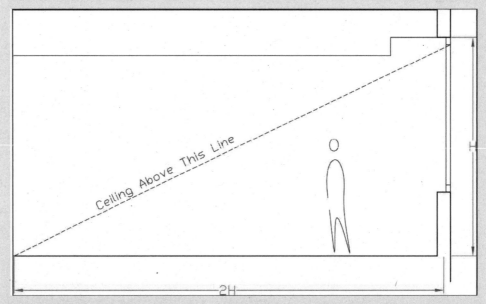

Toplighting Daylight Zone:

❑ The daylit zone under a skylight is the outline of the opening beneath the skylight, plus in each direction the lesser of: 70% of the ceiling height, one half of the distance to the edge of the nearest skylight, or the distance to any permanent opaque partition (if transparent, show VLT) which is farther away than 70% of the distance between the top of the partition and the ceiling. See **Figure 2**.

❑ Achieve a skylight roof coverage that is between 3% and 6% of the roof area with a minimum 0.5 visible light transmittance (VLT) for the skylights.

❑ The distance between the skylights shall not be more than 1.4 times the ceiling height.

❑ Provide a skylight diffuser with a measured haze value of greater than 90% when tested according to ASTM D1003. Avoid direct line of sight to skylight diffuser.

Exceptions for areas where tasks would be hindered by the use of daylight will be considered on their merits.

Figure 2: Toplighting Daylight Zone

In all cases, only the square footage associated with the portions of rooms or spaces meeting the minimum illumination requirements can be applied towards the 75% of total area calculation required to qualify for this credit.

In all cases, provide daylight redirection and/or glare control devices to avoid high-contrast situations that could impede visual tasks. Exceptions for areas where tasks would be hindered by the use of daylight will be considered on their merits.

Potential Technologies & Strategies

Design the building to maximize interior daylighting. Strategies to consider include building orientation, shallow floor plates, increased building perimeter, exterior and interior permanent shading devices, high performance glazing and automatic photocell-based controls. Predict daylight factors via manual calculations or model daylighting strategies with a physical or computer model to assess footcandle levels and daylight factors achieved.

Summary of Referenced Standard

There is no standard referenced for this credit.

Approach and Implementation

A building may have limited daylighting potential due to site or program constraints that limit the orientation of the building, number and size of building openings and floor plate dimensions. Vertical site elements such as neighboring buildings and trees may reduce the potential for daylighting. Evaluate the impact of the building's orientation on possible daylighting options; strive to incorporate shallow floor plates, courtyards, atriums, clerestory windows and skylights into the project to increase daylighting potential. Evaluate the potential to add interior light shelves, exterior fins, louvers and adjustable blinds. See **Figure 3**, which illustrates various daylighting strategies. Glazing parameters directly affect the heat gain and loss of the building which may result in increased energy use. It is important to address the glazing properly not only for energy usage but also for visual quality.

The desired amount of daylight will differ depending on the tasks occurring within each program space. Daylit spaces often have several daylight zones with differing target light levels. In addition to light levels, daylighting strategies should address interior color schemes, direct beam penetration and integration with the electric lighting system. Glare control is perhaps the most common failure in daylighting strategies. Glare is defined as any excessively bright source of light within the visual field that creates discomfort or loss in visibility. Large window areas provide generous amounts of daylight to the task area. If not controlled properly, this daylight can produce unwanted glare and affect the lighting quality. Measures to control glare include light shelves, louvers, blinds, fins and shades. Typically, low luminance ratios and lighting of primary surfaces will enhance visual quality.

Computer modeling software can be used to simulate daylighting conditions and to provide valuable input into the

Figure 3: An illustration of Various Daylighting Strategies

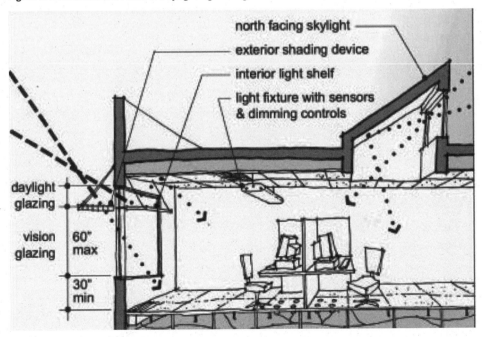

development of an effective, integrated daylighting strategy. Daylighting software produces continuous daylight contours to simulate the daylighting conditions of interior spaces and to account for combined effects of multiple windows within a daylit space.

Photo-responsive controls for electric lighting can be incorporated into daylighting strategies to maintain consistent light levels and to minimize occupant perception of the transition from natural light to artificial light. These controls result in energy savings by reducing electric lighting in high daylight conditions while preserving footcandle levels on the task surface. These types of automatic controls require commissioning and also Measurement & Verification attention.

Core and Shell Considerations

Core and shell building designs typically do not include interior partitions except for those that enclose core spaces. This credit may seem highly achievable for a building with a wide-open floor plate, but this credit is dependant on more than that. The design of the exterior envelope and the depth of the floor plate are also critical for credit achievement. The core and shell project team directly affects the ability of the tenants to accomplish and optimize daylighting of their spaces. Decisions made by the core and shell team can preclude the tenant from achieving this credit in LEED-CI.

Calculations

Compliance with the requirements for this credit may be determined by either following the Glazing Factor calculation methodology (outlined in the following paragraphs) to determine overall glazing factor, or by using daylighting simulation software to determine point-by-point illumination levels (footcandles) measured at desk height (30" above the finished floor).

Areas to include in the daylighting calculations are all areas that could be used as regularly occupied space. Areas that should not be considered include support areas for elevator lobbies, storage, mechanical equipment and restrooms.

The calculation methodology below can be applied to approximate the Glazing Factor for each regularly occupied area in the building. The Glazing Factor (GF) is the ratio of exterior illumination to interior illumination and is expressed as a percentage. The variables used to determine the daylight factor include the floor area, window area, window geometry, visible transmittance (T_{vis}) and window height. This calculation method aims to provide a minimum 2% GF at the back of a space. The Glazing Factor calculation method is designed to identify daylighting conditions based on room and window geometry and visible transmittance based on meeting the performance criteria for overcast sky conditions. Currently this calculation method doesn't take into account light shelves, partitions, significant exterior obstructions or exterior reflective surfaces.

The development of a Daylight Simulation Model is highly recommended where daylighting strategies go beyond the current capability to the Glazing Factor Calculation Method.

Option 1—Glazing Factor

1. Create a spreadsheet and identify all areas that could be regularly occupied. It may be necessary to divide up the floor plate into smaller areas. Determine the floor areas using the construction documents.

2. For each area identified, calculate the window area and use **Table 1** to indicate the acceptable window types. Note that window areas above 7'6" are considered to be daylight glazing. Glazing at this height is the most effective at distributing daylight deep into the interior space. Window areas

Table 1: Daylight Design Criteria

Window Type	Geometry Factor	Minimum T_{vis}	Height Factor	Best Practice Glare Control
sidelighting daylight glazing	0.1	0.7	1.4	Adjustable blinds Interior light shelves Fixed transluscent exterior shading devices
sidelighting vision glazing	0.1	0.4	0.8	Adjustable blinds Exterior shading devices
toplighting vertical monitor	0.2	0.4	1.0	Fixed interior Adjustable exterior blinds
toplighting sawtooth monitor	0.33	0.4	1.0	Fixed interior Exterior louvers
toplighting horizontal skylights	0.5	0.4	1.0	Interior fins Exterior fins Louvers

from 2'6" to 7'6" are considered to be vision glazing. These window areas are primarily used for viewing and lighting interior spaces close to the building perimeter. Window areas below 2'6" do not contribute to daylighting of interior spaces and are to be excluded from the calculations.

3. For each window type, insert the appropriate geometry and height factors as listed in **Table 1**. The geometry factor indicates the effectiveness of a particular aperture to distribute daylight relative to window location. The height factor accounts for where light is introduced to the space.

4. For each window type, indicate the visible transmittance (T_{vis}), a variable number that differs for each product. Minimum T_{vis} is the recommended level of transmittance for selected glazing.

5. Calculate the Glazing Factor for each window type using **Equation 1**. For rooms/areas with more than one window type, sum all window types to obtain a total Glazing Factor for the room/area.

6. If the total Glazing Factor for a room/area is 2% or greater, then the square footage of the room/area is applicable to the credit.

Equation 1: Glazing Factor Calculation

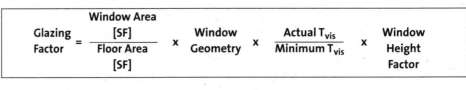

$$\text{Glazing Factor} = \frac{\text{Window Area [SF]}}{\text{Floor Area [SF]}} \times \text{Window Geometry} \times \frac{\text{Actual } T_{vis}}{\text{Minimum } T_{vis}} \times \text{Window Height Factor}$$

7. Sum the square footage of all applicable rooms/areas and divide by the total square footage of all regularly occupied spaces. If this percentage is equal to or greater than 75%, then the project qualifies for this point. (See **Note 1** for further information.)

8. Note that glare control is also required for each window. **Table 3** provides best-practice glare control measures for different window types.

Table 2 provides an example of daylighting calculations for a typical office space. All of the offices are considered to be regularly occupied spaces, while support areas such as hallways, foyers, storage areas, mechanical rooms and restrooms are not considered to be regularly occupied. The example qualifies for this credit because it exceeds the minimum square footage percentage for daylit areas and includes glare control on all windows in daylit rooms.

Option 2—Daylight Simulation Model

1. Create a daylight simulation model for the building, or each regularly occupied space with glazing. The model should include appropriate glazing factors as well as representative surface reflectance settings for interior finishes.

2. For each applicable area, include a horizontal calculation grid at 30" above the floor. This grid will represent the typical work plane height. The calculation grid should be set at approximately 2 foot intervals to provide a detailed illumination diagram for each area. (For larger areas, it may be necessary to increase the grid size for clarity.)

3. Calculate the daylight illumination for each applicable space using the following daylight criteria: clear sky conditions at 12:00 noon on the equi-

Table 3: Common Glare Control Strategies

Description
Fixed Exterior Shading Devices
Light Shelf, Exterior
Light Shelf, Interior
Interior Blinds or Pull-Down Shade
Fritted Glazing
Drapes
Electronic Black-Out Glazing

Table 2: Glazing Factor Tabulation Spreadsheet

Regularly Occupied Space ID	Regularly Occupied Space Name	Regularly Occupied Space Area (sf)	Sidelighting - Vision Glazing					Sidelighting - Daylight Glazing					Glazing Factor
			Geometry Factor	Area (sf)	Actual T_{vis}	Min T_{vis}	Height Factor	Geometry Factor	Area (sf)	Actual T_{vis}	Min T_{vis}	Height Factor	
75% of total regularly occupied floor area	Open Office (Compliance Required Area)	12,600	0.10	2,280	0.9	0.4	0.8	0.10	1,140	0.9	0.7	1.4	2.04
25% of total regularly occupied floor area	Open Office (non-daylit Area)	4,200	NA	0	NA	NA	NA	NA	0	NA	NA	NA	0

Total Regularly Occupied Space Area (sf)	Total Regularly Occupied Space Area with a Minimum 2% Glazing Factor	Percentage of Regularly Occupied Space with a 2% Glazing Factor
4585	3570	78%

nox (March 21/September 21) for the project's specific geographic location. **Figure 4** illustrates a sample daylight analysis for an office space.

4. Create a spreadsheet and identify all regularly occupied areas. Determine the floor area of each applicable area using construction documents. Provide the minimum illumination level (footcandles), determined through the simulation model, for each space.

5. If the minimum illumination for a room/area is 25 footcandles or greater, then the square footage of the room/area is applicable to the credit. (See **Note 1** for further information.)

6. Sum the square footage of all daylit rooms/areas and divide by the total square footage of all regularly occupied spaces. If this percentage is equal to or greater than 75%, then the project qualifies for one point under this Credit.

7. Note that glare control is also required for each window. **Table 1** provides best-practice glare control measures for different window types. Create

another spreadsheet entry that identifies the type of glare control applied to each window type. The type of glare control selected for each window does not affect the daylight factor calculations. **Table 3** provides a listing of common glare control strategies.

Option 3—Daylight Measurement

NOTE 1: This credit can be approached so that 100% of each space does not have to meet the 2% daylight factor or the minimum 25 footcandle requirement. In order to do so, the portion of the space with a 2% (or higher) daylight factor, or 25 footcandle minimum illumination, would count towards the percentage of all space occupied for critical visual tasks. The portion of the space not meeting the daylight factor or illumination criteria would not count towards the compliant area total, but would be considered in the total area calculation. For the calculation spreadsheet, the two portions of the room (the one meeting the minimum daylight factor or illumination and the one not meeting the requirements) would be counted as separate spaces (See **Table 2**).

Figure 2: Sample Daylight Simulation Model Output

The square footage of all compliant spaces is tallied and then divided over the total square footage of all regularly occupied spaces. If the percentage is equal to or greater than 75%, then the project qualifies for one point under this Credit.

Option 4—Prescriptive

Sidelighting

The purpose of this option is to provide projects with a relatively simple method of ensuring that the daylighting credit is met. This method is applicable for relatively standard building designs, primarily rectangular floor plates with a central core. The project team will need to know basic information regarding the building in order to determine compliance. This information is:

❏ Window head height

❏ Window sill height

❏ Window width (per bay)

❏ Bay width

❏ Bay depth to core

❏ VLT (T_{vis})

The calculation should be done for each bay condition in the building (north/south, east/west and corner). The following steps should be used:

1. Determine WA: the Window Area for the bay. This is the window head height less the window sill height that is 2'-6" or greater above the floor, multiplied by the window width(s) per bay.

2. Determine FA: the Floor Area (FA) for the typical bay. This is the bay width times the bay depth to core.

3. Determine WFR: the ration of the Window Area to the Floor Area and is expressed as WA/FA

4. Determine (VLT) (WFR): this is the ratio of visible light transmittance to window to floor area and is expressed as (VLT) (WFR)

5. If this number is between 0.150 and 0.180, the credit has been met for the bay.

6. Each bay condition in the building must meet this requirement.

An example of this calculation is shown below.

Toplighting Daylight Zone

This method is applicable for relatively standard building designs, and may be particularly useful for single floor retail developments. The project team will need to know the following basic information regarding the building in order to determine compliance.

❏ Area of skylights (SA)

❏ VLT (T_{vis}) of skylights

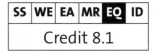
Example Calculation

	N/S bay	E/W bay	Corner bay
Window head height	10	10	10
Window sill height	2.5	2.5	2.5
Window width (per bay)	19	19	78
Bay width	20	20	40
Bay depth to core	40	40	40
VLT (Tvis)	0.86	0.86	0.45
WA			
Window daylight height	7.5	7.5	7.5
Window area (WA)	142.5	142.5	585
FA			
Floor area (FA)	800	800	1600
WFR = (WA/FA)	0.178125	0.178125	0.365625
(VLT) (WFR)	0.1531875	0.1531875	0.16453125

❑ Roof area (RA)

❑ Distance between skylights

❑ Measured haze value of skylight diffuser

The calculation should be done for a typical building condition using the following steps:

1. Determine the skylight roof coverage – this is the ratio of area of skylights to area of roof and is expressed by (SA/RA) (100).

2. Confirm that the skylight diffuser is greater than 90%.

3. Determine the daylight zone(s) in square feet below the skylight, based on the prescriptive criteria.

4. Evaluate the total area (in square feet) of the daylight zone(s).

5. If this total area is 75% or greater than the area of the regularly occupied spaces in the building, the credit has been met.

Combined Sidelighting and Toplighting Daylight Zone

For buildings that have both sidelighting and toplighting conditions a combination of the above two methodologies can be utilized to demonstrate compliance.

Exemplary Performance

This credit may be eligible for exemplary performance under the Innovation & Design section if the project achieves 95% daylighting based on the requirements and guidelines of this credit.

Precertification Submittal Documentation

Provide the LEED-CS Precertification Submittal Template, which includes the following:

❑ Narrative describing how the project intends to accomplish the credit requirements on the credit-specific Submittal Template signed by the appropriate design team member

❑ Confirmation of this intent from the owner/developer on the LEED-CS Precertification Submittal Template

Certification Submittal Documentation

This credit is submitted as part of the **Design Submittal**.

Design and Construction Credit Compliance

The following project data and calculation information is required to document credit compliance using the LEED-CS v2.0 Submittal Templates:

Glazing Factor Calculation Method

❑ Complete the template calculation spreadsheet to demonstrate overall Glazing Factor. The following data is required for input in the template: occupied space area (sq.ft.); area of each type of glazing (sidelighting and toplighting); and visible light transmittance (T_{vis}) for each glazing type.

OR

Computer Simulation Method

❑ Complete the template calculation spreadsheet to demonstrate that the project complies with the minimum illumination levels. The following data is required for input in the template: total regularly occupied space area (sq.ft.); and total regularly occupied space area that achieves a simulated minimum of 25 footcandles.

❑ Provide copies of the applicable project drawings showing the illumination simulation results.

OR

Daylight Measurement Method

❑ Complete the template calculation spreadsheet to demonstrate that the project complies with the minimum illumination levels. The following data is required for input in the template: total regularly occupied space area (sq.ft.); and total regularly occupied space area that achieves a measured minimum of 25 footcandles.

❑ Provide copies of the applicable project drawings showing the illumination simulation results.

OR

Prescriptive Method

❑ Complete the template calculation spreadsheet to demonstrate that the project complies with the minimum illumination levels; that the Sidelighting and Toplighting conditions evaluated constitutes 75% or greater of the building's regularly occupied spaces; and that the applicable prescriptive conditions for Sidelighting and Toplighting have been met.

❑ Provide a typical floor plan drawing with an indication of the typical bay condition that has been evaluated.

❑ Provide a typical floor plan drawing with an indication of the skylight condition that has been evaluated.

AND

❑ Provide a narrative describing any special occupancy areas that have been excluded from compliance. The narrative should include a detailed description of the space function and an explanation as to why the inclusion of views would hinder the normal tasks/function of each excluded area.

For projects that have used computer simulation or physical measurements, please include detailed information describing the method used to determine the daylighting contributions in the building. Include specific information regarding the actual or simulated time of day and weather conditions, measurement equipment or software used, and the calculation method for determining the final daylighting area.

Tenant Sales or Lease Agreement Credit Compliance

This compliance method is not available for this credit.

Considerations

Cost Issues

Specialized glazing can increase initial costs for a project and can lead to excessive heat gain if not designed properly. Glazing provides less insulating effects compared to standard walls, resulting in higher energy use and requiring additional maintenance. However, offices with sufficient natural daylight have proven to increase occupant productivity and comfort. In most cases, occupant salaries significantly outweigh first costs of incorporating daylighting measures into a building design. Studies of schools and stores have shown that daylighting can improve student performance and retail sales (see the Resources section). Daylighting can significantly reduce artificial lighting requirements and energy costs in many commercial and industrial buildings, as well as schools, libraries and hospitals. Daylighting, combined with energy-efficient lighting and electronic ballasts, can reduce the lighting power density in some office buildings by up to 30%.

Environmental Issues

Daylighting reduces the need for electric lighting of building interiors, resulting in decreased energy use. A well-designed daylit building is estimated to reduce lighting energy use by 50 to 80% (Sustainable Building Technical Manual, chapter IV.7, page 90). This conserves natural resources and reduces air pollution impacts due to energy production and consumption.

Daylighting design involves a careful balance of heat gain and loss, glare control,

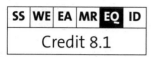

visual quality and variations in daylight availability. Shading devices, light shelves, courtyards, atriums and window glazing are all strategies employed in daylighting design. Important considerations include the selected building's orientation, window size and spacing, glass selection, reflectance of interior finishes and locations of interior walls. Daylit spaces also increase occupant productivity and reduce absenteeism and illness.

Community Issues

Daylighting and outdoor views provide a connection with the building site and adjacent sites, creating a more integrated neighborhood. Daylit spaces can increase occupant productivity and reduce illness and absenteeism.

Resources

Please see the USGBC website at www. usgbc.org/resources for more specific resources on materials sources and other technical information.

Websites

Analysis of the Performance of Students in Daylit Schools

www.innovativedesign.net/ studentperformance.htm

Nicklas and Bailey's 1996 study of three daylit schools in North Carolina.

The Art of Daylighting

http://www.edcmag.com/CDA/ Archives/10e5869a47697010Vgn VCM100000f932a8c0

This *Environmental Design + Construction* article provides a solid introduction to daylighting.

New Buildings Institute's Productivity and Building Science Program

www.newbuildings.org/downloads/ FinalAttachments/PIER_Final_ Report(P500-03-082).pdf

Provides case studies and program report on the benefits of daylighting.

Radiance Software

http://radsite.lbl.gov/radiance/

Free daylighting simulation software from the Lawrence Berkeley National Laboratory

The Whole Building Design Guide, Daylighting

www.wbdg.org/design/daylighting. php?r=ieq

Lighting Controls

www.wbdg.org/design/electriclighting. php?r=ieq

The Daylighting and Lighting Controls sections provide a wealth of resources including definitions, fundamentals, materials and tools.

Print Media

Architectural Lighting, Second Edition by M. David Egan, PE, and Victor Olgyay, AIA, McGraw-Hill, 2002.

"Daylighting Design" by Benjamin Evans, in *Time-Saver Standards for Architectural Design Data*, McGraw-Hill, Inc., 1997.

Daylighting for Sustainable Design by Mary Guzowski, McGraw-Hill, Inc., 1999.

Daylighting Performance and Design by Gregg D. Ander, John Wiley & Sons, 1997.

Sustainable Building Technical Manual, Public Technology Institute, 1996.

(www.pti.org)

Definitions

Glazing Factor is the ratio of interior illuminance at a given point on a given plane (usually the work plane) to the exterior illuminance under known overcast sky conditions. LEED uses a simplified approach for its credit compliance calculations. The variables used to determine

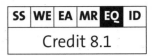
the daylight factor include the floor area, window area, window geometry, visible transmittance (T_{vis}) and window height.

Daylighting is the controlled admission of natural light into a space through glazing with the intent of reducing or eliminating electric lighting. By utilizing solar light, daylighting creates a stimulating and productive environment for building occupants.

Daylighting Zone is the total floor area that meets the performance requirements for daylighting.

Non-Occupied Spaces include all rooms used by maintenance personnel that are not open for use by occupants. Included in this category are janitorial, storage and equipment rooms, and closets.

Non-Regularly Occupied Spaces include corridors, hallways, lobbies, break rooms, copy rooms, storage rooms, kitchens, restrooms, stairwells, etc.

Regularly Occupied Spaces are areas where workers are seated or standing as they work inside a building; in residential applications it refers to living and family rooms.

Visible Light Transmittance (T_{vis}) is the ratio of total transmitted light to total incident light. In other words, it is the amount of visible spectrum (380–780 nanometers) light passing through a glazing surface divided by the amount of light striking the glazing surface. A higher T_{vis} value indicates that a greater amount of visible spectrum incident light is passing through the glazing.

Window to Floor Area Ratio (WFR) is the total area of the window (measured vertically from 2'-6" (or greater) above finish floor to the top of the glass, multiplied by the width of the glass) divided by the floor area.

Daylight & Views

Views for 90% of Spaces

Intent

Provide for the building occupants a connection between indoor spaces and the outdoors through the introduction of daylight and views into the regularly occupied areas of the building.

Can assist tenants in certification under LEED for Commercial Interiors

Requirements

Achieve direct line of sight to the outdoor environment via vision glazing between 2'6" and 7'6" above finish floor for building occupants in 90% of all regularly occupied areas. Determine the area with direct line of sight by totaling the regularly occupied square footage that meets the following criteria:

❑ In plan view, the area is within sight lines drawn from perimeter vision glazing.

❑ In section view, a direct sight line can be drawn from the area to perimeter vision glazing.

Line of sight may be drawn through interior glazing. For private offices, the entire square footage of the office can be counted if 75% or more of the area has direct line of sight to perimeter vision glazing. For multi-occupant spaces, the actual square footage with direct line of sight to perimeter vision glazing is counted.

The core and shell design needs to develop a feasible tenant layout(s) per the default occupancy counts (or some other justifiable occupancy count) that can be used in the analysis of this credit.

Potential Technologies & Strategies

Design the space to maximize daylighting and view opportunities. Strategies to consider include lower partition heights, interior shading devices, interior glazing, and automatic photocell-based controls.

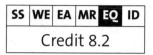

Summary of Referenced Standard

There is no standard referenced for this credit.

Approach and Implementation

There are two calculations required to determine achievement of this credit—Direct Line of Sight to Perimeter Glazing and Horizontal View. The Direct Line of Sight to Perimeter Glazing determination is an area calculation, and confirms that 90% of the occupied area is designed so there is the potential for views from regularly occupied areas. It is based on vision glazing (2'6" – 7'6"), and the location of full height interior partitions. Movable furniture and partitions are not included in the scope of this credit calculation. See **Figure 1**.

One successful design strategy for offices locates open plan areas along the exterior walls, while placing private offices and areas not regularly occupied to the core of the building. The Horizontal Views determination confirms that the available views are maintained. It is recommended that the line of sight used for the determination of Horizontal Views is assumed to be 42" to reflect an average seated eye height. Design teams may, however, wish to utilize alternate view heights for areas with non-typical functions. Maintaining the views for spaces near the core is a primary design objective. See **Figure 2**.

Regularly occupied spaces include office spaces, conference rooms and cafeterias. Areas that need not be considered include support areas for copying, storage, mechanical equipment, laundry and restrooms.

Core and Shell Considerations

Because core and shell project scope would generally have no , or limited, interior build out as aprt of the project scope, the core and shell building design needs to be capable of being built-out by a tenant in such a way as to provide views for 90% of regularly occupied areas. The core and shell design team will need to test this with a feasible tenant layout for the

Figure 1: Direct Line of Sight to Perimeter Vision Glazing, used in the area determination

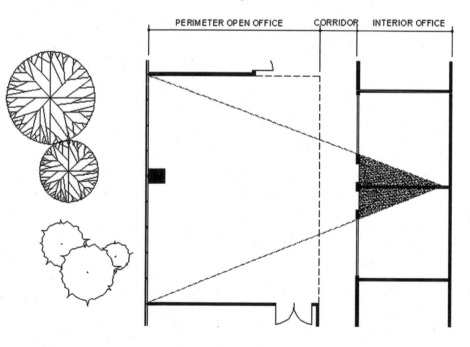

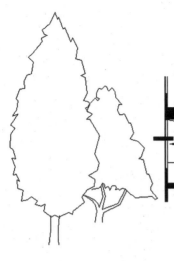

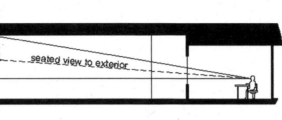

seated view to exterior

building use intended. This layout can be used as part of the submittal.

Commercial office and retail projects will have different design concerns to work through and demonstrate. For an office building the envelope and building geometry will be the main factors in determining whether the project can comply. Retail projects need to consider possible tenant space layouts as they relate to employee use of regularly occupied spaces and how the window placement allows views to the exterior from these spaces.

Calculations

Direct Line of Sight to Perimeter Vision Glazing

1. Create a spreadsheet and identify all regularly occupied rooms/areas. Determine the floor area of each applicable room using construction documents. Using a floor plan, construct line of sight geometries at each window to determine the fraction of the regularly occupied room/area that has direct line of sight to the outdoors. Note: line of sight can pass through interior glazing but not through doorways with solid doors.

2. For private offices, if the percentage of floor area with direct line of sight

Table 1: Determination of Compliance

Room	Regularly Occupied Floor Area [SF]	Plan Area of Direct Line of Sight to Perimeter Vision Glazing [SF]	Calculated Area of Direct Line of Sight to Perimeter Vision Glazing [SF]	Horizontal View at 42 Inches [Yes/No]	Compliant Area [SF]
101 Office	820	790	820	Yes	820
102 Conference	330	280	330	Yes	330
103 Open Office	4,935	4,641	4,641	Yes	4,641
104 Office	250	201	250	No	0
105 Office	250	175	175	Yes	175
Total	6,585				5,966
Percent Access to Views [5,966/6,585] 90.5% Credit Earned					

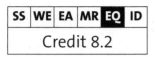
is equal to or greater than 75% (i.e., only the corners are non-compliant), you may enter the entire square footage of that room in the spreadsheet (see **Table 1**) as meeting the credit requirement. If less than 75% of the room has direct line of sight, you must estimate the compliant floor area and enter that value in the spreadsheet.

3. For multi-occupant spaces, such as open work areas and conference rooms, estimate the actual square footage with direct line of sight to perimeter vision glazing.

Horizontal View at 42 Inches

1. Using representative building sections, draw a line at 42" (average seated eye height) across the section to establish the height of the perimeter glazing and any obstruction to it. Draw one or more representative sight lines from a point at 42" in the regularly occupied space(s) to the perimeter vision glazing (see **Figure 2**).

2. For each space where the view, taken at 42" above the floor, is maintained, enter a YES in the spreadsheet in the "Horizontal View" column (see **Table 1**). If a room has direct line of site on the floor plan but does not have an unobstructed view at 42", the floor area of that room may not be counted as meeting the credit requirement and should be marked as NO in the spreadsheet.

Total the area that is determined to meet all criteria above and divide it by the total regularly occupied area to determine if the building meets the 90% access to views requirement.

Exemplary Performance

This credit may be eligible for exemplary performance under the Innovation in Design section however, there is no prescribed threshold for determination of exemplary performance. Projects will be evaluated on a case-by-case basis.

Precertification Submittal Documentation

Provide the LEED-CS Precertification Submittal Template, which includes the following:

❑ Narrative describing how the project intends to accomplish the credit requirements on the credit-specific Submittal Template signed by the appropriate design team member

❑ Confirmation of this intent from the owner/developer on the LEED-CS Precertification Submittal Template

Certification Submittal Documentation

This credit is submitted as part of the **Design Submittal**.

Design and Construction Credit Compliance

The following project data and calculation information is required to document credit compliance using the LEED-CS v2.0 Submittal Templates:

❑ Complete the template calculation spreadsheet to demonstrate overall access to views from occupied spaces. The following data is required for input in the template: occupied space identification, occupied space area (sq. ft.), and area (sq.ft.) of each occupied space with direct access to views.

❑ Provide copies of the applicable project drawings showing the line of sight from interior spaces through exterior windows in both plan and sectional views.

❑ Provide a narrative describing any special occupancy areas that have been excluded from compliance. The narrative should include a detailed description of the space function and an explanation as to why the inclusion of views would hinder the normal tasks/function of each excluded area.

Tenant Sales or Lease Agreement Credit Compliance

This compliance method is not available for this credit.

Considerations

Cost Issues

Additional glazing required to provide access to views can increase initial costs for a project and can lead to increased heat gain if not designed properly. Glazing provides less insulating effects compared to standard walls, resulting in higher energy use and requiring additional maintenance. However, offices with sufficient natural daylight and a visual connection to the outdoor environment have proven to increase occupant productivity and comfort. Daylighting can significantly reduce artificial lighting requirements and energy costs in many commercial and industrial buildings, as well as schools, libraries and hospitals. Daylighting, combined with energy-efficient lighting and electronic ballasts, can reduce the lighting power density in some office buildings by up to 30%.

Environmental Issues

Providing access to views of the outdoors, through the incorporation of vision glazing, enables building occupants to maintain a visual connection to the surrounding environment. The additional glazed area may reduce the need for electric lighting of building interiors, resulting in decreased energy use. This conserves natural resources and reduces air pollution impacts due to energy production and consumption.

When designing for maximum views and daylighting, designers must evaluate and balance a number of environmental factors, such as heat gain and loss, glare control, visual quality and variations in daylight availability. Appropriate shading devices, to control glare and direct beam illumination, must be utilized to provide the highest level of environmental comfort.

Resources

Please see the USGBC website at www. usgbc.org/resources for more specific resources on materials sources and other technical information.

Websites

Analysis of the Performance of Students in Daylit Schools

www.innovativedesign.net/ studentperformance.htm

Nicklas and Bailey's 1996 study of three daylit schools in North Carolina.

The Art of Daylighting

http://www.edcmag.com/CDA/ Archives/10e5869a47697010VgnV CM100000f932a8c0

This *Environmental Design + Construction* article provides a solid introduction to daylighting.

New Buildings Institute's Productivity and Building Science Program

www.newbuildings.org/downloads/ FinalAttachments/PIER_Final_ Report(P500-03-082).pdf

Provides case studies and program report on the benefits of daylighting.

Radiance Software

http://radsite.lbl.gov

Free daylighting simulation software from the Lawrence Berkeley National Laboratory

The Whole Building Design Guide Daylighting

www.wbdg.org/design/daylighting. php?r=ieq

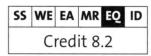

SS | WE | EA | MR | **EQ** | ID

Credit 8.2

Lighting Controls

www.wbdg.org/design/electriclighting.php?r=ieq

The Daylighting and Lighting Controls sections provide a wealth of resources including definitions, fundamentals, materials and tools.

Print Media

"Daylighting Design" by Benjamin Evans, in *Time-Saver Standards for Architectural Design Data*, McGraw-Hill, Inc., 1997.

Daylighting for Sustainable Design by Mary Guzowski, McGraw-Hill, Inc., 1999.

Daylighting Performance and Design by Gregg D. Ander, John Wiley & Sons, 1997.

Sustainable Building Technical Manual, Public Technology Institute, 1996.

(www.pti.org)

Definitions

Daylighting is the controlled admission of natural light into a space through glazing with the intent of reducing or eliminating electric lighting. By utilizing solar light, daylighting creates a stimulating and productive environment for building occupants.

Direct Line of Sight to Perimeter Vision Glazing is the approach used to determine the calculated area of regularly occupied areas with direct line of sight to perimeter vision glazing. The area determination includes full height partitions and other fixed construction prior to installation of furniture.

Horizontal View at 42 Inches is the approach used to confirm that the direct line of sight to perimeter vision glazing remains available from a seated position. It uses section drawings that include the installed furniture to make the determination.

Non-Occupied Spaces include all rooms used by maintenance personnel that are not open for use by occupants. Included in this category are janitorial, storage and equipment rooms, and closets.

Non-Regularly Occupied Spaces include corridors, hallways, lobbies, break rooms, copy rooms, storage rooms, kitchens, restrooms, stairwells, etc.

Regularly Occupied Spaces are areas where workers are seated or standing as they work inside a building; in residential applications, it refers to the living and family rooms.

Vision Glazing is that portion of exterior windows above 2'6" and below 7'6" that permits a view to the outside of the project space.

Innovation & Design Process

Sustainable design strategies and measures are constantly evolving and improving. New technologies are continually introduced to the marketplace and up-to-date scientific research influences building design strategies. The purpose of this LEED category is to recognize projects for innovative building features and sustainable building knowledge.

Occasionally, a strategy results in building performance that greatly exceeds those required in an existing LEED credit. Other strategies may not be addressed by any LEED prerequisite or credit but warrant consideration for their sustainability benefits. In addition, LEED is most effectively implemented as part of an integrated design process, and this category addresses the use of a LEED Accredited Professional in the facilitation of that process.

Innovation & Design Process Credit Characteristics

Table 1 shows which credits were substantially revised from LEED-NC Version 2.2 and which project team members are likely to carry decision-making responsibility for each credit. Innovation Credits that deal strictly with design phase decisions and inclusions (that will not be affected or modified during the construction process) are eligible to be submitted in the Design Phase Submittal. Innovation Credits that rely on the completion of construction to confirm performance must be submitted as a Construction Phase Submittal. The decision-making responsibility matrix is not intended to exclude any party, rather to emphasize those credits that are most likely to require strong participation by a particular team member.

Overview of LEED® Credits

ID Credit 1
Innovation in Design

ID Credit 2
LEED® Accredited Professional

There are 4 points available in the Innovation in Design category.

Table 1: ID Credit Characteristics

Credit	Significant Change from LEED-NC v2.2	Design Submittal	Construction Submittal	Owner Decision-Making	Design Team Decision-Making	Contractor Decision-Making
IDc1.1: Innovation in Design		*	*	*	*	*
IDc1.2: Innovation in Design		*	*	*	*	*
IDc1.3: Innovation in Design		*	*	*	*	*
IDc1.4: Innovation in Design		*	*	*	*	*
IDc2: LEED Accredited Professional			*	*	*	*

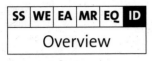

Innovation in Design

1–4 points

Intent

To provide design teams and projects the opportunity to be awarded points for exemplary performance above the requirements set by the LEED-CS Green Building Rating System and/or innovative performance in Green Building categories not specifically addressed by the LEED-CS Green Building Rating System.

Requirements

Credit 1.1 (1 point) In writing, identify the intent of the proposed innovation credit, the proposed requirement for compliance, the proposed submittals to demonstrate compliance, and the design approach (strategies) that might be used to meet the requirements.

Credit 1.2 (1 point) Same as Credit 1.1

Credit 1.3 (1 point) Same as Credit 1.1

Credit 1.4 (1 point) Same as Credit 1.1

Potential Technologies & Strategies

Substantially exceed a LEED-CS performance credit such as energy performance or water efficiency. Apply strategies or measures that demonstrate a comprehensive approach and quantifiable environment and/or health benefits.

Summary of Referenced Standard

There is no standard referenced for this ID Credit. Please refer to the Summary of Referenced Standard section within each LEED-CS credit for relevant standards.

Approach and Implementation

There are two types of innovation strategies that qualify under this credit. The first type includes those strategies that greatly exceed the requirements of existing LEED credits. For instance, a project that incorporates recycled materials or water efficiency measures that greatly exceed the requirements of their respective LEED credits would be appropriate for this credit.

As a general rule of thumb, ID Credits for exemplary performance are awarded for doubling the credit requirements and/or achieving the next incremental percentage threshold. For instance, an ID Credit for exemplary performance in water use reduction (WE Credit 1) would require a minimum of 40% savings (20% = WE Credit 1.1; 30% = WE Credit 3.2, etc.). Exemplary performance is not available for all credits in LEED-CS. Exemplary performance thresholds are listed in the credit sections of the Reference Guide for eligible points.

Because of the market relationship between a building's core and shell, and tenant space build-out, some ID Credits for exemplary performance may be met by mandating that the building's tenants comply with LEED-CS credit requirements. Eligible points are noted within the credit sections of the Reference Guide.

The second type of innovation strategies are those that are not addressed by any existing LEED credits. Only those strategies that demonstrate a comprehensive approach and have significant, measurable environmental benefits are applicable. For example, simple signage in a building would not be considered a significant educational effort by itself. But a visitor's center and interactive display, coupled with a website and video would be an appropriate level of effort for earning an innovation credit.

There are three basic criteria for achieving an innovation credit for a category not specifically addressed by LEED:

1. The project must demonstrate quantitative performance improvements for environmental benefit (establishing a baseline of standard performance for comparison to the final design).

2. The process or specification must be comprehensive. For example, a team that is considering applying for an innovation credit for a green housekeeping program would need to demonstrate that the program applies to the entire project being certified under LEED. Measures that address a limited portion of a project, or are not comprehensive in other ways, may not be eligible in this category.

3. The formula that your project develops for the innovation credit must be applicable to other projects.

Innovation credits awarded for one core and shell project do not constitute automatic approval for similar strategies employed in a future project.

Innovation credits are not awarded for the use of a particular product or design strategy if the technology aids in the achievement of an existing LEED credit.

Approved ID Credits may be pursued by any LEED project, but the project team must sufficiently document the achievement using the LEED credit equivalence process.

Calculations

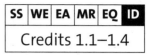

Please refer to the Calculations section within each LEED-CS credit for appropriate calculation submittals.

Submittal Documentation

These credits may be submitted as part of the **Design** or **Construction Submittal** depending on the credit requirements and performance for each proposal.

The following project data and calculation information is required to document credit compliance using the v2.0 Submittal Templates:

❑ Provide the specific title for the ID Credit being pursued.

❑ Provide a narrative statement of the Credit Intent.

❑ Provide a narrative statement describing the Credit Requirements.

❑ Provide a detailed narrative describing the project's approach to achievement of the credit. This narrative should include a description of the quantifiable environmental benefits of the credit proposal.

❑ Provide copies of any specific construction drawings or exhibits that will serve to illustrate the project's approach to the credit. (Note: this may not be applicable to all ID Credit proposals.)

A separate set of submittals is required for each point pursued and no single strategy is eligible for more than one point. Four independent sustainability measures may be applied to ID Credits.

LEED Accredited Professional

Intent

To support and encourage the design integration required by a LEED-CS green building project and to streamline the application and certification process.

Requirements

At least one principal participant of the project team shall be a LEED Accredited Professional (AP).

Potential Technologies & Strategies

Educate the project team members about green building design & construction and application of the LEED Rating System early in the life of the project. Consider assigning the LEED AP as a facilitator of an integrated design & construction process.

Summary of Referenced Standard

There is no standard referenced for this ID Credit.

Approach and Implementation

To become a LEED Accredited Professional, the LEED Accreditation Exam must be successfully passed. To prepare for the exam, it is helpful to attend a LEED Workshop offered by, or authorized by, the USGBC. Workshops include details on prerequisites and credits, calculation and documentation examples, and case studies from projects that have achieved certification.

For more information on workshops and the Accreditation Exam, visit the LEED section of the USGBC website at www. usgbc.org.

Exemplary Performance

This credit is not eligible for exemplary performance under the Innovation in Design section.

Submittal Documentation

This credit is submitted as part of the **Construction Submittal**.

The following project data is required to document credit compliance using the v2.0 Submittal Templates:

❏ Provide the name of the LEED AP.

❏ Provide the name of the LEED AP's company.

❏ Provide a brief description of the LEED AP's project role(s).

❏ Provide a copy of the LEED AP certificate.

Calculations

There are no calculations associated with this credit.

Considerations

LEED Accredited Professionals have the expertise required to design a building to LEED standards and to coordinate the documentation process that is necessary for LEED certification. The Accredited Professional understands the importance of integrated design and the need to consider interactions between the prerequisites and credits and their respective criteria. Architects, engineers, consultants, owners and others who have a strong interest in sustainable building design are all appropriate candidates for accreditation. The Accredited Professional should be the champion for the project's LEED application and this person should be an integral member of the project design team.

Glossary of Terms

Acid Rain

The precipitation of dilute solutions of strong mineral acids, formed by the mixing in the atmosphere of various industrial pollutants (primarily sulfur dioxide and nitrogen oxides) with naturally occurring oxygen and water vapor.

Adapted (Introduced) Plants

Plants that reliably grow well in a given habitat with minimal attention from humans in the form of winter protection, pest protection, water irrigation, or fertilization once root systems are established in the soil. Adapted plants are considered to be low maintenance but not invasive.

Adaptive Reuse

The renovation of a building or site to include elements that allows a particular use or uses to occupy a space that originally was intended for a different use.

Adhesive

Any substance that is used to bond one surface to another surface by attachment. Adhesives include adhesive bonding primers, adhesive primers, adhesive primers for plastics, and any other primer.

Aerosol Adhesive

An adhesive packaged as an aerosol product in which the spray mechanism is permanently housed in a non-refillable can designed for hand-held application without the need for ancillary hoses or spray equipment. Aerosol adhesives include special purpose spray adhesives, mist spray adhesives and web spray adhesives.

Agrifiber Board

A composite panel product derived from recovered agricultural waste fiber from sources including, but not limited to, cereal straw, sugarcane bagasse, sunflower husk, walnut shells, coconut husks, and agricultural prunings. The raw fibers are processed and mixed with resins to produce panel products with characteristics similar to those derived from wood fiber.

Air Changes Per Hour (ACH)

The number of times per hour a volume of air, equivalent to the volume of space, enters that space.

Air Conditioning

The process of treating air to meet the requirements of a conditioned space by controlling its temperature, humidity, cleanliness and distribution (ASHRAE 62.1-2004).

Albedo

Synonymous with solar reflectance.

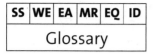

Alternative Fuel Vehicles

Vehicles that use low-polluting, non-gasoline fuels such as electricity, hydrogen, propane or compressed natural gas, liquid natural gas, methanol and ethanol. Efficient gas-electric hybrid vehicles are included in this group for LEED purposes.

Angle of Maximum Candela

The direction in which the luminaire emits the greatest luminous intensity.

Anti-corrosive Paints

Coatings formulated and recommended for use in preventing the corrosion of ferrous metal substrates.

Aquatic Systems

Ecologically designed treatment systems that utilize a diverse community of biological organisms (e.g., bacteria, plants and fish) to treat wastewater to advanced levels.

Aquifer

An underground water-bearing rock formation or group of formations, which supplies groundwater, wells or springs.

Assembly Recycled Content

Includes the percentages of post-consumer and pre-consumer content. The determination is made by dividing the weight of the recycled content by the overall weight of the assembly.

Automatic Fixture Sensors

Motion sensors that automatically turn on/off lavatories, sinks, water closets and urinals. Sensors may be hard wired or battery operated.

Average Annual Building Users

The Average Annual Building Users is the average number of building users occupying the building for an eight-hour schedule per workday taken at the peak use period for the year, the low use period for the year, and the average use period for the year. An average is used because for some building types the occupancy use will fluctuate at different times of the year.

Baseline Building Performance

The annual energy cost for a building design intended for use as a baseline for rating above standard design, as defined in ASHRAE 90.1-2004 Informative Appendix G.

Basis of Design (BOD)

Includes design information necessary to accomplish the owner's project requirements, including system descriptions, indoor environmental quality criteria, other pertinent design assumptions (such as weather data), and references to applicable codes, standards, regulations and guidelines.

Biodiversity

The variety of life in all forms, levels and combinations, including ecosystem diversity, species diversity, and genetic diversity.

Biomass

Plant material such as trees, grasses and crops that can be converted to heat energy to produce electricity.

Bioremediation

Involves the use of microorganisms and vegetation to remove contaminants from water and soils. Bioremediation is generally a form of in-situ remediation, and can be a viable alternative to landfilling or incineration.

Blackwater

Does not have a single definition that is accepted nationwide. Wastewater from toilets and urinals is, however, always considered blackwater.

Wastewater from kitchen sinks (perhaps differentiated by the use of a garbage disposal), showers, or bathtubs may be considered blackwater by state or local codes. Project teams should comply with the blackwater definition as established by the authority having jurisdiction in their areas.

Breathing Zone

The region within an occupied space between planes 3 and 6 ft. above the floor and more than 2 ft. from the walls or fixed air-conditioning equipment.

Building Density

The floor area of the building divided by the total area of the site (square feet per acre).

Building Envelope

The exterior surface of a building's construction—the walls, windows, roof and floor. Also referred to as the "building shell."

Building Footprint

The area on a project site that is used by the building structure and is defined by the perimeter of the building plan. Parking lots, landscapes and other non-building facilities are not included in the building footprint.

Carpool

An arrangement in which two or more people share a vehicle for transportation.

Car Sharing

A system under which multiple households share a pool of automobiles, either through cooperative ownership or through some other mechanism.

CERCLA

Refers to the Comprehensive Environmental Response, Compensation, and Liability Act (CERCLA), commonly known as Superfund. CERCLA addresses abandoned or historical waste sites and contamination. It was enacted in 1980 to create a tax on the chemical and petroleum industries and provided federal authority to respond to releases of hazardous substances.

Chain-of-Custody

A document that tracks the movement of a wood product from the forest to a vendor and is used to verify compliance with FSC guidelines. A "vendor" is defined as the company that supplies wood products to project contractors or subcontractors for on-site installation.

Chlorofluorocarbons (CFCs)

Hydrocarbons that deplete the stratospheric ozone layer.

CO_2

Carbon dioxide

Cogeneration

The simultaneous production of electrical or mechanical energy (power) and useful thermal energy from the same fuel/energy source such as oil, coal, gas, biomass or solar.

Comfort Criteria

Specific original design conditions that shall at a minimum include temperature (air, radiant and surface), humidity and air speed as well as outdoor temperature design conditions, outdoor humidity design conditions, clothing (seasonal) and activity expected(ASHRAE 55-2004).

Commissioning (Cx)

The process of ensuring that systems are designed, installed, functionally tested, and capable of being operated and maintained to perform in conformity with the Owner's Project Requirements.

Commissioning Plan

A document defining the commissioning process, which is developed in increasing detail as the project progresses through its various phases.

Commissioning Report

The document that records the results of the commissioning process, including the as-built performance of the HVAC system and unresolved issues.

Commissioning Specification

The contract document that details the objective, scope and implementation of the construction and acceptance phases of the commissioning process as developed in the design-phase commissioning plan.

Commissioning Team

Includes those people responsible for working together to carry out the commissioning process.

Community

An interacting population of individuals living in a specific area.

Completed Design Area

The total area of finished ceilings, finished floors, full height walls and demountable partitions, interior doors and built-in case goods in the space when the project is completed; exterior windows and exterior doors are not considered.

Composite Wood

A product consisting of wood or plant particles or fibers bonded together by a synthetic resin or binder (i.e., plywood, particle-board, OSB, MDF, composite door cores.)

Composting Toilet Systems

Dry plumbing fixtures that contain and treat human waste via microbiological processes.

Conditioned Space

The part of a building that is heated or cooled, or both, for the comfort of occupants (ASHRAE 62.1-2004).

Construction and Demolition (C&D) Debris

Includes waste and recyclables generated from construction, renovation, and demolition or deconstruction of pre-existing structures. Land clearing debris including soil, vegetation, rocks, etc. are not to be included.

Construction IAQ Management Plan

A document specific to a building project that outlines measures to minimize contamination in the building during construction, and to flush the building of contaminants prior to occupancy.

Contaminant

An unwanted airborne constituent that may reduce acceptability of the air (ASHRAE 62.1-2004).

Conventional Irrigation

Refers to the most common irrigation system used in the region where the building is located. A common conventional irrigation system uses pressure to deliver water and distributes it through sprinkler heads above the ground.

Curfew Hours

Locally determined times when greater lighting restrictions are imposed. When no local or regional restrictions are in place, 10:00 p.m. is regarded as a default curfew time.

Daylighting

The controlled admission of natural light into a space through glazing with the intent of reducing or eliminating electric lighting. By utilizing solar light, daylighting creates a stimulating and productive environment for building occupants.

Daylighting Zone

The total floor area that meets the performance requirements for daylighting.

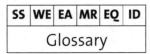

Development Footprint

The area on the project site that has been impacted by any development activity. Hardscape, access roads, parking lots, non-building facilities and building structure are all included in the development footprint.

Direct Line of Sight to Perimeter Vision Glazing

The approach used to determine the calculated area of regularly occupied areas with direct line of sight to perimeter vision glazing. The area determination includes full height partitions and other fixed construction prior to installation of furniture.

Drip Irrigation

A high-efficiency irrigation method in which water is delivered at low pressure through buried mains and sub-mains. From the sub-mains, water is distributed to the soil from a network of perforated tubes or emitters. Drip irrigation is a type of micro-irrigation.

Ecosystem

A basic unit of nature that includes a community of organisms and their non-living environment linked by biological, chemical and physical process.

Embodied Energy

Energy that is used during the entire life cycle of the commodity for manufacturing, transporting and disposing of the commodity as well as the inherent energy captured within the product itself.

Emissivity

The ratio of the radiation emitted by a surface to the radiation emitted by a black body at the same temperature.

Endangered Species

An animal or plant species that is in danger of becoming extinct throughout all or a significant portion of its range due to harmful human activities or environmental factors.

Energy Conservation Measures (ECMs)

Installations of equipment or systems, or modifications of equipment or systems, for the purpose of reducing energy use and/or costs.

ENERGY STAR® Rating

The rating a building earns using the ENERGY STAR Portfolio Manager to compare building energy performance to similar buildings in similar climates. A score of 50 represents average building performance.

Environmental Attributes of Green Power

Include emission reduction benefits that result from green power being used instead of conventional power sources.

Environmental Tobacco Smoke (ETS)

Also known as secondhand smoke, consists of airborne particles emitted from the burning end of cigarettes, pipes, and cigars, and exhaled by smokers. These particles contain about 4,000 different compounds, up to 40 of which are known to cause cancer.

Environmentally Preferable Products

Products identified as having a lesser or reduced effect on health and the environment when compared with competing products that serve the same purpose.

Environmentally Preferable Purchasing

A United States federal-wide program (Executive Order 13101) that encourages and assists Executive agencies in the purchasing of Environmentally Preferable Products and services.

Erosion

A combination of processes in which materials of the earth's surface are loosened, dissolved or worn away, and transported from one place to another by natural agents (such as water, wind or gravity).

Eutrophication

The accumulation of nutrients that encourage dense algal growth. The decay of which depletes oxygen in shallow waters.

Exfiltration

Uncontrolled outward air leakage from conditioned spaces through unintentional openings in ceilings, floors and walls to unconditioned spaces or the outdoors caused by pressure differences across these openings due to wind, inside-outside temperature differences (stack effect), and imbalances between supply and exhaust airflow rates (ASHRAE 62.1-2004).

Exhaust Air

The air removed from a space and discharged to outside the building by means of mechanical or natural ventilation systems.

Ex-situ Remediation

Involves the removal of contaminated soil and groundwater. Treatment of the contaminated media occurs in another location, typically a treatment facility. A traditional method of ex-situ remediation is pump-and-treat technology that uses carbon filters and incineration. More advanced methods of ex-situ remediation include chemical treatment or biological reactors.

Flat Coatings

Coatings that register a gloss of less than 15 on an 85-degree meter or less than 5 on a 60-degree meter.

Fly Ash

The solid residue derived from incineration processes. Fly ash can be used as a substitute for portland cement in concrete.

Footcandle (fc)

A unit of illuminance equal to one lumen of light falling on a one-square foot area from a one candela light source at a distance of one foot.

Formaldehyde

A naturally occurring VOC found in small amounts in animals and plants, but is carcinogenic and an irritant to most people when present in high concentrations—causing headaches, dizziness, mental impairment, and other symptoms. When present in the air at levels above 0.1 ppm (parts per million), it can cause watery eyes, burning sensations in the eyes, nose, and throat; nausea; coughing; chest tightness; wheezing; skin rashes; and asthmatic and allergic reactions.

Functional Performance Testing (FPT)

The process of determining the ability of the commissioned systems to perform in accordance with the Owner's Project Requirements, Basis of Design, and construction documents.

Full-Time Equivalent (FTE)

A measure of building occupants that is equal to one person occupying a building for an eight-hour schedule per workday.

Glazing Factor

The ratio of interior illuminance at a given point on a given plane (usually the work plane) to the exterior illuminance under known overcast sky conditions. LEED uses a simplified approach for its credit compliance calculations. The variables used to determine the daylight factor include the floor area, window area, window geometry, visible transmittance (T_{vis}) and window height.

Graywater (also spelled greywater and gray water)

Defined by the Uniform Plumbing Code (UPC) in its Appendix G, titled "Gray water Systems for Single-Family Dwellings," as "untreated household wastewater which has not come into contact with toilet waste. Gray water includes used water from bathtubs, showers, bathroom wash basins, and water from clothes-washer and laundry tubs. It shall not include wastewater from kitchen sinks or dishwashers."

The International Plumbing Code (IPC) defines graywater in its Appendix C, titled "Graywater Recycling Systems," as "wastewater discharged from lavatories, bathtubs, showers, clothes washers, and laundry sinks."

Some states and local authorities allow kitchen sink wastewater to be included in graywater. Other differences with the UPC and IPC definitions may be found in state and local codes. Project teams should comply with the graywater definitions as established by the authority having jurisdiction in their areas.

Greenfields

Sites that have not been previously developed or graded and remain in a natural state.

Greenhouse Gases

Gases such as carbon dioxide, methane and CFCs that are relatively transparent to the higher-energy sunlight, but trap lower-energy infrared radiation.

Halons

Substances used in fire suppression systems and fire extinguishers in buildings. These substances deplete the stratospheric ozone layer.

Heat Island Effect

Occurs when warmer temperatures are experienced in urban landscapes compared to adjacent rural areas as a result of solar energy retention on constructed surfaces. Principal surfaces that contribute to the heat island effect include streets, sidewalks, parking lots and buildings.

Horizontal View at 42 Inches

The approach used to confirm that the direct line of sight to perimeter vision glazing remains available from a seated position. It uses section drawings that include the installed furniture to make the determination.

HVAC Systems

Include heating, ventilating, and air-conditioning systems used to provide thermal comfort and ventilation for building interiors.

Hybrid Vehicles

Vehicles that use a gasoline engine to drive an electric generator and use the electric generator and/or storage batteries to power electric motors that drive the vehicle's wheels.

Hydrochlorofluorocarbons (HCFCs)

Refrigerants used in building equipment that deplete the stratospheric ozone layer, but to a lesser extent than CFCs.

Hydrofluorocarbons (HFCs)

Refrigerants that do not deplete the stratospheric ozone layer. However, some HFCs have high global warming potential and, thus, are not environmentally benign.

Impervious Surfaces

Surfaces that promote runoff of precipitation volumes instead of infiltration into the subsurface. The imperviousness or degree of runoff potential can be estimated for different surface materials.

Individual Occupant Spaces

Typically private offices and open office plans with workstations.

Indoor Adhesive, Sealant and/or Sealant Primer Product

Defined as an adhesive or sealant product applied on-site, inside of the building's weatherproofing system.

Indoor Air Quality

The nature of air inside the space that affects the health and well-being of building occupants.

Indoor Carpet Systems

Defined as carpet, carpet adhesive, or carpet cushion product installed on-site, inside of the building's weatherproofing system.

Indoor Composite Wood or Agrifiber Product

Defined as a composite wood or agrifiber product installed on-site, inside of the building's weatherproofing system.

Indoor Paint or Coating Product

Defined as a paint or coating product applied on-site, inside of the building's weatherproofing system.

Infiltration

Uncontrolled inward air leakage to conditioned spaces through unintentional openings in ceilings, floors and walls from unconditioned spaces or the outdoors caused by the same pressure differences that induce exfiltration (ASHRAE 62.1-2004).

Infrared or Thermal Emittance

A parameter between 0 and 1 (or 0% and 100%) that indicates the ability of a material to shed infrared radiation (heat). The wavelength range for this radiant energy is roughly 4 to 40 micrometers. Most building materials (including glass) are opaque in this part of the spectrum, and have an emittance of roughly 0.9.

Materials such as clean, bare metals are the most important exceptions to the 0.9 rule. Thus clean, untarnished galvanized steel has low emittance, and aluminum roof coatings have intermediate emittance levels.

In-situ Remediation

Involves treatment of contaminants in place using technologies such as injection wells or reactive trenches. These methods utilize the natural hydraulic gradient of groundwater and usually require only minimal disturbance of the site.

Installation Inspection

The process of inspecting components of the commissioned systems to determine if they are installed properly and ready for systems performance testing.

Interior Lighting Power Allowance

The maximum light power in watts allowed for the interior of a building.

Interior Non-structural Components Reuse

Determined by dividing the area of retained components by the larger of the area of the prior condition or the area of the completed design.

Invasive Plants

Both indigenous and non-indigenous species or strains that are characteristically adaptable, aggressive, have a high reproductive capacity and tend to overrun the ecosystems in which they inhabit. Collectively they are one of the great threats to biodiversity and ecosystem stability.

Laminate Adhesive

An adhesive used in wood/agrifiber products (veneered panels, composite wood products contained in engineered lumber, door assemblies, etc.).

Landfill

A waste disposal site for the deposit of solid waste from human activities.

Landscape Area

Area of the site equal to the total site area less the building footprint, paved surfaces, water bodies, patios, etc.

LEED Project Boundary

The portion of the project site submitted for LEED certification. For single building developments, this will be the entire project scope and is generally limited to the site boundary. For multiple building developments, the LEED Project Boundary may be a portion of the development as determined by the project team.

Life Cycle Analysis (LCA)

An evaluation of the environmental effects of a product or activity holistically, by analyzing the entire life cycle of a particular material, process, product, technology, service or activity.

Life Cycle Cost (LCC) Method

A technique of economic evaluation that sums over a given study period the costs of initial investment (less resale value), replacements, operations (including energy use), and maintenance and repair of an investment decision (expressed in present or annual value terms).

Life Cycle Inventory (LCI)

An accounting of the energy and waste associated with the creation of a new product through use and disposal.

Light Pollution

Waste light from building sites that produces glare, is directed upward to the sky or is directed off the site.

Lighting Power Density (LPD)

The installed lighting power, per unit area.

Local Zoning Requirements

Local government regulations imposed to promote orderly development of private lands and to prevent land use conflicts.

Makeup Air

Any combination of outdoor and transfer air intended to replace exhaust air and ex-filtration (ASHRAE 62.1-2004).

Mass Transit

Includes transportation facilities designed to transport large groups of persons in a single vehicle such as buses or trains.

Mass Transit Vehicles

Vehicles typically capable of serving 10 or more occupants, such as buses, trolleys, light rail, etc.

Mechanical Ventilation

Ventilation provided by mechanical powered equipment, such as motor-driven fans and blowers, but not by devices such as wind-driven turbine ventilators and mechanically operated windows (ASHRAE 62.1-2004).

Metering Controls

Generally manual on/automatic off controls which are used to limit the flow time of water. These types of controls are most commonly installed on lavatory faucets and on showers.

Micro-irrigation

Involves irrigation systems with small sprinklers and micro-jets or drippers designed to apply small volumes of water. The sprinklers and micro-jets are installed within a few centimeters of the ground, while drippers are laid on or below grade.

Mixed-mode Ventilation

A ventilation strategy that combines natural ventilation with mechanical ventilation, allowing the building to be ventilated either mechanically or naturally; and at times both mechanically and naturally simultaneously.

Native (Indigenous) Plants

Plants that have adapted to a given area during a defined time period and that are not invasive. In America, the term often refers to plants growing in a region prior to the time of settlement by people of European descent.

Natural Ventilation

Ventilation provided by thermal, wind or diffusion effects through doors, windows or other intentional openings in the building (ASHRAE 62.1-2004).

Net Metering

A metering and billing arrangement that allows on-site generators to send excess electricity flows to the regional power grid. These electricity flows offset a portion of the electricity flows drawn from the grid. For more information on net metering in individual states, visit the DOE's Green Power Network website at www.eere.energy.gov/greenpower/netmetering

Non-flat Coatings

Coatings that register a gloss of 5 or greater on a 60-degree meter and a gloss of 15 or greater on an 85-degree meter.

Non-occupied Spaces

Include all rooms used by maintenance personnel that are not open for use by occupants. Included in this category are janitorial, storage and equipment rooms, and closets.

Non-porous Sealant

A substance used as a sealant on non-porous materials. Non-porous materials do not have openings in which fluids may be absorbed or discharged. Such materials include, but are not limited to, plastic and metal.

Non-potable Water

Water that is not suitable for human consumption without treatment that meets or exceeds EPA drinking water standards.

Non-regularly Occupied Spaces

Includes corridors, hallways, lobbies, break rooms, copy rooms, storage rooms, kitchens, restrooms, stairwells, etc.

Non-roof Impervious Surfaces

Includes all surfaces on the site with a perviousness of less than 50%, not including the roof of the building. Examples of typically impervious surfaces include parking lots, roads, sidewalks and plazas.

Non-water-using Urinal (also known as a dry urinal)

A urinal that uses no water, but instead replaces the water flush with a specially designed trap that contains a layer of buoyant liquid that floats above the urine layer, blocking sewer gas and urine odors from the room.

Off-gassing

The emission of volatile organic compounds from synthetic and natural products.

On-site Wastewater Treatment

Uses localized treatment systems to transport, store, treat and dispose of wastewater volumes generated on the project site.

Open Space Area

Defined by local zoning requirements. If local zoning requirements do not clearly define open space, it is defined for the purposes of LEED calculations as the property area minus the development footprint; and it must be vegetated and pervious, with exceptions only as noted in the credit requirements section. For projects located in urban areas that earn SS Credit 2, open space also includes non-vehicular, pedestrian-oriented hardscape spaces.

Open-grid Pavement

Defined for LEED purposes as pavement that is less than 50% impervious and contains vegetation in the open cells.

Outdoor Air

The ambient air that enters a building through a ventilation system, through intentional openings for natural ventilation, or by infiltration (ASHRAE 62.1-2004).

Outdoor Lighting Zone Definitions

Developed by IDA for the Model Lighting Ordinance, these definitions provide a general description of the site environment/context and basic site lighting criteria.

Owner's Project Requirements (OPR)

An explanation of the ideas, concepts and criteria that are determined by the owner to be important to the success of the project (previously called the Design Intent).

Paints

Liquid, liquifiable or mastic compositions that are converted to a solid protective, decorative, or functional adherent film after application as a thin layer. These coatings are intended for on-site application to interior or exterior surfaces of residential, commercial, institutional or industrial buildings.

Pedestrian Access

Implies that pedestrians can walk to the services without being blocked by walls, freeways or other barriers.

Percentage Improvement

The percent energy cost savings for the Proposed Building Performance versus the Baseline Building Performance.

Perviousness

The percent of the surface area of a paving material that is open and allows moisture to pass through the material and soak into the earth below the paving system.

Phenol Formaldehyde

Off-gasses only at high temperature, and is used for exterior products; although many of those products are suitable for interior applications.

Porous Sealant

A substance used as a sealant on porous materials. Porous materials have tiny openings, often microscopic, in which fluids may be absorbed or discharged. Such materials include, but are not limited to, wood, fabric, paper, corrugated paperboard and plastic foam.

Post-consumer

Waste material generated by households or by commercial, industrial and institutional facilities in their role as end-users of the product, which can no longer be used for its intended purpose. This includes returns of materials from the distribution chain (source: ISO 14021). Examples of this category include construction and demolition debris, materials collected through curbside and drop-off recycling programs, broken pallets (if from a pallet refurbishing company, not a pallet making company), discarded products (e.g., furniture, cabinetry and decking) and urban maintenance waste (e.g., leaves, grass clippings, tree trimmings, etc.).

Potable Water

Water suitable for drinking and supplied from wells or municipal water systems.

ppb

Parts per billion

ppm

Parts per million

Pre-consumer Content

Defined as material diverted from the waste stream during the manufacturing process. Excluded is reutilization of materials such as rework, regrind or scrap generated in a process and capable of being reclaimed within the same process that generated it (source ISO 14021). Examples in this category include planer shavings, plytrim, sawdust, chips, bagasse, sunflower seed hulls, walnut shells, culls, trimmed materials, print overruns, over-issue publications, and obsolete inventories. (Previously referred to as Post-industrial Content.)

Preferred Parking

Refers to parking spots that are closest to the main entrance of the project, exclusive of spaces designated for handicapped.

Previously Developed Sites

Sites that previously contained buildings, roadways, parking lots, or were graded or altered by direct human activities.

Primer

A material applied to a substrate to improve adhesion of a subsequently applied adhesive.

Prior Condition Area

The total area of finished ceilings, finished floors, full height walls and demountable partitions, interior doors and built-in case goods that existed when the project area was selected; exterior windows and exterior doors are not considered.

Process Water

Water used for industrial processes and building systems such as cooling towers, boilers and chillers.

Property Area

The total area within the legal property boundaries of a site and encompassing all areas of the site, including constructed areas and non-constructed areas.

Proposed Building Performance

The annual energy cost calculated for a proposed design, as defined in ASHRAE 90.1-2004 Informative Appendix G.

Public Transportation

Bus, rail or other transportation service for the general public, operating on a regular, continual basis that is publicly or privately owned.

Rapidly Renewable Materials

Material considered to be an agricultural product, both fiber and animal, that takes 10 years or less to grow or raise, and to harvest in an ongoing and sustainable fashion.

Rated Power

The nameplate power on a piece of equipment. It represents the capacity of the unit and is the maximum a unit will draw.

RCRA

The Resource Conservation and Recovery Act. RCRA focuses on active and future facilities. It was enacted in 1976 to give the EPA authority to control hazardous wastes from cradle to grave, including generation, transportation, treatment, storage and disposal. Some non-hazardous wastes are also covered under RCRA.

Receptacle Load

Refers to all equipment that is plugged into the electrical system, from office equipment to refrigerators.

Recirculated Air

The air removed from a space and reused as supply air (ASHRAE 62.1-2004).

Recycling

The collection, reprocessing, marketing and use of materials that were diverted or recovered from the solid waste stream.

Refrigerants

The working fluids of refrigeration cycles. Refrigerants absorb heat from a reservoir at low temperatures and reject heat at higher temperatures.

Regionally Extracted Materials

For LEED-CS purposes, must have their source as a raw material from within a 500-mile radius of the project site.

Regionally Manufactured Materials

For LEED-CS purposes, must be assembled as a finished product within a 500-mile radius of the project site. Assembly, as used for this LEED definition, does not include on-site assembly, erection or installation of finished components, as in structural steel, miscellaneous iron or systems furniture.

Regularly Occupied Spaces

Areas where workers are seated or standing as they work inside a building; in residential applications it refers to living and family rooms.

Relative Humidity

The ratio of partial density of water vapor in the air to the saturation density of water vapor at the same temperature and the same total pressure (ASHRAE 55-2004).

Remediation

The process of cleaning up a contaminated site by physical, chemical or biological means. Remediation processes are typically applied to contaminated soil and groundwater.

Renewable Energy Certificates (RECs)

RECs are a representation of the environmental attributes of green power, and are sold separately from the electrons that make up the electricity. RECs allow the purchase of green power even when the electrons are not purchased.

Retained Components

The portions of the finished ceilings, finished floors, full height walls and demountable partitions, interior doors and built-in case goods that existed in the prior condition and remained in the completed design.

Return Air

The air removed from a space to then be recirculated or exhausted (ASHRAE 62.1-2004).

Reuse

A strategy to return materials to active use in the same or a related capacity.

Risk Assessment

A methodology used to analyze for potential health effects caused by contaminants in the environment. Information from the risk assessment is used to determine cleanup levels.

Salvaged Materials

Construction materials recovered from existing buildings or construction sites and reused in other buildings. Common salvaged materials include structural beams and posts, flooring, doors, cabinetry, brick and decorative items.

Sealant

Any material with adhesive properties that is formulated primarily to fill, seal, or waterproof gaps or joints between two surfaces. Sealants include sealant primers and caulks.

Secure Bicycle Storage

An internal or external space dedicated to the secure storage of bicycles. This should be available to all building users and may include lockers and storage rooms.

Sedimentation

The addition of soils to water bodies by natural and human-related activities. Sedimentation decreases water quality and accelerates the aging process of lakes, rivers and streams.

Shared (Group) Multi-occupant Spaces

Includes retail sales floors, conference rooms, classrooms and other indoor spaces used as a place of congregation for presentations, trainings, etc. Individuals using these spaces share the lighting and temperature controls and they should have, at a minimum, a separate zone with accessible thermostat and an air-flow control.

Site Area

Synonymous with property area.

Site Assessment

An evaluation of above-ground (including facilities) and subsurface characteristics, including the geology and hydrology of the site, to determine if a release has occurred, as well as the extent and concentration of the release. Information generated during a site assessment is used to support remedial action decisions.

Solar Reflectance (Albedo)

The ratio of the reflected solar energy to the incoming solar energy over wavelengths of approximately 0.3 to 2.5 micrometers. A reflectance of 100% means that all of the energy striking a reflecting surface is reflected back into the atmosphere and none of the energy is absorbed by the surface. The best standard technique for its determination uses spectro-photometric measurements with an integrating sphere to determine the reflectance at each different wavelength. An averaging process using a standard solar spectrum then determines the average reflectance (see ASTM Standard E903).

Solar Reflectance Index (SRI)

A measure of a material's ability to reject solar heat, as shown by a small temperature rise. It is defined so that a standard black (reflectance 0.05, emittance 0.90) is 0 and a standard white (reflectance 0.80, emittance 0.90) is 100. For example, a standard black surface has a temperature rise of 90°F (50°C) in full sun, and a standard white surface has a temperature rise of 14.6°F (8.1°C). Once the maximum temperature rise of a given material has been computed, the SRI can be computed by interpolating between the values for white and black.

Materials with the highest SRI values are the coolest choices for paving. Due to the way SRI is defined, particularly hot materials can even take slightly negative values, and particularly cool materials can even exceed 100. (Lawrence Berkeley National Laboratory Cool Roofing Materials Database)

Square Footage

The total area in square feet of all rooms of a building, including corridors, elevators, stairwells and shaft spaces.

Stormwater Runoff

Water volumes that are created during precipitation events and that flow over surfaces into sewer systems or receiving waters. All precipitation waters that leave project site boundaries on the surface are considered to be stormwater runoff volumes.

Supply Air

The air delivered by mechanical or natural ventilation to a space, composed of any combination of outdoor air, recirculated air, or transfer air (ASHRAE 62.1-2004).

Sustainable Forestry

The practice of managing forest resources to meet the long-term forest product needs of humans while maintaining the biodiversity of forested landscapes. The primary goal is to restore, enhance and sustain a full range of forest values—economic, social and ecological.

System Performance Testing

The process of determining the ability of the commissioned systems to perform in accordance with the Owner's Project Requirements, Basis of Design, and construction documents.

Tenant Sales or Lease Agreement

The contractual agreement for a tenant lease arrangement, or a buyer's sales arrangement.

Tertiary Treatment

The highest form of wastewater treatment that includes the removal of nutrients, organic and solid material, along with biological or chemical polishing (generally to effluent limits of 10 mg/L BOD_5 and 10 mg/L TSS).

Thermal Comfort

A condition of mind experienced by building occupants expressing satisfaction with the thermal environment.

Threatened Species

An animal or plant species that is likely to become endangered within the foreseeable future.

Tipping Fees

Fees charged by a landfill for disposal of waste volumes. The fee is typically quoted for one ton of waste.

Total Suspended Solids (TSS)

Particles or flocs that are too small or light to be removed from stormwater via gravity settling. Suspended solid concentrations are typically removed via filtration.

Underground Parking

A "tuck-under" or stacked parking structure that reduces the exposed parking surface area.

Urea Formaldehyde

A combination of urea and formaldehyde that is used in some glues and may emit formaldehyde at room temperature.

Ventilation

The process of supplying air to or removing air from a space for the purpose of controlling air contaminant levels, humidity, or temperature within the space (ASHRAE 62.1-2004).

Verification

The full range of checks and tests carried out to determine if all components, subsystems, systems, and interfaces between systems operate in accordance with the contract documents. In this context, "operate" includes all modes and sequences of control operation, interlocks and conditional control responses, and specified responses to abnormal or emergency conditions.

Visible Light Transmittance (T_{vis})

The ratio of total transmitted light to total incident light. In other words, it is the amount of visible spectrum (380 – 780 nanometers) light passing through a glazing surface divided by the amount of light striking the glazing surface. A higher T_{vis} value indicates that a greater amount of visible spectrum incident light is passing through the glazing.

Vision Glazing

The portion of exterior windows above 2'-6" and below 7'-6" that permits a view to the outside of the project space.

VOCs (Volatile Organic Compounds)

Carbon compounds that participate in atmospheric photochemical reactions (excluding carbon monoxide, carbon dioxide, carbonic acid, metallic carbides and carbonates, and ammonium carbonate). The compounds vaporize (become a gas) at normal room temperatures.

Wetland Vegetation

Plants that require saturated soils to survive as well as certain tree and other plant species that can tolerate prolonged wet soil conditions.

Window to Floor Area Ratio (WFR)

This is the total area of the window (measured vertically from 2'-6", or greater, above finish floor to the top of the glass, multiplied by the width of the glass) divided by the floor area.

Appendix 1 –
Default Occupancy Counts

Due to the speculative nature of LEED for core and shell projects, the project team may not know the occupant count during the LEED certification process. Because of this, determining and demonstrating compliance with some of the credits can prove challenging and complex. For projects that do not know the final occupant count, a default table has been developed.

The issue of occupant counts is applicable to a number of credits. There are three general areas where it is relevant:

1) The requirements for Alternative Transportation including bike racks, and parking requirements

2) Default numbers needed to determine water use reduction

3) Default numbers needed for Mechanical System Design and Energy Modeling

Core and shell projects that do not have final occupancy counts must utilize the default occupancy counts provided in this Appendix. Projects that DO know the tenant occupancy must use the actual numbers, as long as the gross square foot per employee is not greater than that in the default occupancy count table. If code requirements are less than those in the table, this is acceptable. Default occupancy counts are provided for typical core and shell project types. Project types and circumstances not covered in this Appendix may be considered on a case-by-case basis.

	Gross sf per full time employee			
	General Office	Retail	Medical Office Bldg	R&D -Lab Bldg
SSc 4.2 For bike racks	250	550	225	400
SSc 4.3 For parking requirement	250	550	225	400
SSc 4.4 For car pool requirement	250	550	225	400
WEc 3.1 For water use	(1)*	(1)*	(1)*	(1)*
WEc 3.2 For water use	(1)*	(1)*	(1)*	(1)*
EAc 1 For energy model	250	550	225	400
EQc 1 For ventilation requirements	250	550	225	400
EQc 1 For ventilation requirements	250	550	225	400
EQc 2 For ventilation requirements	250	550	225	400
EQc 6 For individual controls	250	550	225	400
EQc 7 For human contribution to humidity	250	550	225	400

(1) Code or actual, whichever is less

Appendix 2 –
Core and Shell Energy Modeling Guidelines

These guidelines are intended to ensure that projects in different markets with different project teams are approaching the energy modeling requirements in a similar manner, and that a minimum benchmark for energy optimization is established.

1. Create the ASHRAE 90.1-2004 Proposed Building model and Baseline Building model

1.1 Follow the ASHRAE 90.1-2004 Building Performance Rating Method. This is a whole building model inclusive of both core and shell, and tenant space scope. The following describes the prescriptive requirements for developing the whole building modeling of both the known core and shell work and unknown tenant space development.

1.2 Tenant spaces are defined as meeting all the following conditions:

　1.2.1　Components exclusively serve the tenant space;

　1.2.2　Components specifically designed for the tenant space;

　1.2.3　Energy using components are metered and apportioned and/or billed to the tenant;

　1.2.4　The tenant will pay for the components.

1.3 The Core and Shell building is defined as parts of the building that are not tenant space.

2. Proposed Building Model

2.1 Core and Shell Building

　2.1.1　HVAC Systems

　　　2.1.1.1　Model the building system as described in the design documents.

　　　　❑ If the HVAC system is not yet designed, use the same HVAC system as the baseline model.

　2.1.2　Building Envelope

　　　2.1.2.1　Model the building envelope as shown on the architectural drawings.

　2.1.3　Lighting

　　　2.1.3.1　Model the lighting power as shown in the design documents for the core and shell spaces.

2.2 Tenant Spaces

　2.2.1　Lighting

　　　2.2.1.1　Model separate electric meters for the lighting in the core building and the tenant spaces.

　　　2.2.1.2　Choose a space type classification for the building spaces. Use lighting levels shown in chart 9.3.1.2 of ASHRAE 90.1-2004 for the space type use classification.

❏ If the tenant lighting is designed and installed as part of the core and shell work, the project team may model the designed or installed lighting systems.

2.2.2   Receptacle and Other Loads

2.2.2.1 Model separate meters for tenant plug loads and process loads.

2.2.2.2 Use the following values to model tenant plug loads or provide documentation for the modeled loads (see the Process Energy section of EA Credit 1):

2.2.2.3 Computer intensive offices

❏ 2.0 W/sq.ft.

2.2.2.4 General office areas

❏ 1.5 W/sq.ft.

2.2.2.5 Large conference areas

❏ 1.0 W/sq.ft.

2.2.2.6 Corridors

❏ 0 W/sq.ft.

2.2.2.7 Server/computer rooms

❏ 50 W/sq.ft.

2.2.2.8 Other uses

❏ Use diversity in calculations

3. Baseline Building Model

3.1 Core and Shell Building

3.1.1   HVAC System

3.1.1.1 Model the baseline building HVAC system determined from Table G3.1.1A in ASHRAE 90.1-2004.

3.1.2   Building Envelope

3.1.2.1 Comply with the prescriptive requirements of ASHRAE 90.1-2004.

3.1.3   Lighting

3.1.3.1 Model the lighting power in the core and shell areas as determined by the space type classification in chart 9.6.1 of ASHRAE 90.1-2004.

3.2 Tenant Spaces

3.2.1   Lighting

3.2.1.1 Model separate electric meters for the lighting in the core building and the tenant spaces.

3.2.1.2 Use the same lighting power as modeled in the proposed building.

3.2.2   Receptacle and Other Loads

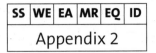

3.2.2.1 Model separate meters for tenant receptacle loads and process loads.

3.2.2.2 Use the same values for receptacle loads as used in the proposed building.

4. Perform Energy Simulation of Proposed Building and Baseline Building

3.1 Simulate building performance for an entire year.

5. Compare Annual Energy Costs of Proposed Building and Baseline Building

5.1 From the simulation, determine the annual energy costs of the budget building and design building.

5.2 Verify that 25% of the overall energy cost is process load.

5.3 Determine the percentage savings for annual energy costs.

Appendix 3 –
LEED-CS Project Scope Checklist

The LEED-CS Project Scope Checklist is intended as a tool for projects to identify and document the core and shell project scope. This document must be submitted with the project certification submittal.

Project Name _____

Project Size (Gross sf) _____

Use Type	Occupancy (Gross sf Per Employee)	Percentage of Total Bldg.
General Office		
Retail		
Medical Office Bldg.		
R & D – Lab Bldg.		

Building Space	Building System	Core and Shell Scope
Main Lobby	Floor finishes	
	Wall finishes	
	Ceiling finishes	
	Air terminal equipment	
	Air inlets and outlets	
	Light fixtures	
	Lighting controls	
Secondary Lobby	Floor finishes	
	Wall finishes	
	Ceiling finishes	
	Air terminal equipment	
	Air inlets and outlets	
	Light fixtures	
	Lighting controls	
Main Corridor	Floor finishes	
	Wall finishes	
	Ceiling finishes	
	Air terminal equipment	
	Air inlets and outlets	
	Light fixtures	
	Lighting controls	
Elevator Lobbies	Floor finishes	
	Wall finishes	
	Ceiling finishes	
	Air terminal equipment	
	Air inlets and outlets	
	Light fixtures	
	Lighting controls	
Secondary Corridors	Floor finishes	
	Wall finishes	
	Ceiling finishes	
	Air terminal equipment	
	Air inlets and outlets	
	Light fixtures	
	Lighting controls	

Building Space	Building System	Core and Shell Scope
Interior Build outs	Floor finishes	
	Wall finishes	
	Ceiling finishes	
	Air terminal equipment Air inlets and outlets	
	Light fixtures	
	Lighting controls	
HVAC	AHUs/RTUs/Air supply equipment	
	Chillers	
	Cooling tower	
	Boilers	
	Primary ductwork	
Electrical	Electrical panels	
	Switchgear	
	Bus duct